HISTORICAL DICTIONARIES OF RELIGIONS, PHILOSOPHIES, AND MOVEMENTS
Jon Woronoff, Series Editor

1. *Buddhism*, by Charles S. Prebish, 1993
2. *Mormonism*, by Davis Bitton, 1994. *Out of print. See no. 32.*
3. *Ecumenical Christianity*, by Ans Joachim van der Bent, 1994
4. *Terrorism*, by Sean Anderson and Stephen Sloan, 1995. *Out of print. See no. 41.*
5. *Sikhism*, by W. H. McLeod, 1995. *Out of print. See no. 59.*
6. *Feminism*, by Janet K. Boles and Diane Long Hoeveler, 1995. *Out of print. See no. 52.*
7. *Olympic Movement*, by Ian Buchanan and Bill Mallon, 1995. *Out of print. See no. 39.*
8. *Methodism*, by Charles Yrigoyen Jr. and Susan E. Warrick, 1996. *Out of Print. See no. 57.*
9. *Orthodox Church*, by Michael Prokurat, Alexander Golitzin, and Michael D. Peterson, 1996
10. *Organized Labor*, by James C. Docherty, 1996. *Out of print. See no. 50.*
11. *Civil Rights Movement*, by Ralph E. Luker, 1997
12. *Catholicism*, by William J. Collinge, 1997
13. *Hinduism*, by Bruce M. Sullivan, 1997
14. *North American Environmentalism*, by Edward R. Wells and Alan M. Schwartz, 1997
15. *Welfare State*, by Bent Greve, 1998. *Out of print. See no. 63.*
16. *Socialism*, by James C. Docherty, 1997. *Out of print. See no. 73.*
17. *Bahá'í Faith*, by Hugh C. Adamson and Philip Hainsworth, 1998. *Out of print. See no. 71.*
18. *Taoism*, by Julian F. Pas in cooperation with Man Kam Leung, 1998
19. *Judaism*, by Norman Solomon, 1998. *Out of print. See no. 69.*
20. *Green Movement*, by Elim Papadakis, 1998
21. *Nietzscheanism*, by Carol Diethe, 1999. *Out of print. See No. 75.*
22. *Gay Liberation Movement*, by Ronald J. Hunt, 1999
23. *Islamic Fundamentalist Movements in the Arab World, Iran, and Turkey*, by Ahmad S. Moussalli, 1999
24. *Reformed Churches*, by Robert Benedetto, Darrell L. Guder, and Donald K. McKim, 1999
25. *Baptists*, by William H. Brackney, 1999
26. *Cooperative Movement*, by Jack Shaffer, 1999

27. *Reformation and Counter-Reformation*, by Hans J. Hillerbrand, 2000
28. *Shakers*, by Holley Gene Duffield, 2000
29. *United States Political Parties*, by Harold F. Bass Jr., 2000
30. *Heidegger's Philosophy*, by Alfred Denker, 2000
31. *Zionism*, by Rafael Medoff and Chaim I. Waxman, 2000
32. *Mormonism*, 2nd ed., by Davis Bitton, 2000
33. *Kierkegaard's Philosophy*, by Julia Watkin, 2001
34. *Hegelian Philosophy*, by John W. Burbidge, 2001
35. *Lutheranism*, by Günther Gassmann in cooperation with Duane H. Larson and Mark W. Oldenburg, 2001
36. *Holiness Movement*, by William Kostlevy, 2001
37. *Islam*, by Ludwig W. Adamec, 2001
38. *Shinto*, by Stuart D. B. Picken, 2002
39. *Olympic Movement*, 2nd ed., by Ian Buchanan and Bill Mallon, 2001. *Out of Print. See no. 61.*
40. *Slavery and Abolition*, by Martin A. Klein, 2002
41. *Terrorism*, 2nd ed., by Sean Anderson and Stephen Sloan, 2002
42. *New Religious Movements*, by George D. Chryssides, 2001
43. *Prophets in Islam and Judaism*, by Scott B. Noegel and Brannon M. Wheeler, 2002
44. *The Friends (Quakers)*, by Margery Post Abbott, Mary Ellen Chijioke, Pink Dandelion, and John William Oliver Jr., 2003
45. *Lesbian Liberation Movement: Still the Rage*, JoAnne Myers, 2003
46. *Descartes and Cartesian Philosophy*, by Roger Ariew, Dennis Des Chene, Douglas M. Jesseph, Tad M. Schmaltz, and Theo Verbeek, 2003
47. *Witchcraft*, by Michael D. Bailey, 2003
48. *Unitarian Universalism*, by Mark W. Harris, 2004
49. *New Age Movements*, by Michael York, 2004
50. *Organized Labor*, 2nd ed., by James C. Docherty, 2004
51. *Utopianism*, by James M. Morris and Andrea L. Kross, 2004
52. *Feminism*, 2nd ed., by Janet K. Boles and Diane Long Hoeveler, 2004
53. *Jainism*, by Kristi L. Wiley, 2004
54. *Wittgenstein's Philosophy*, by Duncan Richter, 2004
55. *Schopenhauer's Philosophy*, by David E. Cartwright, 2005
56. *Seventh-day Adventists*, by Gary Land, 2005
57. *Methodism*, 2nd ed., by Charles Yrigoyen Jr. and Susan Warrick, 2005
58. *Sufism*, by John Renard, 2005

59. *Sikhism*, 2nd ed., by W. H. McLeod, 2005
60. *Kant and Kantianism*, by Helmut Holzhey and Vilem Mudroch, 2005
61. *Olympic Movement*, 3rd ed., by Bill Mallon with Ian Buchanan, 2006
62. *Anglicanism*, by Colin Buchanan, 2006
63. *Welfare State*, 2nd ed., by Bent Greve, 2006
64. *Feminist Philosophy*, by Catherine Villanueva Gardner, 2006
65. *Logic*, by Harry J. Gensler, 2006
66. *Leibniz's Philosophy*, by Stuart Brown and Nicholas J. Fox, 2006
67. *Non-Aligned Movement and Third World*, by Guy Arnold, 2006
68. *Salvation Army*, by Major John G. Merritt, 2006
69. *Judaism*, 2nd ed., by Norman Solomon, 2006
70. *Epistemology*, by Ralph Baergen, 2006
71. *Bahá'í Faith*, 2nd ed., by Hugh C. Adamson, 2006
72. *Aesthetics*, by Dabney Townsend, 2006
73. *Socialism*, 2nd ed., by Peter Lamb and James C. Docherty, 2007
74. *Marxism,* by David M. Walker and Daniel Gray, 2007
75. *Nietzscheanism,* 2nd ed., by Carol Diethe, 2007
76. *Medieval Philosophy and Theology,* by Stephen F. Brown and Juan Carlos Flores, 2007
77. *Shamanism,* by Graham Harvey and Robert J. Wallis, 2007

Historical Dictionary of Shamanism

Graham Harvey
Robert J. Wallis

Historical Dictionaries of Religions, Philosophies, and Movements, No. 77

The Scarecrow Press, Inc.
Lanham, Maryland • Toronto • Plymouth, UK
2007

SCARECROW PRESS, INC.

Published in the United States of America
by Scarecrow Press, Inc.
A wholly owned subsidiary of
The Rowman & Littlefield Publishing Group, Inc.
4501 Forbes Boulevard, Suite 200, Lanham, Maryland 20706
www.scarecrowpress.com

Estover Road
Plymouth PL6 7PY
United Kingdom

British Library Cataloguing in Publication Information Available

Library of Congress Cataloging-in-Publication Data
Harvey, Graham.
Historical dictionary of shamanism / Graham Harvey, Robert J. Wallis.
p. cm. — (Historical dictionaries of religions, philosophies, and movements ; no. 77)
Includes bibliographical references.
ISBN-13: 978-0-8108-5798-8 (hardcover : alk. paper)
ISBN-10: 0-8108-5798-7 (hardcover : alk. paper)
1. Shamanism—History—Dictionaries. I. Wallis, Robert J. II. Title.
GN475.8.H27 2007
201'.4403—dc22

2006031488

∞™ The paper used in this publication meets the minimum requirements of American National Standard for Information Sciences—Permanence of Paper for Printed Library Materials, ANSI/NISO Z39.48-1992.
Manufactured in the United States of America.

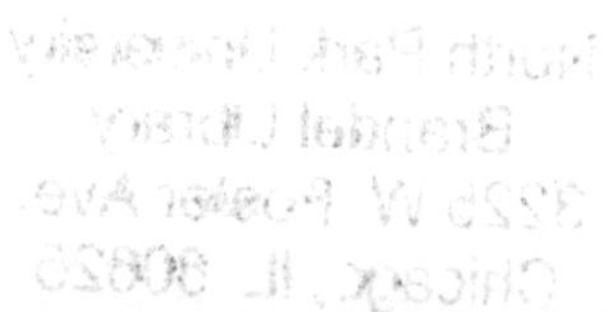

Contents

Editor's Foreword

Shamanism, in many ways, could not be more different from most of the other topics in this series. It is not an established church or an international organization, it does not have a holy book or cross-culturally agreed beliefs, and it has been suppressed over the centuries by more evangelistic religions. Despite this, it is culturally vibrant among people marginalized by colonialism and modernity. However, many of its practices and perspectives have been misinterpreted or reinterpreted. Moreover, the position and functions of the shaman—the central figure—vary greatly from one place to another, which means that there are many different kinds of shamanism. This has been compounded further by a resurgence of interest in shamanism, some of it sensitive and relatively scholarly, some of it wildly speculative and, in an era of globalization, commercially oriented. Additionally, a neo-shamanism has emerged over recent decades that incorporates specific aspects of traditional shamanism, albeit often greatly altered, and it has in a sense given shamanism a new lease on life.

Amidst the uncertainty and confusion, the claims and counterclaims, it is very helpful to have a reference work such as this *Historical Dictionary of Shamanism.* It covers all the time periods from the oldest to the present day, it considers a broad geographical landscape and focuses on areas where shamanism was and sometimes still is most vibrant, it embraces the rather varied forms of indigenous shamanisms and the almost bewildering varieties of neo-shamanism, it deals with major features such as healing and divination or dreams and trance, and it introduces some significant shamans (past and present) as well as writers and scholars. This is done first, in broad overview, in the introduction. The details then appear in the dictionary. Finally, the bibliography, which is actually one of the most important sections, provides a wealth of further sources of information.

This book was written by two eminent specialists on the subject, Graham Harvey and Robert J. Wallis. Dr. Harvey is a lecturer in religious studies at the Open University in Great Britain, where along with shamanism, he focuses on Pagans and indigenous peoples. He has written extensively on shamanism and related issues, including several books, among them *Shamanism: A Reader* and *Animism: Respecting the Living World*. Dr. Wallis is associate professor of visual culture at Richmond University in London, as well as an associate lecturer in humanities at the Open University. He, too, is interested in both historical and contemporary manifestations and has written extensively, most recently publishing *Shamans/Neo-Shamans: Ecstasy, Alternative Archaeologies and Contemporary Pagans.* Between them, they have done a particularly good job of covering the field, explaining its many intricacies, and presenting the material in a clear and comprehensible manner.

Jon Woronoff
Series Editor

Acknowledgments

We have been inspired to engage with shamans and shamanism by many people, including some shamans and many academic colleagues, and a few who are both. A smaller company has been of immense help during the preparation of this book, and we express special thanks to Danielle Bertrand, Jenny Blain, Andy Letcher, and Kenneth Lymer.

Acronyms and Abbreviations

AIM	American Indian Movement
ASC	Altered States of Consciousness; Adjusted Styles of Communication
CIIS	California Institute of Integral Studies
CNRS	Centre National de la Recherche Scientifique
FSS	Foundation for Shamanic Studies
ITA	International Transpersonal Association
NASA	National Aeronautics and Space Administration
NRM	New Religious Movement
SPIRIT	Support and Protection of Indian Religions and Indigenous Traditions
SSC	Shamanic State of Consciousness
UFO	Unidentified Flying Object

Chronology

Shamanism is sometimes said to be the earliest religion, the original religion. In fact, there is no evidence that could prove or disprove such a claim. To the contrary, it is certainly the case that every shaman living today utilizes skills and knowledge that are entirely appropriate to the contemporary world. Shamans and their communities are not "primitive" and do not provide evidence of what the first human ancestors did or thought.

Similarly, it is sometimes claimed that shamanism is a religion eminently suited to the nomadic lifestyle of people who hunt and gather their food rather than growing it or trading it. While it is likely that the first humans were nomadic hunter-gatherers, shamans are employed in almost every conceivable style of culture. While shamans in many places do aid nomadic hunters, Korean shamans solve problems in urban industrial cities, Mongolian shamans have opened clinics in towns, Amazonian shamans have developed chants celebrating outboard motors, and Aboriginal Australian "clever people" are painting works of art that sell in exclusive galleries. Even the allegedly classic style of shamans, that is, those of Siberia, are more likely to be reindeer herders than hunters. Thus, shamans and shamanism do not fit easily with simple evolutionary schemata.

For all these reasons, and because shamans in Siberia are quite different from shamans in the Caribbean, a chronology that traces the history of shamanism could only be misleading, informing us more about Western preconceptions about linear time and history than about the different manifestations of shamanism themselves. If it were possible to date the origins of a particular culture, or its adoption of shamans as religious functionaries, it might then be feasible to produce a time line of that culture's shamanism. However, it is rarely possible to do this. Instead, this dictionary offers only a few tentative dates relevant to archaeological or literary evidence of ancient practices, encounters between Europeans and shamans in particular places, and the publication of several books that have created new forms of shamanism (i.e., neo-shamanism and core shamanism) in the West. Only dates relevant to entries in the dictionary are included.

UPPER PALEOLITHIC PERIOD (FROM PERHAPS AS EARLY AS AROUND 40,000 BCE)

- Caves in Europe, as well as other material/visual culture, are decorated with paintings that have been interpreted as "shamanic art" (there have been suggestions of earlier examples of shamanic rock art elsewhere worldwide—and certainly Eurocentrism should be challenged).

NEOLITHIC PERIOD (FROM AROUND 8300 BCE)

- Europe marks the first use of agriculture, although an "agricultural revolution" arguably overstates the immediate impact; various visual cultures from the period have been interpreted as "shamanic."

BRONZE AGE (FROM AROUND 2500 BCE)

- British artifacts, including decorated daggers and ax heads, as well as gold "jewelry," among other social agencies, from this period arguably reflected status; some scholars have commented on such status-bearers as "shamans."

1766–221 BCE

- Chinese literary texts suggest the existence of *wu* (female shamans) and *his* (male shamans) during the Shang and Chou dynasties.

IRON AGE (FROM AROUND 1000 BCE IN EUROPE)

- "Celtic Druids" are often identified as "Shamans," but these terms are problematic and all too often romanticized.

MIGRATION AGE (FROM AROUND 300–900 CE IN EUROPE)

- Peoples such as the Anglo-Saxons and Norse (Vikings) may have employed shamans before conversion; there is certainly evidence for cross-cultural exchange between these peoples and indigenous communities they encountered, including the Saami.

12TH CENTURY

- Gerald of Wales's *Description of Wales* describes the practice of Welsh *Awenyddion* (entranced diviners).
- Islam's spread through Central Asia leads some shamans to add Muslim saints to their cadre of helpers and to adapt to being more marginal to the religious life of some communities.
- The creation of the Mongol Empire by Chinggis (Genghis) Khan leads to the dominance of Buddhism in large areas of Asia, but shamans continue to serve their communities, as evidenced by 17th-century Buddhist missions in the region; fusions of shamanism and Buddhism evolved when there was no outright persecution.

13TH CENTURY

- The *Saga of Erik the Red* describes a Norse shamanic séance that took place in the 10th century in Greenland and evidences the transition to Christianity.

16TH CENTURY

- An antiwitchcraft movement near Venice, Italy, in this period (according to Carlo Ginzburg) involves claims that the *benandanti*, "those who go doing good," flew to confront malevolent witches.

17TH CENTURY

- Buddhist control of what is now Tuva, north of Mongolia, leads to Lamaist missionary opposition to shamans and shamanism; repression continues under later Chinese and Soviet Russian control.

18TH CENTURY

- Russian colonization of Central Asia leads to Christian persecution of shamans and to the evolution of more individualized, less clan-based authority structures among surviving shamans.
- Russian and other European officials, travelers, and scholars begin to provide accounts of Central Asian shamans. The Tungus word *shaman* generates the German term *schamanen* and then the English *shamanism*. Such narratives become increasingly popular in the following centuries.
- A distinction between male ritual leaders and female mediums begins among the Ainu.
- Christianity is introduced to the Inuit, beginning in Labrador, Canada, sometimes leading to repression but sometimes to creative fusions.
- Enlightenment writers and ideologues, such as Johann von Herder, Johann Goethe, and Victor Hugo, adopt a positive valuation of shamans, consider Orpheus to have been a shaman, and promote individual inspiration, while Diderot and others construct shamans as impostors, among other negative stereotypes.

19TH CENTURY

- Extensive fieldwork research among Siberian shamans begins.
- Alleluia shamanism originates among Amazonian shamans in the Guyana highlands as a response to European colonialism and Christian missionization.
- Comparison with Buddhism leads to the creation of a new indigenous term with which to label shamanism among the Buryats: the *black faith*.
- Allan Kardec initiates a Spiritist movement, Kardecism, in France; it becomes increasingly popular in Brazil.
- Some religious and cultural leaders of Native American nations such as the Lakota and Dakota lead confrontational responses to American colonization; others respond by evolving traditions blending traditional ways with forms of Christianity; and still others encourage the adoption of Christianity as a more or less tem-

porary response to Euro-American domination. New shamanic healing and "world-making," cosmological and culturally reinvigorating ceremonies, are established.

EARLY 20TH CENTURY

- A series of expeditions lead by Knud Rasmussen records Inuit shamanism in Greenland.
- A religious movement called Umbanda is created in Brazil out of a fusion of African, Amazonian, and Euro-Christian traditions.
- The spread of Soviet control leads to repression of shamans and other religious and cultural leaders in Siberia and Central Asia.
- European and Western artists—for example, Vincent van Gogh—are labeled shamans by interpreters who judge some forms of mental illnesses to be shamanic.
- Margaret Murray's claim that Europeans persecuted as "witches" were members of a pagan fertility cult partly inspires the creation of new forms of self-identified Paganism and also encourages the thesis that early witches were led by shamans.
- The Eranos Conferences initiated by Carl Jung bring together scholars of mythology and shamanism with therapists and artists, inspiring developments among neo-shamans.

1950S AND 1960S

- Interest in and experiments with "psychedelics" lead to a popularization of vision-emphasizing interpretations of shamanism and later to "cyberian shamanism" and "entheogen tourism."
- Mircea Eliade's book presenting shamanism as "the archaic techniques of ecstasy" is published, first in French (1951), then in English (1964), and rapidly becomes the focus of considerable scholarly and popular attention.
- Carlos Castaneda's *The Teachings of Don Juan* (1968) is published, attracts the attention of the "psychedelic generation," and inspires an entheogen-focused version of neo-shamanism.

1980S AND 1990S

- Michael Harner's *The Way of the Shaman* (1980) is published and provides a handbook for an even more popular style of neo-shamanism that does not involve hallucinogens and is made available in workshops and New Age–style events.
- Shamanic movements such as Candomblé, Santería, Vodou, Santo Daime, and others spread from South America to other parts of the world, not only as diaspora movements but also gaining non–South American adherents.
- The collapse of the Soviet regime leads to the resurgence of ethnic and local traditions, including shamanism, in many new Asian republics. The support of American neo-shamans generates interesting blends of traditional and neo-shamanic practices and ideas.

Introduction

There are shamans who may be able to heal, and others who may be successful at controlling game animals. Some shamans alter consciousness or use trance, others shape-shift and journey to other worlds. Some mediate between their communities and powerful other-than-human beings. Some become possessed by the spirits of the dead. Other shamans assume third, fourth, or even multiple genders or engage in cross-dressing. Most shamans are animists engaging with other-than-human people, while still others are priests and ritualists. Almost all shamans are skillful performers and even entertainers. Being a shaman may involve a number of these things, or all of them. None of these characteristics should be seen as essential features of shamans or shamanism, however, since this is neither a definitive nor an exhaustively comprehensive list. Any attempt to formulate such a list would, arguably, be naive. Indeed, since some shamans are themselves sorcerers, witches, and tricksters, it is vitally important to stress the tricky, slippery nature of shamanism right from the start.

DEFINING SHAMANS AND SHAMANISM

Shamans are so paradoxical that it is hard to know how to introduce this dictionary without challenging every definition ever offered. Some might think that an easy way out of the dilemma would be to restrict the use of the word *shaman* to its origin with religious officials of some kind among the Tungus-speaking Evenk in Siberia. But even among the Evenk, there are different assessments of what shamans do and who they are. It is even difficult to write about "shamanism" among the Evenk because *-ism* suggests something orderly and systematic that everyone would recognize, which is not the case.

Certainly, shamans are expected to tackle all the mess of reality and make sense of it for their patients, clients, and families. When relationships have broken down, or when health is threatened, or when food stocks are running dangerously low, shamans are commonly called upon to engage with those beings and forces deemed responsible for reestablishing an orderly, healthy, and viable cosmos. But real-life shamans and their communities rarely, if ever, present their understandings of life and their methods of dealing with problems in an orderly thesis, creed, or manifesto. While it is possible to treat a shaman's costume or ritualized actions as a hologram, a representation that includes everything of importance to the shaman, it would be a mistake to think it is possible to reduce shamanism to a few simple phrases.

So the idea that reserving the words *shaman* and *shamanism* for talking about Evenk healers, ritualists, religious leaders, or relationship counselors (or whatever it is proposed Evenk shamanism is *really* about) is not satisfactory. For one thing, if it is acceptable to talk about shamans among Tungus speakers, what about their neighbors who easily recognize similar, but not identical, practitioners of religion, health care, social work, cosmic mediation, knowledge-repository, and more? (No, that list was not edging toward a definition, it was just a trickster tease based on what some shamans do in some places.) And if the term *shaman* applies among the Evenk and their neighbors, why not *their* neighbors? And so it goes on.

Furthermore, just because both Evenk and, for example, some Amazonian shamans might be healers or journey to other worlds, this does not mean that they must be alike in every other way. It is important to attend to the specifics of what shamans do, how they understand the cosmos, and what their communities expect of them. Only carefully researched appreciation of specific, local information should serve as a basis for any comparative or constructive theorizing about what shamans might have in common.

This *Historical Dictionary of Shamanism* acknowledges that there are lots of definitions available, and that they all work perfectly well for some shamans and shamanic activities and not at all well otherwise. It notes some definitions because some people have been quite clear about what they mean by shamans and shamanism. But it does not propose to concur with these or purport to offer definitions of its own. Instead, this dictionary presents information about all kinds of shamans and all kinds of claims about shamanism. When appropriate, it offers critical engagement with these discourses. Lots of entirely different phenomena have been called "shamanism," and although they are all interesting, they are not all one thing. Yet, there are lots of connections, lots of points of contact, between (real or imagined) shamans in one place and shamans elsewhere.

The diversity of practices and traditions that have been labeled "shamanism" is remarkable. Similarly, there remain many areas of considerable debate and disagreement about precisely what makes someone a shaman. Some interpreters are certain that any deliberate use of trance in religion or healing *is* shamanism. Others categorically state that shamans do *not* enter trances. Some identify all forms of possession as shamanism, while others vociferously reject that possibility; indeed, some define shamanism as the *opposite* of possession. If some people present the deliberate alteration of states of consciousness or mind as essentially shamanic, there are plenty of others who will offer evidence for total uncertainty about the nature of consciousness or mind in the first place. As yet, few observers have made much of the fact that shamans in many places ingest brews or inhale snuffs derived from plants that cause vomiting. While the prevalence of vomiting has often been noticed, it has never been treated as *the* definitive practice of shamans. Thus, it is likely that all other definitions might miss possibilities that seem outlandish. But anyone who rejects weird possibilities is bound to fail to understand shamans and shamanism. And so it continues.

HISTORY

Although this is a *Historical Dictionary of Shamanism*, published in a series of historical dictionaries, providing a clear history or neat time line is difficult. Certainly, shamanisms and the variety of perceptions Westerners have of shamans are themselves not without history. One of the earliest encounters with Evenk shamanism is recorded as Nicolas Witsen's evocative woodcut "Priest of the Devil" (from his *Noord en Oost Tartarye*, 1705). This depicts an apparently human figure clad in animal skins with an antler headdress, wielding a drum and beater amid the dwellings of an Evenk community. The figure's clawed feet might represent part of a costume, perhaps linking the priest to bears, but could just as easily indicate that the shaman is himself a devil. It is the otherness of this shaman that is striking, with a cloud of colonialism, skepticism, and missionary zeal distancing some 21st-century viewers from these early encounters with shamans but evidencing attitudes that endure to this day.

After such initial contact with shamans, European explorers went on to engage with similar figures elsewhere, not only in the alleged *locus classicus* of Siberia but also in Southeast Asia, the Arctic, South America, and even Australia. The generic German term *schamanen* became Anglicized as *shaman* and gained wider currency (as noted by Gloria Flaherty, 1992). The reception of picture books of shamans in the 18th century and the consumption of representations of shamans in ethnology and anthropology in the 20th century have consistently been colored by preconception and prejudices. These include Johann Gmelin's (1751) harsh argument that "shamans deserve perpetual labor for their hocus-pocus," Denis Diderot's (1765) Enlightenment characterization of shamans as "imposters who claim they consult the devil—and who are sometimes close to the mark," George Devereux's (1956) psychiatric assessment that shamans are mentally ill, and the more recent proposal from transpersonal psychologists (e.g., Stanley Krippner) that shamans are, to the contrary, indigenous psychotherapists. Shamans are at once a fiction and whatever interpreters want them to be, and yet shamans have continued to shamanize nonetheless. Other contributors to these debates about who or what shamans might be, particularly among Native Americans, have campaigned against the appropriation of indigenous practices by academics and neo-shamans and their representation as "shamanism." All of these shamans and neo-shamans, and especially the discourses in which they are entangled, are of interest in this dictionary.

According to some interpreters of shamanism, a historical slant should have been a gift because, they say, shamanism was the first religion of humanity, the origin of religion, as well as the origin of art and even language, and it continues to exist in many forms in almost every culture alive today. It ought to be possible, the argument goes, to present a time line from the first human right up to the present moment and to fill it with dates and examples of shamans everywhere, from the alleged first shaman painter in the French caves to the use of altered consciousness by today's psychonauts—however contentious, Eurocentric, and indeed chronocentric such a time line might be. But no such time line is provided in this dictionary. Again, the quest for the "original" (presumably Paleolithic) shamans, alongside the origin of art, tells us more about

Western scholars as historians of religion and art, and our own fantasies about shamans, than about prehistoric shamans themselves.

Foregrounding instead the agency of shamans themselves and the authority of indigenous people to define authenticity according to contemporary needs, the dictionary does not insist that "earlier is better," let alone definitive of what shamanism *really* is. Much that shamans do is in relation to the past, as they see and present it. For example, some shamans chant epics in which the cosmos was created by shamanic deities. However, these do not offer claims about origins or "intelligent design," because the point of most such chants is to "re-member" (literally, put back together), reorganize, and improve the cosmos in significant ways. Shamanic performances are one of the ways in which some humans grapple with the problems of the world. Most cosmological chants are intended to be primarily not about the past but about the present and the future. They do not record information about origins, but attempt to establish how things can be from now on. The shaman now chanting *is* the creator. But not all shamans chant cosmological epics—again, this is not a definition or criterion.

Similarly, although the dictionary includes entries about ancient cave paintings (and other rock art) that have been interpreted as the work of shamans, it does not draw a direct line from that art to (or from) contemporary shamanic experience or contemporary artists labeled as shamans. Certainly, no contemporary or recent indigenous culture provides any evidence whatsoever for the earliest human culture or for the earliest shamanism. Indeed, what indigenous people do in any given period is only what they do at that point in their continuing culture and history. The dictionary notes that some academics and some enthusiasts have imagined that contemporary shamans are like—or, more often, regrettably quite unlike—the first shamans. It also notes that such views are polemical and derogatory toward contemporary peoples.

Such polemics can, however, be countered. For example, while Edward Tylor's original theory of "animism" presumed that indigenous people were mistaken in perceiving life in all things (including so-called inanimate objects) and argued that this error defined the entire phenomenon of religion, a "new animism" has recently been theorized. This makes no assumptions about contemporary indigenous religions being vestiges of prehistoric ("original") religions, instead locating shamans as vital agents in creatively mediating between human and other-than-human communities in the present, particularly in instances where indigenous peoples creatively negotiate with colonialism, neo-colonialism, and globalization.

The dictionary provides entries about some indigenous people who have, or are claimed to have, shamans among them, or to practice some form of shamanism. These entries note that there are local words for shamans, and that some indigenous people would prefer to use other words than *shaman* for their healers, ritualists, sorcerers, or wise people. Sometimes this becomes outright denial that their doctors or spiritual leaders are shamans at all. This is certainly true: not everyone called a shaman is anything like any other shaman. However, the point of this dictionary is to engage with this diversity of understanding and to note and comment on some of the many things that are called shamanism.

PSYCHOLOGY, SOCIOLOGY, ANTHROPOLOGY?

"Ologies" are important ways for academics to take a close look at the many things that happen in the world. Shamans have been of interest to almost every academic discipline imaginable. Their performances have been recorded, their relationships mapped, their worldviews charted, their brain chemistry tested, their psychological health checked, their botanical knowledge classified, their transgressions valorized, their gender constructions theorized, and more.

In all the disciplines interested in such matters, different assessments of the nature of shamanism and the character of shamans have been made and promulgated. Roberte Hamayon (1998) summarized Western interest in Siberian shamans as having gone through three broad periods, emblematically labeled devilization, medicalization, and idealization. This is immensely useful, and it can be applied to some studies of shamanism as well as to popular interest (abhorrent or enthusiastic as it may be). But, in the end, it is too neat. Just as shamans can be as ambiguous as tricksters, and just as shamanism can be too fluid to pin down, so academic and popular interests and assessments of shamans have generally been ambiguous. An almost clichéd example of the blend of fear and desire is paraded. In what many consider to be the definitive discussion of shamanism but others deride as hopelessly polemical, Mircea Eliade's *Shamanism* (1964 [1951]) proffered a neat view of "archaic" shamanism that he had to continuously shield from the messy reality of contemporary shamans. Far from revealing what shamanism actually is, he implicitly wanted to make shamans into what he thought they should be. Desire and distaste are illiberally blended into a concoction that has delighted as many people (scholars or otherwise) as it has repelled. Indeed, it is one root from which a whole new style of shamanism has sprouted and flourished.

This dictionary regularly presents ambiguities because ambiguity fits well both with the phenomena of interest (shamanism) and with the study of shamanism (see von Stuckrad 2002).

CONTEMPORARY VITALITY

If ambiguity is important, the roles played by shamans in the contemporary world are of critical interest to scholars in a wide range of disciplines. For a host of reasons (but often to do with a renewed sense of self-determination seeking independence from the globalizing empires of the collapsed Soviet Union or the still dominant colonialism of the West), there is a resurgence of shamanism among many indigenous communities. The dictionary thus engages with many examples of the ways in which people choose to further develop shamanic worldviews and lifeways. In one sense this is straightforward, because shamans seem always and everywhere to have been at the forefront of adopting and adapting new skills to deal with old and new needs. In another sense this is radical, because it forces a recognition that the label "neo-shamanism" wrongly implies an absolute difference between different kinds of shamanism. This does not mean that distinctions cannot be made, but it means that distinctions should not be made for polemical reasons. The differences between Evenk shamans and neo-shamans in the urban West are not necessarily greater than those between Siberian and Haitian shamans. Especially after the deliberate revival of shamanism following the collapse of the Soviet Union, and the vital role many shamans have played in resisting colonialism in Amazonia and elsewhere, it is folly to imagine that "new" means "inauthentic." Shamanism has always evolved, and neo-shamanism is as much an aspect of the evolving culture of the West as Sakha shamanism is an aspect of the evolving cultures of Siberia—and creative engagements between these two in the "global village" disrupt this boundary further.

If shamanism is part of popular cultural dynamics, it is also important in some of the most interesting academic debates. Leaving aside, for now, the place of neo-shamanism in these dynamics and debates, among the most significant contemporary movements is a global swelling or resurgence of indigenous vitality. In part, this is marked both by the assertion of rights over indigenous bodies of knowledge and by rising academic interest in such knowledge (evidenced by a number of recent conferences and publications with significant participation by indigenous scholars). Again, by demonstrating that indigenous cultures and religions are actively participating in and negotiating a globalized world, all this ferment and activity certainly gives the lie to those who would diminish indigeneity, and thus shamanism, as utterly different from Western modernity (including its neo-shamanism). The vitality of indigenous peoples, and the valuing of their knowledge, is both a matter of justice and a reason for considerable academic debate.

This is admirably illustrated in the display board entitled "Our Lives: Now: The 21st Century" in the Smithsonian Institution's National Museum of the American Indian in Washington, D.C. This notes, "We are not just survivors; we are the architects of our survivance. We carry our ancient philosophies into an ever changing modern world." It continues to explain that the "Our Lives" exhibition "is about our stories of survivance, but it belongs to anyone who has fought extermination, discrimination, or stereotypes." Finally, it quotes Gerald Vizenor (1994), who coined the term *survivance*, saying that "it is more than just survival. Survivance means defining ourselves. It means raising our social and political consciousness. It means holding on to ancient philosophies while eagerly embracing change. It means doing what is necessary to keep our cultures alive." This is what shamans do in many cultures today, and while there are issues of neocolonialism at the interface between indigenous shamans and neo-shamans, this also explains why many people (including in Euro-American contexts) are rediscovering the importance of their shamanic inheritance. It also shows why it is important to understand what different cultures understand shamanism to be about.

DICTIONARY ENTRIES

As has already been noted, the dictionary includes entries about most of the phenomena that have been called shamanism. It does not shy away from noting controversies (e.g., about whether shamans are mad, or whether Euro-Americans who claim to be shamans are thieves); indeed, it includes entries about some unpleasant polemics precisely because they help promote consideration about shamans, shamanism, and much else that is important today. There are entries about the past, including ancient European cave art and indigenous practices that are no longer current, notwithstanding the reality that discourse on them endures precisely because they are extinct. Some entries also draw on books and websites that are producing new information, ideas, and views, right up to the last minute. In entries about indigenous peoples and cultures, it should be clear what relates to the past and what is contemporary. Brief entries cannot be all-encompassing or definitive and do not imply that any culture or community is static and unchanging. If any group is characterized as employing shamans, it should be clear that they may also define themselves as Christians, Buddhists, Muslims, or secularists.

The dictionary includes entries about "traditional" shamans and "neo-shamans." All these have been enthusiastically celebrated by some and ridiculed and dismissed by others. Shamanism, if there is an -ism, is too slippery and tricky a phenomenon to be held only by one group. Failure to slip across boundaries and be surprised by new perspectives and possibilities will lead to failure to understand even that which seems familiar. That, at least, is a justification for placing so many disparate matters alongside one another. Thus entries about the Buryats, Celts, Evenk, San, and Sora stand alongside others about hallucinogen tourists, Heathens, techno-shamans, and "wannabe Indians." Entries about Nicholas Black Elk, Mongush Kenin-Lopsan, Maria Sabina, and Thomas Yellowtail bear reading alongside entries about Jan Fries, Gordon "The Toad" MacLellan, Malidoma Somé, the Nephilim, and Austin Osman Spare. Similarly, there are entries about matters that seem to have been accepted as definitive of what shamans do and what shamanism is (e.g., "altered states of consciousness," "trance," "tiered cosmos," "drumming," and "journeying"), along with interventions that disrupt these and argue for new perspectives about, e.g., "adjusted styles of communication," "animism," "becoming-animal," "new-indigenes," and "pragmatism."

Finally, so that this dictionary can contribute to further lively debates about shamans, shamanism, and shamanisms, an annotated bibliography serves as a guide to further study. Whether approached enthusiastically or academically, there are many important matters to consider in relation to shamans. Equally, there are many important matters that might be better understood in relation to the activities and knowledges of shamans.

The Dictionary

– A –

ABORIGINAL AUSTRALIANS. Many of the different language groups and peoples indigenous to Australia speak of "people of high degree" or "**clever people**." These are usually **elders** with unusual abilities and esoteric knowledge who have exceptional skills as counselors and/or diplomats. Clever people deal with **illnesses** and situations that resist the medical and religious knowledge (e.g., the use of particular plants or ceremonies) that is pervasive among traditional Aboriginal communities. Clever people are typically those whose inherent abilities are recognized in childhood, encouraged and reinforced in **initiation** rites, and nurtured throughout life until they can be made full use of by elders.

Academics and Aboriginal culture teachers are divided about whether these traditional **doctors** can be called shamans or compared with shamans elsewhere. Features of Aboriginal cultures and practices that lead some to say that there are Aboriginal shamans include accounts of initiations in which people talk of being abducted, **dismembered**, and reassembled by powerful **other-than-human persons** or, perhaps, "**spirits**." Crystals or other powerful substances are often "sung" or otherwise inserted into bodies (without leaving wounds or outward signs), often providing something like a "third eye" with "x-ray vision." Although the **mastery of spirits** is not part of traditional Aboriginal worldviews and lifeways, engagement with powerful, co-creative beings is important. There are accounts that suggest the importance of **altered states of consciousness**, **ecstasy**, **trance**, or **possession**, but they are not ubiquitous practices of all Aboriginal doctors or clever people. **Journeying** or flying can be part of the clever person's abilities. However, few if any of these seemingly shamanic abilities, experiences, and practices are unique to clever people. In their Aboriginal forms, they arise from and make sense in traditional cosmologies and lifeways for all Aboriginal people. It is probably wise to conclude that clever people do what all Aboriginal people are supposed to do if they live up to what their cultures indicate is appropriate to human behavior. In this sense, the term is equivalent to *elder*, referring to those who are worthy of respect not principally for their age but for their accumulated wisdom and skill.

Similarly, it has been claimed that Aboriginal people have **totem** or **power animals** or plants, like shamans in other cultures. However, on the one hand, the interspecies **clan** relationships of traditional Aboriginal people are not entirely the same as those found elsewhere, since they fit within uniquely Aboriginal conceptions of everything as emerging from "**the Dreaming**," and on the other hand, they are not specific to elders or clever people because every living being comes from the Dreaming and is member of a (totemic/interspecies) clan.

Mircea Eliade misrepresented one Dreaming narrative in support of his construction of shamanism, taking a reference to a pole as equivalent to the *axis mundi* that he claimed to find everywhere among shamans. Far from being about an "escape from history" or a "celestial withdrawal," as Eliade presents it, this and other Dreaming narratives and **rituals** are intimately concerned with what Jonathan Z. Smith (1987) calls "terrestrial transformation and continued presence." That is, the goal of Aboriginal spirituality is a greater engagement with the places in which people find themselves participants.

ABRAM, DAVID (1957–). American cultural ecologist and magician, a proponent of **animism** who argues that Western modernity is a form of willful disconnection from the sensuous realities of the body and the earth. Abram traveled many parts of the world as an itinerant sleight-of-hand magician, living and trading magic with traditional shamans in **Indonesia**, **Nepal**, and the Americas. His work places particular emphasis on the sensorial and linguistic characteristics of the animistic worldview, and stresses the ways in which alphabetic literacy has transformed and often displaced the animistic styles of seeing and speaking common to our oral, indigenous **ancestors**. Abram is highly skeptical of the term *shamanism* because he understands it to imply that shamans are central to, and even revered or worshiped by members of, "shamanistic" cultures. Abram asserts, on the contrary, that traditional shamans or **medicine people** are almost always edge-dwellers, commonly dwelling on the periphery of traditional villages, **mediating** between the human community and the more-than-human community of **animals**, plants, landforms, and earthly elements that surround and sustain the human group. Abram thus asserts that this ecological function—as an intermediary between humans and the rest of an enspirited **nature**—is essential to the craft of the shaman, and that even the shaman's role as a **healer** remains rooted in this more basic ecological function. Hence, for Abram, the shaman always operates in an animistic (rather than a "shamanistic") context, wherein every part of the sensuous cosmos is taken to be animate, sentient, and communicative.

ACHTERBERG, JEANNE (1942–). One of a number of scholars who popularized a psychological approach to shamanism in the 1980s, focusing especially on the "inner" work of the shaman in effecting **healing**. Her volume *Imagery in Healing: Shamanism and Modern Medicine* (1985) details techniques including "guided imagery," such as the visualization of the immune system fighting against illness, and presents evidence for the efficacy of the imagination in promoting health and "wellness." In the vein of the "Mind Body Spirit" movement, Achterberg suggests that there is a necessary connection between the mind and the body and that human imagination is a powerful healing tool in its own right. While the power of the **imaginal** might be recognized, such psychologizing neglects many indigenous facets of shamanisms, from intimate relationships with **other-than-human-persons** (outside "the mind") to the **sorcery** of **dark shamans**. *Woman as Healer* (1991) develops Achterberg's interest in the way in which **women** have tended to be marginalized as healers by their male counterparts in some societies. While she argues that women persecuted during the medieval European **witch** trials were shamans, interpretations of these trials tend to tell us more about our modern prejudices (à la **Margaret Murray**) than about medieval sensibilities. After being diagnosed with cancer, Achterberg rejected Western medicine in favor of a holistic approach to healing, relying on social support webs, guided imagery, and the communal power of prayer (transpersonal medicine). Achterberg is professor of psychology and director of research at the Institute of

Transpersonal Psychology, is a faculty member of the Saybrook Institute, and has been associate professor and director of research in rehabilitation science at Southwestern Medical School in Dallas, Texas.

ADJUSTED STYLES OF COMMUNICATION (ASC). In contrast with the common claim that shamanism is fundamentally a matter of achieving, controlling, and utilizing **altered states of consciousness** (also ASC), it may be preferable to think of shamans as adjusting their styles of communication. In **animist** cultures, shamans are (among other things) **ritual** leaders who **mediate** with **other-than-human persons** by means of respectful etiquette. The advantages of this reconfiguration of "ASC" are that it avoids claims about **individuals**' immediate experiences (which are likely to be inaccessible) and focuses attention on shamanic practices, actions, or **performances**—which are central to the concerns of those who employ shamans and may be seen as signs of the relationship between shamans and those who **possess** or **help** them.

AFRICA. Scholars who distinguish between shamanism and **possession** tend to deny that African religious cultures include shamans or shamanism. However, **Ioan Lewis** among others makes this distinction difficult. He discusses the **Zar** and **Sar** traditions of North and East Africa (prevalent among **Islamic** and **Christian women**) and **Bori** traditions of West and North Africa. Scholars who consider **Caribbean** and African diasporic religions such as **Vodou** and **Candomblé** to be shamanic usually also recognize their roots in West Africa. The **rock art** of the **southern African San** (Bushmen) is widely understood to portray and be part of shamanic **performance** and **cosmology**. Widespread **doctoring** and anti-**witchcraft** or **sorcery** practices are also similar to those clearly identified as shamanic elsewhere. Finally, the **animist** relational cosmologies and epistemologies that give rise to the need for shamans in many cultures are also evident in many parts of Africa, to the extent that, for example, "animist" is often used as the label for many Nigerians who are neither Christian nor Muslim.

AINU. The largest indigenous population of Japan, descending from ancestors who migrated there around 10,000 years ago. The Ainu mainly live in the northern islands of what is now Japan, especially Hokkaido and the Tsugaru Strait area, although in the past they inhabited a wider area and their population was larger. Ainu scholar Sakurako Tanaka distinguishes between ancestral shamans and contemporary **mediums**, *tuskur*. She traces this "decline" to the 17th-century distinction between male ceremonial leaders and female mediums. Tanaka argues that while some mediums have **animal** kin, manipulate animal **spirits**, and lead communal ceremonies, rites, and even **political** confrontation with outside authorities, they can be distinguished from shamans because they do not exhibit **mastery of spirits** but become **possessed** by them. The passivity of the medium allows powerful **other-than-human persons**, *kamuy*, and ancestral **souls** who had **elected** her to reside in her and provide knowledge of the **other world**, **taboos**, and **medicinal** herbs and therefore to diagnose and **heal illnesses** while in an **altered state of consciousness** or **trance**. In recording the skill and knowledge of particular Ainu mediums, Tanaka casts doubt on the value of too strong a distinction between shamans and mediums: the precise nature of human relationships with powerful other-than-human persons varies not only from individual to individual but also according to cultural expectations. If more weight is placed on the choices made by shamans' **helpers** and on the roles played by shamans in their communities, it becomes increasingly difficult to insist that possession and trance are distinct.

ALIEN ABDUCTION. Stories of supposed survivors of **space alien** abductions have some similarities with shamans' **initiation** narratives in which powerful **other-than-human persons** or **spirits** abduct, **dismember**, and reassemble shamanic initiates, especially when they are said to insert powerful artifacts into the abductee's body. They also have parallels in shamanic **healing** narratives, again particularly those in which **illnesses** are caused by the insertion of artifacts into people's bodies or by the abduction of their **souls**. Earlier versions of comparable narratives include abduction or kidnapping by fairies, Indians, gypsies, and devil worshippers. Debate about the implications of these parallels is complicated by their entanglement with commitments to the truth or falsity of claims made.

ALLEGRO, JOHN M. (1923–1988). A member of the team that was translating and supposedly publishing the Dead Sea Scrolls, Allegro reached the controversial conclusion that early **Christian** texts are a coded record of the Essene community's use of **hallucinogenic** mushrooms. Publication of his views in *The Sacred Mushroom and the Cross* (1970) was at least partly responsible for his departure from the official translation team. The full publication of the scrolls (which he had argued for) took place years after his death and has demonstrated that his argument is without warrant. Nonetheless, there are still adherents of the view that "Jesus was a mushroom."

ALLELUIA SHAMANISM. An evolution of **Amazonian** shamanism (particularly in the eastern highlands) influenced by **Christian** missionary discourse (e.g., prophetic promises of a new life, a path to creative powers or "God," and access to new **healing** cures and powerful chants) that began in the late 19th century in the Guyana highlands. Its name derives from the use of various Christian words and phrases in **ritual** chants, songs, and dances. **Neil Whitehead** discusses the rise of this apocalyptic practice in relation to indigenous attempts to deal with the impact of new **illnesses** like smallpox following colonization and the influx of new cultural, **political**, and social situations and technologies. In particular, he notes that *alleluia'san* (practitioners who **perform** this style of shamanism, especially by singing and **chanting**) oppose "**dark shamans**" or *kanaimà'san* and in the process almost marginalize ***piya*** shamans (even though their chief healing role would seem to be required).

ALTAI. The Altai Kizhi, Telengits, Teles, and Teleuts are pastoralists of mixed Turkic-**Mongolian** descent. After the great changes brought by Russian colonization in the 18th century, there arose shamans who, not bound to traditional **clan** structure, took on **spirits** of deceased shamans as their guardians, or **helper-spirits**, and conducted **healing** rituals (Vinogradov 2003). As noted in A. Anokhin's (1924) important early work on Altaic shamanism, the clan-based **white shamans** conducted **rituals** and had "heavenly patrons," who were the benefactors of the clan they belonged to and represented. Anokhin advocated that there were also **black shamans**, as well as "black-white" shamans, but other ethnographers, such as Wilhelm Radloff and Leonid Potapov, did not record such distinctions. Altaic **cosmology** consisted of three levels—a "**tiered cosmos**," consisting of an **underworld**, middle world, and **upper world**—and shamans interacted with the **other-than-human persons** of all these realms.

Impressive Altaic ceremonies featuring a richly **costumed** shaman beating a **drum** and entering a **trance** in order to travel to **other worlds** and communicate with the spirits were observed by several ethnographers. Most famously, Radloff's account has been quoted in numerous subsequent studies, leading **Mircea Eliade** to consider Altaic shamans, in the **locus classicus**, as the most archetypal of all shamans.

During Soviet times, Potapov published work on Altaic shamanism, a topic of study not considered worthy by the antireligious authorities—shamans, along with all religions, were put down with great persecution. The indigenous revitalist religious movement of Ak Jang, the "White Faith" (which had emerged in the Altai in 1904), was initially opposed to shamanism, but itself survived persecution and emerged in the post-Soviet era as a religious and cultural revitalization movement with an ambiguous identity. On the one hand, it now accepts some elements of shamanism, but on the other, it defines itself as nonshamanic (Krader 1956; Dugarov 1991; Vinogradov 2003). There is interest among contemporary Altaians in reclaiming their shamanic past, but there is also a strong push toward reviving Altaic culture and spirituality through Ak Jang. In addition, the books of **Carlos Castaneda** were available in the former Soviet Union, and the Altai has become a destination for **neo-shamans** seeking shamanic gurus and Shambhala (Vinogradov 1999, 41); in *Entering the Circle: Ancient Secrets of Siberian Shamanism Discovered by a Russian Psychiatrist* (1997), **Olga Kharitidi** meets a **Don Juan**–like female Altaian shaman, thus establishing herself in the West as the "Castaneda" of Altaic shamanism.

ALTERED STATES OF CONSCIOUSNESS (ASC). Shamans are sometimes distinguished from other religious or cultural leaders by their ability to deliberately enter distinctive states of consciousness. While these states are sometimes labeled "**trance**" (dissociation from "ordinary reality"), some commentators use terms that are thought to be more narrowly applicable to the experience and practice of shamans, perhaps even as definitive of shamanism rather than other, broader phenomena. **Mircea Eliade** talks of "**ecstasy**" (principally the experience of **soul** flight or **journeying**), while **Michael Harner** prefers "**shamanic state of consciousness**" (a singular state in which realities outside of "normal" perception are experienced).

While **neo-shamanism** is deeply concerned with inner experience and **individual** states of consciousness, there are larger debates about whether there is a single kind of "religious experience" and whether it is possible to speak about unmediated "experience" at all, which make it doubtful that certainty can be achieved about the nature of shamans' states of consciousness or awareness. **Piers Vitebsky** argues that, since there are many different cultural understandings of what shamans do, it is likely that there are many different shamanic states of consciousness. **Caroline Humphrey** and **Urgunge Onon** expand on this by noting a range of states of mind—including different kinds of **dreaming**, assumption of other identities, having visions, the exaltation of calling for blessings, various states of dissociation, fever-induced delirium, and drunkenness—all of which enable Daur **Mongol** shamans, *yadgan*, to access knowledge and experience or perform **rituals**. More significantly, they argue that for both shamans and their communities, what shamans did was more important than any actual state of consciousness. That is, it is less important that shamans actually enter trance or become ecstatic in their mind, experience, or state of consciousness, but vitally important that they demonstrate that they engage with **spirits** or powerful **other-than-human persons**. For example, shamans may demonstrate that they are "journeying" by the **performance** of culturally recognizable acts such as shaking, making **animal** noises, foaming at the mouth, falling to the ground, and so on. Particular actions are associated with, or mean, certain things—for example, lying still, apparently unaware of one's surroundings, indicates that shamans may be "journeying" beyond their bodily and geographic location. If so, it may be better to speak of "**altered styles of communication**" (also ASC) between shamans, their communities, and **otherworld** persons (or spirits). A complementary approach is taken by **Roger Walsh** in arguing that a careful phenomenological approach to what people say they experience permits interpreters to distinguish between shamanic experiences and those of schizophrenics or practitioners of meditation.

In a contrasting trend there is considerable interest in the parallels between brain chemistry and states during shamanic performance and those influenced by endorphins or stimulants such as **ayahuasca** (***yagé***) or **peyote**. A whole style of neo-shamanism utilizing psychoactive plants has evolved as a practical experimental and experiential expression of this interest. Linking a dated theory that the right and left hemispheres of the brain work separately and that nostril blocking can affect brain states, allied to an overemphasis on ASCs, has led **John Pilch** to claim that breathing only through the left nostril can stimulate the right side of the brain and result in ASCs. Questions about conscious states and performative actions continue to be debated. A solution that is applicable to every culture and situation may be impossible or inappropriate, and it may be more useful to attend to specifics.

Although **Michael Winkelman**'s proposal that ASC should stand for "alternate" rather than "altered" state of consciousness has not been widely accepted, his reasoning that "altered . . . implies a static, foundational state" is valid. *See also* ENTHEOGENS; MCKENNA, TERENCE; PSYCHONAUTS.

AMARINGO, PABLO (1938 or 1943–). Peruvian **Amazonian** former ***vegetalista*** whose paintings of "**ayahuasca** visions" were published in a book (1991) he coauthored with Luis Luna (who had met Amaringo during ethnobotanical work with Dennis McKenna). Although the colorful and dramatic paintings draw attention to the visionary results of ingesting ayahuasca and chakruna (*Psychotria viridis*), powerful plant persons and shamans themselves, the book's text not only notes **altered states of consciousness** but, perhaps more importantly, **adjusted styles of** (and abilities in) **communication**. With the aid of ayahuasca, for example, Amaringo heard Amazonian trees weeping as they were cut down and sought **healing** knowledge from helpful **other-than-human persons** or **spirits**. Amaringo ceased shamanizing in 1977 and founded an **art** school to teach painting.

AMAZONIA. The many indigenous peoples of Amazonia (a vast area of South America drained by the Amazon River, including its highland watersheds) traditionally employ and/or fear shamans. A common theme in recent academic discussions of the region's shamanic understandings and practices is the importance of **blood** (i.e., violence) and **tobacco**. There is also a more general interest in the visionary plants or psychoactives, substances, and brews employed by shamans or their clients (especially **ayahuasca**). Perhaps this is not surprising given the large numbers of available plants that are used in the region. As is common elsewhere, **initiation** among Amazonian shamans typically involves **illness** (sometimes self-induced by overconsumption of tobacco), **journeys** to other worlds (sometimes unwilling), **dismemberment**, and relationships with other-than-human

helpers or allies (sometimes including marriage). Shamans' roles in Amazonia are also similar to those elsewhere: **healing**, seeking knowledge, conflict against enemies, and **protection** from **predators**.

Specific elements of particular cultures and variants within the broad Amazonian culture create different stresses from what is encountered elsewhere. In particular, the pervasive division of the animate **cosmos** into predators and prey provides shamans with specific roles. They are commonly associated with **jaguars**, even to the extent of being known as jaguars themselves, placing them firmly on the predator side of the equation. **Eduardo Viveiros de Castro** notes that a shaman's major role in this context is to perceive the underlying (humanoid) person disguised by the clothing of animality, to tell whether the approaching person is a predator or not, and to deal with predators when they do approach. Unlike European-derived culture/**nature** dualism, Amazonian peoples understand that the cosmos is essentially cultural, even monocultural, and that differentiation is not expressed as multiculturalism but as "multinaturalism." What is important, and sometimes vital, is to know when a being is subjectively involved or interested in one, especially if they intend to treat one as prey. But the ability to share the perspective of **other-than-human persons** (e.g., seeing rotten meat as cooked food, as vultures do, or humans as prey, as jaguars do) is dangerous, and shamans manage it only after initiation and training, and even then with care.

At the same time, however, this learned ability leads to degrees of separation between shamans and their human communities. Shamans become suspect and at least potentially dangerous. The notion that shamans may be **transformed** into the appearance (at least) of their **otherworld** helpers or **power animals** or plants may seem romantic (and this may explain its attraction to **neo-shamans**), but in its Amazonian form, it entails a shift away from humanity and human kinship. At its extreme, as in **dark shamanism** or ***kanaimà***, shamans are suspect of becoming **cannibal** predators. In writing about the Warao, Johannes Wilbert notes the association of older shamans with offensive **sorcery** and also with cannibal deities who seek the blood and flesh of humans. Although such betrayals of their own people make shamans suspect, dangerous, and potentially unwelcome, it may also be recognized that they play a **mediating** role with powerful beings who might otherwise entirely destroy and consume humanity.

Both among the Warao and more widely, the more normative and acceptable style of shamanism in the region is concerned with healing and protection from enemies. Many indigenous languages here use words cognate with ***piya*** or *payé*, but according to **Alan Campbell**'s ethnography of the **Wayapí**, these may not be nominative forms (nouns equivalent to *shaman* or *shamanism*) but instead verbal and adjectival forms: activities or particular kinds or styles of activities or active beings. Thus, while some Amazonian peoples employ shamans, others merely recognize particular abilities, actions, or styles as being "shamanic." The influence of Amazonia on the academic and neo-shamanic construction of shamanism is particularly associated with the ethnography of **Michael Harner** among the Untusuri **Shuar** (Jivaro) and **Conibo** and his promulgation of **core shamanism**.

AMBIGUITY. Shamans in many cultures are perceived ambiguously. While they may be called upon to **heal** or **protect** their communities and clients, they may also be suspected of being able and willing to harm people. The difference between a shaman and a **sorcerer** or **witch** is not equivalent to being "one of us" or an enemy. Commonly, "our shaman" may be as suspect of being dangerous and **predatory** as the shamans of enemy groups. Such ambiguous positions may arise from the **initiations** that make shamans different from "ordinary" people. They might enhance the ability of shamans to **mediate** between humans and **other-than-human persons**, but they can result in shamans being marginal to the ordinary life of their communities. In many respects, shamans **perform** roles in indigenous cultures and stories similar to the **tricksters** whose ambiguous or negative acts transform the world. Discussion of "**dark shamans**" (e.g., by **Neil Whitehead**) involve some of the most interesting considerations and examples of ambiguity. **Alan Campbell**'s summary is eloquent: "All very well to be the village **doctor**; but it's not much of a role or an office to be the village killer."

AMERICAN INDIAN MOVEMENT (AIM). Under the banner of self-determination, AIM has campaigned since 1968 for the rights of **Native Americans**, with notable success regarding treaties, sovereignty, and the U.S. Constitution and laws. Following the resolution of the Fifth Annual Meeting of the Tradition Elders Circle in 1980,

AIM in 1984 declared a resolution against the appropriation of Native spirituality by non-Natives and the selling of such material by Native teachers. Such well-known shamans as **Sun Bear**, **Wallace Black Elk**, and **Brooke Medicine Eagle** (named "Ego" here) were singled out as inauthentic spiritual leaders who prostitute Native spirituality for profit. **Neo-shamans** continue to advertise workshops, **vision quests**, retreats, and other "native" ceremonies nonetheless, often at extortionate prices, in which both Natives and non-Natives may participate. Issues of cultural appropriation are complex and culturally specific (e.g., work by **Michael Brown**): in some shamanic communities (such as the **Shuar**), payment for shamanic apprenticeship is not uncommon, while in others (e.g., **Lakota**), fiscal return is not in keeping with tradition. Cultural copyright is a burgeoning issue; for example, the people of Zia Pueblo successfully sued the state of New Mexico for its use of a Pueblo symbol in the state flag.

ANCESTORS. While this word suggests earlier generations, the predecessors of the current generation, its precise meaning varies from one cultural context to another. It is likely that the term is equivalent to "all who have died" in modern European languages. However, even in Europe, the most significant festivals honor specific dead individuals or groups—saints, martyrs, fallen soldiers, and so on—rather than some larger generality. Some indigenous cultures pay considerable attention to deceased members of recent generations but almost entirely ignore those who died longer ago than four generations back. It is equally possible to make offerings to the general community of "the ancestors" without being interested in specific named individuals. The word is also used with reference to co-creative beings who, in **Aboriginal Australian** understanding, may have a **totemic** rather than genetic relationship with humans. In some cultures, shamans may be required to communicate with ancestors or with "the dead," whose demands must be met if they are not to cause harm. Elsewhere, as among the Daur **Mongols**, shamans do not make offerings to ordinary, nonshaman ancestors (or **spirits**), being somewhat removed from ordinary human life themselves.

ANDREWS, LYNN. Best-selling author and **neo-shaman** based in Los Angeles; she has written 18 books, including *Medicine Woman*

(1983), *Jaguar Woman* (1985), and *Dark Sister: A Sorcerer's Love Story* (1995). These books introduce readers to Andrews's personal spiritual transformation from an LA art dealer to a 21st-century neo-shaman after encountering teachers Agnes Whistling Elk and Ruby Plenty Chiefs, who, according to Andrews, are **Native American** members of the Sisterhood of the Shields, a group of 44 indigenous **women** who preserve the secrets of their female shamanic traditions. Andrews offers personal consultations, lectures, and workshops in international locations from Egypt to Hawaii, and in 1994 she established the Lynn Andrews Center for Sacred Arts and Training (Mystery School) offering a four-year professional certification program and bachelor's, master's, and doctorate degrees. The existence of Andrews's teachers and the authenticity of her shamanic teachings have been challenged by scholars, styling her as a female **Carlos Castaneda**, and the **American Indian Movement** and many Native American leaders have publicly denounced her.

ANGAKKOQ. "Visionary and dreamer"; the **Greenlandic** shaman (pl. *angakkut*; also *ilisiitsoq* sing., *ilisiitsut* pl.). Missionary Hans Egede in 1721 offered the first detailed account of shamanism on the west coast of Greenland, describing how the shaman is bound with his head between his legs, his hands behind his back, and a **drum** at his side. The community gathered in the darkness of the house sings for the shaman, who calls on his **spirit helpers** to aid his unfettering. Thus untied, he ascends on a **journey** through the roof of the house to the spirit world, where he consults **ancestor** shamans and then returns to his people with important knowledge to maintain harmony between the worlds of spirits and humans. The Greenlandic angakkoq was a **mediator** between human and **other-than-human persons**, ensuring **taboos** were maintained and attempting reconciliation where they were broken. Sickness was interpreted as a result of breaching taboos, so **healing** required confessions to transgressions on the part of the patient. In her important review of reports by the Egede family of **Christian** missionaries and the Danish ethnographers **Knud Rasmussen** and Gustav Holm, among others, **Merete Demant Jakobsen** follows **Sergei Shirokogoroff**'s assessment of **Siberian** shamanism and characterizes the angakkoq as a "**master of spirits**." The emphasis on control (over the other-than-human people shamans engage with) is fitting for shamanisms of the **Arctic** and parts of **Siberia**, but is not a universal feature of shamanisms. Rather than attempt to pin shamans down to a checklist of features, a decentered approach localizes shamans in specific socio-historical circumstances.

ANIMALS. Shamans engage with animals in a range of significant ways. In societies that live by hunting, shamans may **journey** beyond their physical location or seek the aid of knowledgeable other-than-human **helpers** to locate prey. They may also seek permission from those who control animal groups (a **master or mistress of animals**) before the hunt or offer them gratitude afterward. In **animist** communities (where animals may be considered to be persons or to have **souls**), shamans may be required to **mediate** between their human kin and animals or their "**owners**" who may be offended by the taking of lives. **Bear ceremonialism** and **totemism** form wider contexts in which some shamans also form intimate relationships with particular animals or animal species. In **initiation**, they may bond with animals who become their helpers throughout their careers or lives. Animal communities may also be thought to employ shamans among themselves, and sometimes such shamans visit human shamans. As among humans, some animal shamans can be dangerous and unwelcome, that is, may practice **sorcery**. Particular cultures give priority to particular animals; for example, **jaguars** and anacondas are especially important in **Amazonia**. *See also* POWER ANIMALS.

ANIMAS VALLEY INSTITUTE. Located in southwest Colorado, in the valley of the Río de las Animas Perdidas (River of Lost Souls), and run by Bill Plotkin, "psychologist and wilderness guide" since 1980, the Animas Valley Institute describes itself as "one of **North America**'s longest-standing organizations offering contemporary wilderness rites," including **vision quests**. It offers "**nature**-based programs supporting the recovery and embodiment of the life of the **soul**, the unique truth, passion, and gifts we each were born with." Like other **neo-shamanic** centers, the institute refers to the psychology of **Carl Jung**, especially "**individuation**," to validate its focus on "the mysterious energies within our psyches that guide us on the inward **journey** to soul."

ANIMISM. Arguably the proper label for the type of religion practiced among traditional indigenous people who employ shamans. Rather than being "shamanists" or adherents of "shamanism," these people may be usefully named "animists." While the term was coined by Edward Tylor (a founder of the discipline of anthropology) to define the essence of religion as "the belief in **spirits**" and has played a significant role in theories about the origins of religion, it is used here in a new way. The old theory of animism alleged that indigenous people and the earliest human **ancestors** had made a mistake in believing in spirits. The new theory, associated with **Nurit Bird-David**, **Eduardo Viveiros de Castro**, Signe Howell, and others, sees animism as a relational ontology—the recognition that the world is full of persons, only some of whom are human. In **Irving Hallowell**'s terms, there are human persons and **other-than-human persons**, including rock persons, tree persons, cloud persons, and perhaps "spirit persons."

Animist worldviews and lifeways make it necessary for there to be shamans because (1) humans are relatively weak and need to seek help (in the form of knowledge, **healing**, or defense) from more powerful other-than-human persons and (2) humans often offend other-than-human persons and need **mediators** in order to restore respectful relationships. In this context, shamans may be defined as those persons trained and skilled at working for their community when it is necessary to seek help from or reconciliation with the wider community of life. In turn, as **Graham Harvey** has argued, animism makes shamans both possible and necessary because their roles are about dealing with the problems of a living world.

However, in concluding a discussion of **blood**, **tobacco**, **jaguars**, and shamans, **Carlos Fausto** describes **Amazonian** shamanism as "a predatory animism." This sinister conclusion is based on the fact that the ability of some people (shamans) to interact relationally (e.g., by adoption or alliance) with powerful other-than-human persons (especially jaguars) depends on **predation** in **warfare** and hunting because these are preferred means of affirming one's agency and intentionality rather than being used, preyed upon, by other persons. In short, shamans are necessary in animist communities as both curers and **combatants**.

ARAWETÉ. Indigenous **Amazonian** people whose shamanism is similar in some respects to that of neighboring peoples, and different in others. **Eduardo Viveiros de Castro** summarizes his rich ethnographic account of Araweté shamanism by saying that it

> does not involve any formal **initiation**. Certain recurring **dreams**, especially those featuring the **Jaguar**-Thing, may be signs of a shamanic calling. But what distinguishes a shaman is not his capacity for dreaming (which is also important for a killer), but rather his association with **tobacco**. The usual way of saying someone is not a shaman is *petĩ ã-ĩ*, a "noneater of tobacco." Shamanic training involves a series of sessions of becoming intoxicated by this plant until the person is "made translucent" and the gods come to him.

Unlike other Amazonian shamans, those of the Araweté are not trained by **spirits**—"tutelary spirits do not exist"—but shamans have a broad relationship to all significant **other-than-human persons** in their universe. In addition to tobacco, the other "emblem of shamanism is the *aray* rattle." All adult men possess such rattles and may shamanize to some degree. **Healing** by **sucking** out alien **intrusions** (e.g., **darts**), prevention of assault by enemies and the **illnesses** they may cause, and the returning of detached **souls** are common shamanic practices.

ARCTIC. Indigenous peoples of the Arctic (including parts of Samiland, Norway, Iceland, **Greenland**, Canada, Alaska, and Russia) adapted to its harsh conditions in a variety of ways, and the region is argued by some scholars to be the (or at least *a*) **locus classicus** of shamanism, encompassing the **Inuit**, **Evenk**, **Saami**, and other indigenous communities. Such diversity demonstrates that the concept of a single *ur*-shamanism is inappropriate, yet consistencies across the cultures of the region (e.g., the **mastery of spirits**, **sorcery**, and **healing**) indicate areas of commonality.

ART AND ARTIFACTS. *Art* is a contested term, but the production of visual culture is consistent across shamanisms. Examples might include the impressive visual display of **Siberian** shamans' **costumes** and maps of **spirit** realms on **Saami** shamans' **drums** collected by early ethnographers for display in museum collections. Art in the West tends to be understood as paintings "in the frame" and sculptures "on the plinth" in galleries and museums. Although such a view is Eurocentric, perhaps more fitting to this view of art are the kaleidoscopic paintings of visionary experiences by **Amazonian** *ayahuasceros* and ***vegetalistas***.

Many indigenous peoples consider the objects and sometimes their decoration to be **other-than-human persons** in their own right. While never forgetting the constructed nature of artifacts (e.g., **drums**, masks, **medicine bundles**, and **sucking** tubes) with which they work, they perceive another more active and personal dimension to them. Greg Sarris's writing about the **Pomo** basket weaver and **doctor** Mabel McKay provides some excellent examples of ways in which "**object-persons**" may be treated respectfully.

From prehistory, artistic traditions associated with shamans include a number of **rock art** traditions that have been linked to the **visions** and other **trance** experiences of shamans, from **cave art** of the **European Paleolithic** period and **Southern African** rock art to the megalithic art of **Northern Europe**. In indigenous contexts, some of the most celebrated of shamanic art includes the brightly colored yarn paintings of the **Huichol** (Wixáritari) Indians in Mexico and the split-representation **perspective** art of North America's **Pacific Northwest** coast. Such indigenous shamanic art traditions have been appropriated into the Western dealer-critic system, with Huichol yarn paintings and Pacific Northwest wood carvings, for example, fetching high prices on the "primitive" art market.

A number of modern artists have associated themselves with shamanism or have been labeled shamans by others. The most famous example is **Joseph Beuys** (1921–1986), who depicted shamans in many of his works and made **altered states of consciousness** an integral part of some of his **performance** pieces. Less well known, though no less significant, are occultist and artist **Austin Osman Spare** (1887–1956) and contemporary artist **Marcus Coates**. Marc Chagall (1887–1985) and Vasily Kandinsky (1866–1944) have also been labeled shamans, usually based on the influences of occultism, mysticism, and folklore on their work (as discussed in work by Michael Tucker and Mark Levy), but such sweeping interpretations tend to pay little or no attention to the diversity and contexts of shamanisms, preferring monolithic characterizations. *See also* CALIFORNIAN ROCK ART; SIBERIAN AND CENTRAL ASIAN ROCK ART.

ASIA. *See* BURYATIA; CENTRAL ASIA; CHINA; INDIA; INDONESIA; KOREA; MALAYSIA; MONGOLIA; NEPAL; SAKHA; SIBERIA, NORTHERN AND EASTERN; SIBERIA, SOUTHERN; SIBERIA, WESTERN; SOUTH AND EAST ASIA; TIBET; TUVA.

ATKINSON, JANE MONNIG. In her ethnography *The Art and Politics of Wana Shamanship* (1989), Atkinson discusses the **Wana** of the interior region of east-central Sulawesi in **Indonesia**. As slash-and-burn cultivators, the Wana rely for **mediation** between the worlds of human and **other-than-human persons** on *tau kawalia*, "people spirits" (i.e., shamans). Atkinson addresses the effectiveness of shamans and their **rituals**, focusing on and accounting for the popularity of the *mabolong* or **drumming** ceremony, arguing that ritual can be read anthropologically as symbolic, therapeutic, and a **performance**. **Patients** rely on shamans for **healing**, shamans rely upon their audiences for recognition, and the audience relies upon shamans to maintain community harmony. Shamans must perform well in order to maintain the attention of the audience, by which the community acknowledges the shamanic abilities. The symbolic component of the ritual involves fear of the everyday problems that threaten community life and can be healed only by shamans. Therapeutically, the audience's focus of attention on the often **humorous** shaman rather than on the suffering patient promotes a catharsis in which emotional tensions are eased.

Atkinson asserts that symbolic and performance-based readings are overlooked if too much emphasis is placed on **therapy** as the only goal of shamanic rituals, however, and that the essential role of the community is neglected if the shaman–patient relationship is emphasized. On the other hand, if the ritual is interpreted in terms of its symbolic, therapeutic, and performance-based meanings, the community dynamics of shamanistic ritual become clear.

Atkinson has also written the indispensable article "Shamanisms Today" (1992), offering a critical engagement with discourse on shamans as well as suggestions for future research. Some 15 years later, the study of shamanism is in need of an updated edition.

AWENYDDION. An obscure practice described only briefly by Giraldus Cambrensis (Gerald of Wales) in his *Description of Wales*, written in the late 12th century. The Awenyddion exhibited behavior that is reminiscent of **possession** and other **trance** practices of some shamans, as well as **divination** through **dreams**:

> Among the Welsh there are certain individuals called Awenyddion who behave as if they are possessed. . . . When you consult them about some problem, they immediately go into a trance and lose control of their

> senses. . . . They do not answer the question put to them in a logical way. Words stream from their mouths, incoherently and apparently meaningless and lacking any sense at all, but all the same well expressed: and if you listen carefully to what they say you will receive the solution to your problem. When it is all over, they will recover from their trance, as if they were ordinary people waking from a heavy sleep, but you have to give them a good shake before they regain control of themselves . . . and when they do return to their senses they can remember nothing of what they have said in the interval. . . . They seem to receive this gift of divination through visions which they see in their dreams. Some of them have the impression that honey or sugary milk is being smeared on their mouths; others say that a sheet of paper with words written on it is pressed against their lips. As soon as they are roused from their trance and have come round from their prophesying, that is what they say has happened.

It is difficult to speculate further on the shamanic or even sociopolitical status of the Awenyddion based on Gerald's brief description, although the allusions to shamanic practice are intriguing. Nonetheless, **Druid**-shamans today use this source to reconstruct a practice of oracular seership meaningful for today's Druid communities. In particular, **Philip "Greywolf" Shallcrass** has interpreted the Awenyddion as shaman-like druid-**priests** and has developed the practice as a druid equivalent of the **Heathen** ***seidr***.

AYAHUASCA. Literally, "vine of the dead" in Quechua; also known as ***yagé*** and cognates in various indigenous **Amazonian** languages. A blend of extracts of the Banisteriopsis vine and *Psychotria virdis* or a similar (DMT-containing) plant from which a **vomit**- and **vision**-inducing drink is brewed and ingested by shamans and **healers** in many cultures and religious complexes (including some forms of **Christianity**). For example, ***vegetalistas*** (plant-inspired shamans such as **Pablo Amaringo**), who are justly famous for the elaborate and colorful paintings that represent some of the resulting visions, treat the vine as a powerful **other-than-human person** and teacher.

Marlene Dobkin de Rios demonstrates that ayahuasca is not used as a curative agent, a **medicine** in the Western sense, but "gives the healer entry into the culturally important area of disease causality, enabling him to identify the nature of the **illness** from which a person is suffering, and then to deflect or neutralize the evil magic which is deemed responsible for illness." She has also commented critically on the rise of "ayahuasca **tourism**" conducted by "common drug dealers" rather than "authentic ayahuasca healers," in which Western tourists (including **psychonauts** and others interested in "**entheogens**") are charged for drug experiences disguised as "advanced shamanic training." Dobkin de Rios's background in medical anthropology and psychotherapy provide her with tools for judging the psychotic results of much of this tourism.

Benny Shanon has systematically charted the phenomenology of the ayahuasca experience and characterized it from a cognitive psychological perspective as well as discussing philosophical ramifications. Principally, he characterizes the effects of ayahuasca as manifestations of unusual enhancement of cognitive functioning, creativity, and intuition.

Ayahuasca is central not only to traditional indigenous practices but also to **Santo Daime** and the União do Vegetal that have spread from Brazil to many other countries. These groups were preceded or are paralleled as ayahuasca enthusiasts and missionaries by **William Burroughs**, Allen Ginsberg, Wade Davies, and Dennis and **Terence McKenna**. The psychoactive ingredients of ayahuasca and many other plants were first scientifically analyzed in the 1930s by **Richard Schultes**.

– B –

BALZER, MAJORIE MANDELSTAM (1950–). Research professor at Georgetown University in the Sociology/Anthropology Department and the Center for Eurasian, Russian, and East European Studies (CERES), where she coordinates the Social, Ethnic, and Regional Issues concentration. As a social-cultural anthropologist, Balzer has done fieldwork in the Russian Federation, especially among the Ob-Ugrian Khanty (Ostiak, also called Yugra) of Western **Siberia** beginning in 1976, and the **Sakha** (also called Yakut) of Eastern Siberia since 1986. Among her many publications concerned with these regions, social theory, interethnic relations, religion, and the growth of nationalism, some are concerned with shamans and shamanism, especially in Siberia and the Sakha Republic. In *Shamanism: Soviet Studies of Traditional Religion in Siberia and Central Asia*, she published translations of the work of four Soviet scholars who "begin from the Marxist-Leninist premise that shamanism (like all religion) is obsolete. But they also concede that traditional shamans improved poetry, entertainment, psychotherapy, and occasionally even cures and genuine leadership for their communities." Her publications include important contributions to debates about shamans and their roles and **performances**, as well as constructions of **gender**. Just as **Caroline Humphrey** and **Urgunge Onon** demonstrate that Daur **Mongol** shamans (*yadgan*) are remade by **initiation** into beings closer to **other-than-human persons** or **spirits** than to human beings, so Balzer supports **Maria Czaplicka** and **Bernard Saladin d'Anglure**'s demonstration that shamans are commonly a "third class" or gender that may **mediate** between other persons. Her discussion of **bear ceremonialism** also contributes to discussion of **animist** human relationships with other-than-human persons, **power animals**, and, perhaps, **totems**.

BASILOV, VLADIMIR (1937–1998). Russian ethnographer who published extensively on shamans in **Central Asia** during the latter half of the 20th century. He redressed the scholarly neglect of shamanisms in the region in favor of the "classic" shamanisms of **Siberia** (the **locus classicus**) and demonstrated the endurance and diversity of shamanisms in Central Asia. His seminal book is entitled *Shamanism among the Peoples of Central Asia and Kazakhstan* (1992).

BATAK. Indigenous people from the remaining forests of Palawan, the Philippines. Their shamans share many of the functions of shamans elsewhere, but a principal role is as **mediators** between human communities and **masters** of rice, bees, otters, and other **other-than-human persons** on whose abundance the Batak rely. In regular seasonal **rituals**, especially the *lambay*, shamans take samples of the first honey collected in the forest and seek knowledge about the state of honey resources in the area. If it is indicated that they are too low, the shamans dance while in a **trance** and seek to distribute additional honey. In doing so, they participate in the distributive work not only of bees but also of the Master of Bees, who is ultimately responsible for the dispersal of such resources. Similar engagements with rice and the Master of Rice are equally important and should not be seen as a symbolic function but as a political mediation significant in **resource management**.

BATES, BRIAN. Professor of psychology at the University of Brighton and director of the Shaman Research Program at the University of Sussex. Bates is best known as the author of *The Way of Wyrd* (1983), a novel inspired by historic documents from **Northern Europe**, particularly Anglo-Saxon England, as well as **Carlos Castaneda**'s **Don Juan** mythos, and describing the relationship between an Anglo-Saxon shaman and a young **Christian** monk. *The Wisdom of the Wyrd* (1996) and *The Real Middle Earth* (2002) are follow-up scholarly works that approach the ancient **pagan** religions of Northern Europe as shamanistic. Of particular note is Bates's interpretation of the "Night Mare" charm, or charm "against a Dwarf" in the Anglo-Saxon *Lacnunga* spell book (British Library manuscript Harley 585, c. 1000 CE), according to which a shaman **initiate** is ridden into the **other world** by a *wight* (**spirit**). Bates's work has been influential on contemporary **Heathen** discourse on shamanistic aspects of Northern religion. Bates is also a fellow of the Royal Society of Arts, research director of the Christensen Foundation (Palo Alto) project on recovering the **nature**-based knowledge of ancient England, and senior adviser to the Council of Elders, a project on worldwide indigenous wisdom funded by the Ford Foundation.

BEAR CEREMONIALISM. Among many **Native American**, **Northern European**, and **Siberian** communities, many **rituals** form part of a complex of "bear ceremonialism." **Marjorie Balzer**, for example, draws out the diversities and social tensions involved in what she describes as the complex's most elaborate form, as practiced among the Ob-Ugrian peoples of Western Siberia and the groups living along the Amur River, which forms the border between Siberia and **China**. She writes, "In both regions, the skin and head of a ritually killed bear are placed on a sacred bier and fêted for multiple days." Carnivalesque celebrations, including satirical plays, cross-dressing, uncharacteristic female license, and general bawdiness provide a context in which social tensions are played out, if not resolved. Although shamans are forbidden to shamanize during the festival as celebrated on the Amur, probably because their role as **mediators** between humans and **otherworld** persons is diffused throughout the community, they indicate auspicious timing for the event. Leadership in ritual and communal events, including engaging with **other-than-human persons**, is taken by **elders**, while the events illustrate the broader **animist** ritual and social context in which shamans work.

Juha Pentikäinen presents important discussions of bear cults and folklore in both Finnish and **Saami** cultures. He notes, for example, that there are more than 200 synonyms for *bear* in Finnish, but the actual word was rarely spoken since to do so might provoke an assault by bears. As elsewhere, such **taboo** restrictions are part of the broad animist context in which shamans are employed.

Similar bear ceremonial and discursive complexes could be illustrated with reference to many Native American cultures. Bears play significant roles in **Ojibwe initiatory** and **healing** rituals such as the **Midewiwin**, for instance. This involves bear impersonation by both the shaman presiding over the ritual and initiates, and also participation by otherworld bears as initiators and tempters. In their **trickster**-like **ambiguity**, bears reveal their kinship with shamans and creative beings. **Gerald Vizenor** extends traditional storytelling into urban contexts in a number of his stories about shamans, bears, and "postindian" mixed-blood people. Ojibwe bear narratives and ceremonials (like those that include other **animals**) arise from a wider **totemism**. "Bear shamans" among California indigenous communities may be either shamans who impersonate bears by wearing a **costume** including a bearskin or shamans who gain the ability to **transform** into bears. Sandra Holliman is particularly interested in these shamans' roles as agents of social control, due to the fear inspired by their reputations and uncertainty about their identities or whereabouts. However, she also alludes to other, more positive, abilities, including the fact that they are considered **doctors**.

BECOMING-ANIMAL. In 1980 French philosopher Gilles Deleuze (1925–1995) and psychoanalyst Félix Guttari (1930–1992) published *A Thousand Plateaus*, the second part of *Capitalism and Schizophrenia* (part 1 is entitled *Anti-Oedipus* [1972]). Deleuze and Guttari speak of "vitalism," a sea of constant flow, flux, change, and "becoming," and in chapter 10, entitled "Memories of a **Sorcerer**," they outline how "we sorcerers" engage with becoming by "**becoming-animal**," a form of **shape-shifting** or **transformation** called **theriomorphism**. Unusually for Western philosophy, shape-shifting in this instance should not be read as a metaphor, analogy, or form of mimesis: for Deleuze and Guttari, becoming-animal is not **imaginal** or fantasy but "perfectly real" (1980, 238, also 273–74). In their disruption of Cartesian, Hegelian, and other Western philosophies, and indeed the Modern condition, Deleuze and Guttari might be argued to offer a critical, postmodern methodology for engaging with indigenous realities such as shamanisms and **animism**. Matt Lee examines the Edwardian artist-shaman **Austin Osman Spare** in this light, arguing that Spare is Deleuzian in the sense that he no longer insists on a focus on the "magician" as controller, perceiver, or creator: Sparean sorcery is "a technique not of . . . ego-dissolution but . . . [of engagement] with . . . the ocean of becoming."

BEUYS, JOSEPH (1921–1986). German **artist** who termed himself a shaman. Tartars allegedly rescued Beuys after the Stuka plane in which he was the radio operator crashed in the Crimea during World War II. The Tartars revived him, badly burned and freezing, with fat and felt insulation, and these substances became a primary inspiration for Beuys's work. Beuys regarded the plane crash as an **initiatory**-like experience, likening it to a death and rebirth, and he also endured a long-lasting breakdown that he viewed as a rite of passage essential to being an artist. Beuys's words "Show your wound" espoused the view that vulnerability is the secret to being an artist—the term *wound* here perhaps alluding to the indigenous shaman as a **wounded healer**. The **performance** of *Coyote: I Like America and America Likes Me* (performed in 1974) deployed shamanistic consciousness-altering practices: wrapped in an enormous piece of felt for hours at a time and wearing a felt trilby hat he termed "shamanic," Beuys spent three days in a room caged with a live coyote, accompanied by a tape recording of chaotic turbine sounds. Beuys was an active campaigner for green issues and his environmental art, such as the planting of *7,000 Oaks* (1982–87), has been labeled "community-based social sculpture."

BIRD-DAVID, NURIT (1951–). Anthropologist at the University of Haifa, Israel, whose article "Animism Revisited" is of considerable importance in understanding **animism**, the worldview and lifeways of shamans and their communities. Her research extends the insights of **Irving Hallowell** by discussing her research among the **Nayaka**, a **hunter-gatherer** community of the Gir Valley in the Nilgiri region of South **India**. She has also written insightfully about the **sexual**, marital, and other relational languages and **performances** that express human–**animal** and wider human–**nature** encounters. Her demonstration that **hunting** is frequently spoken of in sexual terms (including "courtship, seduction/abduction, consummation and procreation/reproduction") should be read alongside **Carlos Fausto**'s linkage between shamans, hunters, and warriors that place all in a relation to **predation** and **blood**.

BLACK CARIBS. *See* GARIFUNA RELIGION.

BLACK ELK, NICHOLAS (1863–1950). Also known as Hehaka Sapa. An Oglala **Lakota** whose childhood visions and training enabled him to work as a holy man or **medicine man**: a **healer**, leader, and repository of sacred wisdom. In 1904 he converted to Catholicism and became a catechist among the Lakota. In 1930–31 he began to tell the story of his life and times to **John Neihardt**, a Euro-American poet, who published a version following its translation by Neihardt's son Benjamin and transcription by his daughters Hilda and Enid.

Considerable controversy continues about the nature of Neihardt's book, *Black Elk Speaks* (1961). In addition to the question of whether Black Elk should have told anyone other than another Lakota **holy person** about his knowledge, it has been debated what role, if any, he had in the selection and presentation of elements of his biography in the book. There are discrepancies between Neihardt's book and what his daughter transcribed (as published in 1984 by Raymond DeMallie as *The Sixth Grandfather*). The fact that Neihardt says almost nothing about Black Elk's Catholicism makes it difficult to know whether the two men ever discussed the possibility that Catholic glosses may have been put on earlier Lakota practices or on Black Elk's shamanic experiences and work. A similar critique can be leveled at **Joseph Epes Brown**'s book *The Sacred Pipe* (1971).

The books of Neihardt and Brown are commonly understood to provide a blueprint for what "traditional" Lakota religion was like. In an introduction added in 1979, **Vine Deloria Jr.** celebrated *Black Elk Speaks* as a "great religious classic" and a "North American bible of all tribes" that has greatly aided Native quests for "roots" and affirmation. He wrote, "In Black Elk's visions we have a natural relationship to the rest of the cosmos devoid of the trial-court paradigm but incorporating the theme of a sacrifice so important to all religions in a consistent and comprehensible way." Deloria recognized controversies about the relationship between Black Elk and Neihardt, but considered the status of the book as a sacred text to outweigh questions of redaction and production. (Deloria's own family history may have predisposed him to a more generous reading of the book than that of some critics.)

Black Elk Speaks has continued to be used both by **Native Americans** seeking to strengthen or return to traditional ways and by **New Agers** seeking a model of pristine spirituality. Black Elk (as presented in these books) is iconic for those who imagine Native Americans as being "close to **nature**" and **environmentally** responsible, and therefore as providing a solution to modernity's problems. While such an icon is almost "shamanic" in its transformative power, it is Black Elk's preconversion role as a holy man that contributes to understandings of shamans and their activities. Elements such as his initiatory visions and **illnesses** perfectly exemplify the kind of shamanic narrative preferred by **Mircea Eliade** and many **neo-shamans**. His encounters with **otherworld** persons, the "six Grandfathers" in particular, and his elaborations of Lakota rituals may be taken to be emblematic of the relational, **animist** engagements of holy people. Black Elk cannot now be disentangled from Neihardt's and Brown's selective presentations and must remain an enigmatic and contested figure. In this, he is also iconic of the treatment of Native Americans and other indigenous people in general and shamans in particular.

BLACK ELK, WALLACE (1921–2004). An Oglala **Lakota** who conducted healing and shamanic rituals both for Native and non-**Native Americans**. His conversations with William Lyon (beginning in 1978) led to the publication of *Black Elk: The Sacred Ways of a Lakota* (1990), a series of anecdotes about becoming and being a Lakota shaman. In 1973 he and his wife, Grace, were among the first **elders** to support the occupation of Wounded Knee (site of one of the last massacres of Native Americans by the U.S. military in 1890) by a "Warrior Society" of Native activists of many Nations that became the **American Indian Movement** (AIM). He is also credited with having been instrumental in the passing of the American Indian Religious Freedom Act in 1978. Nonetheless, his willingness to teach a version of Lakota spirituality and **neo-shamanism** to non-Native people, especially those labeled "Rainbow Warriors," led to his naming in AIM's 1984 resolution against those considered disrespectful and exploitative of sacred ceremonies and of the clients they charge to participate. Groups and websites such as Gohiyuhi/Respect and **Center for SPIRIT** list him among "frauds" and "**plastic medicine people**." His take on these conflicting assessments (apart from an encouragement not to engage in conflict) was that he aimed to preserve a "sacred way" while making it accessible to all. The two phases of his life may be marked by his close relationships first with **Leonard Crow Dog** and then with **Sun Bear** (Vincent LaDuke). He was not, as he and others have sometimes claimed, the grandnephew of **Nicholas Black Elk**.

BLACK SHAMANISM. Caroline Humphrey cites the 19th-century **Buryat** scholar Dorji Banzarov as saying that there was no indigenous term for shamanism, but that a recognizable complex of practices and **cosmology** had come to be called "the black faith," *har shashin*, as a "direct contrast with **Buddhism**, which was called the 'yellow faith.'" However, the Buryat and **Sakha** peoples of **Siberia** also distinguish between "black shamans" and "**white shamans**." Black shamans enter a **trance** and descend into the **underworld** as part of their work as **healers** who **combat** various **illnesses**. Unlike the **Amazonian** distinction between curing shamans and "**dark shamans**," *black* and *white* among the Buryat and Sakha peoples are not equivalent to "good" and "bad." However, this contrast is made and elaborated by the Duha Tuvinians and Tuvinians in **Mongolia** and in the Republic of **Tuva**, among whom black is associated with malevolence, "evil deeds," and pollution, according to Benedikte Kristen.

BLACKER, CARMEN. Formerly professor of Japanese in the Faculty of Oriental Studies at the University of Cambridge, Blacker has carried out extensive research on religious practices and folklore, including shamanism, mountain asceticism, and **animal witchcraft** in Japan. Her publications, especially *The Catalpa Bow: A Study of Shamanistic Practices in Japan* (1999), remain central texts in the study of Japanese religions but may not have received the attention they deserve in the wider, more comparative study of shamanism.

BLAIN, JENNY (1949–). Senior lecturer in applied social sciences in the Faculty of Development and Society at Sheffield Hallam University, where she leads the master's program in social science research methods. As an anthropologist studying identity and meaning within today's **Paganisms**, Blain has written extensively on paganism and contemporary **Heathenry**, especially shamanistic ***seidr***, focusing on issues of insider research, the anthropology of **altered states of consciousness**, and **gender**. Her book *Nine Worlds of Seid-Magic: Ecstasy and Neo-Shamanism in North European Paganism* (2002) presented autoethnographic and insider research on contemporary seidr practitioners and shamanistic interpretative work on Heathen religions in **Northern Europe** and contributed to the theorizing of indigenous British and North European shamanisms, as well as to interpretations of Heathenry past (in the Eddas and Sagas) and present (among practitioners). Her journal articles address and contribute to research on shamanisms, Paganisms, **ritual** studies, gender and **sexuality**, folklore, and heritage studies, and her contributions to undergraduate texts (including the introductory sociology text *Think Twice* [2005] she coauthored with Lorne Tepperman) attempt to introduce students to the complexities of thinking about how spirituality and worldview (including **cosmology**) interface with the everyday world. Blain was coeditor and contributor to the volume *Researching Paganisms* (2004), which offered new epistemological, theoretical, and methodological considerations on research in the study of culture and identity, through the case example of new **nature** or earth religions, including her own chapter on seidr. With **Robert Wallis**, Blain codirects the Sacred Sites, Contested Rights/Rites project examining contemporary Pagan engagements with the past, particularly **new-indigenes** at **sacred sites**.

BLOOD. In discussing **Amazonian** shamanism, **Carlos Fausto** notes that to many specialists "the most noticeable fact about this myriad of **neoshamanic** sites and rites is not its profusion but rather the absence of blood and **tobacco**." As **Gerardo Reichel-Dolmatoff** writes, "Shamans and **jaguars** are thought to be almost identical, or at least equivalent, in their power, and each in his own sphere of action, but occasionally able to exchange their roles." The division of all beings between **predators** and prey typically sees shamans and jaguars sharing predatory roles, even when they are not suspect of being **sorcerers**. Among the Asurini do Tocantins, people discover that they have been **elected** to become shamans when they **dream** about jaguars. Fausto also notes that among the Asurini do Xingu shamans are closely related to **spirits** who penetrate human bodies and devour them from within. In all these cases, consuming blood is definitive: it is what jaguars, powerful beings, and shamans do. The consumption of tobacco is important not only as a stimulant but also as a means of covering the "stench of blood." Fausto concludes by defining Amazonian shamanism as "predatory **animism**." He explains that the ability to become familiar with **other-than-human persons** (especially as adopted kin or allies), which permits shamans "to act on the world in order to cure, to fertilize, and to kill," depends on "predation in **warfare** and hunting." Because shamans must be predators in one sense or another, bloodshed (actual or metaphorical) is necessary in every stage of shamanic **initiation** and **performance**.

BOAS, FRANZ (1858–1942). German anthropologist who spent most of his life in the United States and is known as a "founding father" of American (i.e., cultural) anthropology, at Columbia University heading the first Department of Anthropology in the country. Boas advocated an empirical approach to anthropological "science," arguing that a culture must be studied dispassionately in context (an early form of empiricism and participant-observation) not according to the vagaries of ideology (making Boas a founder of cultural relativism). Boas's year with the **Inuit** of Baffin Island in 1883 and his experiences of this culturally sophisticated though apparently technologically primitive society led him to reject the notion of technological evolution—and cultural evolution more generally, as conceived by Edward Tylor, Lewis Henry Morgan, and Herbert Spencer—as indicative of cultural dynamics and success (cultural evolution had been in vogue since the publication of Charles Darwin's theory of evolution, though it differs from Darwin in numerous respects). Instead, Boas advocated local context and history. Among the Inuit, Boas recorded the practices of the ***angakkoq***. Boas also made research trips to the **Pacific Northwest** in the late 1880s, where he studied the diversity of genealogy as well as **art** and shamanism.

BÖN-PO. A **Tibetan** form of **Buddhism** that is likely to have originated as a pre-Buddhist **animism** with shamanic leaders. Some interpreters try to maintain a distinction between Bön and Buddhism, but this ignores both Tibetan self-understandings and many centuries of history. The integration of pre-Buddhist **cosmologies**, practices, and

performances is said to explain the importance of **exorcism** in Tibetan Mahayana Buddhism.

BORI. Discussed by **Ioan Lewis** as a West **African** and **North African** "**possession** cult" arising from the interaction of indigenous religious traditions and **Islam**, and attractive to **women** in particular, perhaps because it gives them a religious role unavailable in their wider society.

BRAIN CHEMISTRY. Western science views the brain as the source of human consciousness, and increasingly sophisticated understandings of brain chemistry have prompted some researchers on shamanism to consider brain chemistry and the role of the human central nervous system as key to understanding **altered states of consciousness** and shamanic experiences. **Neuropsychological** research on altered states has contributed to the shamanistic interpretation of **rock art**, wherein certain geometric shapes termed *entoptic phenomena* that are consistent in visionary experiences may be identified in rock art imagery. In addition, the efficacy of shamanic **healing** has been interpreted as resulting from the release of endorphins (from *endogenous*, meaning "within," and *morphine*, a painkiller), biochemical compounds resembling opiates in their analgesic effects. By attaching themselves to the receptors on nerve cells, endorphins reduce the body's sensitivity to pain—as "natural painkillers" they produce a sense of euphoria. It has been hypothesized that there is an increase in endorphin activity in both **patient** and shaman during shamanic healing, as well as for the shaman during the induction of altered consciousness, such as prolonged dancing and other forms of **deprivation**, since endorphins are linked to endurance. Certain drugs used by shamans may also be linked to endorphin activity: the molecular structure of **peyote** is held to resemble the endorphin *nonadrenaline*, for example. These investigations into brain chemistry and shamanism have prompted **Michael Winkelman** and other scholars to explore **neurotheology**—the idea that the impulse behind shamanism and other religions originates in brain chemistry. *See also* MENTAL HEALTH.

BROWN, JOSEPH EPES (1920–2000). Like **John Neihardt**, Brown is a significant interpreter of the **Lakota** knowledge told to him by

Nicholas Black Elk. Brown's book *The Sacred Pipe* (1971), based on interviews with Black Elk in the winter of 1947–48, deliberately parallels the seven sacraments of Catholicism with seven Lakota **rituals** that are presented as the essence of their religion. While this seems true to Black Elk's evolving spirituality (even as a Catholic catechist, he is said to have supported traditional ceremonies), some question whether it represents traditional understanding. The family history of **Vine Deloria Jr.** lends considerable weight to an interpretation that sincere adoption of some kind of **Christianity** provided a useful and necessary, but temporary, means of survival, but never replaced the foundational "core of traditional religious ways."

BROWN, MICHAEL FORBES. The Lambert Professor of Anthropology and Latin American Studies at Williams College, Massachusetts, Brown authored books including *Tsewa's Gift: Magic and Meaning in an Amazonian Society* (1986), *The Channeling Zone* (1997), and *Who Owns Native Culture?* (2003). Brown's research on **Amazonian** shamanism led him to evaluate engagements between indigenous shamans and **neo-shamans**. As such, he is one of the few scholars to have offered a sensitive yet critical analysis of neo-shamanisms, noting in particular that contemporary practitioners tend to ignore the "Dark Side of the Shaman" such as **sorcery**; he has also problematized the issue of neo-shamanic appropriations of indigenous religions, as well as the "copyrighting" of culture more generally. *See also* SHARON, DOUGLAS.

BUDDHISM. A diverse religion with adherents in most countries. Buddhist leaders have sometimes opposed shamans and shamanism, for example, in **Mongolia**, but never entirely successfully. In most encounters between Buddhists and those who may be considered shamans, both groups and traditions have evolved under the influence of the other. Tantric Buddhism is sometimes said to gain its **ecstatic** and **trance** practices (somewhat distinct from meditation) from shamanism. Similarly, **exorcisms** within **Tibetan** Mahayana Buddhism are sometimes alleged to derive from pre-Buddhist shamanism. It has also been argued that **Bön-po** is a shamanic religion separate from Buddhism.

BURROUGHS, WILLIAM S. (1919–1997). American writer and performer whose correspondence with Allen Ginsberg about **ayahuasca**

or ***yagé*** was published as *The Yagé Letters* in 1963. This was 12 years after he traveled in **South America** to find a cure for his morphine addiction, possibly inspired by his accidental killing of his common-law wife and fellow addict Joan Vollmer. Burroughs's description of the effects of yagé, including the sensation of flight and **journeying** to a "place where the unknown past and the emergent future meet in a vibrating soundless hum," have influenced many later Westerners, especially **psychonauts** or **Cyberian** shamans.

BURYATIA. Located in south-central **Siberia** along the eastern shore of Lake Baikal, and part of the Russian Federation, Buryatia is home to the nomadic hunter, herder, and pastoralist Buryat, of **Mongol** descent and the largest ethnic minority group in Siberia. Buryat peoples live well beyond this border, however, since a historically attested nomadic lifestyle has facilitated movement throughout Outer Mongolia, as well as exchange with the Oirots, Khalkha Mongols, **Evenk**, and others. Until the latter part of the 17th century, present-day Buryatia and adjacent Buryat Mongol regions were an integral part of the Mongolian Empire and had been since the time of Chinggis (Genghis) Khan.

Buryat shamans undergo a series of **initiations** (*šanar*) and attend to a ritual place comprising a specific arrangement of birch trees. They engage with the "**spirit** masters" of the landscape (mountains, valleys, trees, water, etc.) via their **ancestor**-protector **helpers** known as *ongod* (sing. *ongon*) in order to maintain harmony between communities of humans and **other-than-human persons**. The shaman also plays an active role in communal sacrificial **rituals**. **Caroline Humphrey** (1974), for example, documents the lineage ritual for Buxa Noyon, Lord Sky Bull, whereby the shaman calls down Buxa Noyon from the sky to briefly inhabit the shaman, who then imparts a blessing of Buxa Noyon to the attendees. While in other areas, the positions of shaman and chief are distinct, Buryat shamans have been both chief and shaman at the same time.

Tibetan Buddhism and Orthodox **Christianity** have had an impact on indigenous Buryat shamanism. Although the Lamaists have treated shamans harshly, Buddhism has become an important part of Buryat life and there are now "yellow" (Lamaist) shamans. There is a tradition of "**white shamans**" and "**black shamans**" among the Buryat, as there is among the Mongols, and there are also white and black smiths. Distinctions between them can be **ambiguous** but scholarly classifications have tended to reify black and white shamans into ahistorical and universalist abstractions. **Mircea Eliade**, for example, in his search for universal features of shamanism, characterizes white shamans as being able to **journey** only to the **upper world**, while black shamans can access only the **underworld**. Moreover, there are cases whereby calling a Buryat a "black shaman" is tantamount to the label "**witch**" in post-Reformation Europe, with the same brutal consequences.

In the history of scholarly work on Buryat shamans, the Buryat scholar Matvei Khangalov is an important source of late 18th- to early 20th-century ethnography. More recently, Lawrence Krader and Taras Maksimovich Mikhalilov have published notable critical surveys of Buryat shamanism. Since the formation of the Buryat Republic in 1992, a post-Soviet restoration of shamanism has flourished. The assistance of the **Foundation for Shamanic Studies** and its idiosyncratic **core shamanism** has raised issues of neocolonialism for some scholars. Meanwhile, the Circle of Tengerism promotes Buryat shamanism among Westerners, saying: "There are no **taboos**. The spirits choose who they will." Also, there is an official organization entitled the Mongolian Shamans' Association.

BUXTON, SIMON. Founder and director of the **Sacred Trust** and a member of the faculty of the **Foundation for Shamanic Studies**. According to the Sacred Trust website, Buxton "has worked and trained extensively within shamanic traditions for over fifteen years and his work as a shamanic **healer** has been recognized and endorsed by both contemporary shamans and members of the medical community." Buxton practices and teaches **core shamanism**, the "bee shamanism" outlined in his book *The Shamanic Way of the Bee* (2004), and has a shamanic practice in Penzance, Cornwall, England.

– C –

CALDERON, EDUARDO. Peruvian shaman studied by **Douglas Sharon**, whose practices stand at the interface of indigenous shamanisms and **neo-shamanisms**.

CALIFORNIAN ROCK ART. The idea that the **rock art** of California might plausibly be linked to shamanism was revived by David Whitley in a paper entitled "Shamanism and Rock Art in Far Western North America" and developed in detail in his volume *The Art of the Shaman: Rock Art of California* (2000). Whitley revisited ethnographic records, including those on the Shoshone, and established that certain metaphors in these documents referred to the **trance** experiences of shamans. In the rock **art** of the Coso region in the desert of interior southern California, bighorn sheep predominate, yet they were not a major food source, indicating that the rock art was not produced for "**hunting magic**." Whitley argues on the basis of ethnographic records that the prevalence of bighorn sheep engravings is an indicator that the region was viewed as supernaturally potent. Examples of sheep depicted as dead, dying, or being killed may be interpreted as metaphors for trance. The sheep themselves may have been **helpers** assisting shamans to control the weather, among other tasks. According to Whitley, shamans produced rock art as the concluding **performance** of **vision quests** in order to represent their visions and experiences in a graphic medium. As such, the rock art depicts **spirit** helpers and such performances as **healing**, **initiation**, rainmaking, and **sorcery**. Rock art sites were also **sacred sites**, with cracks in the rocks being used as entrances to the spirit world. Whitley has applied this shamanistic interpretive framework to a wide range of sites throughout the Great Basin, and while there has been criticism from antishamanism rock art researchers, this shamanistic interpretation is widely recognized as the most consistent and reliable to date.

CAMPBELL, ALAN T. Anthropologist (then at Edinburgh University) whose book *Getting to Know Waiwai* (1995) is a reflexive ethnography of the **Wayapí** of **Amazonia**. Campbell struggles to find ways to convey the wide range of meanings of the term *payé* (a cognate of ***piya***), which functions as a verb or adjective rather than a noun. That is, people (humans and **other-than-human persons**) can **perform** shamanistic activities or be in a shamanistic state. He notes that some people and states can be "very shamanistic" and others "only slightly shamanistic" and sums up the **ambiguity** of "*payé*-people" by saying that it is "all very well to be the village **doctor**; but it's not much of a role or an office to be the village killer."

CAMPBELL, JOSEPH (1904–1987). American scholar best known for his work on world mythology, as well as a popular public speaker and storyteller. In the first of a prolific number of books on mythology, *The Hero with a Thousand Faces* (1949), Campbell suggests that a universal pattern termed "monomyth" (borrowed from James Joyce) is the essence of, and common to, heroic tales across cultures. His other influential works include *The Masks of God: Primitive Mythology* (1959) and the multivolume, unfinished *World Mythology* (1983–87). The posthumous six-hour PBS broadcast of *Joseph Campbell and the Power of Myth with Bill Moyers* brought Campbell's ideas to a broad audience in 1988. James Hillman remarked, "No one in our century—not Freud, not Thomas Mann, not Levi-Strauss—has so brought the mythical sense of the world and its eternal figures back into our everyday consciousness." **Carl Jung**'s concept of the collective unconscious deeply influenced Campbell, and his notion of the "hero's journey" easily transfers onto shamanistic **journeying**, however generalist such a link might be, neglecting as it does cultural specificity, diversity, and nuance. Campbell taught in the literature department at Sarah Lawrence College in New York and lectured regularly at the Esalen Institute.

CANDOMBLÉ. A **possession** religion originating in Brazil in the interaction of indigenous-, **African**-, and European-derived religious traditions. Practitioners are **initiated** by stages (often following **election** by **other-than-human persons** as revealed by **illness**) into secret knowledge that allows increasing access to the gods, *Orixás*, and the power, *axé*, that can be utilized to improve health, wealth, happiness, and prestige. The Orixás principally originate in West and West-Central Africa, as did the enslaved first practitioners of the tradition, but indigenous **South American** and Catholic **Christian** elements play a role, too. When the Orixás possess their initiates, they **perform** dance ceremonies with **costumes** and actions that reveal their attributes. In the late 20th century, Candomblé gained increasing popularity among people of European origin, spread dramatically throughout and beyond Brazil, and became increasingly public. What **Paul Johnson** defines as *secretism* (the use of **secrecy**, initiations, and revelation) is changing, as apprenticeship within specific lineages and *terreiro*, or "houses of worship," become more public; this seems likely to continue in light of the importance of prestige and local variations in practice. The routinization of the tradition, however, may be illustrated in the hiving off of the martial art of Capoeira from its integral place in Candomblé.

CANNIBALISM. The seemingly ubiquitous fear of cannibalism is expressed in many similar myths and allegations about cannibals in many cultures. Shamans may be expected to **protect** their communities from human or other-than-human cannibals who threaten this form of **predation**. In **Amazonia**, for example, shamans may **mediate** between **otherworld** beings and deities who would otherwise consume the **blood** and flesh of all humans. However, this dangerous allegiance between shamans, especially **dark shamans**, places them among cannibals, vampires, alligators, and human enemies. Nonetheless, even dark shamans, at least when young, may act in a liminal position as **healers** of the **illnesses** caused by aggressors and may **combat** clients' enemies.

CARIBBEAN. A variety of practices evolved in the Caribbean interaction of indigenous-, **African**-, European-, and Asian-derived religious traditions. Some of these (e.g., **Comfa**, Myal, **Obeah**, Quimbois, **Santería** or Lucumí, and **Vodou**) involve **trance** and/or **possession** for the purposes of acquiring knowledge or ability to **heal illnesses** or to **curse** enemies. **Mircea Eliade**'s insistence that shamans exhibit **mastery of spirits** rather than becoming possessed by them has led to the denial that there are shamans in the Caribbean. However, the recognition that leaders of possession cults invite possession and do not always enter trances, but do **perform** acts that signal the presence of **spirits** or **other-than-human persons**, leads **Ioan Lewis** to counter Eliade's construction. In addition to possession, healing, and cursing, other parallels exist between the Creole or hybrid religious traditions of the Caribbean and the practices of shamans elsewhere. These can include **initiation** and training, marriage to an **otherworld** spouse or ally (sometimes leading to distinctive **gender** practices), the suspicion of being a **sorcerer** or magical wrongdoer, and employment by clients.

CARSON, DAVID. Creator of "Medicine Cards," a style of Tarot deck that uses illustrations of **animals**, especially those indigenous to **North America** and of significance to various **Native American** nations, to "receive guidance and **healing** messages from the animals." The cards have become popular in **neo-shamanism**, as they are intended as a "tool to use for personal growth and balanced living." Carson's message blends indigenous themes, such as the importance of respectful symbiotic relationships between humanity and the wider community of life, with a **New Age** emphasis on "realign[ment] with the mystery and love creation offers us."

CASTANEDA, CARLOS (1925–1998). Anthropologist, **neo-shaman**, and author of the **Don Juan** series of books (14 in total with three published posthumously). Castaneda's work has been immensely popular but has been exposed by scholars as an inauthentic ethnography of Mexican shamanism. There is considerable mystery surrounding Castaneda in all aspects of his life and career. He claimed to have been born in Brazil in 1931, but records of his immigration to the United States in the 1950s indicate his birth was in 1925 in Peru. Castaneda studied anthropology at the University of California, Los Angeles, and received an M.A. and Ph.D. for his ethnographic work with Don Juan, a **Yaqui** sorcerer and the inspiration for his best-selling books, the first three of which are entitled *The Teachings of Don Juan: A Yaqui Way of Knowledge*, *A Separate Reality*, and *Journey to Ixtlan*. Interest in psychedelics peaked around the time Castaneda chronicled his use of **peyote**, **datura**, and other **entheogens** with Don Juan in the first two books, yet his third presents readers with non-entheogen shamanistic techniques suitable to a postpsychedelic **New Age** and neo-shamanic audience, indicating that Castaneda's books were more tailored to the countercultural spirituality of the moment than any indigenous reality. Scholars, including **Richard de Mille**, **Daniel Noel**, and Jay Fikes, have exposed Castaneda's ethnography as "fake," while devotees of Castaneda argue that even if the ethnography is inauthentic, the teachings within it remain valid; some even claim they have met Don Juan and practiced shamanism with him.

CAVE ART. European Paleolithic painted and engraved **rock art** imagery, especially in the caves of France (such as Lascaux) and Spain (such as Altamira), has been interpreted as evidence of "**art** for art's sake," **hunting magic**, **totemism**, structuralism—and shamanism. The latter idea has received revived attention since the late 1980s.

Demorest Davenport and Michael Jochim (1988) argued the avian characteristics of the bird-topped "staff" and the simple human stick figure in the Lascaux "shaft scene" might be interpreted as an example of a shaman engaging with and perhaps transforming into a bird spirit **helper**. In the same year, two South African scholars (**David Lewis-Williams** and **Thomas Dowson**), working on **Southern African** Bushman (**San**) rock art, proposed a **neuropsychological model** for interpreting geometric forms in European cave art as **entoptic phenomena**, as well as for interpreting iconic forms as evidence of shamanistic visions and experiences. Lewis-Williams and Dowson's model has been controversial, but while some critics remain "shamanaphobic" (e.g., Bahn 1997, 1998; Solomon 2000; Kehoe 2000), the vast majority of specialists concur that at least a significant proportion of cave art imagery—and similarly that in some other rock art traditions—is likely to be derived from the **altered states of consciousness** associated with shamanisms.

CELTS. Prehistoric Indo-European Iron Age tribes that lived in pre-Roman northwest Europe and colonized Europe west of the Danube from around 1000 BCE; also, speakers of ancient and modern Celtic languages, especially in the modern national regions in **Northern Europe** of Scotland, Ireland, Wales, the Isle of Man, Cornwall, and Brittany. The notion of a "Celtic shamanism" is quite recent, used most often by **neo-shamans** exploring **Druidry** and practices of **altered states of consciousness** among the Celts, although some academics have also examined evidence for these themes.

The term *Celt*, however, is a construct and is contentious. Used by archaeologists to mean the prehistoric Iron Age peoples in northwest Europe, it is nevertheless problematic to define any people as Celtic based on their metalworking and material culture alone. More strictly speaking, the term *Celt* is a linguistic convention, the Celtic language being divided into Brythonic ("P" Celtic) and Goidelic ("Q" Celtic), both of which survive in modern form in parts of Great Britain, Ireland, and France. While it does not therefore denote a racial or ethnic category, *Celt* and *Celtic* endure (among academics and in popular culture) to refer to a distinct people and culture, although these people(s) and their culture remain slippery and difficult to pin down. Archaeologically and historically, it can be difficult to distinguish the ancient Celts from their neighbors (e.g., the **Germanic** tribes), while linguistically and geographically the Celts were regionally variant—Gaulish Celts were similar to but not the same as Irish Celts.

The writers of the *Celtic Twilight* contributed a romantic and a nationalist spin to the image of the Celts and their medieval literature, and some inhabitants of the modern Celtic nations have enthusiastically embraced this identity. *Celt* has an undeniable "currency," and while archaeologists, linguists, and historians have little choice but to battle with its generalizing, nationalist, but useful nature, in popular culture *Celtic* is a buzzword frequently used unreservedly to mean many things, from the **Neolithic** passage tomb of Newgrange to silver jewelry, rock music—and shamanism. The works of **John and Caitlin Matthews** on British shamanism, including *The Celtic Shaman* (1991a) and *Taliesin: Shamanism and the Bardic Mysteries in Britain and Ireland* (1991c), popularized and offered considerable evidence for Celtic shamanic practices and how modern Westerners might use these. Other manuals of practical Celtic shamanism have been contributed by Tom Cowan (*Fire in the Head: Shamanism and the Celtic Spirit*, 1993), Jan Fries (*Cauldron of the Gods: Manual of Celtic Magick*, 2001), and Frank MacEowen (*The Spiral of Memory and Belonging*, 2004). More recently, the Druid **Philip "Greywolf" Shallcrass** has been involved in reconstructive Celtic shamanism, using the practice of **Awenyddion** as described in the late 12th century by Gerald of Wales as a primary source. Scholars are more reluctant to ascribe shamanism (a constructed term itself) to the Celts, but **Leslie Ellen Jones** (author of *Druid, Shaman, Priest: Metaphors of Celtic Paganism*, 1998) and **Robert Wallis** have offered careful, critical analysis of both contemporary practitioners and speculations on ancient Celts, which indicates the term *Celtic shamanism* may not be the oxymoron it first appears.

CENTER FOR SPIRIT. An organization, headquartered in Oakland, California, of **Native American** people dedicated to the preservation and revitalization of American Indian sacred traditions and spiritual practices (SPIRIT is an acronym that stands for "Support and Protection of Indian Religions and Indigenous Traditions"). In addition to supporting Native American communities, the center aims to "insulate the public from fraud manifest in . . . phony, pseudo-Indian workshops" conducted by "**plastic medicine people**." *See also* AMERICAN INDIAN MOVEMENT.

CENTRAL AMERICA. This region, stretching from Mexico to the northwest of Costa Rica, is home to many pre-Hispanic indigenous cultures, including the Olmec, Aztec, and Maya, as well as their Amerindian descendents such as the Quiché and Yucatec. (Some scholars prefer to identify the majority of this region as **Mesoamerica**, beginning only in the center of Mexico, and identifying the areas to the north as having more in common with southern **North American** cultures.) Central American shamanism shares many characteristics with **South American** shamanism, including a complex, multilayered cosmos with human people and **other-than-human persons**, a shamanic calling (through **dreams** or sickness), **initiation** and apprenticeship, an **ambiguous** line between **sorcery** and **healing**, the use of **tobacco** and other nightshades to bring on **altered states of consciousness**, and a sophisticated understanding of **illness** involving **soul loss** and **spirit** attack. There are also shared characteristics with southern North American shamanisms, with the **peyote** cactus used by the **Huichol** (*Wixáritari*) also a part of the **Native American Church**.

Pre-Columbian Aztec **priest**-shamans were called *temoma*, after the sacred bundles they carried on their backs during long journeys, especially the nation's original migration. David Carrasco discusses their **transformative** powers and **mediatory** roles with the deities. Pre-Columbian Mayan shamanism involved priest-shamans who conducted calendrical **divination**, dream interpretation, spiritual healing, and **ritual** sacrifices. The use of fasting, bloodletting, and sleep **deprivation**, perhaps alongside **hallucinogens**, altered the shaman's consciousness and enabled **shape-shifting**. A complex view of **cosmology** informed by planetary observances and including an *axis mundi* at the center of the world permeated Mayan worldviews. Mercedes de la Garza (2002) identifies the Mayan rulers of the classical period as shamans and discusses their initiatory and shamanic practices. Today's Mayan cultures are equally complex and diverse. Quiché shamans continue to observe the 260-day Mayan ritual calendar, with a priest-shaman known as "the keeper of days" who uses the calendar in divination. Quiché shamans in Guatemala also perform blessings and other ceremonies, along with midwifery, dispensing herbal medicine, and a range of medical tasks. Yucatec shamans, on the other hand, endeavor to maintain harmony in human–nonhuman relations through mediation with spirits and by helping people to understand and fulfill their own role in the cosmos.

Interest in indigenous uses of **psilocybin** led **Gordon Wasson** to visit the region and generated a "shamanism **tourism**" industry that had detrimental effects on **Maria Sabina** and others. A more respectful engagement by **Barbara and Dennis Tedlock** has led to a more nuanced but still largely **neo-shamanic** interest in elements of local shamanisms, especially in relation to the **gendered** practices of **women**. Haitian **Vodou**, Cuban **Santería**, and **Garifuna religion**—all "**possession** cults"—are also influential in the region.

CENTRAL ASIA. Indigenous shamanisms, **Buddhism**, and **Islam** meet in this vast landlocked region, and considerable interaction has resulted in many creative fusions and cultural evolutions. Traditionally, the Uzbeks and Tajiks were agriculturalists and pastoralists, while the Kazakhs, Kyrgyz, and Turkmen were nomadic pastoralists. Furthermore, the Tajiks speak an Iranian-based language, while the others are of the Turkic language family. Definitive historical accounts of shamanic practitioners in the region begin around the 18th century CE, and there is evidence from visual culture in the form of Central Asian **rock art**.

Islam was adopted sporadically across Central Asia, beginning in the 12th century, and today these peoples are officially Muslim. Shamans operated outside Islam by conducting healing rituals and séances within their local communities, yet called upon Muslim saints among their cadre of shamanic spirit **helpers**. Furthermore, it was noted by Joseph Castagné that some female shamans did not cover their heads in accordance to Muslim tradition but wore their hair loose.

These shamanisms are historically and culturally contingent as reflected in their known appellations—the Kazakh *baksy*, Kyrgyz *bakshi*, Turkmen *porkhan*, Uzbek *parkhon*, and Tajik *folbin*—yet the close relationships between Central Asian peoples provides clear overlap. The baksy, bakshi, and porkhan can also be bards and play stringed instruments for the recitation of stories and oral epics as well as in shamanic **rituals** in order to engage with spirit helpers; the Uzbek parkhon and Tajik folbin use a tambourine without a drumstick during such rituals. There is a small degree of "**black shamanism**" and "**white shamanism**" among some Kazakh and Kyrgyz, similar to that found among the **Mongols**.

After the establishment of the Soviet Union at the beginning of the 20th century, the purge of religious activities extended from Islam to

Central Asian shamanism. During the latter half of the 20th century, Russian ethnographer **Vladimir Basilov** published numerous articles and his seminal book, *Shamanism among the Peoples of Central Asia and Kazakhstan* (1992), which demonstrated not only the continuing duration and diversity of shamanisms in the region but also the scholarly neglect of the subject in relation to the "classic" shamanisms of **Siberia** (the **locus classicus**). In addition, Basilov (1978) provides a contemporary account of an Uzbek shaman who was forced by the spirits to change **gender** and wear **women**'s **costume**, even though he bore a beard and had four successive wives with children and grandchildren. Since the fall of Soviet Communism, Central Asian shamanisms have been actively revived by a diversity of practitioners not only reconnecting with their shamanic heritage but also, idiosyncratically, re-embracing facets of Islam, as well as adopting elements of **neo-shamanisms**. *See also* ISLAM; SIBERIAN AND CENTRAL ASIAN ROCK ART.

CENTRAL EUROPE. Forms of shamanism among peoples ethnically and culturally related to those of **Central Asia** have been the subject of significant research by **Vilmos Diószegi** and **Mihály Hoppál**. Both have contributed significantly to debates about the possibility of finding shamans in Hungarian folklore and history, especially as examples of Eurasian commonalities. Hoppál has also provided invaluable surveys of studies conducted by Soviet and other Eastern European scholars under Communism. He identifies "traces of shamanistic tradition . . . [especially concerned with control of weather and the use of sieves] in folk narratives and tales" collected recently in Hungary. In contrast with movements that have stressed the distinctiveness of Hungarian/Magyar culture and ethnicity from those of neighboring European nations, especially those in political ascendancy, Hoppál is clear that the figure of the *táltos* in folktales can be identified with the "classic" kind of Eurasian (especially **Siberian**) shaman only by combining disparate elements from discrete folklore and adding missing material. This creative process is well illustrated in the music of Béla Bartók.

CHAGNON, NAPOLÉON (1938–). Professor emeritus of anthropology at the University of California, Santa Barbara, best known for his writings about the **Yanomamo** of **Amazonia**. Chagnon's discussion of Yanomamo shamans (or "shamanizers," since any man can seek the aid of *hekura* "**spirits**" and **perform** functions elsewhere specific to a few individuals) notes processes of **initiation**, uses of **ebene** snuff, **sucking** and other **healing** methods, and **combative** roles. His work became controversial when Patrick Tierney's book *Darkness in El Dorado* alleged that Chagnon had participated in a range of unethical experiments. More lasting criticisms have included challenges to Chagnon's portrayal of the Yanomamo as the most violent people on earth and his commitment to sociobiology.

CHANTING. A large proportion of the **ritual** repertoire and **performance** of shamans in many cultures involves chanting. Both as ritualists leading ceremonies for their communities and as healers conducting **healing** rituals, shamans may use repetitive phonemes, intelligible phrases, or epic poems. These are sometimes combined with other forms of rhythmic repetition, such as **drumming** (perhaps intended primarily to induce and maintain **altered** or **shamanic states of consciousness**) but may take place alone and form the central creative or **transformative** act of shamans. Guilherme Werlang's discussion (and accompanying recorded extract) of the **Amazonian** Marubo people's "myth-chants" is a rich evocation of the "**musical** aspect of Marubo myth . . . or the mythical aspect of Marubo music." He demonstrates that myth and music, words and rhythm, message and melody are inseparable. The shaman chants words and notes that both, at once, mean and achieve the same transformative result: world-creation and people-creation. In this case, and in many others, chanting **mediates** between a particular moment of performance and both past, creative times and recurrent, cyclical re-creation.

CHAOS MAGICK. Emerging out of the Midlands in England, especially the city of Leeds, in the late 1970s and early 1980s, Chaos Magick draws on the ceremonial magic (spelled "magick" to promote a link with ages past) of such figures as **Aleister Crowley**, the practices of "free belief" (appropriating any concept or symbol, not just arcane or indigenous lore, as a focus for effecting magic), **altered states of consciousness** and sigil magic proposed by the artist-occultist **Austin Osman Spare**, and the gothic fantasy literature of H. P. Lovecraft. Chaos Magick gathered momentum in the late 1980s and 1990s with the published works of Phil Carroll (such as *Liber Null* *and Psychonaut*, 1987) and Phil Hine. The title of Carroll's volume *Psychonaut* was borrowed for the song of the same name performed by the gothic rock band **Fields of the Nephilim**, and such **music** alongside that of Coil was important in promoting the **neo-shamanistic** aspects of Chaos Magick. More of a disparate collective of individuals than a "movement" as such, Chaos Magickians tend to practice alone. **Cyberia** thus offers a powerful resource and certainly some aspects of Chaos Magick are shared with **techno-shamanism**.

CHEWONG. An indigenous **hunter-gatherer** and swidden agriculturalist people of the tropical rain forest of peninsular **Malaysia**, whose **animist cosmology** and way of life is discussed by Signe Howell in a number of important publications. The Chewong recognize the personhood of a large number of (but by no means all) other-than-human beings and objects. As in **Amazonia**, Chewong shamans are **initiated** and trained to alter their **perspective** to see as others (especially other-than-humans) see. Initiation, described as "cutting open the eyes," enables this ability by giving the shaman "cool eyes," necessary not only for true **vision** but also for **transformation** into required physical forms. Howell notes that the shaman "does not fulfil any political role within society . . . although he does exercise authority on the cosmological plane." Shamans are required as **healers** because the normally calm and peaceful Chewong are susceptible to disturbances resulting in improper emotions provoked or influenced by an **other-than-human person**. In severe cases, a person's **soul** or smell (integral parts of an individual's being and identity) may be abducted. Generally, **illnesses** and **soul loss** do not result from aggression but from the normal needs of all persons (human or otherwise) to eat; thus they are forms of **predation** requiring a redressing and reassertion of right relationships. Shamans call upon **helpers** and send their souls **journeying** outward (though not necessarily to an **other world**) to retrieve the lost parts of the **patient**. The most valued helpers are the "leaf people," especially because they demonstrate the virtues and values desired by the Chewong: humility and fear rather than prowess and aggression. There are thus evident similarities and marked differences between Chewong culture and shamanism and those of most Amazonian peoples.

CHINA. The history of shamanism in this large Asian country illustrates the variety of possible relationships between shamans and other religious, cultural, and **political** leaders and movements. The Chinese character *wu* is often translated as "female shaman" or "shamaness," and the character *his* as "male shaman." However, both characters can be applied to people who act in similar ways regardless of their **gender**. References to shamans may be found in Shang and Chou dynasty literatures (i.e., 18th–3rd century BCE), in which they act as **diviners**, oracles, **exorcists**, and **healers**, communicating with deities, **ancestors**, and guardian **spirits** while **possessed** or in a **trance**. Shamanic **performances** are recorded in which shamans dance to **rhythmic drum music**, self-mutilate to demonstrate their powers, and are considered to **journey** beyond their physical location to engage (sometimes **sexually**) with their **helpers**. Shamans also have the role, of some importance in Chinese and neighboring cultures, of killing ghosts, *kuei*. **Priestly** leaders of Confucian, Taoist, and **Buddhist** movements sometimes adopted the duties of shamans (especially **mediating** between human and **other-than-human persons**), but just as often belittled or persecuted shamans as **sorcerers**. In the Communist era, shamans have continued to serve local communities as **mediums**, exorcists, and **purifiers** of homes and villages (especially in southeastern China), but they have no official status and have been persecuted. Even in Taiwan, shamans may have a low social status compared to the more respectable, liturgically centered priests.

CHRISTIANITY. Claims that the founders of Christianity—Jesus Christ and his disciples—were shamans have been made on the basis of the prevalence of **healing** and **exorcism** in the Bible. **John Allegro**'s claim that Christianity began among a group who ate hallucinogenic **mushrooms** is no more likely than the popular myth that **Santa Claus** was a shaman. **John Pilch**'s interpretation of Jesus as a shaman (or "**holy man**," as Pilch prefers) is largely founded on the privileging of "sky **journeying**" (following **Michael Winkelman** and **Roger Walsh**). The many competing understandings of the "historical Jesus" and of earliest Christianity make any theory based on a single theme or issue highly unlikely.

Nonetheless, contact between Christianity and indigenous, **animist**, and shaman-employing cultures has often resulted in clearly shamanic fusions and **possession** cults. Many **Caribbean** and **South American** religious traditions, such as **Vodou** and **Umbanda**, creatively blend **African** and local **cosmologies** and **performances** with forms of Christianity. Although the majority of these blend Roman Catholic imagery of saints with significant deities from other traditions, Orthodox Christians can also be attracted to shamanic practices, as in the **Zar** possession cult in Ethiopia. While Protestant Christians generally oppose religions other than their own, Pentecostalist movements in Africa and **Central America** can fuse indigenous antipossession and anti-**witchcraft** practices with **trance** or **ecstatic visionary** performances. The **Spiritual Baptist** movement, originating in Saint Vincent but now also in the United States, creatively fused African-derived trance practices with revivalist Christianity. Also in the United States, the **Native American Church** typifies an indigenizing movement that fuses elements of Christianity with **Native American** and Central American (especially **Huichol** or Wixáritari) religious cultures.

CHURCHILL, WARD (1947–). A Creek/Cherokee Métis (part Native American) and professor of ethnic studies at the University of Colorado. A prolific author about **Native American** issues, especially in relation to Euro-Americans, Churchill is a fierce critic of "**white shamanism**" as taught by "**plastic medicine people**" to "**wannabe Indians**" (a practice he also labels "spiritual hucksterism"). He sees the appropriation of Native American religious traditions and identities as a form of intellectual or spiritual theft parallel to that of the taking of the Black Hills and its gold in the late 19th century. Churchill's books, especially *Fantasies of the Master Race* (1992) and *Indians Are Us?* (1994), have provided much of the terminology used by opponents of "appropriation" by **neo-shamans**. His criticism of such practices and groups should be read in the context of his wider critique of U.S. hegemony and continuing colonialism.

CIRCLE OF THE SACRED EARTH. An organization founded by Roy Bauer in the United States, describing itself as a "church of **animism** fostering shamanic principles and practices." Alongside "shamanic **healing**, counseling, and **journeying**," it offers rites of passage, Reiki, and "crystal healing."

CLANS. Ioan Lewis states that "shamanism is tied to the Tungus [**Evenk**] clan structure of which, indeed, it is an essential component," thereby situating shamans in their communities and social contexts in a way that few other interpreters have done. Noting that Evenk clans, like those in many other indigenous and **animist** cultures, include not only living humans but also **ancestors**, **other-than-human persons**, and **spirits**, Lewis encapsulates much of what might be labeled **totemism**, that is, the understanding that humans are intimately related not only with their genetic ("**blood**" or "uterine") kin but also to a range of other persons, not all of whom are human or mortal. Within this social context, Lewis argues, the shaman as **master of spirits** "is essential to the well-being of the clan, for he controls the clan's own ancestral spirits and other foreign spirits which have been adopted into its spirit hierarchy." Left outside of the clan relationship, "free spirits" can be "extremely dangerous . . . pathogenic . . . sources of the many diseases" that afflict people. Shamans, therefore, **mediate** among members of the clan and between the clan and hostile beings, and they also **combat** "noxious" spirits and seek to cure **the illnesses** they cause. The collaborations between **Caroline Humphrey**, Nicholas Thomas, and **Urgunge Onon** have resulted in similarly important and rare discussions of the **political** and social contexts in which shamans live and work. They demonstrate, for example, that shamans can work with emperors on behalf of imperial conglomerations of clans, and that they can be distinguished from **elders**, who also lead clans and engage with **ancestors** in particular ways.

CLEVER PEOPLE. A term used with reference to knowledgeable and skilled **Aboriginal Australian elders**, **healers**, and **ritual** leaders. Thus, it is equivalent to "shamans" in some cultures and to "**medicine people**" among many **Native Americans**.

CLIFTON, CHAS S. (1951–). A lecturer in English at Colorado State University, Pueblo, with particular interests in **nature** writing, Clifton is the editor of a series of books about contemporary **Paganism**. One of these is entitled *Witchcraft and Shamanism* (1994), in which he has a chapter exploring possible sources for reconstructing historical European shamanic practices and ideas. Clifton's more recent research has been about "flying ointments" that were alleged to enable early modern **witches** (i.e., those accused of malevolent **sorcery**) to fly and have been proposed as European analogues of **Amazonian ayahuasca** and similar substances that induce **visions** or

altered states of consciousness. His conclusion is that such ointments are merely a literary motif, a plot device in narratives about the unnaturalness of alleged witches. His self-syndicated column (and blog site), "Letters from Hardscrabble Creek," includes a number of astute and entertaining observations on debates and claims about contemporary shamanisms, such as his humorous essay entitled "Training Your Soul Retriever."

COATES, MARCUS. British **artist** whose work explores the interface between what it is to be human vis-à-vis "**nature**," particularly through video installations. In *Journey to the Lower World* (2005), Coates made a shamanic **journey** for a group of residents in a Liverpool tower block (apartment building). In the video, we see the community gather in one resident's small living room, while Coates prepares himself by donning a red-deer-antler-and-hide costume. With an audiotape of shamanic **drumming** in the background, Coates begins his journey, which is viewed on a second videoscreen. Taking the elevator to the ground floor works as a metaphor for the journey to the lower world. Footage of various birds (a moorhen and sparrowhawk, for instance) represents the creatures Coates encounters as **spirit helpers** in his journey. Returning to the ordinary world by elevator, Coates then recounts his shamanic experiences to the audience, and the community seems uncertain as to whether the **neo-shaman** has offered anything of value to their needs.

Unlike other artists who engage with shamans as romantic visionaries in synch with community needs, Coates's installation raises issues of uncertainty and **humor** in shamanic practice. The reason for the journey is community oriented, but the community, with giggles and whispers, is uncertain about this neo-shaman and may not be convinced he is genuine. This might compare with the down-to-earth, everyday, and **sexual** humor in some indigenous rites. Coates's **performance** itself is tongue-in-cheek, but at the same time there is a tension in the air, and the artist seems committed to the efficacy of the rite. Here, too, the tension, uncertainty, and unpredictability of the performance is not unlike indigenous shamanisms and is reminiscent of **Michael Taussig**'s (1987) deconstruction of the traditional Western model of shamanisms perpetuated by masculist observers in which shamans are perceived to be largely male, dominating figures who control social relations and charismatically master their communities and whose rites always end in success.

COMBAT. A major role of many shamans is to defend their communities from enemy shamans, **witches,** or **sorcerers**, as well as **predatory** or aggressive **other-than-human persons** or **spirits**. The ability to know what is happening at a distance may be drawn on as an "early warning system," just as it may aid in the investigation of the origins of **illnesses** and other negative phenomena. It is not always enough that shamans identify the source of aggression, though, and they may be expected to engage in combat themselves, either by joining other warriors or by shamanizing with harmful intent. This is part of what leads **Carlos Fausto** to describe **Amazonian** shamanism as "a predatory **animism**."

COMFA. In the interaction between indigenous-, African-, European-, and Asian-derived religious traditions in Guyana, Comfa evolved as a **possession** and ceremonial complex in which **protection**, problem solving, and **healing** may be offered to clients. The name derives from the Twi *O'komfo*: "**priest**, **diviner**, or prophet/soothsayer." Until the 1950s, Comfa referred to the worship and propitiation of the "Watermamma." Kean Gibson notes that "anyone who becomes spiritually possessed on hearing the beating of **drums**, or who becomes possessed without apparent reason . . . are said to 'ketch comfa.'" But it can also refer to communal events led by a host and celebrants who invite possession and **mediate** between clients and **other-than-human persons** or **spirits**. These beings who **elect** to work through entranced celebrants include **ancestral** members of all the ethnicities that contribute to Guyana's multicultural population. Each ethnically identified being plays a stereotypical role and is recognizable in the **trance** "work." One example of this that also illustrates another link with shamanic **initiation** and **performance** elsewhere is that "Spanish spirits . . . demand **sexual** relations" with a practitioner of the opposite **gender**. In **Siberia** and elsewhere, this would be talked about as "marriage" and would lead to **transvestitism**, but in Comfa, "Spanish spirits" are identified as "prostitutes" and the few who work with them are labeled "promiscuous homosexuals and lesbians." As elsewhere in the Caribbean, this acceptable possession tradition is often opposed to **Obeah**.

CONIBO. A people of the Peruvian Upper **Amazon**. Interest in Conibo culture and shamanism is largely dominated by interest in their use of **ayahuasca** or ***yagé***. Halfway through the year **Michael Harner** spent with them (1960–61), he felt drawn "to study their spiritual life, the **cosmology** and their religion" and was told that there was only one way to learn: not by asking questions but by taking the shaman's drink, *ayahuasca*. Nonetheless, Harner's "**core shamanism**" definitively rejects the use of hallucinogens even while asserting that it is rooted in methods of achieving **altered states of consciousness** and **journeying** to **other worlds** that would be recognizable to Conibo shamans. Ayahuasca **visions** are understood by Conibo shamans to be provided by "eye **spirits**" and include dramatic and vivid formal designs and patterns with **healing** properties. When these touch the shaman, they become songs and can then be sung into a **patient**.

CORE SHAMANISM. Term used by **Michael Harner** and colleagues, including **Sandra Ingerman**, at the **Foundation for Shamanic Studies** to define the key features of shamanism, specifically the **journey** to **other worlds** in a willfully induced (controlled) **altered state of consciousness** "in order to acquire knowledge, power, and to help other persons" (Harner 1990 [1980], 20). The emphasis on the shamanic journey derives from **Mircea Eliade**'s understanding of shamanism as an "archaic technique of **ecstasy**." The approaches of both Harner and Eliade are problematic in their universalizing of diverse and discrete, culturally situated shamanisms into a monolithic category to be palatable to Western audiences. Harner has reached tens of thousands of practitioners globally in workshops teaching core shamanism, in which **drumming** (and other monotonous or **rhythmic** sounds) is used to induce a **shamanic state of consciousness**. Core shamanism arguably has the greatest currency as a shamanic practice today, not only among Westerners but also those indigenous communities reviving their own shamanic traditions with the assistance of core shamanists, including some **Native American**, **Saami**, **Inuit**, and **Central Asian** tribes.

COSMOLOGY. Shamans and their communities usually share a cosmology, a view of the world, that includes an understanding of both how everything works and how it began. Generally, shamanic cosmologies are **animist**, although **neo-shamanism**'s modernist framework is demonstrated by its central focus on **individuation** and its **therapeutic** practice. Many indigenous origin myths attribute the creation of the world or cosmos to a number of cooperating and competing **other-than-human persons**, including **tricksters**. But it is commonplace to consider that the actions of all living beings continuously co-create the world, intentionally or otherwise. Shamans may be required to **mediate** between communities and persons whose co-creativity is contradictory, or they may seek to mitigate the results of a creative activity that endangers their community or clients (*see* SAN).

A fundamental problem in understanding shamanic cosmologies (and hence everything that shamans do) is raised by the question of what the world is like. Modernist (post-Enlightenment) cultures are founded on a hierarchical dualism that contrasts "**nature**" with "culture" (as object versus subject, materiality versus consciousness, and so on). Shamans and their animist communities may see and experience the world entirely differently. **Eduardo Viveiros de Castro** demonstrates the importance of **perspectivism** in relation to **Amazonia** (and his argument is supported elsewhere). The shaman's job is "to see as others see." On the basis that all living beings share a single culture but perceive one another differently because there are "multiple natures," manifest forms or masks, shamans are required to see past the "multinaturalism" to the cultural being. They can then determine the probable intentions of others, especially those who are likely to be **predators** on human communities.

Classic accounts of shamanic cosmologies from many cultures suggest a tripartite model of the cosmos—an understanding of a three-**tiered cosmos** consisting of an **underworld**, this world, and an **upper world**. Shamans are required because these worlds are interconnected and their inhabitants influence each other in significant and sometimes dangerous ways. Beings from the upper or lower worlds may attack a shaman's community, inflicting **illnesses** and preventing hunting. Especially in **Mircea Eliade**'s model of shamanism which privileges this cosmology, shamans are by definition people who can **ecstatically journey** between the worlds on behalf of their communities. In **neo-shamanism**, the **other worlds** are often taken to be interior to individual shamans or their clients, or archetypal and ideational locations (the "**imaginal**"). Thus, shamanic journeying becomes an "inner" experience parallel to **Jungian** and other therapeutic techniques such as **visualization**.

COSTUMES. What shamans wear is often of considerable importance to the fulfillment of their roles. Costumes may not be mere decoration or artistic embellishment but **helpers** as significant as the **other-world** or **other-than-human persons** with whom the shamans work. However, considered as **art and artifacts**, shamanic costumes may illustrate their understanding of the cosmos and advertise their skills. The donning of costumes may be an important part of shamans' **performances**, and some wear different costumes to achieve different purposes (e.g., among the **Altai** different costumes are worn to ascend into the **upper world** or descend into the **underworld**). Where **transvestitism** is important, cross-dressing may be an important indicator of shamanic ability or training.

CREIGHTON, JOHN. In his volume *Coins and Power in Late Iron Age Britain* (2000), Creighton draws on **neuropsychological** analyses of **rock art** to argue that the geometric and distorted anthropomorphic imagery on Iron Age (**Celtic**) coinage may be derived from **altered state of consciousness** experiences, possibly influenced by **entheogenic** plants such as the opium poppy, cannabis, or henbane, for which there is some archaeological evidence in **Northern Europe**. He goes on to suggest that altered consciousness and coin production were agentic in the negotiation and contestation of power, among **Druids**, for instance, with the coin—its color, precious metal composition, indication of status, mythological imagery, and so on—beguiling those who came into contact with it. Imagery on coins, **visionary** or otherwise, might be deemed too limited in content, and the coins themselves too diminutive, for such an analysis to be reliable. Creighton's interpretation of the basketry compass work of the Latchmere Heath mirror in a similar light—mirrors offering passages to **other worlds**—is perhaps more convincing. There is scope for this data to be considered alongside other sources in order to grasp the likelihood of "Celtic shamanisms." Creighton is positive about the likelihood of finding residues of entheogens in British prehistoric contexts and the insights this might provide into prehistoric religions.

CROW. Native American nation, also known as Absaroke and Apsáalooke. Their reservation in Montana is a small fraction of territory recognized as theirs by treaties with the federal government of the United States in 1851 and 1868. Their traditional lifeways were similar to those of other Plains Indians, nomadic bison-hunting peoples, and their traditional religion included similar ceremonial practices, including the sun dance and **sweat lodges**. Noted **medicine people** among the Crow include **Pretty Shield**, **Thomas Yellowtail**, and **John Pretty on Top**. Some such people are **healers**, but others never heal, instead leading ceremonies on behalf of the community, usually **mediating** with **other-than-human persons**.

CROW DOG, LEONARD (1942–). Sicangu (Brûlé) **Lakota medicine man**, "road man" in the **Native American Church**, and coauthor with **Richard Erdoes** of *Four Generations of Sioux Medicine Men* (1995). Erdoes records Crow Dog's narration of a "cross-fire ceremony" in the book *Lame Deer: Seeker of Visions* (1972), which he cowrote with **John (Fire) Lame Deer**. In this, he says of **peyote** that it opens "three doors . . . makes me recognize myself, makes me understand the people, makes me understand the world." Crow Dog was a significant spiritual leader at the **American Indian Movement**'s occupation of Wounded Knee in 1973, where he revived the Ghost Dance, saying that his great-grandfather had been the last ghost dancer to surrender in 1890.

CROWLEY, ALEISTER (1875–1947). British writer and occultist who gained notoriety in the media as a practitioner of black magic and the "wickedest man in the world." Though self-styled as "The Great Beast 666," Crowley's system of "magick" is equally associated with the maxims "Love is the Law, Love under Will" and "Do what thou wilt," which were embraced by a number of self-empowerment groups in the second half of the 20th century. Crowley became interested in the occult while studying at Cambridge and joined the Golden Dawn, where he met such luminaries as poets W. B. Yeats and Victor Neuberg and novelist Arthur Machen. In 1904 in Cairo, Crowley received *The Book of the Law* through the **medium** of his wife Rose, a treatise which he claimed inaugurated the "new aeon" or **New Age** of Horus. Crowley founded the Abbey of Thelema in Cefalu, Sicily, where he hoped to attract followers to his new "Law of Thelema," but the venture had limited success. Crowley wrote prolifically, his most notable works being *Magick* (1973), the novel *Moonchild* (1929), and the voluminous journal *The Equinox*, of which he was editor. Crowley died in near obscurity in a boardinghouse near Hastings in Kent, but has nevertheless had a major influence on contemporary esotericism. Contemporary Western shamans whose practices include the working of magic owe much of their knowledge and practice to Crowley, as well as to fellow occultist **Austin Osman Spare**.

CUNNING FOLK. Scholars such as Owen Davies and **Emma Wilby** have distinguished between beneficent "cunning folk" and maleficent "**witches**" in early modern Britain. While cunning folk might offer **healing**, help find lost objects, **divine** the future, and establish the whereabouts of criminals, witches caused **illness**, infertile crops, and even death. Cunning folk often had "familiar **spirits**" as allies in their work and made **journeys** to the spirit world, elf home, or land of the fairies, while witches consorted with devils and made nocturnal travels to the Sabbath. Much of this nomenclature is tied up with the discourse of the witch trials, but the distinction between cunning folk and witches is demonstrable if markedly permeable. In her detailed examination of encounter-narratives between cunning folk and familiars/witches and their devils, Wilby argues convincingly, if perhaps overstating the case, that "coherent and vigorous 'shamanistic **visionary** traditions' existed in many parts of Great Britain during the early modern period."

CURING. *See* DOCTORS; HEALING; ILLNESSES; MEDICINE.

CURSING. Invoking curses is a significant ability attributed to shamans in many cultures. It may either be thought of positively (as a means of protecting a shaman's community, perhaps as a form of **combat** against enemies) or negatively (as a sanction against disrespect within the community or an aspect of **sorcery**). This is part of the **ambiguity** of shamans and their activities in many cultures. The specific form and method of cursing employed, or suspected of being employed, varies.

CYBERIA. Drawing conceptually on the vast tundra of **Siberia**, "Cyberia" (see Rushkoff's 1994 volume of the same title, for instance) refers to the virtually vast region of the Internet. For contemporary cyber shamans, the Internet is a powerful resource, not only for networking and communication but also as a **divinatory** device and source of **otherworldly** (hyperreal) knowledge. **Chaos Magickians** who use **altered states of consciousness** and **Austin Spare**'s concept of "free belief" (appropriating any concept or symbol, not just arcane or indigenous lore, as a focus for effecting magic) may use Cyberia as a potent magickal forum. Cyberia interfaces with **techno-shamanism** in a number of ways, including the accessibility through the Internet of electronic **music** that is held to affect brainwave patterns and thereby induce **trance**.

CZAPLICKA, MARIA ANTONINA (1886–1921). Polish-born cultural anthropologist best known for her fieldwork among indigenous **Siberian** communities, published as *Aboriginal Siberia* (1914). Czaplicka documents Siberian shamanism as a form of "Arctic hysteria": "To be called a shaman is generally equivalent to being afflicted with hysteria." The work is important for being one of the few original ethnographies of Siberian shamanism in English and for examining the discourse on shamanism as a form of psychosis. *See also* MENTAL HEALTH.

– D –

DANCE OF THE DEER CENTER FOR SHAMANIC STUDIES. Established in 1979 by **Brant Secunda**, grandson of the Mexican **Huichol** (*Wixáritari*) shaman Don José Matsuwa, with the mission "to preserve the Huichol culture and its shamanic practices and traditions." The center supports Secunda's program of teaching Huichol shamanism throughout the world, including pilgrimages, **vision quests**, and conferences, in order to "reunite people to the source of all life in order to help **heal** the earth, our communities, and ourselves." While there is a distinct **New Age** flavor to this discourse and the term *vision quest* is not indigenous to the Huichol, all financial profits go directly to the Huichol (although it is not stated to what extent Secunda and Don José's family may personally benefit).

DARK SHAMANS. A distinction is commonly drawn in **Amazonia** between "curing shamans" and "dark shamans." This should not be interpreted, however, as "our shamans" versus "enemy shamans" because *all* shamans may potentially act against their family and neighbors and not only against enemies. The alignment of dark shamans with **cannibal** deities may be a specific form of shamanic **mediation**

by which the extreme **predation** of the deities is lessened by a diminished level of violence committed by shamans. Noting that there are "three distinct but related shamanic complexes: ***piya***, ***alleluia*** and ***kanaimà***," **Neil Whitehead** discusses kanaimà (a particular form of dark shamanism) at length, describing it as a form of "assault **sorcery**" that "involves the mutilation and lingering death of its victims."

DARTS. In many cultures, it is thought that **illnesses** may be the result of assault by **sorcerers**, **witches**, enemy shamans, or even aggrieved "friendly" shamans. In many cases, these hostile forces fire darts and other **intrusions** that can be seen only by **healing** shamans. The removal of darts, sometimes by **sucking** cures, can be a significant part of a shaman's job.

DATURA. The use of hallucinogens is not universal to shamanisms, but many shamans, especially in **South America**, engage with culturally recognized plants as **other-than-human persons** in intimate relationships that enable powerful **visions**. Datura is one such **entheogen**, a variety of the Solanaceae (potato) family (which also includes deadly nightshade, henbane, **tobacco**, and mandrake) with a range of species widely distributed globally (common names include jimsonweed, devil's apple, thorn apple, devil's weed, stinkweed, and moonflower). Use of the plant to induce visions is focused on the Americas, especially Mexico and the American Southwest, with speculation that many **Central American** cultures were familiar with datura's hallucinogenic properties. Most famously but erroneously, the shamanic use of datura was promoted by **Carlos Castaneda** in his **Don Juan** mythos—yet Edward Spicer, an anthropologist and a specialist in **Yaqui** culture states: "I know of no information or reference concerning Yaquis using *Datura*." Ingestion is, however, prevalent in South America where various "tree daturas" (*Brugmansias*) are used in **ayahuasca** and **San Pedro** brews.

Datura ingestion is held to produce the effects of **transformation** into **animal** form and **spirit** flight. As such, datura use has been linked to European folklore on werewolves, and **Michael Harner** and other scholars attribute the riding of Medieval **witches** on broomsticks to datura use in the witches' salve or brew. **Chas Clifton** counters such claims as a misreading of a literary motif rather than as ethnographic historical data; that is, witches are identified in narratives as people who can fly, and evidence can be provided for the inadequacy of entheogen explanations.

The active hallucinogenic constituents of datura are the tropane alkaloids, especially hyoscyamine, scopolamine, and atropine, which are concentrated in the seeds. These alkaloids have a stimulating effect on the central nervous system (e.g., increasing heart rate) while simultaneously depressing the peripheral nerves (e.g., dehydration of mucus membranes), producing a period of agitation and visions often followed by a prolonged sleep. Overdose is fatal, so shamans who engage with the plant have sophisticated recipes for managing dosage.

DAYAK. Indigenous people of Borneo, **Indonesia**, and **Malaysia**. Their **animist** religious culture necessitates the employment of shamans as **healers** and intermediaries with **other-than-human persons** and Dayak **ancestors** who inhabit the rain forests. With the increasing destruction of Indonesian rain forests, Dayak culture is both threatened and a source of resistance. Dayak shamans have been part of antiglobalization and antiforestry protests.

DE HEUSCH, LUC. *See* HEUSCH, LUC DE.

DE MILLE, RICHARD. De Mille became suspicious that elements of **Carlos Castaneda**'s **Yaqui** "ethnography," and indeed the shaman-informant **Don Juan** himself, were inauthentic—an elaborate fiction. He wrote a lengthy volume entitled *Castaneda's Journey: The Power and the Allegory* (1976) assessing the veracity of Castaneda's work in meticulous detail, with the follow-up work, *The Don Juan Papers: Further Castaneda Controversies* (1980) presenting arguments from both camps. De Mille pointed to the unavailability of Castaneda's field notes due to their mysterious accidental loss or destruction, as well as to inconsistencies in dates, locations, and so on. In one specific example of plagiarism, the "waterfall jumping" of Don Juan's fellow sorcerer Don Genaro replicates **Barbara Myerhoff**'s experience of watching the **Huichol** shaman **Ramón Medina Silva** perform this feat. Supporters of Castaneda point to the "validity" of the Don Juan mythos in speaking "truths" that stand outside ethnographic fact, whether the original ethnography was invented or not. Nonetheless, de Mille, **Daniel Noel**, and Yaqui representatives have conclusively debunked Castaneda.

DEER TRIBE. Also known as the Métis Medicine Society. A global organization that promulgates a blend of **Native American** religious traditions, **neo-shamanism**, and **New Age** spirituality through lecture tours, workshops, publications, websites, retreats, and study groups available to "anyone who seeks knowledge, **healing**, spiritual self-development and physical mastery." As a registered nonprofit organization, it seeks tax-deductible donations of money (as well as donations of "time, talents, and energy") through its website, especially for the construction of a "Spirit House of Beauty."

DEFENSE. *See* PROTECTION.

DELORIA, VINE, JR. (1933–2005). Standing Rock Sioux and Santee Dakota; professor emeritus of history and religious studies at the University of Colorado in Boulder. Among Deloria's many important publications are *Custer Died for Your Sins: An Indian Manifesto* (1969), *God Is Red* (1973), *American Indians, American Justice* (1983), *For This Land* (1999), and *Singing for a Spirit: A Portrait of the Dakota Sioux* (2000). A collection of his writings is available as *Spirit and Reason: The Vine Deloria, Jr., Reader* (1999). In *Singing for a Spirit*, Deloria rewrites his family history, including material rejected and disorganized by Sarah Olden in *The People of Tipi Sapa* (1918). This includes the **initiation** and work of Deloria's **medicine man** great-grandfather, Saswe, who became an Episcopalian **Christian** in 1873, three years before his death. Not only does his account offer an insight into the initiation and role of **holy people** among the Yankton (Dakota) in the late 19th century but it also casts light on the adoption of Christianity among indigenous people, including their shamans. Deloria argues that his people "adopted the hymns rather than the doctrines of Christianity" and that the new religion aided their transition into the new life of reservation confinement. Here and in a foreword to the 1979 edition of *Black Elk Speaks*, Deloria provides an explanation for the full participation of **Nicholas Black Elk** and other holy people in publishing their life stories: at the "right time," these early-20th-century books would aid "traditionalists" in disseminating their traditional practice among another generation making yet another cultural transition and reasserting autonomy and agency. He regularly notes the easy coexistence of indigenous forms of Christianity and the continuance of traditional knowledge and at least some practices, especially in noting his family's intimate relationship with **other-than-human persons**, for example, the Thunders. Deloria's writings also contain fierce criticisms of Euro-American engagements with **Native Americans**, including the appropriation of spiritual traditions and their commoditization by "**plastic medicine men**" and their clients who "treat the world like a spiritual delicatessen."

DEPRIVATION AND OVERSTIMULATION. Rhythmic dancing, monotonous singing, **chanting** and **drumming**, prolonged fasting, hyperventilation, flagellation and other forms of pain, and light deprivation all mark ways in which shamans may deprive or stimulate the senses in order to induce **altered states of consciousness**. Such practices are not universal to shamanisms, but they are a consistent feature since such practices facilitate **altered styles of communication**—enabling intimate relationships with **other-than-human persons**.

DESCENT OF INANNA*.** A mythic poem dating from around 1750 BCE, surviving in at least 30 inscribed clay tablets with more than 400 lines of text and rediscovered in the excavation of Nippur, the ancient Sumerian religious and cultural center (now in Iraq). The principal interpreter, Samuel Noah Kramer, worked with folklorist and storyteller Diane Wolkstein to present an evocative understanding of this and other material relating to Inanna, the Sumerian goddess of heaven and earth, also known to the Akkadians as Ishtar. Wolkstein represented the descent according to **Mircea Eliade**'s assertion that shamanic **initiation** follows a universal pattern that includes death, **dismemberment**, and rebirth. Another Inanna myth in which the goddess has a tree made into a throne and a bed has also been interpreted in the light of Eliade's claims that shamans universally ascend into the **upper world** via trees or poles. The popularization of this understanding of shamanism particularly follows from the psychology of **Carl Jung** (himself influential on Eliade). A preeminent example of this is in Sylvia Perera's popular *Descent to the Goddess: A Way of Initiation for* ***Women (1981). Websites promulgating the notion that Inanna's descent was a shamanic initiation and Jungian integrative process continue to proliferate. However, a straightforward reading of the text shows that Inanna did not return from the **underworld** changed in any way and did not conduct shamanic **rituals**.

Rather, she descended into the realm of the shadowy dead to witness the funeral of her brother-in-law, the Bull of Heaven. The shamanic initiation theory is an entirely new myth that fits a **neo-shamanic** understanding perfectly and Sumerian mythology not at all.

DEVEREUX, PAUL (1945–). British researcher of earth mysteries whose work has furthered scholarly attention to the archaeology of shamanism and opened up the topic to a broad audience beyond academia, as well as contributing to debates in academia—archaeology in particular. As editor of the earth mysteries journal *The Ley Hunter*, Devereux recently revised the notion of ley lines as intentional links between prehistoric and historic sites (first suggested by Alfred Watkins), or as the spiritual arteries of the earth, to the "**spirit** tracks" used by shamans during out-of-body travel. The argument is contentious (deconstructed by Alby Stone in *Straight Track, Crooked Road* [1998]) but has injected new energy into the interpretation of ley lines. Devereux has also explored the prehistoric use of psychedelics for inducing **altered states of consciousness** in *The Long Trip: A Prehistory of Psychedelia* (1997), with particular attention to shamanism and **rock art** and other visual cultures. His work, as a member of the Dragon Project Trust, on the **power** of place also attends to shamanism in discussing the effects of electromagnetic and other anomalies at **sacred sites** that may affect human consciousness. The recent Dream Project by the Dragon Project Trust, involving collaboration between Devereux and **Stanley Krippner**, indicates that **dreams** are indeed influenced by scientifically unknown factors at sacred sites.

DIONYSIAN MYSTERIES. Dionysus was a Greek deity of wine, **ecstasy**, and liberation. **Rituals** and stories devoted to him evolved over the centuries and are commonly interpreted as beginning as a celebration of intoxication and eventually becoming a path to rebirth. Ecstatic **initiation** and **trance possession** by the deity, especially when accompanied by **drumming** and the seeking of oracular knowledge from the **underworld**, are sometimes interpreted as shamanic. Aristophanes' play *The Frogs* (c. 400 BCE) seems to record an element of the Mysteries, a **journey** to and from the underworld, but suggests theater rather than carnival or possession.

DIÓSZEGI, VILMOS (1923–1972). Hungarian ethnologist and research fellow of the Hungarian Academy of Sciences in Budapest. In addition to his extensive work on **Siberian** shamans, published as *Popular Beliefs and Folklore Tradition in Siberia* (1968), Diószegi has explored the process of becoming a shaman, regional diversity, and traces of shamanism in Hungarian folk beliefs. Since Diószegi's death, **Mihály Hoppál** has edited two volumes of his work—*Shamanism in Siberia* (1996) and *Shamanism: Selected Writings of Vilmos Diószegi* (1998). *See also* CENTRAL EUROPE.

DISMEMBERMENT. A common feature of many stories of **initiations**, especially of shamans. Powerful **other-than-human persons**, **ancestors**, or **spirits** take the prospective initiate (often against their will) and tear or cut them apart, often killing them and/or eating them. Sometimes this happens after the initiate has been taken away from their everyday surroundings, perhaps into an **underworld** or **other world**. It is usually followed by the insertion of sources of power, help, or ability into their bodies. For example, there are accounts of the initiation of **Aboriginal Australian** "**clever people**" that include the insertion of crystals either as empowering substances or as magical weapons. There are also accounts of **illnesses** being inserted into **Siberian** shamans to enable them to **heal** their community of these illnesses. Shamans initiated in this way speak not only of the pain of the process but also of their fearful uncertainty that they would survive it. However, survival entailed being reassembled or literally re-membered and sent home to learn how to use their new abilities properly.

Dismemberment and reassembly is not only about the acquisition of new powers and abilities. It indicates that shamans are made or remade differently from other people. For example, the Daur **Mongols** (discussed by **Caroline Humphrey** and **Urgunge Onon**) understand that people's bones come from their fathers and their flesh and **blood** from their mothers; the word for the "bone joint," *uye*, is the same as that for "patrilineal generation." So when initiates are dismembered, they are torn out of their people's kinship system and turned into a different kind of being, at least partially an other-than-human person or a spirit. At the same time, the new *yadgans* (Daur shamans), having already experienced death and doing so again each time they shamanize, are unlike **elders**, who are still approaching death and thus have a different relationship and ceremonial engagement with **ancestors**.

DIVINATION. The acquisition of information via supernatural means; derived from the Latin *divinare*, meaning "to foretell" or "to discover something." Divination may involve consulting a specialist, such as a shaman, or may—particularly in contemporary Western contexts—be conducted for oneself. Observing the meaning of **dreams**, the casting of lots (bones, stones, sticks, playing cards, etc.), reading patterns in **nature** (such as the flight of birds or the movement of the planets), and scrying (gazing at a crystal ball or into a pool of water) all mark examples of how almost any device might be put to use in divination and demonstrate the ubiquity of divination across cultures. The prophesying of future events from the entrails of a sacrificed animal (extispicy) among the Scythians, for instance, marks one specific indigenous instance of the practice. In antiquity also, Tacitus describes the use of lots from a nut-bearing tree in Germania, and although it is not clear whether the marks on them were runes, today's **Heathens** use the runes in divination, attributing a shamanic connection due to the vision ot the runes witnessed by the shaman-god **Odin**, a master of ***seidr***—and seidr itself is used in prophesy today. Similarly, **Druid** shamans often ascribe a divinatory role to the "**Celtic**" *ogham* script, and there are efforts to reconstruct the practice of **Awenyddion**. Among many indigenous communities, shamans are considered to be repositories and seekers of knowledge, using divination to find knowledge inaccessible locally. **Saami** shamans watch the movements of a "frog" (sometimes a collection of interlocked metal rings) across their decorated **drums** as they strike them. Diviners may seek to identify the perpetrator of **sorcery** or the originator of some insult to **other-than-human persons** responsible for the presence or absence of **animals** for hunting. Dreams may also be treated as opportunities for divination: what a shaman dreamed could be interpreted as indicative of the likely result of any attempt to **heal illnesses** during the next day.

DOBKIN DE RIOS, MARLENE (1939–). American medical anthropologist and clinical psychologist; professor of anthropology at California State University, Fullerton. Best known for her interest in

ayahuasca and other plant use in **Amazonia** and especially Peru, Dobkin de Rios's many publications include *Visionary Vine* (1972) and others interested in "shamanic techniques of **healing** and psychotherapy." She clarifies the fact that ayahuasca is not used as a curative agent, a **medicine** in the Western sense, but "gives the healer entry into the culturally important area of disease causality, enabling him to identify the nature of the **illness** from which a person is suffering, and then to deflect or neutralize the evil magic which is deemed responsible for illness." She has also written insightfully about the "ayahuasca **tourist**" industry in which Amazonian tradespeople are finding increasingly lucrative employment in offering ayahuasca sessions as "advanced shamanic training." She argues that these are rarely if ever conducted by "authentic ayahuasca healers" but rather by "common drug dealers" whose clients are frequently left with psychotic and physical health problems. This is all the more interesting given her argument that shamanic healers do not give psychotic patients ayahuasca but have an arsenal of other **therapeutic** techniques (including store-bought medicines) as well as means of declining to treat patients whose illnesses are beyond their powers.

DOCTORS. In many indigenous cultures, shamans are **healers**. As the local equivalent of Western doctors, they seek the causes and cures of **illnesses**. However, since their medical practice exists in an **animist** context, it is frequently either spiritualized or demonized in Western discourse. For example, the use of the term ***medicine people*** with reference to **Native American** religious leaders can be interpreted in a way that privileges allegedly metaphysical "powers" rather than recognizing the importance of the people's skill as healers. On the other hand, the term *witch doctor* in many **African** contexts is often taken to place these people among suspect workers of magic rather than recognizing their role as **combatants** against **witches** *and* the illnesses they cause. In both cases, local medical knowledge is highlighted by indigenous terms and denigrated or misinterpreted in many Western contexts. Many indigenous people, for instance, the **Karuk**, prefer the term *doctor* to the term *shaman*.

DON JUAN. An alleged **Yaqui** sorcerer and informant to **Carlos Castaneda** and the central character in his prolific series of Don Juan books, including *The Teachings of Don Juan: A Yaqui Way of Knowledge*,

A Separate Reality, and *Journey to Ixtlan*. Castaneda received an M.A. and Ph.D. for his ethnographic work with Don Juan but **Richard de Mille**, **Daniel Noel**, and Jay Fikes, among other scholars, have deconstructed Castaneda's Don Juan as an invention, with more in common with a psychedelic audience of the late 1960s and **New Agers** since, than with authentic Yaqui practices that creatively fuse indigenous and **Christian**, specifically Catholic, traditions. Don Juan's teachings on the use of **datura**, **peyote**, and other **entheogens** were particularly appealing to 1960s psychedelic readers as well as to **neo-shamans** since then.

DOWSON, THOMAS A. South African archaeologist and **rock art** researcher. Dowson initially drew attention to enigmatic geometric imagery in **Southern African** rock art traditions and later, with **David Lewis-Williams**, proposed a **neuropsychological model** for the shamanistic interpretation of this and other rock art traditions. In his work on the Southern African material and European **cave art**, Dowson has foregrounded the sociopolitical contexts of individual shamans as artists and developed a shamanistic approach composed of three "elements of shamanism": shamans are agents who alter consciousness; these **altered states of consciousness** are accepted as ritual practices by the agent's community; and knowledge concerning altered consciousness is controlled in effecting certain socially sanctioned practices. These elements offer a line of approach that dispenses with "shamanism" as a metanarrative in order to embrace cultural diversity, specificity, and nuance—crucial especially when examining shamanistic rock art which, critics have suggested, appears to make all rock art "the same." Dowson has most recently advocated **animism** as an interpretative tool enabling a refining of the shamanistic approach to rock art. He is also known for his writing on queer archaeologies and other indigenous or prehistoric visual culture, including the art of Benin.

DREAMING, THE. In **Aboriginal Australian** English, or in translations of Aboriginal traditional terms, the Dreaming refers to the process by which places and emplaced life was created, ordered, and socialized. It is only loosely related to terms for **dreams** and is not a time-related concept like "creation" in **Christian** and some other **cosmologies**; that is, it does not refer to past acts of a Creator but to present responsibilities of all life. Many Aboriginal culture teachers prefer to speak of "the Law" rather than the Dreaming to avoid misunderstandings of a similar nature to these. The concept is related to shamanism in that "**clever people**" are those who live most closely according to the Dreaming.

DREAMS. Some people understand that to dream is to **journey** in the **other world**, or that the dream world is the real one and that what is seen there will happen here sooner or later. Dreams may therefore be seen as opportunities for **divination** or as **visions** of the future. Dreams usually need interpreting: dreams of particular **animals** may warn of the need to be wary of poison. **Carlos Fausto**'s (2004) discussion of **blood** and **tobacco** ideas in **Amazonia** entails consideration of dreams as a prime means by which shamans seek to control enemies (especially other-than-human ones), making them allies and even pets who will help the shaman **heal** or harm others. Dreams may also be **initiatory**: to see particularly powerful **other-than-human persons** is to know that one has been **elected** to become a shaman. Greg Sarris's account of the life of Mabel McKay, a **Pomo doctor** and weaver, provides an illustration of reliance on dreams as modes of communication between shamans and their **helpers**.

Note that the **Aboriginal Australian** term ***the Dreaming*** is not primarily concerned with dreams. Rather, it is a rough translation equivalent for a variety of indigenous terms, only some of which refer to revelatory dreams.

DRUGS. *See* ENTHEOGENS.

DRUIDS. A type of **Pagan**, both in antiquity among the **Celts** and in the present among contemporary Celtic Pagans. *See also* AWENYDDION; JONES, LESLIE ELLEN; MATTHEWS, JOHN and CAITLIN; NORTHERN EUROPE; SHALLCRASS, PHILIP ("GREYWOLF").

DRUMS AND DRUMMING. Rhythmic sounds and movements are commonplace in shamanic **performance**. In **Mircea Eliade**'s construction of shamanism as "the techniques of **ecstasy**," the creation of rhythm is the primary technique that induces ecstasy or the **altered states of consciousness** that he claims define shamanism. It is certainly true that shamans in many cultures make use of drums and other instruments, along with **chanting** and movements. Drums may not only be decorated with **cosmological** symbols but also themselves represent the cosmos and its inhabitants. In addition to their use in achieving **trances** or other **altered states of consciousness**, drums might also be aids in **divination** or in **journeying** to **otherworld** locations. Nonetheless, considerable variations exist in the use of drums. Some **Siberian** shamans use their drums to create not rhythmic but arrhythmic noise. Many **neo-shamans** following **Michael Harner** typically utilize a particular drum rhythm that is claimed to induce the desired "**shamanic state of consciousness**," but claimants disagree on what that rhythm should be (3–4 beats per second or 4–7 beats per second are common). **Techno-shamanic** or "rave" "trance dances" often follow the same pattern. At the interface of indigenous and Western practitioners, and in an ironic postcolonial twist, Harner's **Foundation for Shamanic Studies** has introduced its own idiosyncratic drumming technique to communities where traditional practices have been lost (for example, in parts of post-Soviet Russia) and the drum may never have been used.

DRURY, NEVILL (1947–). Australian author whose introductory and survey work on shamans, **Pagans**, and esotericism (e.g., *The Elements of Shamanism*, 1989; *Magic and Witchcraft: From Shamanism to the Technopagans*, 2003) has opened up "shamanism" to a broad audience and popularized **neo-shamanic** practice. Drury's book *The Shaman and the Magician* (1982) made useful observations on the similarities between some indigenous shamanisms and various Western occult traditions, particularly in light of **altered state of consciousness** practices. Drury's discussion of the Edwardian artist **Austin Osman Spare** and Australian **witch** artist **Rosaleen Norton** (*Pan's Daughter*, 1993) are particularly noteworthy in this regard. Clearly, however, caution should be exercised when casually unifying disparate cultures with "shamanism" as a singular, unified discourse.

DUBOIS, THOMAS. DuBois has examined **Saami** engagements with Norse communities, arguing that there was far more contact than previously thought, to the point that creative religious exchange ensued. The practice of ***seidr*** was shared to an extent, although it is unclear to what extent Viking seidr derives from Saami shamanic practices. **Neil Price** has advanced the argument archaeologically, attending to examples of

Saami and Norse burials where **gender** and cultural conventions are disrupted, interpreting these as examples of seidr practitioners.

– E –

EARTH MYSTERIES. *See* DEVEREUX, PAUL; SACRED SITES; STONE, ALBY.

EBENE. A snuff prepared from the beans of an **Amazonian** tree of the nutmeg family (genus *Virola*), which is either snorted through tubes (sometimes bird bones) or blown into the nostrils, inducing **purifying vomiting** and dramatic, **musical visions** and **altered styles of communication** (especially through singing) between shamans and significant **other-than-human persons**, including **animals**, plants, and the earth. By this means, shamans learn and **perform cosmological** and **healing** songs and **chants**. Unlike some other plant derivatives with similar effects, ebene is also used recreationally by other people, as it can result in displays of affection and emotion that are normally socially constrained.

ECSTASY. Shamans are sometimes distinguished from other religious or cultural leaders by the ability to achieve an **altered state of consciousness** which **Mircea Eliade** labeled "ecstasy." The etymology of this originally Greek word implies an ability to "stand outside" oneself. It is often used as a synonym of **journeying** and an antonym of **possession**, because Eliade claimed that shamans control or **master spirits** rather than losing control.

EDWARDS, BROOKE. *See* MEDICINE EAGLE, BROOKE.

ELDERS. Shamans are rarely the only social and ritual leaders in their communities. **Caroline Humphrey**, **Urgunge Onon**, and **Marjorie Balzer** clarify the role of shamans by discussing the differences between them and elders. There are ceremonies that shamans **perform**, and others that elders perform. Sometimes shamans are specifically barred from participating in ceremonies run by elders; at other times, they can be present but must not shamanize. The **bear ceremonial** complex demonstrates that the distinction between shamans and elders is not necessarily that shamans engage with the **other world**, **spirits**, or **other-than-human persons** and elders do not. Rather, shamans and elders may do similar things in different ways, or elders sometimes do what shamans do more expertly and powerfully, or in more fraught or dangerous situations. Shamans are sometimes defined as those who have already experienced death during the **initiation** rites, which remake them as distinct kinds of people from elders, who are those approaching death. Similarly, the intense and intimate relationships evolving from initiation and shamanic performance may entail obligations to their otherworld or other-than-human kin and companions that prevent shamans from doing certain things. For example, shamans may be barred from hunting because **animals** will know of their approach (although, as with bear ceremonialism, they may indicate auspicious times and places).

ELECTION. From the perspective of **other-than-human persons**, or **spirits**, who **initiate** or work with shamans and/or cause **illness**, phenomena commonly interpreted as **possession** or **trance** should really be labeled "election." An understanding of shamans and their work may be advanced by noting that humans may not always be in charge or responsible for the choices made and actions taken by such beings. From many shamans' perspectives, their activities may be the outworking of **otherworld** agency rather than human cultural practice.

Bernard Saladin d'Anglure also uses the term to refer to the practice of some individuals among **Siberian** and **Arctic** peoples to choose their own **gender** and/or gendered relationships and performances.

ELEMENTS OF SHAMANISM. *See* DOWSON, THOMAS A.

ELIADE, MIRCEA (1907–1986). Historian of religions and fiction writer who was born in Romania but lived most of his life as an exile in France and the United States, where he became professor of the history of religions at the University of Chicago. Eliade authored the most widely read academic book on shamanism: *Shamanism: Archaic Techniques of Ecstasy* (1964 [1951]). In it, he not only presents ethnographic data from many diverse cultures but also marshals them to support a theory about the nature and influence of shamanism.

Eliade insists that shamans do not become **possessed** but rather exhibit **mastery of spirits**, with whom they engage while in an **altered state of consciousness** called ***ecstasy*** that is interpreted by shamans as **journeying**. That is, shamans go to meet and master **other-than-human persons** in various **other worlds**. They achieve such states and are supported in such journeys by the use of various standardized "techniques," including **drumming**, **chanting**, and forms of **deprivation and overstimulation**. Eliade asserted the ubiquity of a mode of **initiation** in which neophyte shamans were **dismembered** and reassembled following **illnesses** induced by **spirit** beings whom shamans either defeated or contracted as **helpers**.

Shamanism is "archaic" not in the sense of being antiquated or obsolete, but as the primary or foundational religious experience that underlies *all* other religions. Further, its most ancient and original forms began and continued among **hunter-gatherer** peoples, especially those of **Siberia**. In fact, Eliade presented a version of Siberian and **Central Asian** data as the "pure form" of shamanism from which all other practices (e.g., those that use hallucinogens) degenerated.

When read alongside Eliade's works about ostensibly different religious and cultural phenomena, it becomes clear that a single project motivated him—namely, the encouragement of an allegedly exalted spiritual practice with which to confront the materialism of communism and, to a lesser degree, capitalism. The religious edifice he constructed is vast, but can be illustrated by his situating of "journeying to other worlds" in the context of claims about the cosmic *axis mundi* or *omphalos* that links **upper**, middle, and **underworlds**, while allowing a distinction between the ways in which shamans and **priests mediate** between the worlds. Eliade definitely (and definitively for many **neo-shamans**) privileged journeys to upper-world or celestial realms, again presenting other destinations as indicating degenerate forms of shamanism.

Eliade's shamanism is a new myth, rooted in some verifiable observations and some misrepresentations of particular local cultures, which he applied universally. Jonathan Z. Smith details some of Eliade's misrepresentations, such as that of an **Aboriginal Australian** "**Dreaming**" narrative as being concerned with celestial journeying and authority, whereas it is actually concerned with "terrestrial [earthly, this-worldly] transformation and continued presence." In abstracting shamans from their local, **political**, cultural, social, temporal, and other contexts, he both misrepresents shamans (and their practices, **cosmologies**, and communities) and points the way toward **Michael Harner**'s "**core shamanism**" and similar neo-shamanic practices. Much of his project can also be paralleled in the works and thought of **Carl Jung**, who told Eliade at the Eranos Conference in 1952 that "the modern world is desacralized, that is why it is in a crisis. Modern man must rediscover a deeper source of his own spiritual life." As **Daniel Noel** states, in considering the intimate link between Eliade's fiction writing and his books about religion, especially shamanism, "The core of soul of the West's idea of shamanism is not factual at all, but fantastic, fictive, a work of imagination." Although criticizing Eliade's willful (re)construction of the "-ism" of shamanism, Noel intends this to encourage a renewed celebration of the powerful "practice of mindful imagination." In this sense, Noel presents Eliade and Jung as the West's leading shamans.

ELKIN, ADOLPHUS P. Australian anthropologist at Sydney University and author of *Aboriginal Men of High Degree* (1945). In contrast with pervasive denigrations of **Aboriginal Australians** in general and their "**doctors**" or "**medicine people**" in particular, Elkin argued that "the real medicine man is a professional individual of special training whose personality, from the point of view of the community, reaches a high degree of normality." He notes claims about **initiatory dismemberment** and the insertion of crystals and other powerful objects, but counters assertions about the psychological ill-health of "men of high degree" by referring to their otherwise normal social and relational behaviors.

ENTHEOGENS. Etymologically, *entheogen* derives from Greek *entheos*, "**possessed** by a god" (which is related to the modern English *giddy* and Old English *gidig*, "possessed by a god/**spirit**") and *genous* "produced." Hence *entheogen* is literally "generate god or spirit within." The term has currently gained popularity in describing consciousness-altering substances such as the **peyote** cactus, **datura**, **ayahuasca** vine, and LSD. Related terms are arguably more pejorative, overly generalist, or too specific: *drugs* is vague and retains negative associations, while *visionary plants* excludes a number of naturally occurring and synthesized substances and also unhelpfully privileges vision over other senses; *psychedelic* refers also to a specific, contentious era, and *hallucinogen* inevitably has connotations of mental aberration (illness) as does *psychoactive* in the prefix *psycho-*. *Entheogen* appears to be more sensitive to shamanic, rather than illegal or "recreational," use of these substances, but **Andy Letcher** argues that it presumes a monotheistic ontology. Moreover, indigenous accounts attest that these substances are understood not as significant for what Western science would term active chemical agents, but as **other-than-human persons** in their own right, especially as **helpers**. Hence, for *ayahuasceros*, it is the brew itself that is crucially important rather than the chemical constituent DMT, since the brew is carefully produced and comprises a number of plant-people who help the shaman call upon **altered styles of communication** with other-than-humans. Notably, none of the popular Western terms discussed here recognize the importance of the **purifying** and **purging** aid given by significant helpers. *See also* ALTERED STATES OF CONSCIOUSNESS; HOFFMAN, ALBERT; SAN PEDRO; SHULGIN, ALEXANDER.

ENTOPTIC PHENOMENA. Entoptics (from the Greek, meaning "within vision"), also known as phosphenes, are complex and diverse luminous geometric images derived from the human central nervous system, produced specifically within the optic cortex and characteristic of certain **altered states of consciousness**, including shamanistic **trances**. Links between entoptics, altered consciousness, and shamanisms have been explored in a number of visual culture studies. Entoptics have been vociferously debated in **rock art** research in particular, due to their use in a **neuropsychological model** proposed by the **Southern African** rock art researchers **David Lewis-Williams** and **Thomas Dowson** in order to establish the origins of some rock art imagery in altered-consciousness and related shamanistic practices.

ENVIRONMENTALISM. Shamans cannot strictly be identified as environmentalists because, as **animists**, they are members of a large community of life rather than being surrounded by an impersonal environment or "**nature**." However, the common indigenous requirement to be respectful and even humble in one's relationships with all persons (humans as well as **other-than-human persons**) generally leads to ecologically responsible lifestyles. Shamans in many places are centrally concerned with **resource management**. In an important article entitled "From Cosmology to Environmentalism" (1995), **Piers Vitebsky** argues that at the same time as an "intensely local kind of knowledge [i.e., that of shamans] is being abandoned [in many indigenous cultures] in favour of various kinds of knowledge which are cosmopolitan and distance-led," "shamanism" is being co-opted to support environmentalist and **therapeutic** projects. He illustrates this with reference to the changing culture of the **Sora** of **India** and the **Sakha** (Yakut) of **Siberia**. The Sora are increasingly exchanging their intensely local culture as they become linked into larger markets and contexts: for example, their crops become food and commodities, where they had once carried **ancestral** "**souls**." The Sakha, however, are finding shamans and shamanism iconic in the evolution of a cultural and ethnic identity that fits the needs of their new republic.

All this illustrates and takes place within a larger context of a struggle between globalization (homogenization) and local diversity. It should not be reduced to or mistaken for a contrast between **neo-shamanic** "appropriation" and indigenous decline. Indigenous shamans, in some places at least, are appropriating methods and idioms that *may* aid their peoples' survival and even full participation in global affairs with some degree of autonomy and agency. However, environmentalists do often use representations of indigenous people (especially **Native Americans**) as icons to support their cause.

Vitebsky matches his list of four "key characteristics which [are] reasonable to see as distinctively shamanic" with an insight into the problematic reinvention of shamanism in environmentalist (and therapeutic) contexts. He argues that shamanism's "*local* nature is co-opted" but immediately relocates the environmentalist or therapist in new ways. Its "*holistic* nature is shattered," but because it remains a "cardinal value," it is replaced by the "weaker concept of globality." Its "*eristic* nature suffers a variable fate in the new therapies [because they are "less gutsy"] . . . but becomes a driving force in the heroic side of environmental campaigning." Finally, its "*dissident*, or anti-centrist nature is likewise retained and enhanced ('alternative')." Vitebsky's argument is supported by reference to the role-play by shamans and shamanism in the practice and discourse of environmental movements among indigenous peoples and in the West. Many activists in the anti-road and "social justice" (i.e., antiglobalization) movements identify as or with shamans.

ERDOES, RICHARD. American coauthor of a number of biographies (or partial autobiographies) of significant **Native Americans**, including **John Lame Deer** and **Leonard Crow Dog**, along with a number of other relevant books such as his collection of "**trickster** tales." In an epilogue to *Lame Deer, Seeker of Visions* (coauthored with Lame Deer, 1972), Erdoes narrates his "first encounter with the American West" and his early acquaintance with Indians. These demonstrate that experiences of numinous **nature** and gregarious, **humorous** people are at the core of Erdoes's work. In contrast with the collaboration between **Nicholas Black Elk** and **John Neihardt**, Erdoes is explicit about his motivations and creative role.

ETHNOMUSICOLOGY. Music, **rhythm**, **chant**, song, **drumming**, and other instrumental **performances** are significant aspects of much shamanic work and have been studied by this branch of musicology devoted to musics rooted in particular cultures, especially indigenous ones. Shamanic music has been considered in relation to a number of issues, especially its role in inducing **trance**, **ecstasy**, and **altered states of consciousness**, as well as in the theorizing of performance.

EUROPEAN PALEOLITHIC. The Old Stone Age, a chronological period extending from around two million years ago to around ten thousand years ago, depending on the area at issue, and encompassing the rise of early modern humans (Cro-Magnons) in Europe. The European Paleolithic is part of the "three-age system" (of Stone Age, Bronze Age, and Iron Age), but these antiquarian classifications are arbitrary at best, suggestive of unifying periods of time, and it is misleading to define peoples by their tool use alone. The period is best known for the so-called origin of **art**, marked by **cave art** (most famously in France and Spain, though not restricted to these areas), some of which has been interpreted as derived from **altered states of consciousness**. Shamanism is often cited, in turn, as the **origin of religion**. The search for origins, though, must be situated within the Eurocentric concerns of Western discourse and may tell us more about ourselves than the people of the Paleolithic. Indeed, the emphasis on

"European Paleolithic" itself is Eurocentric, disrupted by Paleolithic finds—including plausibly shamanistic art—elsewhere in the world. *See also* NEOLITHIC.

EVENK (TUNGUS). The term *shaman* derives from the Tungus language group, the largest of the northern group of the Manchu-Tungus languages, and the nomadic **reindeer** herding Evenk (formerly known as the Tungus) comprise the largest indigenous **Siberian** Tungus-speaking group. The Evenk territory is huge, covering about a million square miles of the taiga in Northern Siberia, from the River Ob in the west to the Okhotsk Sea in the east, and from the Arctic Ocean in the north to Manchuria and Sakhalin in the south. One of the earliest encounters with Evenki shamanism is recorded as Nicolas Witsen's illustration (a wood-cut from his *Noord en Oost Tartarye*, 1705) labeled "Priest of the Devil." Since then, the Evenk have been the subject of many anthropological studies, the most recent being **Piers Vitebsky**'s The *Reindeer People: Living with Animals and Spirits in Siberia* (2005).

EXORCISM. Shamans can be distinguished from the victims of **possession** not because they do not become possessed by **otherworld** persons or **spirits** (despite the claims of **Mircea Eliade**) but because they can be called upon to exorcise those who are unwillingly controlled by **predatory** beings. Shamans are, by definition, people who form intimate (even **sexual** and/or marital) relationships with **other-than-human persons** who can overwhelm others and inflict **illness** or bad luck on them. **Combat** between possessing beings and shamans is, therefore, a key part of shamanic **initiation**, being, and **performance**. **Ioan Lewis** distinguishes between shamanism and possession cults in which no form of possession is welcome. Exorcism can be a part of both religious complexes, but it is more **ambiguous** in the case of shamans because they exorcise with the aid of beings who are, to some degree at least, in possession of the exorcising shaman.

EXTRA PAY. Term proposed by **Graham Harvey** referring to the ways in which Western (scholars and **neo-shamans**) might contribute to shamanisms in a reciprocal (decolonizing) way. Harvey borrows from Lewis Carroll's Alice book, *Through the Looking Glass* (1872), in which Humpty Dumpty, according to Harvey, proposes that he can "use a word to mean just what he wanted it to mean, 'neither more or less.' If a word like *glory* or *impenetrability* is made to work hard, carrying unusual or idiosyncratic meanings, Humpty Dumpty says he 'pays it extra.' 'Shamanism' is now a hard working word" (Harvey 1997, 106). In his *Shamans/Neo-Shamans* (2003), **Robert Wallis** offers a critical examination of neo-shamans, including an analysis of how they pay "shamans" extra by valuing the term and adding and combining new things with it—from regarding the term *shaman* as honorific rather than a commodity (your community rather than yourself calls you a shaman) and actively engaging in causes for indigenous self-determination, to expressing perceptions of shamanic practice that involve danger and uncertainty where other neo-shamans romanticize, decontextualize, and psychologize these issues.

– F –

FAUSTO, CARLOS. In an important article with particular reference to the Parakanã, Fausto defines **Amazonian** shamanism as "**predatory animism**." In an elucidating comment, he contrasts **neo-shamanism**, which is "turned on the remodeling of **individual** subjectivities," with Amazonian shamanism, "concerned with producing new persons and social relationships from the stock of human and nonhuman subjectivities existing in the **cosmos**." Fausto also notes that these understandings of shamanism are distinguished by the use or avoidance of **blood** and **tobacco**. He might also have listed **vomiting** as a distinguishing sign. Fausto's understanding of animism, like that of **Irving Hallowell** and **Nurit Bird-David**, is that it is a view of the cosmos as being full of persons, only some of whom are human. But, he argues, the problem of "interacting verbally and establishing relationships of adoption or alliance" that enable shamans to "act on the world in order to cure, to fertilize, and to kill" (i.e., quintessentially shamanic engagements) is that persons (intentional agents) can either act on or be acted upon by others. In Amazonian understandings, people can either be predators or prey. By **initiation** and increasing skill, shamans become expert at gaining and controlling "a surplus of intentionality and agency" and an ability to see and use the **perspective** of the Other, especially of enemies. **Predation**

links shamans with **jaguars** and other powerful **other-than-human persons**, as well as with hunters and warriors, as is demonstrated by discourses and, perhaps, practices involving the consumption of blood. Similarly, the use of tobacco is a **transformative** act that first initiates and later enables shamans to see like or as jaguars. This alteration of perspective is also discussed by **Eduardo Viveiros de Castro**.

FIELDS OF THE NEPHILIM. Also known as the Nephilim or Nefilim. British rock band established in 1983 who came to prominence with the gothic subculture of the late 1980s and early 1990s—with devoted fans to the present. The Nephilim (Hebrew for "the fallen ones") are announced in the Book of Enoch, and Carl McCoy, lead singer and lyricist for the band, describes them as the first shamans. McCoy is an occultist and **neo-shaman** whose inspiration derives from the Western occult tradition and indigenous sources. The title of the song "Moonchild" (1988) is derived from occultist **Aleister Crowley**'s novel of the same name. "Psychonaut," allegedly recorded in **ritual**-like circumstances by candlelight and accompanied by incense, is also the title of a book on **Chaos Magick** by Phil Carroll. The song includes an incantation "zi dingir kia kanpa / zi dingir anna kanpa," meaning "**spirit**, god of the earth, remember / spirit, god of the sky, remember," allegedly in Sumerian/neo-Babylonian and from the *Necronomicon* (originally by H. P. Lovecraft), and the video includes footage of McCoy in a sun dance rite. The Nephilim's enigmatic and mystical lyrics engage with magical, shamanistic, and occult themes, some of them sourced from McCoy's automatic-writing experiences, and both McCoy's **art** and lyrics are often inspired by the work of the occultist and artist **Austin Osman Spare**.

FLAHERTY, GLORIA. Flaherty's volume *Shamanism and the Eighteenth Century* (1992) has made a major contribution to the historiography of the term *shaman*. Immediately upon "discovery," shamans were molded to the preferred stereotypes of Westerners, from "juggler" and charlatan to mentally ill and socially estranged. Flaherty is particularly interested in the reception of the term in Europe and the metamorphosis of the "**artist**" into the "shaman of higher civilization."

FOUNDATION FOR SHAMANIC STUDIES (FSS). A nonprofit educational organization located in Mill Valley, California (formerly the Center for Shamanic Studies in New York, established in 1983), founded and directed by **Michael Harner**. The FSS aims to "preserve and revive indigenous shamanism," offers "urgent indigenous assistance," conducts research on shamanic **healing** and the "mapping of nonordinary reality" (MONOR), and seeks to "revive shamanism in the East and the West" (www.shamanism.org). The foundation teaches "Harner Method" **core shamanism** in a worldwide workshop program, ranging from the beginner course "The Way of the Shaman: The Shamanic **Journey**, Power and Healing" to yearlong shamanic practitioner training programs. The FSS is also known for its monetary contributions to those they designate "**living treasures** of shamanism," such as Wangchuk, an elderly **Tibetan** shaman living in exile in **Nepal**. Scholars have commented on the problematic nature of defining a "core" shamanism when shamanic practices are so diverse worldwide and on the neocolonial role of the foundation as "arbiter and authority over who is and who is not a 'true shaman'" (Johnson 1995, 172).

FREYJA. Norse goddess interpreted as a shaman-type figure by some **neo-shamans**, scholars, and **Heathens**, due to her prowess as a ***seidr*** practitioner.

FRIES, JAN. German **neo-shaman**, occultist, and magickian who has been influential in Europe in promoting a form of "freestyle shamanism" that emphasizes **trance** work in **nature** without necessary reference to a specific tradition or traditions. As such, Fries has been influenced by the work of **Austin Osman Spare** in particular, especially his use of sigils to effect magick, as well as the focus on individual gnosis in **Chaos Magick**. Yet, in addition to his acultural *Visual Magick: A Manual of Freestyle Shamanism* (1992), Fries has published the acclaimed *Helrunar: A Manual of Rune Magick* (1993) and more recently *Cauldron of the Gods: Manual of Celtic Magick* (2001), which clearly draw on established traditions.

FURST, PETER T. Anthropologist specializing in shamanisms, hallucinogens, and **art**, especially the use of **peyote** by and art of the **Huichol**

(*Wixáritari*) in Mexico. Furst is professor emeritus of anthropology and Latin American studies at the State University of New York at Albany (where he previously chaired the Department of Anthropology) and a research associate with the University of Pennsylvania Museum. His edited volumes *Flesh of the Gods* (1972) and *Hallucinogens and Culture* (1976) raised awareness of the institutionalized, cross-cultural use of **entheogens** (rather than dismissing entheogen use as socially aberrant or peculiar), and Furst was elected foreign fellow by the Linnean Society for his work on sacred plants.

Furst's initial ethnographic fieldwork took him to Warao country in the Orinoco Delta of Venezuela. With his colleague **Barbara Myerhoff**, he was the first non-Huichol to undertake the pilgrimage to Wirikùta to harvest **peyote**. Furst encouraged the Huichol, who were producing votive objects (carved gourds lined with beeswax and decorated with brightly colored wool yarn and beads) to work on new "narrative" works consisting of yarn on beeswax fixed on flat plywood. In this way, he brought Huichol "yarn paintings," and the shaman-artist **Ramón Medina Silva** in particular, to a broader audience, with the article "The Art of 'Being Huichol'" (1978), of particular significance. In addition, the recent volume *Visions of a Huichol Shaman* (2003), the catalog of an exhibition at the University of Pennsylvania Museum of Archaeology and Anthropology in 2004, champions the work of the leading Huichol artist José Benítez Sánchez, known for the curvilinear style he pioneered in the 1970s.

In a long-running dispute between Furst and Jay Fikes, the latter questions the legitimacy and accuracy of Furst and Myerhoff's ethnographic work on the Huichol, as well as their "Western" influence on Huichol "tradition." In ***Carlos Castaneda****: Academic Opportunism and the Psychedelic Sixties* (1993), Fikes argues that Furst helped Castaneda to fabricate descriptions of **rituals** by exaggerating or misrepresenting such practices as waterfall jumping and peyote enemas, thereby assisting Castaneda's literary celebrity and furthering Furst's and Myerhoff's careers as experts on Huichol shamanism. Furst's response—that Fikes is a "paranoid," "overprivileged white anthropologist"—is equally highly charged. Furst and Fikes accuse one other of attempting to destroy the other's reputation and career. The legal wranglings are not resolved at the time of writing.

– G –

GALDANOVA, GALINA R. Buryat ethnologist of Buryat, **Mongolian**, and **Siberian** shamanisms. She is senior researcher and Mongolian finds keeper at the Institute of Oriental, Mongolian, and **Tibetan** Studies of the Siberian Branch of the Russian Academy of Sciences.

GARIFUNA RELIGION. The Garifuna (also known as Black Caribs) are the descendents of **Africans** and the indigenous Carib people of Saint Vincent in the **Caribbean**. The survivors of a British deportation to Honduras continued the evolution of Carib religion and language. **Paul Johnson** summarizes their traditional religion as having

> aspects typically associated with some West African groups, like the use of **drums** to induce possession **trance** by **ancestors**. It also shows Carib features, like the shaman (*buyei*) who blows smoke on a patient's afflicted body to extract penetrations. And it reveals Catholic features, like the importance of baptism and images of the Virgin and saints in homes.

As in other Caribbean, **South American**, and **Central American** shamanic religions, the main ceremonial event, the *dügü*, involves **spirit possession** so that aggrieved ancestors who are causing **illness** become present to be offered "food, rum, praises, and even simulated **sex**." For their **performance** in this multiday event, shamans dress in "clothing ordered from 'African' clothiers of New York" and compare their "work to more well-known African systems of Yoruba and **Vodou**." The ceremony is also marked as "traditional" by its demonization by evangelical **Christians**.

GENDER. In particular local cultures, the question of gender may be a significant determinant of shamanic ability, acceptability, and authority. However, it is rarely as simple a matter as saying "among this group, shamans are always male, while among that one, they are always female." While it is true that most shamans in **Korea** are female and most **Siberian** shamans are male, there are counterexamples in both areas. Neither is it always the case that male shamans are more valued that female shamans. **Piers Vitebsky** notes, for example, that among the **Sora**, "male shamans work mostly in the 'lesser' tradition of **divining** and **healing**, while funerals are conducted by shamans of the 'great' tradition, who are mostly **women**." He also notes that female shamans among the Sora "sometimes hold a sword or axe as they go into **trance**" in order to engage in **combat** with enemies and dangerous **other-than-human persons**. In contrast, some male shamans in Siberia wear female dress. In other cases, as **Marie Czaplicka** notes, shamans' **costumes** may combine features peculiar to the dress of both sexes and indicate that they are some other gender entirely.

To further complicate the matter, shamans may marry **spirits** of the same gender as themselves and, for example, a male shaman may sometimes be "female" in relation to a spirit husband. On the other hand, a Sora shaman marries both a man of a different lineage to her own (so that her children increase her husband's line) and the "spirit son of her predecessor, who is her own aunt" (so that the child of this spirit-kin incestuous marriage will stay within her lineage). With reference to similar data and possibilities, **Bernard Saladin d'Anglure** notes that a binary model (opposing male and female genders) cannot make sense of the role of shamans in **Inuit** and other cultures. His "ternary" model demonstrates that the **mediating** role played by shamans (both between other members of their societies and between human and other-than-human persons) requires a more fluid or dynamic perception of gender. Shamans' ability to mediate arises from their "**third gender**" position and role.

Shamans may, then, be biologically male or female, costumed as either male or female or both, and married both to human and other-than-human spouses of the same or opposite gender. They may also be primarily employed by men or women to deal with situations that are largely concerned with men or women in particular cultures (often but not always coded as "public" versus "private," or "community" versus "family" concerns). A further complication arises when we note that among the Inuit, at least, the third gender of shamans is part of a wider mutability of gender: children may be understood to have decided which gender to be before or at birth, their genitalia more or less rapidly adapting to their decision. Yet other children receive the name of a deceased relative of the opposite gender and then **perform** that gender role for as long as they carry the name. These widespread **transformations** are what makes it possible to understand shamans as not belonging entirely "either to the class of males or to that of females, but to a third class, that of shamans," as Czaplicka says, and also as essential mediators between all the many constituent elements, beings, and situations of the **cosmos**, as Saladin d'Anglure demonstrates.

A similar point is also illustrated in relation to **initiatory dismemberment** and reassembly. As if all of this were not challenging enough to European-derived notions of gender, among the **Ojibwe** and speakers of cognate Algonquian language, a grammatical distinction is made not between male and female genders but between animate and inanimate genders. That is, in these **animist** cultures and languages, persons and personal actions are spoken of differently to objects and impersonal events.

For all these reasons, the addition of a feminine ending *-ka* to the Tungus masculine term *shaman* by a few **neo-shamans** wishing to speak of "female shamans" fails to engage in any interesting way with the possibilities raised by indigenous shamanic constructions and performance of gender. **Barbara Tedlock**'s *The Woman in the Shaman's Body* (2005) offers a guide to reclaiming or reimagining shamanism for contemporary women, but despite its foundation in considerable research both among indigenous communities and in ethnographic literature, it presents a picture of shamanism almost entirely equivalent to that of **core shamanism.**

GERMANIC. Language group of **Northern Europe** specific to Germany but with direct links to the languages of Scandinavia (e.g., Old Norse) and English. Germanic peoples include the Ancient Germans, Anglo-Saxons, Icelanders, Danes, Swedes, and Norwegians. Ancient Germanic **pagan** religion, including practices interpreted as shamanic such as ***seidr***, are being revived and reconstructed by today's **Heathens**.

GINZBURG, CARLO. Professor of Italian Renaissance studies at the University of California, Los Angeles, who is best known as a pioneer of "microhistory" (examining a small period of history in meticulous detail to reveal more general information) as applied to the *benandanti* ("those who go doing good"), a late-16th- to mid-17th-century group of peasants in the Friulian countryside near Venice, Italy, whose anti-**witchcraft** actions involving such supernatural activities as **spirit** flight (or **journeying**), were themselves, like those of **cunning folk** in Great Britain in the early modern period, persecuted as witchcraft practices. Ginzburg's claim that the benandanti are evidence of an enduring European fertility cult is too much of an interpretative leap for many historians to accept, especially given the backlash against **Margaret Murray**'s comparable, if arguably less nuanced and poorly researched, thesis. Ginzburg develops this idea, proposed in *The Night Battles: Witchcraft and Agrarian Cults in the Sixteenth and Seventeenth Centuries* (1983), and in the follow-up volume ***Ecstasies****: Deciphering the Witches' Sabbath* (1991), with the more general—and therefore even more difficult to swallow—claim that descriptions of night flights and battles across Europe and Asia are indicative of a persistent shamanic substrate.

GOODMAN, FELICITAS (1914–2005). Anthropologist who claimed that various prehistoric remains and the imagery of certain indigenous **artistic** traditions point toward specific stances or "postures" that can automatically induce a **trance**. Ethnographic instances include "the bear posture," based on a carving of a shaman and a bear **spirit** from **North America**'s **Pacific Northwest**. By adopting the pose of the shaman, according to Goodman, any human can potentially enter an **altered state of consciousness**. One prehistoric example is the **cave art** of the so-called wounded man depicted in the shaft scene of the famous cave of Lascaux in the Dordogne, France: Goodman suggests that if we take the bird-headed stick and bison as upright, the wounded man is positioned at a 37-degree angle, and that by achieving this angle (with some form of support), trance can be induced. In *Where the Spirits Ride the Wind: Trance Journeys and Other Ecstatic Experiences* (1990), Goodman provides numerous examples of these trance postures, as well as evidence for the efficacy of the postures in altering consciousness.

From the perspective of rock art research, the argument regarding the "wounded man" marks a good example of how such imagery is inappropriately interpreted with the Modern, 18th-century definition of art. Not only is there no reliable reason to compare cave paintings with two-dimensional canvases; there is also nothing to suggest where "up" is in the paintings—they are not to be viewed as "framed" or subject to modern Western aesthetic rules. Certainly there are demonstrable connections between the postures some shamans assume and altered consciousness (**San** shamans in **South-**

ern Africa, for example), but the assumption that simply sitting as an "**African diviner**" or reclining at a 37-degree angle automatically induces a trance is debatable.

In the vein of **core shamanism** and transpersonal psychology, Goodman's argument depends on an acultural and monolithic shamanism and the decontextualizing and universalizing of prehistoric and indigenous shamanisms for Western consumption. In 1978 Goodman founded the Cuyamungue Institute in Ohio to "preserve the ancient tradition of **ritual** body postures as a doorway to the realm of spirit and non-ordinary consciousness known as Alternate Reality," and the institute continues this work today.

GREENLAND. The world's largest island, situated in the **Arctic**, Greenland has indigenous **Inuit** and immigrant Danish inhabitants. The Inuit ***angakkoq*** (shaman), discussed by such scholars as **Knud Rasmussen** and **Merete Demant Jakobsen**, **mediates** between human and **other-than-human persons**, in order to maintain harmony and make reparation for **taboo** breaking. Greenland's strong historic connections to Scandinavia gave rise to one of the most important records of **Heathen *seidr*** practices, the Saga of Erik the Red, which describes a séance at a Viking farmstead in Greenland.

GREENWOOD, SUSAN. Anthropologist and **Pagan** teaching undergraduate courses on shamanism and **altered states of consciousness** at the University of Sussex in Great Britain. Greenwood has written widely on **nature** religion and magic, taking a critically sympathetic approach to issues of identity, **gender**, feminism, morality, and the **environment**. She is the author of two important volumes on magic: *Magic, **Witchcraft** and the **Otherworld*** (2000), exploring British Paganisms and **neo-shamanisms**, especially **wicca**, as expressed through concepts of the other world; and *The Nature of Magic: An Anthropology of Consciousness* (2005), which theorizes magic as a form of altered consciousness itself. In the latter volume, Greenwood deals with a general concept of "magical consciousness," on the one hand, and localized **animistic** engagements with living landscapes, on the other, although the tension between the general and particular is not resolved: the concept of animism itself might sidestep the need for a concept of a singular, universal (to humans) magical consciousness.

GRIM, JOHN (1946–). Professor of religion at Harvard University and cofounder and codirector (with Mary Evelyn Tucker) of the Forum on Religion and Ecology. Grim's published research has engaged with **Native American** and other indigenous religions, religion and ecology, **ritual**, and mysticism in the world's religions. His book *The Shaman* (1983) discusses **Ojibwe** shamanic ritual complexes (including the **Midewiwin**), **performance**, and **cosmology**, but he has also engaged with shamans in **South and East Asia** and the Philippines.

GROF, STANISLAV (1931–). Internationally known psychiatrist, one of the founders of transpersonal psychology, and a pioneer of LSD research. Grof's early research on the clinical uses of psychedelics began at the Psychiatric Research Institute in Prague, where he was principal investigator of a program systematically exploring the heuristic and **therapeutic** potential of LSD and other psychoactive substances. Grof went on to become chief of psychiatric research at the Maryland Psychiatric Research Center and assistant professor of psychiatry at the Henry Phipps Clinic of Johns Hopkins University, Baltimore, Maryland. His research on LSD was published in the form of numerous articles and books, including *LSD Psychotherapy* (1980), *The Cosmic Game* (1998), and *Psychology of the Future* (2000).

As one of the founders of transpersonal psychology, he established the International Transpersonal Association (ITA), and at the Esalen Institute in Big Sur, California, he developed holotropic breathwork with his wife, Christina Grof. Holotropic breathwork is "a powerful approach to self-exploration and **healing** that integrates insights from modern consciousness research, anthropology, various depth psychologies, transpersonal psychology, Eastern spiritual practices, and mystical traditions of the world" (www.holotropic.com). The process combines accelerated breathing with evocative **music** in a safe setting in order to induce "a non-ordinary [**altered**] **state of consciousness**," which is reminiscent of **core shamanism** practice.

– H –

HAITI. *See* CARIBBEAN; VODOU.

HALIFAX, JOAN. According to her website, Joan Halifax Roshi is "a **Buddhist** teacher, Shaman and anthropologist," having been a faculty member of Columbia University, the University of Miami School of Medicine, the New School for Social Research, the Naropa Institute, and the California Institute for Integral Studies. She founded the Upaya Sen Center in 1990. Her work on shamanism includes *Shamanic Voices: A Survey of Visionary Narratives* (1979), chronicling the practices of a variety of individual shamans, including the Mexican **Mazatec** Indian *curandera* **Maria Sabina** and **San** (Bushman) healer Old K'xau. *Shaman: The Wounded Healer* (1982), a richly illustrated "coffee table" book, has made shamanism accessible to a wide audience and popularized the role of the shaman as a **wounded healer**—someone who has endured an often life-threatening **illness** but, with the assistance of **other-than-human persons**, has been **healed** in order to become a shaman and healer. Such an **initiatory** sickness is not unusual in indigenous shamanisms, though not universal. The concept of shaman as wounded healer must be contextualized as a device enabling Western understanding rather than a universal indigenous reality and is simultaneously a problematic metanarrative lacking nuance.

HALLOWELL, A. IRVING "PETE" (1892–1974). Anthropologist at the University of Pennsylvania whose research among the **Ojibwe** of south-central Canada between 1930 and 1940 led him to coin the influential phrase "**other-than-human persons**" to speak of Ojibwe understandings of the nature of a thoroughly relational, **animist** world inhabited by persons both human and otherwise. Given the care with which he notes that persons of all kinds have **transformative** abilities, some more developed and practiced than others, it is important to realize that *human* may also be a fluid term: Someone who appears human at one point may take on a different shape at another time. It remains true, however, that the most radical challenge to Western notions of personhood is the Ojibwe and broader Algonquian understanding that humans are not the definitive type of person. In some cases, of particular importance to the work of shamans, human persons are weak and need the considerable **help** and/or **protection** of other-than-human persons. Hallowell's respectful approach to the people he studied led him to argue for the necessity of taking their worldviews seriously, and his publications include careful and insightful discussions with regular reference to the authority of his informants and friends, especially along the Berens River,

Manitoba, and especially Chief Berens, whom Hallowell regularly cites as a coresearcher and significant intellectual influence.

In addition to work that provides a good foundation for understanding the animist context in which shamans live and work, and in which their knowledge fits with their wider culture, Hallowell also discussed more specifically shamanic ceremonial complexes such as **Midewiwin**, "Shaking Tent," and Wabanowiwin. There is some difference of opinion about whether the publication or even discussion of some of these ceremonies and associated narratives is appropriate, although Hallowell certainly gave away fewer details than some other writers and it is evident that his discussion was motivated by respect throughout. Also, Hallowell engaged carefully with the changing cultural, socioeconomic, **political**, and **environmental** situation of those he studied. He did not reify the "traditional" past as the only topic of importance to scholars, and he notes indigenous agency in evolving forms of both traditional practice and **Christianity** to suit the changing times.

HALLUCINOGENS. *See* ENTHEOGENS; HOFFMAN, ALBERT.

HAMAYON, ROBERTE. French linguist and ethnologist. Hamayon has conducted extensive research on **Mongolian** peoples and shamanism in Mongolia, **Siberia**, and **China**. She has drawn attention to the negative connotations of isolating **trance**, **ecstasy**, and **altered states of consciousness** as defining features of shamanisms in Siberia, these having been used to demonize shamans in the past, and argues that in consequence these terms are of little use in informing our understanding of what shamans do. Hamayon theorizes about shamans, **sex**, and **gender** in Siberian shamanism, arguing that shamanic séances among the **Evenk** (Tungus) and **Buryat** are themselves "sexual encounters." As such, she argues that the "marriage" between shamans and their **helpers** is more significant in understanding what these shamans do than the ecstasy, **mastery of spirits**, or **journeying** emphasized by other scholars. Hamayon's work has also clarified the relationship between shamans and community in pre-Soviet Siberia: shamans secured "good luck" for hunters, and the ceremony at which this is effected involved the interplay of "game" (hunted animals) and "games" (entertainment and contests), enhancing our understanding of relationships, especially reciprocity, in shamanistic communities. Hamayon was a researcher (1965–74) at the French Centre National de la Recherche Scientifique (CNRS), and since 1974 she has been director of studies at the École Pratique des Hautes Études, Science of Religion Section. She is the founder of the Centre for Mongolian and Siberian Studies and its journal, *Études mongoles et sibériennes*.

HARNER, MICHAEL. Arguably the most prominent figure in the introduction of practical shamanism to Westerners and its reintroduction into indigenous communities, via the **Foundation for Shamanic Studies** in Mill Valley, California, a nonprofit educational organization of which Harner is director and founder. Harner and colleagues offer workshop programs in "Harner Method" **core shamanism**.

Harner studied shamanism as an anthropologist and shamanic practitioner among the Untusuri **Shuar** (Jivaro) peoples of Ecuador and the **Conibo** of the Peruvian **Amazon**, as well as in western **North America**, in the Canadian **Arctic**, and in **Northern Europe** among the **Saami**. Having been a professor at Columbia and Yale universities, the University of California at Berkeley, and the New School for Social Research in New York, Harner has led a distinguished academic career. As an anthropologist, his publications include *The Jivaro: People of the Sacred Waterfalls* (1972) and *Hallucinogens and Shamanism* (1973). Nonetheless, Harner is best known for introducing practical shamanism to the West, in *The Way of the Shaman* (1980).

HARVEY, GRAHAM (1959–). Lecturer in religious studies at the Open University, Great Britain. In addition to an edited volume (2003) collecting some of the most significant writings about shamans, their activities, and their worldviews, Harvey has written about the "new **animism**" and other works that engage with the wider indigenous religious contexts in which some shamans work. His writings about **Pagans** include discussion of shamanic influences and practices in the movement. He has also coedited a volume (with Karen Ralls, 2001) concerned with "indigenous religious **musics**" to which a number of significant **ethnomusicologists** contributed, several discussing music and **trance** and developing **Gilbert Rouget**'s argument.

HASLUND-CHRISTENSEN, HENNING (1896–1948). In addition to collecting sound recordings of **Mongolian** folk singing and **musical** instruments (e.g., *The Music of the Mongols*, 1943) during his five expeditions to **Central Asia**, Haslund-Christensen was a founder of the Danish Expedition Foundation (1945) and provided valuable ethnographic information on Mongolian shamanism in his classic of travel literature, *Mongolian Adventure: 1920s Danger and Escape among the Mounted Nomads of Central Asia* (2001).

HAWAII. The Huna tradition said to be indigenous to Hawaii has become popular among **neo-shamans** and is disseminated in workshops and via the internet. The term *Huna* refers to teachings or wisdom held and sometimes disseminated by experts, *kahuna*; the term *kahuna* is cognate with other Polynesian terms (e.g., Maori *tohunga*) meaning "expert." It can be applied to all kinds of experts—**priests**, carpenters, singers, canoe builders, or anyone else with a recognized and prized skill. However, it is often interpreted by nonindigenous people as a claim to more mystical or shamanic powers. That *Huna* may mean (temporarily hidden or elite) knowledge does not necessarily equate with shamanic knowledge. While few academics accept claims of widespread Pacific or Oceanic shamanisms, proponents of Huna (e.g., **Serge Kahili King**) are vociferous in asserting indigenous roots. However, it is likely that the idea originated with Max Long's claims that Hawaiian friends taught him the basis of his "Huna Fellowship" system, established in 1945. Certainly, more recent books and websites replicate and elaborate from Long's ideas, adding ideas and practices derived from wider neo-shamanism. Long's **spiritualism** is now reexported as Hawaiian shamanism. Elements of indigenous traditions may be incorporated to give local flavor—for example, the Pleiades star cluster is important in many Oceanic cultures, but some Huna proponents identify it as the home of the **space aliens** who brought their wisdom to Hawaii.

HEALING. Among the most significant duties performed by shamans are concerned with healing clients from **illnesses**. Sometimes illnesses are understood to be **otherworld** persons aggressively assaulting humans, either because they are by nature malevolent or as revenge against human insults. Alternatively, illnesses may result from the assault of **sorcerers** or **witches**, perhaps by shooting **darts**

into people's bodies to make them ill. Shamanic **initiation** may involve **journeys** to the homeland of illness-beings, either to gain their **help** in healing or to defeat them on behalf of the shaman's kin group. Often initiation involves **dismemberment** and reassembly after powerful helpers or objects are inserted into the new shaman's body.

Healing techniques vary considerably, but often take place in elaborate communal **ritual performances**. A refusal to recognize indigenous **doctoring** abilities has often led to a denial that they can really heal or to a reluctant admission that shamanizing may have psychological results. **Neo-shamanism** is often solely **therapeutic**, especially focusing on **individual** psychological concerns, converting otherworld journeying into "inner journeys" and offering "**soul retrieval**" as a mode of **Jungian** psychotherapy.

HEATHENS. At the time of conversion to **Christianity** in Iceland, the terms *kristni* and *hedhni* made a simple distinction between Christendom and Heathenry, the latter meaning "people of the heath," referring to those who practiced their **pagan** religion outside on the heathland rather than inside a church building. *Heathen* only later became a derogatory term, and Heathens today are reclaiming the term to positively describe themselves and their communities. Today's Heathens are engaged in an ongoing process of creative self and community discovery and re-enchantment, reconstructing ancient **Northern European** pagan practices, such as the shamanistic practice of ***seidr***, and making them relevant to a (post)modern world.

HEHAKA SAPA. *See* BLACK ELK, NICHOLAS.

HEINZ, RUTH-INGE. Scholar of comparative religion and psychological anthropology and a research associate at the Center for Southeast Asian Studies, University of California, Berkeley. Heinz authored the volume *Shamans of the 20th Century* (1991), offering one of the first detailed accounts of **neo-shamanic** practice alongside that of indigenous shamans, with the intent of demonstrating that shamanism is a vibrant religion thriving in an increasingly globalized world. Heinz characterizes the shaman as a **mediator** between the sacred and profane, and in locating "**trance mediums**" alongside shamans and others who alter consciousness, Heinz's approach aligns with that of **Ioan Lewis** in broadening the term *shaman* for application outside the **locus classicus** of **Siberia** and the **Arctic**. More recently, Heinz has proposed a model of "**alternate states of consciousness**" (2003), based on a scale from dissociation to mind-expansion, with the determining factor of control over the state indicating ability. As such, Heinz includes shamanistic **journeying** alongside mediumistic and **possession** trances, and the role of control in her model aligns with **Michael Harner**'s definition of **core shamanism**.

HELPERS. Shamans are often marginal figures, but they are rarely solitary. In some cultures, they are aided by apprentice shamans or by other types of **ritualists**. Where **trance** is a significant part of what shamans do, they may regularly rely on the support and physical protection of someone who remains grounded in daily reality and awareness. **Neo-shamans** are often aided by a **drummer** or a recording of rhythmic drumming. While **healing**, **journeying**, and other shamanic practices may require skills gained by **initiation** and/or training, it is common for these to be contained within communal rituals and other more public **performances**. In addition to human helpers, many shamans rely on other-than-human helpers. Some cultures privilege powerful, shamanic **animals** (e.g., **jaguars**) or plants (e.g., **ayahuasca**) as the primary helpers of shamans. Terms like ***spirit*** are often used to refer to **otherworld** helpers. In all these cases, the fact that such potential allies or helpers have their own interests and ambitions makes them **ambiguous** and, at times, dangerous allies.

Mircea Eliade's insistence that shamanism is the control or "**mastery of spirits**" rather than **possession** is certainly overstated, but it does point to the frequency with which shamans struggle to maintain control for the benefit of themselves, their clients, and their communities. Eliade's claim also undervalues the understanding that shamans are **elected** by their eventual helpers, who may continue to make significant demands on them. However, his influence on neo-shamans has blended with that of **Jungian** therapeutic approaches and **individualization** to enable people like **Sandra Ingerman** to invite would-be (neo-)shamans to "visualize an animal that you love and respect and let it carry out the . . . actions" of a "guardian animal."

HEUSCH, LUC DE (1927–). Professor of anthropology at the Free University of Brussels, Belgium. Following **Mircea Eliade**'s categorical distinction between shamanism as "**mastery** of **spirits**" and

possession as "being controlled by spirits," Heusch presented them as opposing moves: the "ascent of man to the gods" versus the "descent of the gods on (and into) man." From this, he elaborated a "geometry of the soul" that deserves consideration as a religious text, but not as an appraisal of ethnographic data about the real life and work of shamans.

HINDUISM. Various elements of Hindu practice have been claimed to be shamanic, especially by those interested in local, village practice rather than the more philosophical and **priestly** Hinduism of the Brahmin caste and texts. The problem of what to include as "Hindu" and how this might relate to shamanism can be illustrated with relation to the Ayyavazhi religion of southern **India**. Ayyavazhi is generally included as a Hindu movement, but seems to require recognition as a distinct practice. Some adherents make use of **divination** to seek the cause of **illness** and to find appropriate **healing** methods. Even if such practices are shamanic (which is debated), they are not always positively valued or encouraged. In **Piers Vitebsky**'s discussion of the **Sora**, he notes both distinctions between indigenous practices and Hinduism, and the integration of Hindus into Sora shamanic practice, especially as the posthumous or "**spirit**" marital partners of shamans.

HIP HOP. *See* PERKINSON, JAMES W.

HMONG. Southeast Asian people originating in Laos; many now live in **North America**. Traditionally an **animist** culture, the Hmong employ shamans as **healers** and **mediators** in disruptive situations. **Illnesses** and other problems may be understood to result from disruption and lack of cohesion among the **souls** that inhabit each person's body. Such souls are supposed to cooperate to form the individual, but may act independently and require a shaman's attention. Illnesses and bad luck may also be caused by unwanted **possession**, which requires shamans to **journey** to the **other world** in **performances** that can be public or seen only by individual clients or **patients**. Journeying is supported by **helpers rhythmically** hitting gongs when guided by the shaman, who wears bell rings on each hand. **Divination** using split buffalo horns may aid understanding of the cause and solution of problems. Shamans also play significant roles in maintaining and developing traditional culture, especially when faced with **Christian**

missions and the dominance of Western modernist society. Thus, they offer a further illustration of the **political** dimensions of shamanism. *See also* SOUTH AND EAST ASIA.

HOFFMAN, ALBERT (1906–). Swiss chemist who synthesized the hallucinogen LSD (d-lysergic acid diethylamide), a chemical derived from the ergot fungus he had been working on in order to develop new drugs for the firm Sandoz. While the drug initially offered unremarkable effects in preliminary laboratory experiments in 1938, Hoffman accidentally discovered the powerful psychedelic properties of LSD when, acting on a "peculiar presentiment," he synthesized a fresh batch of the chemical in 1943. An "extremely stimulated imagination" resulted from brief, accidental exposure to the chemical, and so, intrigued, Hoffman ingested what he assumed to be a conservative dose of a 250-millionth of a gram—actually a massive dose—and then rode his bicycle home, where he experienced "fantastic and impressive" effects. Hoffman's "problem child" or "medicine of the soul" (he used both terms) has had a profound effect on the lives of thousands of people, from those who have had bad "trips" to those who have appreciated their experiences as being benign, spiritual, and/or "shamanic."

LSD ingestion prompted many psychedelic-experience seekers in the Euro-American psychedelic boom of the 1960s to explore shamanism, especially with the publication and subsequent popularity of **Carlos Castaneda**'s **Don Juan** mythos, which gave accounts of **entheogen**-induced shamanic experiences, and the promotion by **Timothy Leary** (the "high priest" of acid) of LSD as a cure to social normativity. The potential of LSD in "psychedelic **therapy**" to treat such **mental health** disorders as neurosis, psychosis, schizophrenia, and depression yielded fascinating, if contradictory, results (reactions among subjects varied) for transpersonal psychologists, psychiatrists, and psychotherapists such as **Stanislav Grof**, before LSD was made illegal across the world in 1966 and scientific research was heavily regulated (leading to a drying up of funding and interest). While the drug remains illegal, there is renewed scientific investigation, and LSD, along with the synthesized chemicals mescaline (from **peyote**, described by **Aldous Huxley**), DMT (an active agent in **ayahuasca**, promoted by **Terence McKenna**), and ibogane (from the root of the West **African** plant **iboga**), is a major a source of inspiration to many **techno-shamans**, **psychonauts**, and other **neo-shamans.**

HOLY PEOPLE. A term for religious leaders among many **Native American** nations, who may be comparable with shamans elsewhere. ***Medicine people*** is a similar term, emphasizing the **healing** abilities and sacred powers of these people. "Holy man" and "holy woman" are also used by **John Pilch** to refer to ancient Mediterranean and biblical healers and **visionaries**, such as Jesus Christ, whom he considers the equivalent of shamans. *See also* BLACK ELK, NICHOLAS.

HOPPÁL, MIHÁLY. Hungarian ethnographer with wide interests in the shamanisms of Eurasia, particularly those of **Siberia** and Hungary. In addition to important ethnographic publications, Hoppál has surveyed ethnographic films about shamans and their activities, and he has discussed both historical material and contemporary shamanism, particularly with regard to those involved in the "cultural revivals" of various post-Soviet republics in Asia. Hoppál has also collaborated in important coedited publications with **Anna-Leena Siikala**, **Juha Pentikäinen**, and Otto von Sadovszky.

HORWITZ, JONATHAN. Neo-shamanic practitioner who founded the **Scandinavian Center for Shamanic Studies** in 1986, and with **Annette Høst** offers such basic and advanced workshops as "The Shaman's **Journey**," "Shamanic Counselling Training," and "**Soul Retrieval** Training." Horwitz was a faculty member of the **Foundation for Shamanic Studies** for eight years, and the practices of Horwitz and Høst are very much influenced by **core shamanism**, including Høst's work on Nordic (**Northern European**) ***seidr***. As a practitioner, Horwitz has been critical of anthropological approaches to shamanic practice as **performance**, sensing a devaluing of genuine experience and the "reality" that shamans actually engage with **spirits**. This practitioner perspective is a fitting response to atheistic, empiricist, and skeptical scholars, but does neglect the important contribution the discourse of performance offers to studies on shamanism in moving analysis away from the veracity of belief to the nuances of what shamans do.

HØST, ANNETTE. Neo-shamanic practitioner operating with **Jonathan Horwitz** at the **Scandinavian Center for Shamanic Studies** (founded in 1986), which offers a variety of workshops. Høst's work focuses on Nordic (**Northern European**) ***seidr***, which she began studying with the Swedish group *Yggdrasil* and has since developed in her own unique direction.

HUICHOL. The *Mara'akate* (sing. *mara'akame*) of the Huichol (*Wixárika*, pl. *Wixáritari*), in the central Mexican Sierra Madre Occidental, make an annual pilgrimage of hundreds of miles into the Wirikùta Desert, the ancestral homeland, in order to harvest the **peyote** cactus. The shamans "hunt" the peyote in the form of a deer, firing prayer arrows at the cactus so that it may be safely harvested. The peyote is crucial to **ritual** life, allowing shamans to "see with our hearts," and this dynamic maintains harmony between human and **other-than-human persons**. Peyote **visions** are recorded in vibrantly colored yarn paintings, which entered the **art** market in the 1970s and can fetch high prices. The creation myth about the first shaman describes how jealous male shamans **dismembered** Takutsi Nakawe in order to steal her power. Recalling this myth aids understanding of the **gendered** reality of Huichol shamanic work: today both men and **women** may become shamans, but men take public roles while women are more secretive for fear of **sorcery**.

Dreams are crucial: for Huichol living in the sierra (rather than close to towns and cities), for instance, the governor and tribal authorities are chosen through the dreams of shamans. Shamans also preside over rituals marking the annual cycle of rainy and dry seasons. Shamans may be marked out from birth, chosen due to a prolonged **illness**, or their proclivity for smoking the sacred **tobacco** in childhood can be a sign of future shamanhood, while those who choose to become shamans are perceived to have the most difficult path. Over a five-year apprenticeship, the chaste **initiate** observes dreams and interprets these with the assistance of an **elder** shaman, often a family member.

Huichol ethnography, by which the Huichol themselves were exposed to a wider audience, was pioneered by **Barbara Myerhoff** and **Peter Furst**, who worked with the shaman **Ramón Medina Silva**. Jay Fikes draws attention to problematic areas of the "Delgado-Furst-Myerhoff collaboration," including uncanny resemblances between the exploits of **Carlos Castaneda**'s (fictional) **Don Juan** and their own informants. Fikes also examines the negative impact that popularization by "Castaneda partisans" of Huichol shamanism has had on the Indians. Their work, along with that of Castaneda, brought psychedelic-experience seekers from North America in the 1960s, who disrupted local lifeways. Following in the wake of Furst, Myerhoff, and Castaneda, such contemporary shamans as **Brant Secunda** and Prem Das are now offering teachings in Huichol shamanism across the world. One positive effect is financial remuneration to the Huichol via the profits of Secunda's **Dance of the Deer Center for Shamanic Studies**. Secunda and Prem Das have nonetheless rewritten native practices for a global and **New Age** market: Secunda conducts **vision quests** and expensive pilgrimages (to Alaska, parts of Europe, and other "exotic" locations), while Prem Das, a disciple of Hari Das Baba, has blended yoga with the Huichol traditions he learned from Huichol shaman Don José.

HUMOR. Shamanic **initiation** and work can be deadly serious, but it can also employ considerable humor. Elements of **bear ceremonialism** and of **sexual** encounters within shamanic **performance** illustrate this. Some shamanic initiation and **healing** accounts insist on the need to make **otherworld** persons, especially aggressive ones, laugh in order to gain **mastery of the spirits**. The link between shamans and **tricksters** can also involve considerable humor, while **combative** shamanism may include satirical comedy.

HUMPHREY, CAROLINE (1943–). Professor of anthropology at Cambridge University. Humphrey has carried out research in **Siberia** and **Mongolia** in the Soviet and post-Soviet periods, as well as in **India**, **Nepal**, Inner Mongolia, and Manchuria. Her research interests include shamanism, theories of **ritual**, and socialist/postsocialist economy and society. With Nicholas Thomas, she coedited *Shamanism, History, and the State* (1994) and contributed an important chapter on the **political** role of shamans in the Manchu state. With **Urgunge Onon**, she coauthored *Shamans and Elders* (1996), which explores the role of shamans in Daur Mongol societies, carefully distinguishing them from **elders**. Both books are important engagements with the political and social place of shamans in their cultures and redress an imbalanced view of shamanism as a separate domain of life identifiable as "religion." The latter book is also among the most detailed accounts of historical and near-contemporary Mongolian shamans and their practices, roles, and relationships with other religious functionaries. It uses "shamanism" to refer to "the entire conglomeration of ideas about beings in the world which includes the shaman," and "shamanship" to refer to the shaman's practice or **performance**.

HUNA. *See* HAWAII.

HUNTER-GATHERERS. A lifeway employed by the majority of indigenous peoples, especially shamanic communities, involving the hunting of such game as deer, fish, and whales and the gathering of shellfish, fruit, honey, and so on. The terms *gatherer-hunter* and *thoughtful forager*, though problematic in their own right, have been used to iterate the prominence of gathering over hunting and to challenge the hierarchy of "man the hunter" and "woman the gatherer." But these **gender** divisions of labor are often permeable. "Hunter-gatherer" retains currency, although it is overtly simplistic to define a people based on their economic strategy alone (the same could be said of modern Westerners as "capitalists"). Shamans are crucially important in many hunter-gatherer communities, especially those more dependent on hunting, where harmony between human and **other-than-human persons** is disrupted by the violence (killing for food) they inevitably do to one another. Shamans are indispensable as relationship brokers between human and other-than-human people, in persuading game to become a hunter's quarry, and to make reparation for the breaking of **taboos**. As a slippery academic construct, while shamanism tends to be associated with hunter-gatherers, it might equally be applied to such contexts as farming (e.g., the megalithic **art** of post–Agrarian Revolution Europe and its possible origin in an **altered state of consciousness**) and capitalism (e.g., the **Korean** kam).

HUNTING MAGIC. The notion that shamans believe they can control game via magical means and so ensure a successful hunt. The concept tends to signify stupidity and/or superstitious belief in magic on the part of the peoples at issue. Hunting magic was an idea popularized by Sir James Frazer (1854–1941) in his infamous *The Golden Bough* (1890) and informs us more about the prejudices of Victorian male armchair anthropologists than about indigenous practices and knowledges. Hunting magic has since been applied to and become erroneously synonymous with the making of **rock art** and **European**

Paleolithic cave art in particular: hungry hunters painted images of their quarry in the false belief that by jabbing spears at these effigies, or painting mortal wounds on them, this game could be successfully hunted in the bush. Despite its prevalence, this interpretation is supported by little or no evidence (e.g., most of the **animals** depicted were not primary sources of food). A more nuanced understanding of hunting magic and the role of shamans in it is facilitated by the new **animism**. Shamans, certainly, may undertake **journeys** into the **other world** in order to seek out game and **mediate** with **other-than-human persons** or **spirits** in order to negotiate success for hunters, usually making agreements or sacrifices in turn, such as the establishing and regulating of certain **taboos**. In this sense, hunting magic is more like **resource management** than foolish superstition.

HUTTON, RONALD. Professor of history at Bristol University in England. Hutton has written a critical history of British **paganism** (*The Pagan Religions of the Ancient British Isles: Their Nature and Legacy*, 1991) and modern **witchcraft** (*The Triumph of the Moon*, 1999), both of which attend in part to alleged shamanistic aspects of these religions from prehistory to the present. Hutton has also written two books on shamanism, the latter of which (*Shamans: Siberian Spirituality and the Western Imagination*, 2002) offered discussion for an English-speaking audience of scholarly work on **Siberian** shamans that had previously been available only in Russian. Hutton's contribution is to demonstrate the historical construction of "shamanism" while attending to consistent features of Siberian shamans and to contrast these with the recent engagements of **neo-shamans** with Siberian spirituality.

HUXLEY, ALDOUS LEONARD (1894–1963). English author, poet, and philosopher, perhaps most famous for his utopian novel *Brave New World* (1932b) and such important nonfiction as *The Art of Seeing* (1932a), *The Perennial Philosophy* (1946), and *The Devils of Loudon* (1952); grandson of Thomas Huxley and brother of Julian Huxley. An account of Huxley's experiments with the drug mescaline is published in *The Doors of Perception* (1954), with rich and celebratory descriptions of the hallucinations and detailed analysis of the mystical and social implications of his experiences. The follow-up volume *Heaven and Hell* (1956) balances the positive experiences with what have since been termed "bad trips" and contributes descriptions of the effects of LSD. In *Brave New World*, the drug "soma" serves as a major tool of the totalitarian state, while in *Island* (1962), Huxley's last major work, the drug "moksha" is central to the doomed utopia of Pala—and both of these novels likely draw on Huxley's own experiments with **entheogens**. Huxley's work has had a major impact on psychedelic audiences—**Jim Morrison**'s band the Doors took its name from Huxley's 1954 book—and his work continues to have an influence on many **neo-shamans**. The fact that Huxley requested an injection of LSD on his deathbed lends greater weight to his status as a **visionary** and shaman among neo-shamans.

– I –

IBOGA. *Tabernanthe iboga*, or simply iboga, is a common shrub in parts of West **Africa** that contains the active **entheogenic** constituent indole alkaloid *ibogane*. There are numerous Bwiti sects that fuse African **animist** and **Christian** monotheistic belief systems, having spread from Gabon and Cameroon to the Congo, Zaire, and Equatorial Guinea. One reason for this success is that Bwiti is considered to be a monotheistic universal religion accessible to anyone prepared to approach iboga with respect and humility. Bwitists scrape off the bark from the roots of the plant and grind this into a powder, which is eaten in massive doses over some days, producing one of the most potent and long-lasting **altered-state-of-consciousness** experiences known. Under the influence of iboga, experients often describe meeting a powerful entity that represents the **spirit** of the plant and/or "god" and are able to **heal**, **divine** the future, and engage with **ancestral** spirits. A notable effect of iboga is **vomiting**, which, like other emetic entheogens, is seen by those ingesting it as offering important spiritual **purification**. In the West, the potential of iboga as a treatment for addiction, especially opiate addiction, is being explored with compelling results.

ILLNESSES. Among many **animist** communities, illnesses may be considered to be **other-than-human persons** or **spirits** in their own right. Elsewhere they may be caused by the actions of **sorcerers, witches**, or aggressive enemy shamans. In particular, illnesses may be thought to be inserted into bodies by **darts** thrown by such **predatory** beings. In either case, **healing** may be a necessary role for shamans in such communities. They may **mediate** with **otherworld** or other-than-human persons to resolve whatever problem caused them to intrude into human bodies, they may **combat** the invading beings, or they may apply local medical or **doctoring** methods to remove the intruding dart or other substance. In some cases, illnesses result in some aspect of **patients** being alienated from themselves, and shamans may need to **journey** in search of that part (e.g., lost, stolen, or damaged **souls**) and return it to their patients.

IMAGINAL. Describing the realm of consciousness or the **other world** in which shamans **journey** during **altered states of consciousness**, according to **Jungian** psychologists. The term was applied to shamanisms and **neo-shamanisms** most explicitly by **Daniel Noel** in his book *The Soul of Shamanism: Western Fantasies, Imaginal Realities* (1997), in which he argues that Jungians such as James Hillman provide "indispensable resources for arriving at another New Shamanism: an imaginal shamanism for Western seekers" that does not appropriate from indigenous shamans but contributes something new and important to the world. The term theorizes shamanic altered states in a way that is easier for Westerners unfamiliar with **trances** to understand, but the connotations of "imagination" also raise issues of whether *imaginal* engages sufficiently with the "reality" of shamanic experiences. *See also* BECOMING-ANIMAL.

INDIA. Piers Vitebsky argues that "shamanism [in India and widely throughout **South and East Asia**] is often the religion of earlier, aboriginal tribes" but is never entirely separate from the now dominant regional religions of **Hinduism**, **Islam**, **Buddhism**, and **Christianity**. His fieldwork among the **Sora**, a jungle-dwelling "scheduled tribe" (a group recognized as indigenous under Indian constitutional law) on the borders of Orissa and Andhra Pradesh, illustrates his argument here and in many other discussions. For example, in addition to male and female shamans (all called *kuran* but distinguished by **gender**), Sora villages have a "hereditary earth **priest** whose performance does not involve **trance**." Additionally, kuran gain their shamanic powers by marrying high-caste Hindu **spirits** in the **underworld**, for example, "warriors and kings who for centuries have wielded **political** and economic power over the Sora." It seems likely that the Sora are typical of the situation for many other scheduled tribes.

INDIVIDUATION. Under the influence of modernism, the stress on individual, "inner" experience and reality has been significant both in studies of **shamanic/altered states of consciousness** (including **trance** and **possession**) and in **neo-shamanic cosmology** and **performance**. Early studies that presented shamans as psychologically ill or damaged people, and more recent ones interested in **brain chemistry**, exemplify scholarly attempts to situate shamanism within psychology. Neo-shamanism is influenced by **Carl Jung**'s privileging of "individuation" as a **therapeutic** goal, and therefore typically presents **journeying** as self-exploration. **Paul Johnson**'s "case study in **New Age** Ritual Appropriation" also identifies the influence of Sigmund Freud in interpretations of "**soul loss**" as equivalent to repression and trauma.

INDONESIA. A number of peoples indigenous to this Southeast Asian archipelago employ shamans. *See also* ATKINSON, JANE MONNIG; CHEWONG; DAYAK; SOUTH AND EAST ASIA; WANA.

INGERMAN, SANDRA. **Neo-shamanic** practitioner and author. Ingerman's most well-known book is *Soul Retrieval: Mending the Fragmented Self* (1991), outlining the practice of **soul retrieval** as taught by **Michael Harner**'s **Foundation for Shamanic Studies**, of which she was educational director. She has also written the sequel, *Welcome Home: Following Your Soul's Journey Home*, and is the author of a number of other volumes and CDs on neo-shamanic practices, including *Shamanic* ***Journeying****: A Beginner's Guide.* Soul retrieval, as it is presented by Ingerman and the foundation, involves **visualization**, guided meditation, and the **healing** of psychological ills more than the actual (perceived or otherwise) retrieval of lost **souls** as in indigenous shamanic contexts—for example, the **Greenlandic** ***angakkoq***. Ingerman holds an M.A. in counseling psychology from the California Institute of Integral Studies and teaches workshops on shamanism worldwide.

INITIATION. Shamans are sometimes distinguished from other religious or cultural leaders by a particular style of initiation. In contrast with **priests**, who are normally educated by other priests in the technical procedures and necessary knowledge for sacrificial and ceremonial practice, shamans are often said to be selected against their will by **otherworld** persons or **spirits** who abduct, **dismember**, and reassemble them as new shamans. During these frightening and sometimes painful experiences, neophyte shamans may have powerful objects inserted into their bodies that will provide them with the power or ability to **heal** and help their people and/or **curse** and **combat** enemies. In some cases, the beginning of initiation is marked by the onset of **illness**. Whereas "ordinary" people may be killed by these illnesses, shamans may have to struggle to overcome and **master** the aggressing beings rather than being overwhelmed and destroyed by them. To survive and return from **ecstatic journeying** or **trance** is to be remade as a shaman, perhaps with the ability to heal the particular initiatory disease or condition. Similarly, when other people are abducted, they may become **possessed** and require the services of a shaman to return them to full health and ordinary life.

In some cases, the initiate meets powerful otherworld **helpers** or allies, and they may even marry otherworld persons. The intimate relationships established between shamans and their otherworld helpers or spouses may entail **taboos**, prohibitions or expectations that also distinguish shamans from their communities. For example, a male shaman married to a male **other-than-human person** may have to dress in female attire, either throughout life or only when performing shamanic work. Aspects of **Nicholas Black Elk**'s biography exemplify a tradition that failure to abide by initiatory regulations may lead to abandonment by one's helpers or a decline in one's shamanic abilities. Shamans among the **Mapuche** of Chile are supposed to renew their initiation regularly in complex communal ceremonies that refresh their relationships with otherworld helpers.

In Haitian **Vodou**, marriages are such a regular aspect of initiation that marriage contracts are drawn up specifying the respective duties of both partners. **Alfred Métraux** (1959) includes a copy of a contract that specifies that the human partner, Madame Andrémise Cétoute, "must consecrate Tuesday and Thursday to her [spirit] husband Damballah without ever a blemish on herself," while Monsieur (also "citizen") Damballah Toquan Miroissé's "duty is to load his wife with good luck so that Madame Cétoute will never know a day's poverty." The contract includes the advice that "it is with work that spiritual and material property is amassed" and concludes, "in execution of article 15.1 of the Haitian Code. They hereto agreed in the affirmative before qualified witnesses." While the legal language of this contract may be unique to Vodou, it is entirely typical of the establishment and obligations of relationships between shamans and their otherworld companions in many other places.

In addition to such relational introductions, initiates may gain a first experience of the techniques they will employ when working for their communities. They may learn locally appropriate ways to ingest hallucinogens, such as **ayahuasca** or ***yagé*** (treated as a powerful plant person) among **Amazonian** shamans; how trance and/or possession is performed or revealed to clients; the use of **drums**, rattles, or other **rhythm**-making instruments; forms of **chanting**; the wearing of appropriate **costume**; and so on. Such lessons may begin in other worlds but continue under the tutelage of more experienced shamans. When **Michael Harner** sought to understand **Conibo** shamanism, he was told that he could learn only by experiencing what shamans experience when inspired by ayahuasca. Scholars are divided about the lengths to which it is appropriate to go in order to understand what other people take for granted or wish to explain, but Harner is not alone in taking this initiatory journey.

It should also be noted that although the pattern of illness, abduction, dismemberment, and revelation of knowledge and techniques in the other world may be typical of the experience of many shamans, it is not the only mode of initiation. **Sora** shamans are far from unique in being apprenticed to relatives who teach them the role and accompany them while **dreaming** and in other forms of trance. Amazonian shamans seeking shamanic knowledge commonly pay more experienced shamans to teach necessary techniques and chants. It is perhaps safest to conclude only that the gift of becoming a shaman can be inherited, desired, or feared, but it is always up to otherworld or other-than-human persons to decide if they will work with and support someone as a shaman. Only in some cases do they impose their will by the process that is sometimes mistakenly said to be a universal marker of shamanism.

Neo-shamans also often seek initiation.

INTERNATIONAL SCHOOL OF SHAMANISM. A school based in Atlanta that offers individual and group seminars and workshops, consultations, **healing**, rites of passage, and other services which aim to align an individual's mind, body, and spirit and reconnect people with the sacredness of **nature**. It was founded by Thomas Richard Lake, who is described as "an anointed shaman" and has studied with **North American,** Mexican, and **South American** (Brazilian and Peruvian) shamans; his interest in shamanism derives from a background in theology and holistic psychotherapy. Like similar **neo-shamanic** organizations, the school has more in common with **New Age** metanarratives of shamanism than with indigenous shamanisms embedded in local and community contexts.

INTRUSIONS. Illnesses are often thought to be caused by the **intrusion** of artifacts (e.g., **darts**) or **predatory** beings into a body. A significant part of a shaman's role can be **doctoring**, especially in order to remove such intrusions. They may also be required to seek the responsible aggressor and **combat** them.

INUIT. Indigenous communities of the **Arctic** coasts of **Siberia**, Alaska, Canada, and **Greenland** (formerly known as Eskimos), well known for their hunter-fisher lifestyle and documented initially by such ethnographers as Martin Frobisher, G. F. Lyon, **Franz Boas**, Edmund James Peck, and **Knud Rasmussen**. These reporters tell us that the work of **mediating** between the **animist** worlds of humans and **other-than-human persons** is termed *angakuniq* (or derivations of this); Boas informs us that on Baffin Island, "the persons, who can see the souls of men and of **animals** and are able to visit **Sedna** [a **Master of Animals**] are called *angakkut*," while according to **Merete Demant Jakobsen**, the Greenlandic ***angakkoq*** ("visionary and **dreamer**") is a "**master of spirits**." Consistently across Inuit cultures, shamans maintained harmony and made reparation for **taboo** breaking by acting as a broker between human and other-than-human people, having the ability to approach these beings in the correct way (without causing offense). The breaking of taboos might lead a **spirit** to steal the **soul** of the taboo breaker, so the shaman would undertake the **journey** to the spirit realm in order to restore the soul and therefore health of the patient. Famine might also result from offense caused to the spirits of hunted animals, and again the shaman would be called upon to restore the imbalance in relationships. Despite these benevolent actions, there are reports that some shamans used

witchcraft in competing with other shamans and in order to kill enemies. Upon its arrival (from the 18th century in Labrador and spreading thereafter), **Christianity** had a massive impact on shamanistic practices, driving them underground in some places but with a creative fusion of the two evident elsewhere; today, there is a precarious relationship between them.

ISLAM. Some varieties of Islam have been labeled shamanic or shamanistic. **Ioan Lewis** discusses possession cults called **Sar** or **Zar** in North and East **Africa**, and the similar **Bori** cult in West and **North Africa**. It is sometimes claimed that the Alevīlik or Alevis, originating in Turkey, blend Shi'a and Sufi Islamic elements with pre-Islamic Turkic shamanic practices and ideas. However, to interpret the dervishes as **performing** a "**trance** dance" may be to focus on their techniques rather than their purpose or role in society, and at that level these communal dancers may not be accurately considered shamans.

– J –

JAGUARS. A number of **Amazonian** peoples identify shamans as jaguars. Usually this is stated strongly ("shamans are jaguars"), not metaphorically ("shamans are like jaguars"). Western interpreters seem to find it difficult to accept the equation at face value, e.g., **Gerardo Reichel-Domatoff** seems to struggle to write: "Shamans and jaguars are thought to be almost identical, or at least equivalent, in their power, each in his own sphere of action, but occasionally able to exchange their roles." However, a full appreciation of the nature of shamans in the region requires acceptance that the obvious meaning is intended: shamans *are* jaguars. Jaguars are not valorized as noble and elusive representatives of a pristine **nature** over against the cultural world of humanity. Nor, therefore, are shamans being celebrated as "close to nature," "noble savages," or exemplary **environmentalists**. The precise point of the claim is an equivalence rooted in **predation**: just like jaguars, the preeminent predators of Amazonia, so shamans are "predatory **animists**" (to paraphrase **Carlos Fausto**'s phrase). The choice is a straightforward one between being a predatory or being prey: everything is either one or the other (not only or always "essentially," but in lived reality). By **initiation** and practice, shamans ally themselves with predators, especially jaguars but also deities and **spirits** that seek to eat human flesh or drink human **blood**. The accusation that they are or may be **cannibals** has been made both by indigenous people and by European or Euro-American observers. However, from their perspective as jaguars, they are not cannibals. Fausto also notes that the importance of blood and **tobacco** in Amazonia is almost precisely the inverse of the **neo-shamanic** marginalization or ignorance about both.

In **Eduardo Viveiros de Castro**'s writings, another aspect of the jaguar–shaman relationship is central. Shamans are people (humans or **other-than-human persons**) who can shift their **perspective** to see as others (predators or prey) see. They see beneath the diverse physical forms to the underlying, real cultural realities. That is, most humans see jaguars as **animals** who eat raw meat, but shamans can see them as they see themselves: as humanoid persons who eat cooked food as cultured beings. They can also see humans as jaguars see them: as prey. Shamans may then **combat** the predatory enemy approaching in the form of a jaguar or they may form an alliance and prey among humans. Failure to appreciate these resonances of claims about jaguar–shaman relationships makes it difficult to explain the full **ambiguity** and danger of the role played by shamans.

JAKOBSEN, MERETE DEMANT. Jakobsen's volume *Shamanism: Traditional and Contemporary Approaches to the* ***Mastery of Spirits*** *and* ***Healing*** (1999) reviews previous work on the **Greenlandic *angakkoq*** and contrasts this with **neo-shamanic** practices. While noting the positive benefits of neo-shamanisms for its practitioners, she points out that these practices are far removed from the challenging and potentially dangerous role of the angakkoq, who walk between the worlds of human and **other-than-human persons** and **mediate** engagements between them.

JAPAN. *See* AINU.

JIMSONWEED. *See* DATURA.

JIVARO. *See* SHUAR.

JOHNSON, PAUL C. Visiting associate professor in history at the Center for Afroamerican and African Studies and Latin American and **Caribbean** Studies at the University of Michigan, Ann Arbor. Johnson is the author of the award-winning book *Secrets, Gossip and Gods: The Transformation of Brazilian Candomblé* (2002), which explores the role of "secretism" in this and other religions. Instead of the dubious notion of "syncretism," which suggests that there are "pure forms" of religions and cultures that may be corrupted when they encounter one another, Johnson proffers a richer understanding of the way in which persecuted and marginal Creole or hybrid groups, cultures, and practices survive and even thrive. In an article that compares research among practitioners of **Candomblé** and those of **Garifuna religion**, he refines the utility of the term *indigenous* by exploring the way in which these two religions "extend" and "indigenize" the practices and identities of their practitioners and their wider cultures.

JONES, LESLIE ELLEN. In her volume *Druid, Shaman, Priest* (1998), Jones discusses the **Celtic Druid** as a shaman, not only examining ancient evidence but also critically engaging with **neo-shamanic** manifestations of Celtic shamanism. Regarding the former, Jones concurs with other scholars in arguing that the terms *Celt* and *shaman* are constructed and problematic, but that shamanistic aspects can reliably be discerned in such literature as the Welsh poet Taliesin and warrior-hero Owein ap Urien. Addressing neo-shamanism, she focuses on the work of **John Matthews**, commenting especially on the contrast between Matthews's apparently accessible and "safe" practices vis-à-vis the more challenging, even dangerous path of other, indigenous shamanisms. Jones is quick to dismiss Matthews's practices as lightweight and **New Age**, but Celtic shamanism today is by no means singular, and there are practitioners who not only integrate their practices into the challenges of everyday life but also engage with the "dark side" of the shaman, such as **Philip "Greywolf" Shallcrass**.

JOURNEYING. Spirit journeying, **soul** flight, or **ecstasy** are often taken to be essential and even definitive features of shamanisms. **Neo-shamans**, particularly practitioners of the **core shamanism** proposed by **Michael Harner** and taught by the **Foundation for**

Shamanic Studies, significantly influenced by **Mircea Eliade**, view what Harner has termed "journeying" as crucial to their mode of shamanism and universal to all shamanisms. But while the practice is common in the **locus classicus** of **Siberia**, not all shamans journey in this way, and to emphasize this feature over others neglects the diversity of shamanic practices. **Ioan Lewis** coined the term ***soul projection*** to label this aspect of shamans' work.

JUDAISM. This religion is rarely perceived to have shamanic elements, although those who confuse mysticism and shamanism may consider the Kabbalah to be shamanic. **Ecstatic visionary journeys** to Judaism's equivalent of an **upper world**, that is, heaven, were commonplace in ancient Jewish literature. However, Rabbi Gershom Winkler claims to have learned from **Native Americans** in the southwestern United States and discovered parallels between their shamanism and large areas of traditional Judaism, if understood in a new way. Largely he means that Judaism celebrates earthly life, recognizes a wider-than-human community as significant, and can include, if not an entirely **animist**, at least a pantheistic worldview. Winkler's "shamanic Judaism," taught through retreats and workshops of his Walking Stick Foundation, is in most respects quite similar to other forms of **neo-shamanism**, even if it refers to ancient and medieval Jewish mystical and magical texts; it is all about "sacred circles," "**animal totems**," and the use of feathers. Other similarities include his association with **David Carson**, whose Medicine Cards offer a form of Tarot with Native American symbolism.

JUNG, CARL G. (1875–1961). Swiss founder of psychotherapy. Jung's ideas and techniques have had considerable influence on **neo-shamans**, including their explicit use of **visualization** and common stress on **individuation**. Jung has been described by **Dan Noel** as a shaman himself, "because he opened up shamanic **healing** possibilities to an entire culture: ours." He also calls Jung "a modern Merlin" and discusses his "**initiatory** descent to what he called the objective psyche, [which led] to the insight that inner images are the **soul**'s substance, [and] provides the radical psychological legacy realized in the work of the post-Jungian **imaginal** psychologists." Noel's definition of this version of "Western shamanism" is a "soulful spirituality, in artful touch with **dreams** and imaginings, including especially those which connect us to our wounding, can be a shamanic spirituality of imaginal healing." This admirably summarizes the project and work of many of Jung's psychotherapeutic heirs, including James Hillman, and is evident in Sylvia Perera's treatment of the ***Descent of Inanna***. It is also a fine summary of what Jung may have intended in his many books, lectures, and other work and encapsulates his inspirational role in the Eranos Conferences at Ascona, Switzerland, in which many formative thinkers of the 20th century, especially the Jungians and mythologists influential on neo-shamanism, participated.

– K –

KALWEIT, HOLGER. German ethnologist and psychologist who has studied shamanism in **Hawaii**, the **North American** Southwest, Mexico, and **Tibet**. Kalweit is the author of several books in German, as well as the founder of two psychotherapeutic methods, darkness therapy and **nature** psychotherapy, which draw on shamanic practices. In the now-classic *Dreamtime and Inner Space: The World of the Shaman* (1988), Kalweit presents accounts of shamans worldwide and compares these with psychological research into **altered states of consciousness**, proposing that shamans are "astronauts of inner space." More recently, *Shamans, Healers and Medicine Men* (2000), as with other volumes by psychotherapists, presents yet another grand survey of shamans worldwide as **healers** and focuses on personal relationships, arguing that shamanic healing is "not merely the alleviation of symptoms but entails a **transformation** of one's relationship to life."

KANAIMÀ. The predominant form of **dark shamanism** in **Amazonia**. **Neil Whitehead** defines it as "assault **sorcery**," which involves the "mutilation and lingering death of its victims." Not only is an understanding of all forms of dark shamanism necessary in relation to particular ethnographic discussions; it also aids appreciation of the inadequacy of Western dualisms that try to separate "(our) good shamans" from "(their) bad sorcerers." The pervasive importance of **predation** and **perspectivism** are also clarified by recognition of the role of these practices and discourses. As in the **Caribbean**, kanaimà can function as an assertion of agency and autonomy among indigenous peoples under colonialism. This is also important in recognizing the malleability and continuing evolution of "traditional" indigenous notions of what shamans might be and do.

KARDECISM. Beginning as a spiritualist movement called Spiritism, founded by the self-named Allan Kardec in France in the mid-19th century, but reaching its most popular contemporary form in Brazil, Kardecism now blends European-derived **Christian** esoteric and spiritualist traditions with **African** (e.g., **Umbanda**) and indigenous **Amazonian** traditions. Following group singing and **drumming**, individuals become **possessed** and are spoken through by **spirits** who advise and instruct the group or clients. The movement stresses moral and charitable lifestyles and practices, insisting that liberation is not only spiritual but also social and practical.

KARUK. A people indigenous to northwestern California who typically refer to their shamanic **healers** and **ritualists** as "**doctors**," *êem*. Traditionally considering themselves to live at the center of the world, their primary ritual (recently revived) is the "Fix the Earth" ceremony (sometimes called "world renewal"). This and other ceremonies may be considered to be living persons in their own right, communicating and caring for the **animist** community of humans and **other-than-human persons**. Julian Lang's *Ararapíkva* (1994) translates creation stories told to John Harrington in 1926 and includes details about **sucking** cures, songs, basket weaving, and **medicine** plants.

KATZ, RICHARD. Clinical anthropologist whose research in the late 1960s on **San** (Bushmen) **healing** practices in the Kalahari Desert is published as the seminal volume *Boiling Energy: Community Healing among the Kalahari Kung* (1982). Katz adopted a method of participant-observation grounded in sociological theory, and his work outlines the importance of the **trance** or healing dance to community well-being. Anthropological research in this area has been crucial to the shamanistic interpretation of **Southern African** and other **rock art** traditions. In the late 1970s Katz continued his research with fieldwork on healing and **witchcraft** in Fiji, published as *The Straight Path of the Spirit: Ancestral Wisdom and Healing Traditions in Fiji* (1999). Katz is currently professor of cross-cultural psychology at the University of Saskatchewan (First Nations University of Canada).

KELLY, KAREN. Neo-shamanic practitioner living in Cambridge, England, who studied with **Jonathan Horwitz** of the **Scandinavian Center for Shamanic Studies**. With a background in **core shamanism**, Kelly offers **healing** to private clients, edits *Spirit Talk* ("a core shamanic newsletter"), and co-facilitates the London Open Drumming Group, which brings neo-shamans together to **drum** and **journey**.

KENDALL, LAUREL. American anthropologist best known for her books about **Korean** shamans: *Shamans, Housewives, and Other Restless Spirits* (1985) and *The Life and Hard Times of a Korean Shaman* (1988). She presents the results of her fieldwork among rural and urban shamans largely from the perspective of the shamans themselves rather than their clients or wider culture. She notes: "Korean shamans first drew my interest as **women** ministering to women. I was inspired by a burgeoning anthropological interest in the little-studied female side of ethnography" (1985, 178). While this draws attention to the predominance of women in *kut*, shamanic rituals, both as shamans and as clients seeking healing or solutions to problems, it contrasts with Korean feminist and academic writing, both about shamans and about women, that reveals the marginality of shamanism. Kendall may overestimate the importance of shamans in Korean culture or feminism, but her work is important in challenging pervasive claims that shamanism is the preserve only of **hunter-gatherer** cultures.

KENIN-LOPSAN, MONGUSH. President of the Society of **Tuvan** Shamans, founder and honorary chairman of Tos Deer (Nine Skies), the centralized religious organization of shamans in the Republic of Tuva, as well as a senior researcher at Aldan-Maadyr (Sixty Rebels), the Tuvan national museum. Kenin-Lopsan has been a major force in the revival of traditional spiritual practices in Tuva since the decline of Soviet Communism. He collaborated with the **Foundation for Shamanic Studies** on a conference in 1993 for the "rehabilitation of shamanism in Tuva," and following the conference, the president of Tuva stated that both shamanism and **Buddhism** would be "equally respected in the modern Tuvan Republic." Kenin-Lopsan has also been declared a "**living treasure** of shamanism" by the Foundation for Shamanic Studies. Tuvan shamanic clinics resemble doctors' surgeries in some ways, with treatment rooms and diagnosis based in part on Western techniques (e.g., taking the pulse and temperature), with shamanic work integrated into the consultation, and all board-certified Tuvan shamans carry a membership card. Kenin-Lopsan is also a professor on the School of Shamanic Studies program in Tuva, offering teaching in Tuvan shamanism to non-Tuvans. *See also* HEALING.

KHARITIDI, OLGA. In her book *Entering the Circle: Ancient Secrets of Siberian Wisdom Discovered by a Russian Psychiatrist* (1997), Kharitidi suggests that her experiences with indigenous shamans began at a psychiatric hospital in Novosibirsk, **Siberia**, with a patient whose mental **illness** was apparently caused by his call to be a shaman. Following in the footsteps of **Carlos Castaneda** and **Lynn Andrews**, Kharitidi's unwitting introduction to shamanism is portrayed as a true story that can bring meaning and spiritual purpose to the lives of her readers. The book is described as "Castaneda à la Russe" by **Michael Harner**, and there are clear similarities between Kharitidi's work and that of Castaneda. Her book portrays misleading stereotypes, suggesting shamanism is a "proto-tradition, a basic tradition . . . able to preserve very important archaic rituals and beliefs that have not changed as a result of social and cultural influences." Kharitidi describes her precognitive **dreams** of the "lady in the ice" found on the Ukok Plateau, near the borders of Kazakhstan, **Altai**, and **China**, and these dreams culminate in the appearance of Belovidia, the Siberian homeland of a "long-forgotten, advanced, esoteric civilization." Besides this decontextualizing and romanticizing of shamanism, Kharitidi does, however, draw a distinction between her own **neo-shamanism** and that of the indigenous shamans she learned from, not claiming to be a shaman or initiated as one, and she also emphasizes the community role of shamanic practitioners—aspects often overlooked by neo-shamans who misrepresent shamanisms.

KIM, CHONGHO (1954–). Korean scholar whose doctoral research at the University of New South Wales, Australia, entailed fieldwork among Korean shamans, their clients, and wider society. In contrast with **Laurel Kendall**'s interest in shamans' perspectives and her desire to study a **gendered** phenomenon, Kim was intrigued by the paradox of the persistence of the marginalized and somewhat covert practice of shamanism and its role in Korean society. Even the reactions of his own family to his researching shamanism provide evidence of the ambiguity of the tradition: even relatives who admit to having paid for a *kut*, **ritual**, evidenced embarrassment that Kim was researching the topic. He also illustrates the paradox by referring to the fact that Kendall was researching and writing at the same time as another scholar, Clark Sorensen, who was also interested in Korean peasants and industrialization but never mentions **spirits** or shamans. Kim is explicit that the difference between the books of Kendall and Sorensen is not surprising, because they focus on two sides of a Korean "cultural discrepancy" between the "ordinary world" (Sorensen) and the "field of misfortune" (Kendall). Kim's own work is concerned with the fault line between those two coexisting but antagonistic worlds in Korean culture.

KING, SERGE KAHILI. Leading proponent of the **Hawaiian** *Huna* tradition. The addition of the family name Kahili to his name derives from his adoption by a *kupua*, or "shaman of the Hawaiian tradition," at the age of 18, three or four years after his father had initiated him in Huna. King also studied with West **African** shamans. His many books and lectures convey his stress on down-to-earth practicality and his rooting of shamanism in urban reality. Like most **neo-shamans**, he portrays shamanism as helping others to know themselves better, a form of **healing** entirely fitted to modernity.

KOREA. Shamanism in Korea is almost entirely a **women**'s phenomenon: both shamans and their clients are normally women. Shamanic **rituals**, *kut*, involving **trance** and the entertainment of **ancestral** and other **spirits**, are commonly requested out of a sense of need, for example, when other means of **healing** or problem resolution fail, and are often kept secret even within a family. **Chongho Kim** cites the results of a Korean Gallup poll that indicated 38 percent of the Korean population (or around 10 million people) had resorted to a shaman. Nonetheless, except in folkloric or cultural performances, shamanic **music** is far from popular, and the entire practice remains marginal. Kim argues that **Laurel Kendall**'s research is limited by its focus on shamans' views and practices and that it mistakes the phenomenon for a feminist spirituality. In contrast, he is interested in the paradox of a widespread practice that continues to be deemed shameful. Korean shamanism is also interesting in presenting a significant contrast with the common presentation of shamanism as a religion of **hunter-gatherers**: in Korea it has long been practiced in a rural agrarian context and has made the transition into urban industrialization, albeit without losing its marginal status. Shamanism in Korea is summed up by Kim as existing within "the field of misfortune" rather than "the ordinary world." It is not an honored tradition but rather a necessity that seeks the cause and solution of seemingly intractable problems of relationships, **illness**, and employment. *See also* GENDER.

KRIPPNER, STANLEY. Professor of psychology and director of the Center for Consciousness Studies at the Saybrook Graduate School, San Francisco, and past president of the Association for Humanistic Psychology, the American Psychological Association, and the Parapsychological Association. Krippner has written profusely on empirical research relating to the efficacy of shamanic and other forms of **healing**, as well as on the broader, related topics of parapsychology, psychotherapy, and consciousness studies. He is the coauthor of *The Realms of Healing* (1977) and *Healing States: A Journey into the World of Spiritual Healing and Shamanism* (1986), both with Alberto Villoldo, as well as *Spiritual Dimensions of Healing: From Tribal Shamanism to Contemporary Health Care* (1992) with Patrick Welch. Krippner's psychological approach to shamanic healing insists that the human mind has an innate ability to heal (itself, the body, and the mind and body of other people) and that shamans, as the "first psychotherapists," are exemplars of this technique. Such an approach represents shamanism in a form accessible (both intellectually and experientially) to modern Westerners as well as to scientific analysis. Shamans themselves understand their practices rather differently, focusing on engagements and relationships with **other-than-human peoples**, yet the psychological metaphor has increasing currency among some at the interface of indigenous shamans and **neo-shamans**, where it enables cross-discourse dialogue and understanding.

– L –

LA BARRE, R. WESTON (1911–1996). American anthropologist and ethnologist best known for his studies of **peyotism** among **Native**

Americans, particularly the Kiowa and the **Native American Church** in the 1930s and 1960s. La Barre also conducted research among the Aymara of Peru. The Smithsonian Institution has an extensive archive of his field notes and correspondence in all these areas.

LAKOTA. Indigenous nation originating in and around the Great Plains of the center of **North America**. Their **holy people** serve as repositories of knowledge, ceremonial leaders, **healers**, and **mediators** with significant **other-than-human persons**. Influential but contested presentations of the **initiation** and practice of their shamans include works by **John Neihardt** and **Joseph Epes Brown**, both of whom write about **Nicholas Black Elk**.

LAME DEER, JOHN (FIRE) (1900 or 1903–1976). Oglala **Lakota** *wichasha wakan*, **holy man** or **medicine man**, who also earned a living as, among other things, a rancher, rodeo rider, and reservation police officer. Lame Deer initiated the collaboration with **Richard Erdoes** that resulted in their coauthoring of *Lame Deer, Seeker of Visions* (1972). For Erdoes, the project was evidently **initiatory** as he went on to coauthor a number of significant biographies and other works with **Native American** authors in a similar conversational style.

In the book, Lame Deer describes his life and that of his people and explains Lakota ceremonies and practices—not only "traditional" ones such as **vision quests**, the sun dance, and **healing** rituals but also recent indigenous developments such as the **Native American Church** rooted in **ritual** ingestion of **peyote**. He says of the *wichasha waken* that "such a one can cure, prophesy, talk to the herbs, command the stones, conduct the sun dance or even change the weather, but all this is of no great importance to him. These are merely stages he has passed through. . . . He has the *wakanya wowanyanke*—the great vision." Going on to talk about the importance of listening rather than preaching, Lame Deer stresses the vital importance of following one's (initiatory) vision that establishes one's particular way of relating to the powerful **other-than-human persons** of the world. He also talks about the vital importance of places, especially the Black Hills, and how their sacrality continues to lead to various forms of protest about dominant American abuse of the land, its waters, minerals, and life. This should not be mistaken for an **environ-**

mentalist message, however, because it is about the place of humanity in the community of life.

Lame Deer's shamanism is an aspect of a broader **animism**. His motivations for recording his life story and knowledge are both to guarantee the continuity among his people and other Native nations of the practices he discusses and to "save the white man from himself" by pointing out the folly of an obsession with gold or money. This book and websites about Lame Deer regularly refer to the **humor** with which he presented himself and his interests, and even desperately serious concerns. Lame Deer's son, Archie Fire Lame Deer, followed his father as a respected holy man and passed the tradition on through his family.

LAPPS. *See* SAAMI.

LEARY, TIMOTHY (1920–1996). Clinical psychologist and counterculture drug guru. With a Ph.D. in clinical psychology, Leary founded the Harvard Center for Research in Personality in 1958. After eating a number of "magic **mushrooms**" (**psilocybin**) in 1960, Leary underwent "the deepest religious experience of my life," leading to his clinical experiments (on student guinea pigs) with LSD, initially funded by the military. Leary subsequently became disillusioned by academia, "dropped out" of Harvard, and established the privately funded international Foundation for Internal Freedom in 1963. Leary became the most vocal and controversial spokesperson for drugs, particularly psychedelics and especially LSD, as an indispensable aid to human development. His message to "tune in" (by taking LSD), "turn on" (to the counterculture), and "drop out" (of mainstream society, or at least challenge its ideology) was particularly attractive to young people, and Leary, as "high priest of drug culture" was frequently challenged by, spent some time on the run from, and was imprisoned by the authorities. *See also* ENTHEOGENS.

LETCHER, ANDY (1968–). British scholar of religion whose work has focused on the role of the bard in contemporary **Paganism** and **entheogenic neo-shamanism**. His research on the latter, *Shroom: A Cultural History of the Magic Mushroom* (2006), chronicles Anglo-American **psilocybin** use, offers a discourse analysis of psychedelic experience, and critically engages with the arguments of key thinkers on hallucinogenic **mushrooms**, principally **Gordon Wasson**, **Timothy Leary**, and **Terence McKenna**, whose ideas have permeated popular culture and led to a number of myths about entheogen use worldwide.

Wasson suggested the magic mushroom produced the religious impulse in humans during the **European Paleolithic**, spreading globally via cultural diffusion. He produced evidence to support his theory from a wide variety of problematic sources, such as identifying fly agaric as the Vedic Soma. Wasson also proposed that European cultures have been either "mycophilic" or "mycophobic," a worldview enduring in folk memory. Letcher argues that Wasson's discourse derives from Frazerian cultural evolution with "fossils" of folk memory (of mushroom use) preserved. Wasson also overemphasizes the importance of fly agaric use: in **Siberia** (the **locus classicus** of shamanism), fly agaric is used only in two small areas, mainly recreationally, and not by shamans.

Assessing the work of Wasson, Leary, and McKenna as a whole, Letcher argues that these thinkers promoted entheogens as essentially benign and psychedelic experience as essentially the same across cultures and across entheogens (with LSD discourse having a major role in this perception). Yet, such experience is diverse and always culturally mediated. Considering the loaded terms *psychedelic*, *entheogen*, *drugs*, and the like, Letcher finds no suitable, nonpejorative alternative and employs all of them so as not to privilege one discourse over another.

LEWIS, IOAN M. (1930–). Professor emeritus of anthropology at the London School of Economics and author of *Ecstatic Religion: A Study of Shamanism and Spirit Possession* (1971). His wide-ranging research is important as a clarification of the relationship between **trance** (an interior state of disassociation) and **possession** (a culturally mediated interpretation of trance as the intrusion of **spirits** or **otherworld** beings), between official and marginal cults (often distinguishable by the **gender** of the main performers), and between control by and **mastery of spirits**. Lewis regularly contests **Mircea Eliade**'s construction of shamanism, generally seeing it as a system imposed on more diverse data. Demonstrating that possession is a performance established and interpreted by particular cultures, he challenges Eliade's (and **Sergei Shirokogoroff**'s) assertion that shamans master but are not mastered by spirits. Noticing that practitioners invite possession similarly undermines Eliade's schema. As such, Lewis broadens the use of the term *shamanism* beyond the **locus classicus** of **Siberia** and the **Arctic**, specifically to **Africa**.

Lewis's abiding interest, however, is in the relationship between cults and experiences of possession and the wider social order. Paying attention to details of who gets possessed, what benefit they or others derive from the possession, what social mechanisms contain or are contested by possession cults, what role degrees of social power play in all this, and how shamans and their work fit into **clan** and other social contexts enables a far richer understanding of the phenomenon than claims about "true" and "degenerate" forms of shamanism. Lewis engages with the **Sar**, **Zar**, and **Bori** cults of East, North, and West Africa, in which **women** play significant roles despite their general marginality in locally dominant forms of **Christianity** and **Islam**.

LEWIS-WILLIAMS, J. DAVID. South African **rock art** researcher who proposed a shamanistic interpretation (also known as the "**trance** hypothesis") to some of this diverse imagery. Attending to the similarities between the **Southern African** material and **European Paleolithic cave art**, Lewis-Williams and **Thomas Dowson** developed a **neuropsychological model** for establishing whether a given rock art tradition is derived from **altered states of consciousness**, and if so, how it is shamanistic, within its specific community context. Lewis-Williams has also written a volume on cave art (*The Mind in the Cave*, 2002) and the European **Neolithic**. Lewis-Williams is professor emeritus of rock art at the University of the Witwatersrand, Johannesburg.

LINDQUIST, GALINA. Swedish anthropologist whose important fieldwork on **neo-shamanisms** in Sweden (1992–95) resulted in a doctoral thesis published as *Shamanic* ***Performance*** *on the Urban Scene: Neo-Shamanism in Contemporary Sweden* (1997). Lindquist examines the group *Yggdrasil* in particular, and the way that indigenous and ancient shamanisms are relocalized in contemporary contexts, with such practices as ***seidr*** reenchanting practitioners' lives, promoting "fuzzy community," and resulting in a "new internal tradition." From a practitioner perspective, Lindquist's understanding of neo-shamanic **ritual** as a form of imaginative "play" and performance might seem to demean neo-shamanic experience (as suggested by **Jonathan Horwitz** and others), yet Lindquist's work was formative in the emerging study of neo-shamanism, and this sort of approach usefully moves analysis away from the myopic focus on definition and what a shaman *is* to the complexity of what shamans do.

LIVING TREASURES AWARD. The **Foundation for Shamanic Studies** (FSS) makes this award to "exceptionally distinguished" indigenous shamans "where their age-old knowledge of shamanism and shamanic **healing** is in danger of extinction." "Living treasure" designation includes an annual lifetime stipend enabling these shamans to continue their shamanic work. It has been awarded to **Tibetan** shaman Wangchuk, living in exile in **Nepal**, as well as to shamans in the **Amazon**, Brazil, **Siberia**, and **Tuva**. The award also enables the FSS to study these shamans and record their practices for posterity. The benevolent intentions of the foundation notwithstanding, critics have raised questions of the long-term implications of such an award and the position of the FSS as arbiter of who is and who is not a "real" shaman worthy of their fiscal recognition.

LOCUS CLASSICUS. A purist approach identifies **Siberia** as the classic example of shamanism, since this is where the term *shaman* originates, among the **Evenk**. Some scholars include the **Arctic** as part of this region because a consistent feature of these shamanisms, following **Sergei Shirokogoroff**'s work in Siberia, is the **mastery of spirits**.

LOWER WORLDS. *See* UNDERWORLDS.

– M –

MACLELLAN, GORDON ("THE TOAD"). British **environmental** educator and **performer** who runs Creeping Toad Education, Training and Workshops with the mission of helping people "discover their own ways of valuing the 'specialness' of their homes, schools, neighborhoods and the wildlife that surrounds us," ranging from children's pond dipping and mask making to storytelling, sacred dance, and encounters with the fairy realm. MacLellan has described himself as "sort of a shaman," bridging communities and environments, and to many **Pagans** in Great Britain, he has indeed earned the title of shaman. MacLellan says that there are three overlapping kinds of shamans: "personal **healers** . . . who help people listen to themselves; community healers . . . who help people listen to each other; and patterners . . . who help the community listen to/relate to the world around them." His educational work and publications fall largely into the last category.

MALAYSIA. Shamans in Malaysia (called *bomoh*, *pawing*, or *dukun* in various languages), **heal illnesses** by **exorcism** or by dealing with the **other world**, **other-than-human persons**, or **spirits** who inflict problems or bad luck. Shamans may serve as **doctors** within their **Christian**, **Islamic**, **Hindu**, or indigenous societies and sometimes across religious and ethnic boundaries. In discussing **gendered** and **political** distinctions and relationships in relation to Malaysian shamans, **Ioan Lewis** also provides examples of the **sexual** nature of some human relationships with other-than-human persons or **possessing** or **electing** spirits. He notes that a Muslim woman who claimed to have had a child by a "spirit to which she was 'married' was fined by an Islamic court for committing adultery." In contrast, he also discusses the "mystical marriage" between a Malay bomoh and his "spirit bride" that lasted for 13 years, resulted in the birth of two "spirit children, a boy and a girl," and ended in divorce. Happily, the divorced bomoh continued to be guided and medically advised by his ex-spirit wife.

MAPUCHE. A Chilean indigenous people among whom the revitalization of shamanism was a significant part of the cultural resurgence and **political** activism that resisted and critiqued the oppressive Chilean regime in the 1970s and beyond. Traditionally, a shaman, *machi*—whose association with **healing** is indicated by the similarity of the term *machitun*, "a healing ceremony"—renewed her (sometimes his) relationship with **spirit helpers** in complex, communal ceremonies that included renewal of the shaman's *rewe*, a **totemic** post, and altars. Communal **rituals**, *gillatun*, were supposed to take place every four years (four being a sacred number) and renewed social and intercommunal relationships. The reorganization of both shamanic and communal renewal ceremonies provided a focus for the indigenous rights movement in Chile. As elsewhere, shamans do not choose the profession, but inherit the role from a parent or other relative who **elects** his or her successor and passes their spirit on as a helper. The onset of **initiation** is marked by **illness** and is usually unavoidable. During **trances**, the spirit speaks through the shaman, but a special translator, a *zugumachife*, is required to convey the meaning of messages about healing. Shamans are both ritual leaders (although requiring the support of several other kinds of ritualists) and repositories of knowledge about the past and communal concerns. Mapuche communities are ambivalent about their shamans and about the value of continuing the revitalization of shamanic and other traditional practices.

MARA'AKATE. *See* HUICHOL.

MASTER OR MISTRESS OF ANIMALS. Shamans in many cultures are required to **mediate** between their community and the powerful **other-than-human persons** who control the existence and movements of **animals**. Offenses against animals or against the Master or Mistress of Animals (or of particular animal species, e.g., seals or **reindeer**) may result in the absence of animals, the failure of hunting, and severe famine. This is also an aspect of the role of shamans as **resource managers**. Among the best known controllers of animals is an **Arctic** underwater **otherworld** female known to **Inuit** and related peoples by various names, but now most often as **Sedna**.

MASTERY OF SPIRITS. Shamans are sometimes distinguished from other religious or cultural leaders by their ability to control or master **spirits** or other **other-than-human persons**. For example, it may be the shaman's job to gain control of hostile beings who cause **illness** by overpowering ordinary people. They may **combat** beings who cause **possession** or "**soul loss**." However, it is now clear that **Mircea Eliade** and **Luc de Heusch** overstate the distinction between shamans who master spirits and their clients and members of "possession cults" who are mastered by spirits. In **Siberia**, the **Arctic**, **Greenland**, and many other places, shamanic **initiation** and **performance** require a degree of control by **otherworld helpers**. It is more useful, then, to consider the empowering relationships between shamans and other-than-human persons to be reciprocal to some degree.

MATTHEWS, JOHN AND CAITLIN. British **neo-shamans** who, following their work on "the Western mystery tradition," pioneered the study and practice of "**Celtic** shamanism." John Matthews's *The Celtic Shaman* (1991a) and *Taliesin: Shamanism and the Bardic Mysteries in Britain and Ireland* (1991c) not only offered considerable evidence for ancient Celtic shamanic practices, such as analysis of the medieval Welsh poet Taliesin as a shaman, but also popularized how modern Westerners might use these sources in their own neo-shamanisms. This work has been scrutinized by such academics as **Ronald Hutton**, **Leslie Ellen Jones**, and **Robert Wallis**, who problematize, among other issues, the application of the term *shaman* to medieval sources that are enigmatic, incomplete, and often poorly translated. Jones comments on the contrast between Matthews's apparently accessible and "safe" practices vis-à-vis the more challenging, even dangerous, path of other **indigenous** shamanisms, and she dismisses his practices as lightweight and **New Age**. Wallis agrees, but adds that Celtic shamanism today is by no means singular and that there are practitioners who not only integrate their practices into the challenges of everyday life but also engage with the "dark side" of the shaman. Caitlin Matthews's solo-authored work includes *Singing the Soul Back Home: Shamanism in Daily Life* (1995), concerned especially with **soul retrieval**. Following the lead of the Matthewses, there are now numerous volumes on Celtic shamanism, including those by Tom Cowan, **Jan Fries**, and Frank MacEowen.

MAZATEC. People of southern Mexico in **Central America**. The Mazatec's shamanic **healing** use of **mushrooms** aided **Richard Schultes** in isolating a curative agent useful in the development of a new heart drug. Their blend of indigenous **animism** and Catholic **Christianity** resulted in their naming of the powerful sage species *Salvia divinorum* after the Virgin Mary as "Ska Maria Pastora." Although it is valued by **psychonauts** and some **neo-shamans** as an aid in exploring and **altering states of consciousness**, salvia's Mazatec use is primarily as an aid to **purification** prior to healing and **divination**. The **visions** it inspires are understood to require singing to aid incorporation into everyday life and health.

MCKENNA, TERENCE (1946–2000). Psychedelic thinker, writer, and conspiracy theorist whose experiments with LSD, DMT, and especially magic **mushrooms** (**psilocybin**) led him to proselytize the perceived benefits of **entheogen** use in his books and on the lecture circuit. McKenna proposed that a number of separate psychedelics (psilocybin, DMT, ibogane, and LSD) are more shamanic than such drugs as ketamine and **datura**, because they alone occasion experiences of other beings (including the "machine elves"). He went further, to not only essentialize *all* psychedelic experience as essentially shamanic (involving encounters with **spirits**) but to also argue that magic mushrooms played a pivotal role in human evolution. In McKenna's archaic Eden, magic mushroom ingestion triggered the religious impulse and language, as an aphrodisiac promoted reproductive success, and low doses produce visual acuity and made humans better hunters. McKenna tied all of these ideas into a cosmic theory wherein the universe is perceived to evolve with discrete moments of change toward complexity, which can be predicted using the I Ching oracle, with the next ingression of novelty due in 2012, an important date in the Mayan calendar. The ingestion of psychedelics is crucial in McKenna's schema, enabling contact with the extraterrestrial beings who steer cosmic evolution. The teleology of this equation notwithstanding, McKenna's assumption that "tripping" early humans were more successful than straight ones not only is difficult to take seriously but also tells us more about his own psychedelic agenda than about the past. Nonetheless, McKenna's discourse retains persuasive power among the psychedelic community, with his pro-psychedelic message available in numerous books and audio recordings and disseminated in the sample McKenna "raps" in dance music, most famously "Re:Evolution" by the British psychedelic-influenced electronic music group **The Shamen**.

MEADOWS, KENNETH. One of a number of **neo-shamanic** authors whose books in the 1980s and 1990s, such as *Shamanic Experience: A Practical Guide to Contemporary Shamanism* (1991), popularized shamanic practice, especially drawing on **Native American** spirituality. That such a title as the early *Earth Medicine: A Shamanic Way to Self-Discovery* (1989) remains in print is a testament to the popularity of this sort of approach and the **medicine wheel** teachings in particular. Meadows's notion of "shamanics" styled shamanism as a technique for personal growth among Westerners, rather than something that was embedded in social relations or negotiations with **other-than-human persons**. Meadows has also written a book on runes entitled *Rune Power* (1996), largely born from his rather bizarre suggestion in *Earth Medicine* that there are similarities between runic **divination** and the Native American medicine wheel. Just as his many books have been vilified by Native Americans campaigning against the exploitation of their traditions, many **Heathens** are critical of his **New Age** and psychological-reductionist interpretations of runes and Heathen traditions.

MEDIATION. A central role for shamans in many indigenous cultures, especially where food **resources** and **illnesses** come from, and are controlled by, masters in **other worlds**.

MEDICINE. A term that is particularly common in discussions of **Native American** religious traditions and practices. In part, it draws attention to the **doctoring** or **healing** powers and abilities of **medicine people** (e.g., **Thomas Yellowtail**, **Nicholas Black Elk**, and **Pretty Shield**). It also refers to power provided in **initiatory** and respectful ongoing relationships between **holy people** and the **other-than-human persons** who **elect** and **help** them. There is considerable debate about whether indigenous terms such as *wakan* (**Lakota**), *manitou* (**Ojibwe**), and *baaxpee* (**Crow**) refer to "metaphysical energies" (which might be tapped somewhat like a "mystical electricity") or to persons who teach and provide the required abilities and social position for an **initiated** leader or healer to do his or her work. Clearly these words have rich and resonant ranges of meaning and should certainly not be limited by their translation as "power," as is commonplace among **neo-shamans**.

MEDICINE BUNDLES. Among many **Native American** peoples, it is common to gather sacred and powerful stones, herbs, and other **object-persons** into bundles that then serve as the focus of respectful ceremonialism (including elaborate **rituals** when the bundles are unwrapped and everyday signals of polite etiquette). They can be stored in family homes or in tribal/national repositories. The bundles and their constituent members can be considered to be persons in their own right, as shown by the offering to them of **tobacco** and other expressions of respect.

MEDICINE EAGLE, BROOKE (1943–). Also known as Brooke Edwards. Métis (i.e., of Anglo and **Native American** parentage) author and popularizer of a version of **neo-shamanism**. Medicine Eagle is described as a "global earthkeeper" who "prepares us for that 'golden age' when we will live in harmony and grace upon a renewed earth." Her website defines a "true shaman" as "one who holds the golden dream in her heart until it comes true on Mother Earth." She anticipates a "new time" of harmony, cooperation, respectfulness, and good relationships that will replace the "passing time" of division and discord. In this, she blends leitmotivs typical of indigenous discourse (e.g., "respect") with those of **New Age** (e.g., the "essential self" and a Westernized version of Feng Shui). Medicine Eagle was named in the 1984 resolution of the **American Indian Movement** against those considered disrespectful and exploitative of sacred ceremonies (especially **sweat lodges** and **vision quests**) and of the clients they charge to participate. Native American groups and websites such as "Gohiyuhi/Respect" and the **Center for SPIRIT** cite her as a "fraud" and unlikely to be enrolled as a member of the **Crow** Nation.

MEDICINE FATHERS. In the biography of **Thomas Yellowtail**, a **medicine man** of the **Crow**, there are regular references to "medicine fathers" who **elect** and **initiate** medicine people, giving them instructions about **ritual**, **healing** or **doctoring** techniques, and the **taboos** (requirements and restrictions) that will constrain and, if adhered to, empower them. These include **other-than-human persons**, for example, the Little People, and medicine people of previous generations. *See also* SEVEN ARROWS.

MEDICINE PEOPLE. Also medicine men and medicine **women**. A term cognate with **holy people** among many **Native Americans** that may be comparable to shamans elsewhere. ***Medicine*** not only emphasizes abilities to **heal** people from **illnesses** but also refers to sacred powers and/or abilities gifted to **elected** people at **initiation** and dependent on proper, respectful use throughout life. Specific plants, stones, **rituals**, and **chants** may also be labeled "medicine."

MEDICINE WHEEL. The term was first applied to the Big Horn Medicine Wheel monument and **sacred site** on Medicine Mountain, part of northern Wyoming's Big Horn Range. The wheel consists of an 80-foot-diameter circular arrangement of stones, with 28 rows of stones radiating from the center to form spokes that meet an encircling stone rim. There are five smaller stone circles around the wheel's periphery. It is thought to have been built around 200 years ago by **Native Americans**, with the 28 spokes symbolizing the days of a lunar month. As a more general concept, the medicine wheel has come to refer to a set of Native American teachings based around the construction of a hoop with four quarters and/or six cardinal directions representing creation and (human and **other-than-human**) people's relation to it. The precise correspondences vary from tribe to tribe and the medicine wheel has become an important symbol of pan-Indian identity.

Sun Bear (Vincent LaDuke), allegedly of **Ojibwe** and Euro-American descent, who founded the Bear Tribe Medicine Society, had **visions** directing him to share the teachings of the medicine wheel with Natives and, controversially, non-Natives. At medicine wheel gatherings, participants can undertake **sweat lodges**, pipe rituals, and crystal **healing** ceremonies, all themes from Plains Indian and Ojibwe traditions adapted by Sun Bear and fused with **environmentalism** and **New Age** self-help and **therapeutic** themes to form the "medicine wheel teachings." Sun Bear's teachings have inspired countless people and provided them with empowering methods for living their lives in a "sacred manner," but Métis teachers like Sun Bear have been ostracized and criticized by Native American activists (especially among the **American Indian Movement**) who question his ancestry and the authenticity of his teachings and have physically disrupted his workshops. Alice Kehoe traces the idea of the medicine wheel to what was originally "a minor item in Cheyenne life, little wooden hoops used primarily in a game of skill" (1990, 200). **Vine Deloria Jr.** identifies Kehoe and other contributors to James Clifton's *Invented Indian* (1990) as neocolonial arbiters over what is and what is not "tradition," especially given their consensus that current perceptions of Indianness are invented and therefore not traditional. Similarly, **Ward Churchill** labels this "new racism."

MEDIUMS. Shamans are sometimes distinguished from "mediums," a term most often applied to people, generally in Spiritualist or Spiritist movements, who enter **trances** and **possession** states and allow the dead or "**spirits**" to speak through them to clients. The most common reasons for making this distinction are that mediums appear more passive than shamans, may be controlled by the spirits rather than **masters of the spirits**, and do not **journey** to **other worlds** but instead expect to be visited by the spirits. Since these features are certainly not absent among shamans, the distinction cannot be absolute. More tellingly, both trance and possession—indeed, all putative **altered states of consciousness**—are culturally mediated and interpreted **performances** and may neither be completely distinguished nor held to be entirely passive.

MELANESIA. A subdivision of **Oceania** or the Pacific Islands (along with **Polynesia** and **Micronesia**), spreading from New Guinea in the west to Norfolk Island in the east. It does not always refer to clear cultural or geographical distinctions. Various Melanesian peoples have been identified as having **animistic** cultures and employing shamans. Ira Bashkow, for example, writes about the Papua New Guinean Orokaiva's version of the widespread taro cult in which prophecy, **spirit possession**, and shamanism confronted colonialism and reasserted indigenous vitality and sovereignty. This local form of "cargo cult" began in 1912 ana enabled people to consider and engage with their integration into globalized consumerist modernism. Garry Trompf's discussion of Melanesian religion notes the induction of **trance** among the dancers in a taro cult who chewed wild strawberry leaves and blew out scented breath or smoke. Robert Wallis has contributed a critical discussion of shamanism, ethnography, and rock art in Malakula, Vanuatu.

MENTAL HEALTH. Shamans have been characterized as psychotic, schizophrenic, epileptic, neurotic, or otherwise mentally ill by a number of authors during the 20th century and especially since **Maria Czaplicka**'s notion of "**Arctic** hysteria" (1914). Having witnessed the apparently bizarre, violent, and disturbing shamanic performances of Siberian shamans, Czaplicka argued that the harsh arctic environment (including lack of light and essential vitamins) led to shamanism as a peculiar form of institutionalized mental illness—although she does argue that shamans are accomplished in retaining control over these "fits" of hysteria. In a similar vein, an ethnographer in **Melanesia** in the 1930s, John Layard, identified the *bwili* or "flying **tricksters**" of Malakula (Vanuatu, Melanesia) as epileptic shamans due to their uncontrolled shaking, on the one hand, and **otherwordly** feats including **transformation** into **animals**, on the other. Layard concluded that the bwili's epilepsy was a form of institutionalized shamanism. Classifying shamans as mentally ill immediately reinforces their status as Other and exotic, revealing more about our peculiar fetishes as Westerners than the reality of indigenous shamanisms. Psychoanalytic anthropologist George Devereux argued in the 1950s and 1960s that Mohave shamans were neurotic, while Andreas Lommel supposed that the mental illness of **European Paleolithic** shamans led to artistic creativity in the form of **cave art**.

Western artists of the 20th century have also often been defined as shamans, with their **art** the result of a somewhat beneficial mental illness—Vincent van Gogh's alleged epilepsy being one example. Parallels have been drawn by Julian Silverman in the late 1960s between shamans and schizophrenics, but while the latter are paranoid, socially distant, and unable to control their experiences, shamans are better known for their intense mental concentration (Kehoe 2000), social embeddedness/efficacy, and often a degree of control over their **altered state of consciousness**. Indeed, Richard Noll (1983) has convincingly outlined a "state-specific" approach to the "schizophrenia metaphor" for shamans, effectively deconstructing the idea.

The inversion of shaman-as-psychotic to shaman-as-psychotherapist emerges in the 1960s with experiments on psychedelics. Psychotherapists were quick to see **Carl Jung** as a shaman and psychotherapy as a modern form of shamanic work, as among the work of **Stanislav Grof**, **Stanley Krippner**, and **Ralph Metzner**. Refreshing as this is in revising the idea that shamans are mentally ill, it has its own problems, especially as a restrictive psychological metaphor for shamanisms. Whatever the discourse, it is clear that socially effective shamanic practice must be regarded as mentally sound in its context—shamans may resist "normal" classifications, but they are not "mad."

MESOAMERICA. Cultural and ecological region within **Central America** but with a northern boundary within central Mexico. The fluidity of boundaries here, as elsewhere, militate against drawing absolute distinctions. For example, if "Central America" is open to cross-fertilization to the north and south, so too is Mesoamerica. The **Yaqui** (Yoeme) and **Huichol** (Wixáritari) exemplify cultural and geographic border crossings.

MÉTRAUX, ALFRED (1902–1963). Swiss ethnographer of **Vodou** in Haiti and surveyor of **Amazonian** and Guyanese shamanism, conducting fieldwork in the late 1940s. Métraux was the author of *Voodoo in Haiti* (1959), a work still cited by more recent scholars of Haitian and **Caribbean possession** religions. His definition of a shaman is "a person who maintains by profession and in the interest of the community an intermittent commerce with **spirits**, or who is possessed by them." Métraux notes that the intensity of "religious experience" makes shamans both privileged and marginal. His account of the **initiation** and **performance** of shamans includes the ingestion of **tobacco** and "bark infusions," **vomiting**, **journeying** (especially to the **other world**), possession, **healing** by fumigation and **sucking** (especially to remove "invisible **darts**"), and the **ambiguity** of shamans who might be **sorcerers**. Métraux also says that the shaman "is above all the individual who uses, for the benefit of all, the superior power of the spirits and who thwarts their evils if necessary."

METZNER, RALPH. Internationally known psychologist and one of the pioneers of LSD research at Harvard University in the 1960s before academic research on the subject was halted. Metzner coauthored *The Psychedelic Experience* (1964) with **Timothy Leary** and Richard Alpert, which used the **Tibetan** Book of the Dead to guide LSD and other **entheogenic** experiences, including instructions for how to approach a psychedelic session. Metzner was academic dean (1979–88) and academic vice president (1988–89) of the California Institute of Integral Studies and teaches there on **altered states of consciousness**, psychotherapy, and eco-psychology. His volume *The Well of Remembrance* (1994) explored **Northern European** mythology and "shamanism" from a psychological perspective. He is also cofounder and president of the Green Earth Foundation, "an educational organization devoted to the **healing** and harmonizing of the relations between humanity and the earth." Most recently, Metzner authored ***Ayahuasca**: Hallucinogens, Consciousness and the **Spirit** of Nature* (1999) and *Sacred **Mushroom** of **Visions**: Teonanacatl* (2005), and he has been on the Board of Advisers for the Center for Cognitive Liberty and Ethics since 2000.

MEXICO. *See* CENTRAL AMERICA.

MICRONESIA. A subdivision of **Oceania** or the Pacific Islands (along with **Polynesia** and **Melanesia**), inclusive of more than 2,000 islands east of the Philippines. Like the other subdivisions, it does not always refer to clear cultural or geographical distinctions. Among references to shamans in the region is a Chamorro **trickster** tale (retold by Bo Flood) in which a shaman called Lepe' pee' l mo'ng defeats a **cannibal** monster having first brewed a **protective** potion. **Combat** against malevolent beings is also important in Ifaluk, where shamans are required to **exorcise possessed patients** or clients and thereby restore social harmony (as discussed by Melford Spiro). The possessing agents are ghosts whose malevolence continues from their bad character during life. Shamans are aided by beneficent ghosts (again, those who established themselves as good people during life). As among the **Chewong** of **Malaysia**, Ifaluk shamanic stories and activities serve to encourage people to be cooperative, helpful, and sharing rather than aggressive and greedy.

MIDEWIWIN. Ojibwe ceremonial complex, entailing an unfolding or hierarchical series of **initiations** involving **transformation** and **healing** rites and including elements of **bear ceremonialism**. While the complex is supposed to be secret, it has been discussed by a number of scholars, including **John Grim**. It also features in the translations and creative fiction of **Gerald Vizenor** (e.g., in *Summer in the Spring* and *Bearheart: The Heirship Chronicles*).

MIDWIVES. Midwives in some cultures can have much in common with shamans, especially **election** by powerful **helpers** from **other worlds**. Elsewhere, midwifery may be a role of shamans themselves. Susan Sered (1992) includes midwives among the "**women** as **ritual** experts" she discusses. However, the claim that those persecuted as **witches** in early modern Europe were really village midwives and **healers** has been shown to be based on inadequate research.

MISTRESS OF ANIMALS. *See* MASTER OR MISTRESS OF ANIMALS.

MONGOLIA. Mongolia is a landlocked **Central Asian** country of grassland, mountains, and desert that today is bordered by Russia to the north and **China** to the south. In the 13th century, a confederation of nomadic, shamanistic tribes was united as the Mongol Empire by Chinggis (Genghis) Khan. His successor, Kublai Khan, made **Buddhism** the new religion of his empire, but Buddhism waned with the decline of the Mongol Empire. In the 16th century, Altan Khan, a distant descendant of Chinggis Khan, adopted "Yellow Hat" **Tibetan** Buddhism as the religion of the Mongols and bestowed the title of "Dalai Lama" on the Tibetan spiritual leader. Lamaist missionaries institutionalized Buddhism into Mongolia by the 17th century, persecuting shamans as they did so (terming Buddhism the "yellow faith" and shamanism the "black faith"), to the extent that Buddhism persisted through Communism and is the state religion of Mongolia today. Nonetheless, it is clear that many features of Mongolian Buddhism absorbed shamanistic practices. An important early work on the black faith of the Mongols was written by the **Buryat** Mongol scholar Dorji Banzarov (1846).

The territory of the Mongols was split into Inner Mongolia, controlled by the Chinese, and Outer Mongolia, which became a Soviet republic. In the Mongolian S.S.R., as in the rest of the Soviet Union, religious activities were repressed, and both shamanism and Lamaism were brutally suppressed. During the second half of the 20th century, Walter Hessig published several important works on Mongol shamanism, while **Vilmos Diószegi** conducted much-needed ethnographic fieldwork on the state of shamanism in the 1960s. In post-Soviet times, as in other parts of Central Asia, there has been a revival of shamanism, and an official organization entitled the Mongolian Shamans' Association has been established. One of the most important studies on Mongolian shamanism, by **Caroline Humphrey** (with Daur Mongol **Urgunge Onon**), *Shamans and Elders* (1996), details historical and near-contemporary Mongolian shamans and their practices and roles. Humphrey and Onon argue for an approach to Mongolian shamanism not as a singular or even coherent "religion," distinct from daily life, but as historically and socially constituted, comprising different types of knowledge and experience and recalling discussions of new **animism**.

MORRISON, JIM (1943–1971). Born James Douglas Morrison. Lead singer and songwriter of the late 1960s–early 1970s American rhythm-and-blues-, blues-, and jazz-influenced psychedelic rock band the Doors. The band's name was taken from **Aldous Huxley**'s book *The Doors of Perception* (in turn borrowed from William Blake's poem "The Marriage of Heaven and Hell": "If the doors of perception were cleansed, everything would appear to man as it truly is, infinite"), chronicling Huxley's experiments with mescaline and LSD. With his saturnine good looks, exuberant stage presence, and cryptic lyrics, Morrison attained cult status among fans. He has been labeled a shaman due to his experiments with LSD and other drugs, the symbolic content of his improvised lyrics/poetry, his bohemian California lifestyle, and his interest in mysticism. Morrison's wild, **ecstatic**, and magnetic stage **performances** in his alter ego, the Lizard King—involving shouting, screaming, and playing dead on the stage floor, as well as dancing as an eagle with arms outstretched—are visually reminiscent of shamanic rites. Oliver Stone's biopic *The Doors* (1991) provides a particularly shamanic interpretation, associating Morrison with **Native American** mythology and desert **vision quests**, as well as the poetry of William Blake and Arthur Rimbaud and the philosophy of Friedrich Nietzsche. Keen to be taken seriously as an artist, Morrison published two books of poetry in his lifetime, *An American Prayer* (1970) and *The Lords and the New Creatures* (1971); he also directed the film *A Feast of Friends*. Morrison died in Paris in 1971 at the age of 27; the registered cause of death was heart attack, but rumors of a heroin overdose persist.

MURRAY, MARGARET (1863–1963). British Egyptologist who made an important contribution to that subject but is probably best known for her work *The Witch-Cult in Western Europe* (1921), which proposed a pan-European, pre-**Christian** religion extending from the **Neolithic** to the Medieval **witch** crazes, wherein groups of 13 witches worshipped a fertility god. Murray expanded her thesis in *The God of the Witches* (1931) with the "old religion" involving the worship of a horned god, and going back to shamans of the **European Paleolithic** (represented in the **cave art** of the period such as the antlered shaman or "**sorcerer**" of Les Trois Frères in France). Despite criticism from historians for misrepresenting evidence and drawing problematically on Sir James Frazer's outmoded concept of "sacred kinship," Murray's work was taken seriously by many and extended into the public arena with an entry on witchcraft in the *Encyclopaedia Britannica*. While it was crucial in the development of modern **Paganism** and especially modern Pagan witchcraft or **Wicca**, Murray's thesis has been deconstructed by such historians of witchcraft as Keith Thomas and especially **Ronald Hutton**'s recent work *The Triumph of the Moon: A History of Modern Pagan Witchcraft* (1999), which has been influential among Pagans themselves.

MUSHROOMS. While **entheogen** use is often perceived to be prevalent in shamanism worldwide, few indigenous shamans have made mushroom use an important part of their practice. Most of these are located in **Central America** and **South America**. Ob-Ugrian and Finno-Ugrian shamans are most noted for their ingestion of *Amanita muscaria* or fly agaric mushrooms, but while this practice continues today among Khanty shamans of Western **Siberia**, fly agaric use in the **locus classicus** of **Central Asia** and Siberia is mainly recreational.

One major reason for the overemphasis on mushrooms is that the mycologist **Gordon Wasson** suggested fly agaric was the Vedic "Soma" and that "magic mushrooms" more generally produced the religious impulse in humans. Wasson "discovered" the **Mazatec** Indian *curandera* **Maria Sabina** in the 1950s and held Sabina's **healing** ceremonies involving the **psilocybin** mushrooms to be the archetypical residue of a prehistoric mushroom cult. These ideas were picked up by **Timothy Leary**, who described eating a number of psilocybin mushrooms in 1960 as "the deepest religious experience of my life," leading to his countercultural mantra "tune in, turn on, drop out." **Terence McKenna** has since echoed both Wasson's and Leary's views, adding his belief that mushrooms and other entheogens facilitate communication with extraterrestrial entities (**space aliens**) crucial to the transcendence of the human race. Overemphasis on mushrooms also lead to **John Allegro**'s suggestion, based on his reading of the Dead Sea Scrolls, that "Jesus was a mushroom" and to interpretations of earliest **Christianity** as a mushroom and shamanic cult.

In his volume *Shroom: A Cultural History of the Magic Mushroom* (2006), **Andy Letcher** argues that the discourses of these thinkers tell us more about their own predilections than about indigenous shamans or entheogens. He also discusses the significant role played by magic mushrooms in **Cyberian** shamanism and **Pagan animism** and among **psychonauts**. As with the adoption of **ayahuasca** by many **neo-shamanic tourists**, it is notable that it is the **vision**-inducing or hallucinogenic effects of mushrooms and other entheogens that are the chief focus of enthusiasm rather than their **purgative vomiting** effects. In contrast, Sabina emphasized that the need to induce vomiting for **purification** as central to shamanic and healing **rituals**.

MUSIC. In addition to the making of **rhythmic** sound aided by **drums**, rattles, bells, and other instruments, shamans in many cultures sing or **chant** in the course of the **rituals** they conduct. Some of this music has **healing** intent and/or properties, some **purifies** or educates listeners, while other examples cause effects (e.g., **illness**) at a distance. Some shamanic chants are said to be revealed by **other-than-human persons** or **otherworld helpers**, for example, powerful plant persons such as **ayahuasca**. Some songs or chants are taught by an elder shaman to **initiates**. They may involve special languages known only to shamans and can involve complex **cosmological** myth recitals that reestablish and adjust the order of the cosmos or of relationships, disturbance of which causes illness, famine, or social problems.

Recordings of indigenous "shamanic," **neo-shamanic**, and **techno-shamanic** music are available. In addition to groups that identify themselves as shamanic such as the **Shamen** (who worked with **Terence McKenna**), others acknowledge the influence of shamanic ideas and practices. For instance, Santana's album *Shaman* has a companion website in which Carlos Santana says that "a Shaman is a spiritual healer who brings balance to mind, body, heart and spirit with colors, sound, herbs and song, creating unity and harmony in the world"; it also suggests reading books by **Mircea Eliade**, **Michael Harner**, McKenna, **Ruth Heinze**, and **Mihály Hoppál**, and Otto von Sadovszky.

MUTWA, CREDO (1921–). Prolific Zulu writer who styles himself variously as shaman, **medicine man**, and **witch doctor**. Mutwa's books have been about **healing**, **ritual**, **cosmology**, and mythology. His promulgation of the notion that **African** peoples and spiritual traditions derive from contact with **space aliens** have not diminished his popularity among his main readership of **neo-shamans**.

MYERHOFF, BARBARA (1935–1985). One of the earliest anthropologists of **Huichol** (*Wixáritari*) shamanism, Myerhoff was one of the first non-Huichol (with **Peter Furst**) to participate in the annual pilgrimage to Wirikùta to gather the **entheogen peyote**, as detailed in her book *Peyote Hunt* (1974). Much of Myerhoff's ethnographic material engaged with the shaman **Ramón Medina Silva**. In the Department of Anthropology at the University of Southern California, her research on the anthropology of **ritual**, life histories, and **women** and religion (especially **Judaism**) was influential, and Myerhoff's work also reached beyond academia with popular books, film, and theater.

– N –

NATIVE AMERICAN CHURCH. Founded in Oklahoma in 1918 and creatively fusing elements recognizable from earlier indigenous religious traditions and movements of **North America** and **Central America** (especially those of the **Huichol** or Wixáritari) with elements of **Christianity**, the Native American Church attracts adherents from many **Native American** nations in both urban and reservation locations. It is sometimes described as "peyotism" because of the sacramental use of **peyote** buttons in **purification** and prayer. This is not to be confused with an encouragement of "psychedelic experience," hedonism, or **altered states of consciousness** for their own sake. The church's **ritual** teachings and practices are allied to a strong ethical and communal focus. Peyote is important as an **other-than-human person** and **helper**, sometimes identified with Jesus Christ, who aids people to restore respectful relationships and live appropriately (including without addiction to alcohol). Peyote is valued more for opening the "heart," that is, as an inspirer of love and compassion, and the stomach, as a **purifying purgative**, than for any hallucinatory effects. The main ritualist or "road man" is sometimes compared to a shaman in the way he leads and serves his community. In rituals, the road man is supported by a number of other important officials, but all members of a local group are expected to participate fully in night-long meetings in which everyone is a participant rather than an observer. Thus, the church provides another example of a democratized form of shamanism, typical of Native America more generally.

NATIVE AMERICAN SPIRITUALITY. Since there are hundreds of distinct **Native American** Nations, many containing more than one distinctive traditional religious practice, it should be clear that the phrase "Native American spirituality" refers to a fictional conglomeration. Most often it privileges a version of **Lakota** spirituality, appropriating elements such as the **sweat lodge** and **vision quest** from their cultural context to make them available in non-Native cultures. Far from aiding an appreciation of Native American religious traditions, this piecemeal approach generates misunderstanding of the role **medicine people** and ceremonies play. The phrase is often used in **whiteshamanism** and by those accused of being "**plastic medicine people**" or frauds.

NATIVE AMERICANS. A significant number of traditional Native American cultures have employed and sometimes continue to employ people who have been labeled "shamans." Indigenous terms that are sometimes translated as "shaman" often refer to **doctoring**, especially the common "**medicine people**," but may also acknowledge the **ritual** expertise and **mediating** functions of "**holy people**." The **animism** of some Indian nations includes a democratized or diffuse shamanic engagement with **other-than-human persons** by potentially anyone. Others delegate specific roles to **initiated** and trained individuals, who may become well known far beyond their own community. Many Native Americans object strongly to the misappropriation of religious traditions by non-Native people, especially when this leads to the charging of extortionate fees for spiritual activities and when used to construct a romanticized "**Native American spirituality**." *See also* NORTH AMERICA.

NATURE. One aspect of the common Western perception that indigenous peoples, especially **hunter-gatherers**, are "close to nature" is that shamans and shamanism provide helpful leads in restoring human respect for the world. The fact that this close-to-nature view was once valued negatively ("primitive savagery") should encourage careful reflection on the culturally determined and shifting idealism of such views. The **environmentalism** of indigenous people and shamans may or may not be evidenced in particular contexts. However, as Bruno Latour concludes from reading diverse relevant ethnographies, it is more likely that most indigenous peoples do not know of any place that could be called "nature." **Eduardo Viveiros de Castro** demonstrates that in **Amazonia** there is a common perception that all living beings (and in these **animist** communities that probably means all existences) have one common culture: they eat cooked food, live in constructed dwellings, abide by or break kinship rules, are hospitable or predatory, and may require shamans or shamanic powers or abilities. However, he further notes, in contrast with the Western notion of multiculturalism and a single "nature" (or "mono-naturalism"), indigenous Amazonians understand that the single culture shared by all life is masked by "multinaturalism." In this context, shamans are those trained and experienced in perceiving the cultural person hidden by the mask of apparently different natures. This is especially important when a "natural" appearance masks a predatory activity. So, a **jaguar** may be an **animal** passing by, but it may instead be intent on **predation** against humans, who require shamanic defense.

While this specifically Amazonian **perspectivism** may not be applicable elsewhere, it does exemplify the pervasive absence of a dualistic contrast between "nature" and "culture" among most indigenous peoples. In animistic communities, for example, what appears to Westerners to be nature is understood to be "the community of life" or, in Latour's terms, "the collective." However, among **neo-shamans** the perception that shamanism encourages respectful environmentalism is important. It encourages practices that take place in rural or wilderness environments, participation in ecological **protection** or enhancement projects, and lifestyles respectful of the wider, other-than-human living world. **Gordon MacLellan**'s work as an environmental educator illustrates the outworking of shamanic practice and environmentalism. The pervasive perception of indigenous intimacy with nature and spirituality sometimes (as in the biography of **Richard Erdoes**) combines with a sense of the numinous power and beauty of "natural" places to establish an initial interest in indigenous peoples in general and shamans in particular.

NAYAKA. A **hunter-gatherer** community of the forested Gir Valley in the Nilgiri region of South **India**. Their relational epistemology is discussed in **Nurit Bird-David**'s article on **animism** (1999). The centrality of sharing—of space, things, and actions—in Nayaka life expresses their perception that they live *with* persons, not all of whom are human, who relate with others in various ways, especially as kin (defined here and among many other hunter-gatherer peoples as those with whom one shares and relates socially, more than those related by descent or genealogy). Nayaka relationality includes not only human persons (*avaru*) but also **other-than-human persons** (e.g., elephants, rocks, or hills), *devaru*, a term that expresses "we-ness" or emergent community. Human and other-than-human persons discover their personhood at the same time that they learn to relate socially in culturally appropriate or respectful ways, not before or apart from that. In other words, Nayaka engage with the world as a community of persons, some of whom are interested in engaging respectfully with human persons. They seek to know how their experiences are the result of encountering persons (i.e., beings who relate). As Bird-David puts it, the Nayaka seek to understand how "things-in-situations relate to the actor-perceiver and, from the actor-perceiver's point of view, to each other." Skill in respectful relating is nurtured in events in which approximately one-fifth of the men (and, in principle if rarely in actuality, **women**) of the community perform as devaru while in **trance** states. By doing so, they "bring to life" the devaru, who are invited to engage in conversation and other **performative** acts. Thus, a mutual enabling and sharing is made evident to the community in trance performance of relational encounters. More experienced performers gain increasing recognition and appreciation. While such experienced performers may not entirely warrant the label "shaman," their trance performances and roles in the community have significant parallels with shamans elsewhere. The Nayaka are also of interest here, however, because they illustrate significant features of the animism that makes shamans possible and necessary.

NEIHARDT, JOHN (1881–1973). Poet and writer (Nebraska's poet laureate for 52 years) who published a version of the biography of **Nicholas Black Elk**, a **Lakota holy man.** Brought up on a Nebraska farm, Neihardt had an experience that inclined him not only toward poetry rather than technology but also toward the study of mysticism. He describes flying across the universe and being spoken to by the voice of a "ghostly brother." A reading of Vedantic philosophy added impetus to what he experienced as a demand to become a mystic. Reece Pendleton argues that these experiences, inclinations, and experiences prepared Neihardt for his friendship and literary work with Black Elk. It is interesting to speculate what role "mysticism" played in Neihardt's selective presentation of aspects of Black Elk's biography. The failure of the book to make an impact before the 1960s suggests that it required a rereading in the light of rising interest in shamans and indigenous people (albeit as **environmentalist** and countercultural icons) to replace Neihardt's more mystical intentions. Or perhaps it is simply that Neihardt lacked the shamanic language to understand his experience and thus mistook it for mysticism until he encountered Black Elk. According to Raymond DeMallie, Black Elk interpreted Neihardt's vision to him as a shamanic calling by an Indian **spirit** guide. All of this raises questions about the interpretation of shamanism and its relationship with other kinds of religious experience and practice.

NEOLITHIC. "New Stone Age," a period assigned in Europe to the development of agriculture or the Agricultural Revolution, although **hunter-gatherer** activity endured well into the period, and it is misleading to characterize a people's culture based on their economic strategy or tool use alone. Neolithic **art**, particularly the geometric images of various megalithic monuments in northern France, eastern Ireland, and northern Wales, have been interpreted as **entoptics** indicative of an origin in an **altered state of consciousness** by some archaeologists, including Richard Bradley, Jeremy Dronfield, **David Lewis-Williams**, and **Thomas Dowson**. *See also* EUROPEAN PALEOLITHIC.

NEO-SHAMANISM. Also neo-Shamanism, neoshamanism, new shamanism, **whiteshamanism**, contemporary shamanism, urban shamanism, Western shamanism. A term applied by scholars to engagement with, application of, or appropriation from indigenous or prehistoric shamanism by Westerners (mostly those of European descent) for personal or community **healing** and empowerment. With an increase in **entheogen tourism**, there are now many books recounting neo-shamanic experiences, one of the most compelling of which is Daniel Pinchbeck's *Breaking Open the Head: A Visionary Journey from Cynicism to Shamanism* (2002).

Worldwide, the most popular practice is that of **core shamanism** taught by **Michael Harner**, founder of the **Foundation for**

Shamanic Studies, to Westerners as well as Native people seeking to revive their own traditions. A number of indigenous and Métis (part-indigenous) shamans have also taught neo-shamans, including **Sun Bear** and **Brooke Medicine Eagle**, while the teachings of **Nicholas Black Elk** are also popular. Other key figures in the United States are **Carlos Castaneda**, who popularized shamanism with his series of books on the fictional **Yaqui sorcerer Don Juan**, and **Lynn Andrews**, who styled the **medicine wheel** teachings for non-**Native Americans**. Other neo-shamans have turned to prehistoric indigenous traditions in **Northern Europe** in order to reconstruct ancient shamanisms for contemporary **Wiccan**, **Celtic**, and Norse **Pagan** practice, most notably the **Heathen** practice of ***seidr*** and **Druidic** revival of **Awenyddion**. Key figures in Great Britain include the environmental educator **Gordon "the Toad" MacLellan** and the founders of Eagle's Wing for Contemporary Shamanism, Leo Rutherford and Howard Charing, who offer **drumming** and other workshops. Most recently, the **Sacred Trust**, founded and directed by **Simon Buxton**, has become the most prominent organization for neo-shamans in Great Britain. Such magazines as ***Sacred Hoop*** and ***Shamans' Drum*** serve as resources to practitioners seeking information on shamans and workshop programs.

Those who genuinely feel their practices are authentic and not dissimilar from indigenous traditions might deem the term *neo-shaman* offensive. Nonetheless, neo-shamanic practices do tend to romanticize indigenous shamans, neglect the negative aspects of "**dark shamans**," and be more consumer-oriented and based on self-growth. Others directly appropriate indigenous traditions despite clear opposition from such groups as the **American Indian Movement**. **Native American spirituality** has been a focus of contention in this regard, as some **elders** have openly taught non-Natives, while others have condemned the commodification of their spiritual practices.

Taking a more nuanced approach than those who might be termed "**wannabe Indians**," the title "shaman" is viewed as honorific by practitioners such as MacLellan, whose efforts are aimed at community education and healing rather than self-oriented personal development. The boundary between indigenous/prehistoric shamans and neo-shamans is increasingly permeable, as accelerating numbers of Westerners engage with indigenous shamans directly, and vice versa, such as in **ayahuasca** and **peyote** ceremonies. The study of neo-shamanism, and its cognate contemporary Paganism, gained coherency and respectability in the 1990s with work by **Graham Harvey**, Marion Bowman, **Ronald Hutton**, and others. Ethnographies of neo-shamanisms have been offered by **Jenny Blain**, **Galina Lindquist**, and **Robert Wallis**.

NEPAL. An ethnically and religiously diverse country bordered by **Tibet** and **India**. **Hindu**, **Buddhist**, and **animist** Nepalese may employ shamans or attend shamanic **performances** for **healing** or **mediation** with **ancestors** and significant **other-than-human persons**, especially when dealing with death. Among those who have been considered shamans are the *jhankri* and *dhami*. Stan Mumford discusses the roles of Tibetan lamas and Garung shamans in Nepal, considering their "exchanges with the **under world**, demon **exorcism**, recalling the **soul**, and the famed guiding of consciousness in the Tibetan death rite." Charlotte Hardman's publications, especially about the Lohorung Rai, provide detailed information about shamanic **cosmologies**, methods, and tools in the context of a careful consideration of indigenous approaches to emotion and understandings of selfhood. **Piers Vitebsky** points to a distinction between the practices of the Himalayan Nepalese and those of the southern lowlands, in which only the former "**journey**" while the latter invite **possession**. Nepal is among the destinations for shamanism **tourists** who have paid particular attention to the Gosainkunda Lake pilgrimages that attract Nepalese Hindus for a full-moon celebration that also involves shamanic **initiations** accompanied by **drumming**.

NEPHILIM. *See* FIELDS OF THE NEPHILIM.

NEUROPHYSIOLOGY. *See* BRAIN CHEMISTRY; NEUROPSYCHOLOGICAL MODEL; NEUROTHEOLOGY.

NEUROPSYCHOLOGICAL MODEL. David Lewis-Williams and **Thomas Dowson**'s neuropsychological model, set out in their *Current Anthropology* article "The Signs of All Times: Entoptic Phenomena in Upper Paleolithic Art" (1988), proposes three loosely defined and fluid stages in the progression of **trance**. In the first, "**entoptics**," stage, subjects spontaneously perceive entoptics, classified into six principal types: grids, lines, dots, zigzags, catenary curves, and filigrees. In the second, "construal," stage, subjects attempt to make sense of these geometric shapes and construe them into culturally recognizable forms: a Western subject may perceive an entoptic grid and may construe it into the string-grid of a tennis racket, while a **San** (Bushman) shaman may construe an entoptic grid into the shape of the honeycomb associated with powerful bee **spirit-helpers**. In the third, "entoptics and iconics," stage, subjects may perceive both entoptic and culturally derived iconic imagery. In this latter stage also, when the trance is at its most intense, subjects may feel they are a part of their imagery: in one neuropsychological experiment, a subject thought of a fox and instantly became a fox; the *therianthropes* (composite human–**animal** images) in San **rock art** and **European Paleolithic cave art** may be associated with such experiences. In all three stages, imagery is subject to seven principles of visual transformation: replication, fragmentation, integration, superpositioning, juxtapositioning, reduplication, and rotation.

Lewis-Williams and Dowson applied their model to European Paleolithic cave art, which is without directly relevant ethnography, and demonstrated the strength of their model by applying it to two rock art traditions that are known ethnographically to be linked to shamanistic practices: San rock art, on which their earliest research is based, and rock art imagery from the Coso range in far western **North America** (developed by David Whitley). Since its dissemination in published form, the neuropsychological model has been applied to a vast corpus of imagery as diverse as northwest European megalithic **art** (by Jeremy Dronfield), **Aboriginal Australian** rock art, and British Iron Age coinage. Critics such as Paul Bahn question the value of a model that appears to sweepingly interpret all artistic traditions with geometric images according to shamanistic trances. Proponents of the model contest its indiscriminate use also, arguing that too often it is applied uncritically in a search for entoptics. Such a search for similarities has a misleading premise—equating entoptics with shamanism—and neglects to account for trance stages 2 and 3, the principles of **transformation** steering the perception of imagery, and the heterogeneity of rock art (and other visual culture) and shamanisms.

More recently, a more rigorous and critical approach to neuropsychology and shamanisms in rock art research has developed. As a matter of course, the neuropsychological model must be applied in its entirety in order to retain its integrity and effectiveness as a valuable interpretative tool: identification of endogenous forms, principles of transformation of visual imagery, and specific cultural contexts of iconic images. Furthermore, Dronfield has reformulated the loosely classified "entoptics" or "subjective visual phenomena" into specific "endogenous diagnostic" categories. Moreover, a "shamanistic approach" has been theorized by Dowson that not only embraces the diversity and difference of shamanisms and rock art but also has wider implications for how shamans are understood anthropologically and archaeologically, particularly in light of the new **animism**. This refinement of approach suggests that while an "entoptics" bandwagon has passed, the shamanistic interpretation remains at the forefront of rock art research.

NEUROTHEOLOGY. The idea that the impulse behind shamanism and other religions originates in **brain chemistry**, put forward in **Michael Winkelman**'s *Shamanism: The Neural Ecology of Consciousness and Healing* (2000). Winkelman explains the cross-cultural commonality of shamanism and other **healing** practices in terms of a biological imperative: Since all humans are capable of altering consciousness and such **altered states of consciousness** are derived from the human central nervous system, so shamanism specifically is "humanity's original healing practice." *See also* NEUROPSYCHOLOGICAL MODEL.

NEW AGE. New Age can be defined as a popularization of historical European esoteric traditions, making the pursuit of self-knowledge accessible to the contemporary **individualized**, globalized, and consumerist world. A catch phrase used by many adherents asserts, "You are god, you are god, you are god." New Age promotes the notion that the "true self" is an inner reality in contact with a generous **cosmos** and in need of self-awareness and harmonious or holistic living. Many adherents interpret shamanism as a quest for this requisite inner self-knowledge, translating **journeying** to **other worlds** into "inner journeys." Similarly, New Age's individualistic notion of the "**soul**" encourages interest in a particular, **neo-shamanic** and **therapeutic** understanding of "**soul retrieval**."

NEW-INDIGENES. A term coined by **Jenny Blain** and **Robert Wallis** to refer to emerging identities in Great Britain (and elsewhere, e.g., in **North America**) among contemporary **Pagans** and other new **nature**, earth, and alternative religions. Acting as **individuals** and/or "neo-tribes," new-indigenes identify themselves as intrinsically linked to the living, **animistic** landscapes in which they live and take heed of those indigenous voices (particularly **Native Americans**) who suggest that rather than appropriate their traditions, **neo-shamans** should re-embed their spirituality in their own "native" land. New-indigenes tend to be polytheistic and animistic, engaging in their daily lives with a diversity of **other-than-human persons** who are perceived as active agents in their own right rather than as **spirits** separate from matter. New-indigenes live in landscapes which themselves have intrinsic agentic properties—are "living"—and are not simply palimpsests cultured by human acts. Some new-indigenes are proactive in protest culture where roads and other building projects threaten woodland, derelict land, and other havens for other-than-human people. Many Pagans in particular establish relationships with their local "**sacred sites**," which may require campaigning for access to them on auspicious occasions (notably, Stonehenge), as well as claiming a say in their management.

NOEL, DANIEL C. (1936–2002). A scholar of the psychology of religion and myth (particularly **Celtic** and **Native American**), religion and the arts, and **Jungian** studies, Noel taught and lectured widely in the United States and overseas, most recently as professor emeritus in the Mythological Studies Program at Pacifica Graduate Institute, Carpinteria, California, and visiting professor of liberal studies in religion and culture at Vermont College, Norwich University, Montpelier, Vermont. Recognized as an authority on Carl Jung and Joseph Campbell, he is the author of *Paths to the Power of Myth: Joseph Campbell and the Study of Religion* (1990), and he wrote a critical response to **Carlos Castaneda**'s fictional anthropology entitled *Seeing Castaneda: Reactions to the "Don Juan" Writings* (1976). Noel's neo-Jungian approach to shamanism, as exemplified in *The Soul of Shamanism: Western Fantasies, Imaginal Realities* (1997), proposed that **neo-shamanism** originates in the works of "shamanovelists" (such as **Mircea Eliade** and Castaneda) and "shamanthropologists" (including **Michael Harner**) and that, as such, shamanism is a Western construct. Noel argued that the figure of Merlin as shamanic psychopomp, activated by the power of the imagination ("**imaginal**"), offered a shamanism that was more suitable to Westerners than to indigenous practices or previous neo-shamanisms derived from these (e.g., the **entheogen**-based shamanism of Castaneda).

NORSE. *See* HEATHEN; NORTHERN EUROPE; PAGAN.

NORTH AFRICA. Due to the emphasis on **Siberia** and the **Arctic** as the **locus classicus**, alongside the rare extension of the term into **Southern Africa**, and the fact that **Islam** and **Christianity** have heavily missionized indigenous peoples in the region, shamanism has only rarely been discussed in the northern part of **Africa**. A major work of reflexive anthropology by Vincent Crapanzano on **spirit possession** in Morocco entitled *Tuhami: Portrait of a Moroccan* (1980), however, presents an interpretive ethnography of an illiterate tile maker who believes himself to be married to a camel-footed she-demon. Tuhami is a master of magic and a storyteller, and he endures nightly visitations from demons and saints including 'A'isha Qandisha, the she-demon from whom he seeks liberation. Such themes of possession, "demons," and magic are not unusual in Islamic folklore here and elsewhere. To assume that referring to Tuhami and other practitioners as shamans is an interpretive leap is to miss the point: rather, shamanism can work hard as an active tool in disrupting conventional nomenclature and practice, exposing neocolonial stereotypes and facilitating alternative avenues of approach.

NORTH AMERICA. Shamanism has been identified among a wide range of indigenous nations in North America, from the **Yaqui** living around the Mexican border to the **Inuit** of the **Arctic**. Objections have been raised to the use of the word *shaman* with reference to religious and cultural leaders in North America on the grounds that the term is specific to **Siberian ritualists** and that there are local names for the different kinds of leaders recognized by particular indigenous nations. It is often true that "**holy people**," "**medicine people**," "**doctor**," or "ritualist" are better translations of many of these terms. Similarly, distinct roles are performed by those labeled in particular ways within a single community, for example, the *Tcisaki*, *nanandawi*, *wabeno*, and *meda* among the **Ojibwe**. The issues are similar with reference to words like *religion* that are drawn from other cultural contexts and require considerable care if they are not to convey misinformation about specific local contexts and cultures. Nonetheless, there are considerable similarities between **Native American** ritualists, **healers**, and spiritual leaders and those labeled "shamans" elsewhere.

North America is also the origin of much **neo-shamanic** activity, from **Sun Bear**, who argued that "**Native American spirituality**" should be shared among a wider community of non-Natives, and **Carlos Castaneda**'s **Don Juan** mythos, to **Michael Harner**'s proposal of a "**core shamanism**" free of cultural specificity. Other Native Americans—for example, those affiliated with the **American Indian Movement**—have criticized Sun Bear and non-Native "teachers" such as Castaneda and Harner for appropriating Native American knowledge, traditions, and practices, often suggesting that Euro-American neo-shamans should reclaim their European shamanistic traditions, as practiced among the **Celts** and other **Northern Europeans**.

NORTHERN EUROPE. Shamanistic themes have been identified, with some speculation, in the pre-**Christian pagan** religions across northern Europe, the "Old North." While it is likely that prehistoric communities in the region had shamanistic practitioners, identifying these individuals or their traditions as specific examples is controversial. The oldest evidence is that of **European Paleolithic cave art**, particularly in France and more recently northern England, some examples of which contain geometric shapes known as **entoptics** that are held to be specifically derived from some **altered states of consciousness**, as well as anthropomorphic images including therianthropes thought to depict shaman–**animal** composites or **theriomorphism**. From the Mesolithic period (Middle Stone Age), a find of perforated antler frontlets at the site of Star Carr in Yorkshire, England, may have comprised part of a headdress, perhaps used in shamanic rites. The **rock art** of **Neolithic** and Bronze Age structures has also been examined vis-à-vis entoptic phenomena, with the Neolithic passage tombs of Ireland receiving the most attention.

The Northern religions of the **Celtic**, Norse, Anglo-Saxon, and related peoples have also been cited as shamanistic, primarily due to the style of their **art** as well as recurrent mythological themes in various literary sources that were written in the Christian era but may refer to earlier pagan traditions. Key examples here are the Celtic practice of **Awenyddion**, described by Gerald of Wales, in which a **priest** may enter a **trance**, and a detailed description of a ***seidr*** séance in the Saga of Erik the Red, according to which a seeress communicates with **spirits** in order to divine supernatural knowledge for a Norse community in **Greenland**. The Germanic god **Odin** and goddess **Freyja** may display shamanic themes: the *Hávamál* in the Poetic Edda records Odin's self-**initiation**, in which he hangs from a tree for nine nights, pierced by his own spear, in order to receive the **vision** of the runes, and Freyja is said to have taught Odin the practice of seidr, for which he is accused of *ergi* (unmanly behavior).

Such examples as these have inspired a number of contemporary Pagan **neo-shamanic** practices and beliefs, including the notion of a shamanic "Old Religion" among some **Wiccans**, derived in part from **Margaret Murray**'s thesis that medieval **witchcraft** reaches back to the Paleolithic era. The recent **Druidic** reconstruction of Awenyddion has been pioneered by **Philip "Greywolf" Shallcrass** of the British Druid Order. The better-known **Heathen** reconstructions of seidr began with the work of **Diana Paxson** and the Hrafnar group in California, but there are now manifestations in Great Britain, largely due to the work of **Jenny Blain**, and elsewhere in Europe. Such innovative revivals and reconstructions attest to the vitality of neo-shamanisms in the early 21st century.

NORTON, ROSALEEN (1917–1979). An **artist** who was born in New Zealand but lived and worked in Australia and gained notoriety as the "**witch** of King's Cross." Norton's creative output included such paintings as "Lucifer," "Witches Sabbat," and "Individuation," and the dark, erotic content of these and other works led to trials for obscenity. The **altered states of consciousness** Norton engaged with in her occult and art practices (if the two may be so disengaged) have been associated with shamanic practices.

– O –

OBEAH. A **Caribbean** term with at least two distinct uses: It can label an accusation of malevolent **sorcery**, but it can also refer to practices that have evolved from the interaction of indigenous-, **African**-, European-, and Asian-derived religious traditions. Reference to "Obeahman" or "Obeahwoman" usually indicates dislike and distrust of those accused of malevolence and inappropriate engagement with **spirits**. It can even be used to allege that, through **mastery of spirits**, someone controls the dead and makes them serve evil interests. Practitioners themselves may speak only of "going to a man" or "going to a woman" for them to "work." However, they may define Obeah as doing either "dirty work" or "good work" (although some are said to do "everything"). This parallels the **ambiguity** of shamanic work elsewhere, as practitioners utilize their knowledge and relationships with **other-than-human persons** who act as **helpers** or allies to offer **protection** and advice, especially on how to gain one's desires or to injure enemies and prevent them harming clients, perhaps by causing **illness**. Alongside various ceremonial practices, herbalism is significant. The term itself is a Creolized form of the Ashanti term *Obayifo* ("**witch**") or *obeye* ("beings that inhabit witches"). Obeah practitioners were among the leaders of rebellions against slavery and provided some means of asserting agency among oppressed groups. Ceremonies, especially those that included **drumming**, were therefore outlawed in various places. Practitioners of Obeah can be members of **Christian**, **Hindu**, and other congregations at the same time. Similarly, Obeah practice often contradicts the stereotype that it is the preserve of impoverished descendents of slaves—rather, it has adherents in all social and ethnic strata of society. It is of the essence that Obeah and similar Caribbean traditions are Creole and popular traditions.

OBJECT-PERSONS. A term that attempts to express in English the indigenous notion that many objects are not inanimate, "mere representations," or **art** but rather are persons or agents in their own right. The term might apply to natural objects, such as stones, and to artifacts (objects of human manufacture) such as baskets. **Drums**, **medicine bundles**, fetishes, masks, and images of divinities or **ancestors** illustrate some examples of significant object-persons with whom shamans in particular cultures might engage and whose active participation in shamanic **performance** they may seek.

OCEANIA. Although some scholars insist that shamanism is the preserve of circum-**Arctic** regions, the peoples who live in the many islands of Oceania in the Pacific often employ religious leaders who use **trance** and manipulate sources of power to engage with **other-than-human persons** to the benefit of their communities or in their defense against aggressors. If the boundaries between shamans, on the one hand, and **mediums** and prophets, on the other, are fluid, the subject matter for consideration is vast. Also, since shamans elsewhere are frequently employed as **diviners** and **mediators** and are frequently accused of being **sorcerers** or **witches**, plenty of Oceanic equivalents can be found. It has become traditional to divide the islands of Oceania into **Polynesia**, **Micronesia**, and **Melanesia**. Regional influences from **South and East Asia**, **Aboriginal Australia**, **North America**, and **South America** have also been present in traditional cultures even prior to the effects of colonialism and globalization.

ODIN (ODINN). Norse god interpreted as a shaman-type figure by some scholars, **neo-shamans**, and **Heathens**, particularly due to his ability as a ***seidr*** practitioner.

OJIBWE. Also known as Anishinaabeg, Ojibwa, and Chippewa. A **Native American** people now living in the Midwest of the United States and south-central Canada. Their Algonquian language makes a grammatical distinction between animate and inanimate **genders**; that is, it marks persons and personal actions differently to objects and impersonal events. While this indigenous people's preferred self-definition, Anishinaabeg, identifies them as human persons, they speak of a wide range of **other-than-human persons** (e.g., rock-persons, tree-persons, and thunder-persons). Honorific terms like *grandparent* are used to indicate respectful relationships not only with human relatives but also with honored rocks and other personal beings. Research among one band of Ojibwe by **Irving Hallowell** has been influential among more recent scholars of **animism** and shamans such as **Nurit Bird-David**. Within the broader animism of the traditional Ojibwe worldview and lifeways, there are specific ceremonial practices that may be considered shamanic, for example, the **Midewiwin**. **John Grim**'s book *The Shaman* focuses on different types of shamans among traditional Ojibwe: **diviners**, **healers**, **dream** interpreters, seekers and repositories of knowledge, and **mediators** with other-than-human persons, among others.

ONON, URGUNGE (1919–). A Daur **Mongol** who is the manager of the Mongolia and Inner Asia Studies Unit at Cambridge University. His collaboration with **Caroline Humphrey** in recording and discussing his people's changing culture, in which shamans and **elders** led **clans** in particular ways, is among the most important recent studies of shamanism. It is one of the few studies that interprets shamans not only in a religious frame but also, more significantly, in a **political** and social one.

ORIGINS OF RELIGION. Many theories about how religion began propose that shamanism is the earliest religion of humanity. This is rooted in the notion that **hunter-gatherer** societies are closest to the first human cultural groups and that such groups are more truly shamanic than urban dwelling or settled gardening societies. **Mircea Eliade**'s definitions of shamanism as "the archaic techniques of **ecstasy**" and of "authentic shamanism as the preserve of hunter-gatherers" (in contrast with allegedly degenerate forms found among peoples with other subsistence patterns) misleadingly enshrine these notions in wider imagination.

ORPHIC MYSTERIES. Like the Sumerian ***Descent of Inanna*** epic, the mysteries of the Greek hero Orpheus have been interpreted as being shamanic. In part, this is because Orpheus descended into the **underworld** to restore his dead wife to life. He is also the archetypal mystagogue or **initiator** and revealer of mysteries. However, like other classical-period mysteries, those of Orpheus privilege restraint rather than excess. The main link between Orpheus and **ecstasy** is in the stories of his frenzied **dismemberment** by female devotees of **Dionysus** annoyed by Orpheus's rejection of all deities except the sober, solar Apollo. This is hardly an encouragement of **trance** or **possession** among his initiates. Nonetheless, **Gloria Flaherty** (1992) shows that Orpheus was considered preeminent among shamans, themselves considered preeminent religious virtuosi, by 18th-century Enlightenment writers such as Johann von Herder, Johann Goethe, and Victor Hugo. But it is as an inspired poetic **performer** rather than as an entranced **otherworld journeyer** that Orpheus is considered shamanic, thereby making the term too vague to be useful.

OTHER-THAN-HUMAN PERSONS. A phrase coined by **Irving Hallowell**, influenced by the **Ojibwe** of southern-central Canada. It refers to the widest possible community of living beings. For example, in the Ojibwe language not only are humans, **animals**, fish, birds, and plants living, relational beings, but so too are **object-persons** such as rocks and certain weather systems (the thunder-beings). The word ***spirits*** is sometimes attached to other words, as in *rock spirit* or *tree spirit*, to suggest that some rocks or trees are different from others. Hallowell's phrase has gained currency because it does not misrepresent the indigenous thought and experience that some rocks, trees, and storms act as persons: that is, as relational, intentional, conscious, and communicative beings. This worldview and lifeway is now being called **animism**, which makes shamans both possible and necessary.

The phrase should not be misunderstood to imply that humans are the standard against which other "persons" might be compared. Rather, the phrase arises among humans trying to talk with other humans. It is implicit that eagles might speak of eagle-persons and other-than-eagle persons, and so on. The understanding that humans are not the only persons also involves the notion that not all shamans are human. In **Amazonia**, for example, it is common knowledge that the most powerful shamans (or persons with shamanistic abilities, *payé*) are anacondas. **Ambiguity** and uncertainty about the way in which an other-than-human person relates or acts toward humans may require human shamans to seek to alter their **perspective** to see what others see and then deal appropriately with the resulting knowledge.

OTHER WORLDS. Many shamanic **cosmologies** posit the existence of lands, realms, or dimensions accessible to shamans after **initiation** and training. These are rarely if ever equivalent to the transcendent realms posited by monotheistic religions (e.g., heaven and hell). They are perhaps best understood as alternative lands, access to which is made by unusual means (for ordinary humans): descent into an **underworld**, ascent into an **upper world**, or nonphysical **journeys** over vast distances. Many of these other worlds are the primary home of significant **other-than-human persons**, or **spirits**. Where these include the beings who control **animals**, birds, or fish in this world, shamans may be responsible (as **resource managers**) for **mediation** to ensure that hunters or fishers encounter sufficient prey to meet the needs of their community. Where the otherworld persons control diseases or are "spirits of **illness**," shamans' roles may include seeking powerful aid in **healing** or mediation to divert the negative attention of **predatory** beings. Some other worlds are the eventual destination of the dead, in which case shamans are unique in being able to journey there before their deaths and—the important bit—return again. That this is always a dangerous pursuit is illustrated by the need for initiation and the aid of powerful **helpers**. When shamans form intimate relationships with otherworld persons, it can affect their social standing and role, and even their **gender**.

OWNERS. Shamans in some societies are said to engage with **otherworld** or **other-than-human persons** who "own" **animal** species or all animals. Permission may be sought from such beings before a hunt, and gratitude and apologies may be offered for the taking of lives afterward. This is a significant part of shamans' roles as **mediators**.

– P –

PACIFIC ISLANDS. *See* MELANESIA; MICRONESIA; OCEANIA; POLYNESIA.

PACIFIC NORTHWEST. Among the 11 recognized **Native American** nations of the **North American** Pacific Northwest coast, there are numerous village community identities, and shamans are prominent figures: for the Tsimshian, "Of all the people, the shaman, or **medicine man**, is the most powerful seer, and with the help of the **spirits**, the shaman sees beyond the present world and uses this understanding to look after the people." The Gitxsan "believe human beings are neither separate nor different from natural objects, **animals** and spiritual entities. . . . The *haalayt-dim-swannasxw* [shamans] . . . see things not ordinarily visible and [are able to] visit non-human realms" ("Listening to Our Ancestors: Native Art on the North Pacific Coast," National Museum of the American Indian, Washington, D.C.).

Transformation is a key theme in the shamanism of the region, as expressed in **art**: split representation, for instance, a stylistic convention that maximizes representation rather than naturalistic depiction and is most famously discussed by **Franz Boas** in *Primitive Art* (1955), allows as many identifying and characteristic features as possible to be depicted at once. This means **clan totems** will be immediately recognizable to the viewer: a killer whale, for example, will always have teeth and a dorsal fin, the beaver will always have two large incisors, and the hawk always has a hooked bill. Split representation refers to the reflection of an image based on a bilateral axis, and further, in some instances we see the body of an animal split lengthways and then opened out, embodying a transformation of the creature, a form of **dismemberment**.

Masks worn in such ceremonies as the potlatch take this element of transformation further. During the potlatch ceremony, the clan or family history is traced back to a time when there was no boundary between humans and animals. Often constructed with eyes and a mouth that open and close, such masks are worn by shamans in order to "see" into the spirit world. Other masks with human faces that open out to reveal animals within, such as the ubiquitous raven, assist shamans in transforming into these **other-than-human persons**. Frequently, the shaman's rattles convey the importance of transformation and the permeability between the worlds of humans, animals, and spirits: a shaman figure lies on the back of a raven, with his tongue extended to meet the tongue of the frog set in his belly, in order to absorb the potency required to engage with these other-than-humans. This sophisticated and complex **cosmology** has been appropriated and decontextualized in the **neo-shamanic** "**trance** postures" taught by **Felicitas Goodman**: it is assumed that by simply standing in the pose of the human figure in a shaman-and-bear "spirit" carving, any human can potentially reach an **altered state of consciousness**. Such interpretations may be empowering for Westerners, but they are incongruous with indigenous practices and may, indeed, be interpreted as a form of disrespectful cultural theft.

PAGANISM. Label applied to distinct religious phenomena, including "indigenous religions" and a series of new and/or reconstructed ancient indigenous European traditions. It is a self-designation of various subgroups, including but not limited to **Druids**, **Heathens**, and **Wiccans** or **Witches**. Some practitioners of **Chaos Magick** also consider themselves to be Pagans.

PARAPSYCHOLOGY. Scholars and others interested in parapsychological, psychic, or "psi" phenomena and experiences (e.g., telepathy, clairvoyance, clairaudience, psychokinesis, and precognition) have considered shamans as possible subjects for understanding, refuting, or validating competing arguments. The Parapsychological Association provides a good example of the range of relevant interests, citing Maria Luisa Felici's discussion of **North American** Indian shamans; **Stanley Krippner**'s book concerned with the "spiritual dimensions of **healing**"; Serena Roney-Dougal's consideration of **altered states of consciousness**, **brain chemistry**, psychosis, and hallucinogens; and Bruno Severi's discussions about altered states of consciousness and **ayahuasca** use among the Shipibo **Conibo** of **South America**. For obvious reasons, there are parallels between these interests and those of psychologists and of **Jungian**-influenced **neo-shamans**. However, while the publications mentioned focus particularly on questions of interiority and experience, they do also attend to social roles and **performative** issues, at least in passing.

PATIENTS. Since shamans may often be the primary **doctors** in their communities, **healing** people attacked by other **combative** shamans, **other-than-human people**, or **sorcerers** and **witches**, it is evident that many of their clients are patients. However, in parts of **Amazonia**, shamans may gain recognition as senior shamans by the number of their "bonded patients," that is, those who have been successfully healed but cannot afford to compensate the shaman for their dangerous exertions.

PAXSON, DIANA. Contemporary **Heathen** whose Hrafnar group in San Francisco was one of the first to reconstruct ***seidr***. The practice has taken on a distinctly different identity in Great Britain under the auspices of **Jenny Blain**, and in Scandinavia with the work of **Annette Høst**. Paxson has also established a deity **possession** practice in her group. Paxson noticed how traditional shamanic societies often incorporated possession into their rites, and to build on the fragmentary Nordic evidence with contemporary possession techniques, she studied and took part in the **rituals** of an **Umbanda** community in San Francisco. Regarding the Norse sources, in the Saga of King Óláfr Tryggvason (Flateyjarbók 1), an idol of the fertility god Freyr is described as being carried around the country in a wagon, accompanied by his "wife," a **priestess**. The hero of the tale, Gunnar, fights with the idol and takes its place, whereupon the Swedes are delighted that the god can now feast and drink and are even more pleased when his "wife" becomes pregnant. If interpreted as a possible example of possession, as Paxson suggests, then it may have been common practice among the Swedes for people to take on the part of a deity and let the deity speak through them when needed. Gunnar, then, is the "shaman," or whoever else was accompanying the priestess before being usurped by him: Gunnar's struggle with Freyr would actually be a fight with the previous shaman. Alternatively, or in addition—for each interpretation is not mutually exclusive—Blain suggests the possibility that a "spirit-marriage" is described, similar to examples in **Siberia**, with the wife as the "shaman": she has a spirit-spouse, Freyr, and a human-spouse, Gunnar, which is customary for the Swedes but is incomprehensible to the Norwegians, who assume Gunnar must be impersonating Freyr. And if Freyr is said to speak, this must "really" be Gunnar speaking, rather than the priestess relaying Freyr's messages. Attending to these sorts of interpretations, Paxson has combined ethnographic analogy with Norse sources to reconstruct a Heathen possession technique for the present.

PENTIKÄINEN, JUHA (1940–). Professor of religious studies at the University of Helsinki, Finland, who has devoted a lifetime's research to Finnish folk and popular religion, shamans and "shamanhood," bear folklore and cults, and similar topics, both in relation to Finland and more widely. In *Oral Repertoire and World View* (1978), Pentikäinen details interviews with a traditional Finnish **healer**, who was also considered a shaman or a **witch**. His more recent discussions of shamans and their practices and worldviews are important for bringing together careful local ethnography with a clear grasp of broad surveys.

PERFORMANCE. Shamans are people who perform particular roles in communities. They are recognized and valued by those communities precisely for their abilities to perform such roles. Often, they are also performers in the sense that they conduct or lead more or less public and dramatic events, ceremonies, or **rituals**. Discussions of shamanic performances usually refer to the **art and artifacts** (sometimes perceived as "**object-persons**") with which they work, such as **musical** instruments, **costumes**, and mirrors. More theoretical attention to the concept has also been offered. Thomas Csordas (1996) argues that all too often what scholars mean by "performance" is a ritual as a whole, without attention to the details within it as performances, and he calls for "experiential specificity"—attention to those invisible details central to shamans' experiences. It is here, however, that shamans are most open to charges of invention. Many travelers' tales and early ethnographies focused on shamans' **tricks**—ventriloquism or juggling, for example—and concluded that everything shamans did was similarly done only for show.

While **Jonathan Horwitz** and others have objected that the term *performance* appears to suggest pretence, **sham**, acting, or role-play, it is used in the scholarly sense to refer to definitive shamanic activities. Nonetheless, many shamans do make full use of acting abilities and even trickery or shamming. In his article on "Shamans and **Sex**," **Ioan Lewis** refers to the "theatrical 'play acting'" of **Siberian** shamans rutting with **animal** partners. Also, Siberians are not alone in noting the necessity of entertaining and/or tricking **otherworld** persons ("**spirits**") in order to gain **healing** power or to survive while **journeying** in hostile environments.

Edward Schieffelin usefully complicates matters by asking who—spirit or shaman—is the performer: for the New Guinea Kaluli, it is the spirit whose performance is judged. In addition, he suggests that rather than being credulous and accepting, the community may form a critical, evaluative, and sophisticated audience of the shamanic performances.

Jenny Blain and **Robert Wallis** suggest a phrase that is more cumbersome but avoids associating "performance" with "fake" or "role-play." They argue that shamans negotiate within a cultural framework, interact with spirits, and in this way "actively accomplish meanings" through the construction of relations between human and other-than-human worlds.

PERKINSON, JAMES W. (1951–). Professor of philosophy and religious studies at Ecumenical Theological College, Detroit. Perkinson is the author of *Shamanism, Racism, and Hip Hop Culture* (2005) in which he argues that hip hop culture is shamanic because it continues an indigenous **African** diasporic shamanic and **trickster** practice of taking that which oppresses people (i.e., "**spirits**") and **mastering** it to **heal** the community. Simultaneously, he argues that the dominant white culture of the United States is a form of **witchcraft**.

PERSPECTIVISM. A central theme of **Eduardo Viveiros de Castro**'s writing about **Amazonian** shamans and their wider societies puts the ability to see from another's perspective at the center of what shamans do. If powerful persons, especially shamans and **sorcerers**, might *appear* in different physical forms—for example, that of a **jaguar** or a human—it can be vital to see what is *really* there. But the issue is larger than this, because Amazonian **cosmology** entails the notion of a single culture shared by all living beings (fish, birds, **animals**, plants, deities, humans, and others) but masked by divergent appearances of physical nature. So, while most humans see jaguars as animals who eat raw meat, and peccaries as prey animals, jaguars and peccaries see themselves as living in homes and eating cooked food. Meanwhile, jaguars and peccaries see humans as prey and **predators**, respectively. Shamans see the cultural reality obscured by the multiplicity of **nature**. This contrasts with Western modernity in which a single nature (of stable physical, material reality) provides a foundation for the multiplicity and diversity of (human) cultures. Where modernity has "multiculturalism," Amazonia has "multinaturalism." But, more significantly, where modernity worries about solipsism (do we think the same?), Amazonians worry about **cannibalism** (do we taste the same?). In such a context, the most valued roles of shamans are associated with knowledge, **combat**, and **healing**. Signe Howell summarizes data from among the **Chewong** of **Indonesia**, and many other **animist** societies, which show that a common part of apprentice shamans' **initiation** and training is "learning to see in a new way." Thus Viveiros de Castro's argument may be applicable to all shamans.

PETERS, LARRY G. (1942–). Peters is one of a number of scholars-turned-shamans, such as **Michael Harner**, who have undertaken anthropological fieldwork with shamans and undergone experiences that led them to become shamans themselves and thereafter to teach **neo-shamans**. Peters is a professor of anthropology and psychology at the California Graduate Institute of Professional Psychology and Psychoanalysis in Los Angeles and a board member of the Society for the Anthropology of Consciousness. He has carried out fieldwork in **Nepal**, **China**, **Mongolia**, and **Siberia** and is self-termed a "**Tibetan** Shaman" using shamanic counseling and other psychotherapies "to promote psycho-spiritual integration" in his clients. Peters's teaching methods and **healing** practices are firmly situated in the tradition of Harner's **core shamanism**, and indeed he is a research associate with the **Foundation for Shamanic Studies**.

PEYOTE. Name derived from the Nahuatl word *peyotl* for the buttons of a cactus indigenous to Mexico and the southwestern United States. Its ingestion is central to the rituals of the **Native American Church** and **Huichol** (*Wixáritari*) shamans. Academic and enthusiastic interpreters often privilege the **vision**-inducing or hallucinogenic effects of peyote, as they do with other plant and **mushroom** derivatives, and portray its emetic, **vomit**-inducing properties as an unfortunate side effect. However, vomiting is central to many shamanic rituals, **purifying** participants and preparing them for encounters with significant **other-than-human persons**, including **adjusted styles of communication** with the plant-persons themselves. **Carlos Castaneda**'s early books stressed the need for peyote's help in achieving consciousness of other **helpers** who would aid one in seeking a good way to live. Louis Lewin published the first systematic study of the pharmacology of peyote in 1886, and included it among the "Phantastica" (rather than the "Inebriantia," "Exitantia," "Euphorica," or "Hypnotica") in his encyclopedic classification of drugs and psychoactives (*Phantastica*, 1924). The first English translation of Lewin's book (1931) was read almost immediately by **Aldous Huxley** and had a considerable impact on him, resulting in years of experimentation in **altering states of consciousness** as a form of mysticism. Edward Anderson's book (1996) publishes more recent research about the "divine cactus."

PILCH, JOHN J. Biblical scholar at Georgetown University, Washington, D.C., and the University of Pretoria, South Africa, who argues that Jesus Christ was a "**holy man**" whose ability to achieve **altered states of consciousness** and **journey** to the **upper world** established his ability to **heal**. He draws on a range of cultures and theories to make his case.

PIYA. Various similar and related words in diverse **Amazonian** languages refer to the kind of shamans who have the ability to **heal illnesses** or commit violence (**predation**). In some languages (e.g., that of the **Wayapí** discussed by **Alan Campbell**), cognate terms are not nouns but verbs and adjectives and should be translated as "shamanize" or "shamanic." **Neil Whitehead** distinguishes piya from **alleluia** and **kanaimà** practices and practitioners. Although all might be dangerous, it is only "kanaimà'san" (practitioners of kanaimà) who are by definition "assault **sorcerers**." Piya shamans "are primarily sought after to heal."

PLASTIC MEDICINE PEOPLE. A term applied to **Native Americans** who perform ceremonies or teach traditional knowledge to Euro-Americans or anyone else who is willing to pay. It can also be applied to "**wannabe Indians**" and "wannabe shamans" (non-Native people who "want to be" Native and shamanic). The term is usually an accusation leveled against **New Age neo-shamans** by such critics as the **American Indian Movement**, the **Center for SPIRIT**, **Ward Churchill**, and Gohiyuhi/Respect. **Wallace Black Elk** is often listed as an example.

The term "plastic medicine man" applies literally to Playmobil's toy #3877, which claims to represent either an "Indian" or "Native American" **medicine man** and illustrates the point that disrespect flows both ways. It has been pointed out that Playmobil does not offer toy versions of other religious leaders (there is a Druid in its catalog, but no rabbi or pope), and that the company's Native American collection brings together elements of entirely separate indigenous cultures. The title of Al Carroll's contribution to *They Call Us "Indians"* (Banfield 2005), "Would You Buy a Plastic Eucharist from This Man? When Curiosity about Natives Turns to Abuse," suggests a link between the metaphor and literal plastic representations.

POLITICS. In **Mircea Eliade**'s construction of shamanism, political involvement is a sign of degeneracy among shamans. He prefers to present them as **ritualists** and religious leaders rather than as community leaders, let alone the allies of emperors. Similarly, the universalization of shamanism by **Michael Harner** and other promoters of **core shamanism** and **neo-shamanism** typically divorces the practice from local political concerns. In contrast, **Caroline Humphrey**, **Urgunge Onon**, and Nicholas Thomas demonstrate the intimate relationships between **Mongolian** and **Chinese** shamans and emperors and **elders**. Similarly, Mercedes de la Garza argues that the Mayan rulers of the classical, precolonial period were shamans because they "acquired [their divine quality] through strict **initiation** rituals . . . as well as through continual ascetic practices," including locally significant forms of "self-sacrifice." A reinsertion of shamans into their lived realities requires full engagement with their political and other communal roles. Even neo-shamans, for all that they may wish to devote themselves to "spirituality," are integral members, if not significant players, in the expansion of Western hegemony precisely because some of them insist on universalism and the separation of religion from politics.

POLYNESIA. A subdivision of **Oceania** or the Pacific Islands (along with **Micronesia** and **Melanesia**), including islands in a vast triangular area of the Pacific Ocean between **Hawaii**, New Zealand, and Rapa Nui (Easter Island), that does not always refer to clear cultural or geographical distinctions. Claims have been made that shamans can be identified in traditional cultures throughout the region but are complicated by controversy about the projection of **neo-shamanic** interpretations onto **ritualists** and **healers** of various kinds. Claims about Hawaiian shamanism are particularly fraught.

POMO. An indigenous people of California. Greg Sarris has written both biographical and fictionalized accounts of the life and work of traditional **doctors** such as Mabel McKay. He describes their **healing** practices (e.g., **sucking**), reliance on **dreams** and **otherworld helpers**, **combat** with "poisoners" or **sorcerers**, **initiatory illnesses**, **visions**, and use of songs and other **music**. As elsewhere, it is clear that doctors and sorcerers use similar methods but seek different ends. Sarris also discusses the importance of basket weaving and usage in Pomo and neighboring **Native American** peoples' **cosmologies** and shamanic practices. McKay treated her baskets, including those displayed in museums, as **other-than-human persons** or **object-persons** in their own right.

POSSESSION. Shamans are sometimes distinguished from other religious or cultural leaders by their ability to deliberately enter a **trance** that is sometimes considered to be equivalent to possession. **Mircea Eliade** and **Luc de Heusch** categorically distinguish the two phenomena because they defined possession as involving a loss of control to **spirits** and a concomitant inability to **master the spirits**. If *trance* is defined as an **altered state of consciousness**, then *possession* can be defined as either "being controlled or directed by an **other-than-human person** or spirit" (from an experiential perspective) or "the **performance** of culturally recognizable signs that someone is a vehicle through which another being is acting." While some interpreters see trances as permitting and leading to possession, others are insistent that both are sets of practices or behaviors—performances rather than states of mind. **Caroline Humphrey** notes that the important matter for shamans and their communities is rarely the **individual**'s inner state of mind (which is considered inaccessible to others), but the fact that particular actions identifiable as possession or trance indicate that the shaman is communicating with **helpers** or **journeying** to gain knowledge and abilities beyond those of other people.

Ioan Lewis counters Eliade's and Heusch's schema by pointing to the regularity with which the "classic" shamanic **initiatory** and biographical accounts from **Siberia** and the **Arctic** include possession. He also details the parallels between "possession cults"—for example, the **Zar**, **Sar**, and **Bori** in **Africa** and **Vodou** in the **Caribbean**—and shamanism. Noting that phenomena understood as evidence of possession in one culture may be interpreted as madness or hysteria (sometimes caused by **mushroom** ingestion or "tarantism"), Lewis undermines the notion that these are entirely psychological experiences. Finally, he demonstrates that Eliade's and Heusch's formula is derived from their wider, religious perspective rather than from the data themselves. It can be concluded, therefore, that possession is an aspect of the **election** of shamans by **otherworld** persons who wish to communicate, help, or empower initiated individuals and continues to form a mode of relationship between shamans and their helpers. This help may include aiding others who are possessed or who have suffered "**soul loss**" under assault by powerful other-than-human persons. In Lewis's concise formulation, shamans may seek to cure these forms of **illness** by "**soul projection**." He also draws on the work of **Sergei Shirokogoroff** to conclude that shamans may be either (or both) "hostages to the spirits" and their **sexual** and/or marital partners. Shamans might, then, be defined as people who welcome possession as an aspect of (sexual/marital) relationship with spirits and be distinguished from the victims of unwanted possession, who may be the subject of **exorcism** by shamans (or other religious specialists, where there is no notion of acceptable possession).

POWER ANIMALS. A significant portion of the practice of **neo-shamanism**, including almost all early workshops in the style of **Michael Harner**'s **core shamanism**, involve guided **visualization** or meditation—sometimes glossed as "**journeying**"—in search of a "power animal" or "**totem**." Usually these are considered to be integral parts of an individual's "true self." They are the closest **helpers** and guides in further journeying and shamanic work. Power animals usually take the form of dolphins, wolves, eagles, horses, and the like, indicating a Western bias for what are perceived to be benevolent and/or powerful beings. Neo-shamans also tend to recall **Mircea Eliade**'s and **Sergei Shirokogoroff**'s emphasis on the **mastery of spirits** in retaining control over their engagements with power animals. Some neo-shamans, **Heathen** and other polytheistic **Pagan** practitioners in particular, have developed more sophisticated engagements with **other-than-human persons**, viewing the nomenclature "power animal" as indicative of a **New Age** understanding of shamanism rather than an **animistic**, **new-indigenous** one.

PRAGMATISM. Indigenous shamanisms tend to disrupt the binary sacred–profane boundary imposed by Western observers, avoid transcendentalism, and embed practice in pragmatic day-to-day community (human and **other-than-human**) relations. The relationship between shamans and clientele among the **Native American** Gitxsan community of the **Pacific Northwest** offers a salient example: "The fees for **doctoring** might be ten blankets, prepaid, for each **patient**, or it might be as little as one blanket. But if the doctored person died afterwards, the blankets were returned" ("Listening to Our Ancestors: Native Art on the North Pacific Coast," National Museum of the American Indian, Washington, D.C.).

PREDATION. A significant theme of many **Amazonian** cultures is that there are basically two kinds of beings—predators and prey—each of which is divided into three major groups: **spirits**, people, and **animals**. However, all living beings (and in these **animist** cultures that might mean all beings) see themselves as humans. Thus, a spirit (as seen from a human **perspective**) might see itself as a human preying on animals, while an animal (again as seen from a human perspective) might see itself as a human preyed on by spirits; people (from a human perspective) see themselves as humans preyed on by spirits and predatory animals. A shaman's job therefore includes achieving the perspective of others—"seeing as they see"—and making use of the resulting knowledge to achieve particular goals. Similar **cosmological**, social, and relational understandings (of importance for **resource management** and **mediation**) are discussed in relation to **Siberian** peoples by **Roberte Hamayon** and **Ioan Lewis**.

PRETTY ON TOP, JOHN. Cultural director and speaker for the **Crow**/Absaroke Nation who succeeded **Thomas Yellowtail** as **medicine man** and Sun Dance chief in 1985. He was chosen for this role by **Seven Arrows**, the "**medicine father**" and chief of the Little People (who, in this culture, live inside mountains) who had **elected** and instructed previous medicine people and Sun Dance chiefs. In 1986 Pretty on Top was selected to represent all **Native Americans** at the world prayer meeting sponsored by Pope John Paul II at Assisi, Italy. He is listed on **Center for SPIRIT**'s website as rejecting **Brooke Medicine Eagle**'s claim to be a traditional medicine woman, saying, "The book she published is so far away from Crow spirituality she's not recognized anywhere in our traditional ways."

PRETTY SHIELD (1856–1944). Medicine woman of the Apsáalooke ("Children of the Large-Beaked Bird," often now called **Crow**) during the 19th-century transition to reservation life. She told her life story to Frank Linderman through an interpreter and using sign language, and he published it as *Red Mother* (1932), later reprinted as *Pretty-Shield: Medicine Woman of the Crows*. This includes Pretty Shield's narration of everyday life, as well as her **medicine** practice and **dream visions**, and is considered "easily the feminine equivalent of **Neihardt**'s *Black Elk Speaks*." Her husband, Goes Ahead, was one of the scouts for the U.S. Seventh Cavalry's assault on the **Lakota** that culminated in the Battle of the Little Big Horn. Pretty Shield's granddaughter, Alma Snell, authored a memoir of life with her grandmother, *Grandmother's Grandchild* (2000).

PRICE, NEIL. Archaeologist whose exhaustive analysis of Norse–**Saami** relations in *The Viking Way* (2002) indicates that there was much creative cultural exchange. In particular, Price attends to the practice of ***seidr*** and the way in which a number of burials of Saami and Norse, which themselves disrupt **gender** and cultural boundaries, may be interpreted as practitioners of seidr—that is, as shamans.

PRICE-WILLIAMS, DOUGLASS. Professor emeritus in anthropology at the University of California, Los Angeles, who has, as part of his research into psychological anthropology and cross-cultural cognitive studies, written extensively on shamanism, **altered states of consciousness**, **dreaming**, and **alien abduction**. With **Larry Peters**, Price-Williams argued for an "experiential approach" to shamanism in the early 1980s, part of the wider interest in insider and experiential anthropology gaining coherency at that time. More recently, he has been exploring dreaming as an interactional activity, rather than "the dream" being a thing in itself, as well as the cross-cultural consistencies in descriptions of UFO close encounters and shamanic **initiations** and **rituals**.

PRIESTS. Shamans are commonly distinguished from priests in academic discussions of distinctions between kinds of religious leaders. Although some cultures recognize that there are some situations in which a person may act as both shaman and priest, or shaman and **elder**, such roles are often distinct. The defining practice of priests is the offering of sacrifices on behalf of their communities or of the world. **Caroline Humphrey** and **Urgunge Onon** demonstrate the sacrificial duties of elders but not shamans in **Mongolia**. In **Amazonia**, shamans may offer sacrifices, especially as part of their **mediating** role between deities and human communities. Thus the distinction is not a universal one. It is likely that the preference for shamans over priests in contemporary Western imagination is rooted in intra-**Christian** polemics of Protestants against Catholicism and alleged **ritualism** and misconstrues the significance of both religious functionaries.

PROTECTION. A significant role of shamans in many indigenous communities is to provide protection from enemies of various kinds, including **sorcerers**, **witches**, **predators**, enemy shamans, annoyed **ancestors**, **illnesses**, and even deities. They may protect by obtaining knowledge of impending attack, by offering **mediation** for breaches of **purity** or insults to **other-than-human persons**, or by **healing** illnesses with the aid of powerful **otherworld helpers**. In **Amazonia**

and elsewhere, shamans' ability to alter their **perspective**, to see as another sees, can enable them to see past material forms to understand the real nature of a potential predatory or prey **animal**, human, or **spirit**. Among some Amazonian peoples, a chief role for a community's shaman is to indulge in mild acts of predation (bloodletting) against their neighbors in order to protect them from far more aggressive assaults by **cannibalistic** deities. Among the **San** in **Southern Africa**, healing **rituals** are guarded by those who ward off the co-creative deity and ancestors who made the world a harsh place, while others seek the energy to heal.

PSILOCYBIN. A hallucinogenic or **entheogenic** alkaloid (4-phosphoryloxy-N, N-dimethyltryptamine) of the tryptamine family present in many species of fungi, the best-known being the genus *Psilocybe*, including *Psilocybe cubensis* and *Psilocybe semilanceata* (Liberty Cap), popularly known as "magic **mushrooms**" or "shrooms." Psilocybin mushrooms are found in many places worldwide, and the use of them is especially associated with those cultures that have domesticated cattle, since many species are dung living.

Gordon Wasson identified psilocybin, along with fly agaric (*Amanita muscaria*) and other mushrooms, as part of an "archaic mushroom cult" that spread across the globe from ancient Europe. **Timothy Leary**, on the other hand, promoted magic mushrooms as the key to transforming society and unlocking human consciousness, while **Terence McKenna** held magic mushrooms and other entheogens to be the triggers for achieving cosmic consciousness. All of these authors assumed mushroom use was intrinsically a shamanic occupation and that it was both widespread and archaic in origin. **Andy Letcher** has convincingly deconstructed this discourse, arguing that, apart from accidental ingestion in Europe (recorded as "poisoning") and the deliberate recreational and sacramental use since the first recorded instance in 1970, the "folk evidence" supposed by Wasson is unverified and, outside Europe, the role of the magic mushroom use has been exaggerated.

The principal location for magic mushroom use is Mexico, where half the world's species exist, and it is here that Wasson met and went on to celebrate in print the **Mazatec** Indian *curandera* **Maria Sabina**, who privileged the help of mushrooms in inducing **vomiting** at least as much as she sought their aid in inducing **visions**. Nonetheless, magic mushrooms play significant roles in **Cyberian** shamanism and **Pagan animism** and among **psychonauts**.

PSYCHEDELICS. *See* ENTHEOGENS; HOFFMAN, ALBERT; SHULGIN, ALEXANDER (SASHA).

PSYCHOACTIVES. *See* ENTHEOGENS.

PSYCHONAUTS. A term sometimes applied to **neo-shamans**, **Chaos Magickians**, **techno-shaman**s, those ingesting **entheogens**, some **Pagans**, and other contemporary Westerners exploring the realms of **altered states of consciousness**. Where astronauts travel into space, psychonauts undertake **journeys** to inner space—be it defined as the mind, the human consciousness, the subconscious/unconscious, or an external cosmic reality. The term is most memorable as the title of "a manual of the theory and practice of magic" (1987) by Phil Carroll and of a major song by the gothic rock band **Fields of the Nephilim**.

PSYCHOTECHNOLOGIES. Term used by **Mircea Eliade** to refer to the strategies shamans use to **alter states of consciousness** and thereby achieve "**ecstasy**"—from **drumming** and dancing to fasting and **chanting**, alongside other forms of sensory **deprivation and overstimulation**—but Eliade was dismissive of **entheogen** use, erroneously seeing this as a degenerate practice. Since such "psychotechnologies" might easily be associated with other religious practices as well, they should not be overemphasized as indicative of "shamanism," with recent trends focusing more on what shamans do in their engagements with **other-than-human persons**.

PURGATIVES. Many shamanic **rituals** and **performances** include the ingestion of plants that result in **vomiting**. Some observers, including enthusiastic participants (e.g., **Gordon Wasson**) have mistaken this for an unfortunate and embarrassing side effect, but the pervasive indigenous understanding is that this is the key thing: it is an absolutely necessary act of **purification** aided by powerful **other-than-human persons**. **Maria Sabina**, for example, insisted that if a **patient** or client did not vomit with the **help** of mushrooms, as **ritualist** and **doctor** she would have to do so. Many of the plants valued as inspirers of **visions** or **altered states of consciousness** are at least equally important as emetics (inducers of vomiting) and aids toward purity.

PURITY AND PURIFICATION. All cultures make some division between what they consider "normal" and what they consider "abnormal"; some also categorize certain things, events, and acts as either "sacred" or "profane" and have procedures for keeping them apart or dealing with contact between them. Anthropologist Mary Douglas has written important works about these issues. Shamans are often required to **mediate** between people, or between humans and **other-than-human persons** (e.g., **animals**, **ancestors**, or **spirits**), because someone has offended someone else. This central part of their function as **ritualists** reestablishes "purity" in the relationships. Also, significant portions of many shamanic rituals involve purification, especially those utilizing **purgatives** (which may also result in **visions**) and those initiating **altered styles of communication** between shamans and their **helpers**. **Maria Sabina** talked about the importance of purificatory purgatives in the **healing** process, both for the *curandera* and for the **patient**.

– R –

RASMUSSEN, KNUD (1879–1933). Early 20th-century ethnographer of the **Greenlandic** ***angakkut*** who was born in Greenland, the son of a Danish missionary and a local **Inuit** woman. In 1910 Rasmussen and his colleagues established the "**Arctic** Station of Thule," from which the Thule Expeditions set out in order to map areas of Greenland and explore Inuit cultures. During the most famous of these, the four-year Fifth Expedition, Rasmussen made extensive records of Inuit lore and shamanistic practices. His contribution to the study of Greenlandic shamanism and role as an advocate of the Inuit has been discussed by **Merete Demant Jakobsen**.

REICHEL-DOLMATOFF, GERARDO (1912–1994). Colombian anthropologist with particular interests in **Amazonian** peoples, especially the Tukano and Desana in Colombia. In addition to general publications about the cultures of these people and their neighbors, Reichel-Dolmatoff wrote specifically about shamans (or *payé*), **cosmology**, mythology, and "narcotic drugs," including **tobacco** and **ayahuasca**. In *The Shaman and the Jaguar* (1975), he summarized that the

> principal spheres of a *payé* are the curing of disease, the obtaining of game **animals** and fish from their supernatural **masters**, the presiding over **rituals** in the individual life cycle, and defensive or aggressive action against personal enemies. In all these aspects the role of the *payé* is essentially that of a **mediator** and moderator between superterrestrial forces and society, and between the need for survival of the individual and the forces bent on his destruction—sickness, hunger and the ill will of others.

In his contribution to **Peter Furst**'s book about "the ritual use of hallucinogens," Reichel-Dolmatoff argues that "the purpose of taking [*yagé*] is to return to the uterus" and thence to the creation of the cosmos and the establishment of society. Both knowledge and **purification** are obtained in this context. Reichel-Dolmatoff's work is also notable for informing the shamanistic approach to **rock art** and its attention to **entoptic phenomena**: when Tukanoans were asked to draw their mental imagery, they tended

> to fill the pieces of paper he gave them with rows of formalized and reduplicated geometric motifs comparable with their painting of the same motifs on the walls of their houses. The Tukano identified these reduplicated forms as images derived from what they themselves recognized as the first stage of their **trance** experiences; there can be little doubt of their entoptic origin. (Reichel-Dolmatoff 1978, 12–13)

REINDEER. Many **Arctic** cultures (including the **Saami** and the Chukchi) subsist by reindeer herding. Not surprisingly, reindeer play a role in their shamanic narratives, **rituals**, and **cosmologies**. Among the **Siberian** Chukchi, for example, shamans sometimes ascend to the **upper world** by riding a reindeer. A modern myth has developed that **Santa Claus** was originally a shaman.

RESOURCE MANAGEMENT. A significant role for shamans in many indigenous cultures, part of their **mediatory** and **political** functions. Shamans may engage with particular **animals**, plants, birds, fish, and similar **other-than-human persons** on whom their communities rely (especially for food) in order to guarantee the availability of future "resources." Examples include **Batak** shamans' participatory role in dispersing honey and rice, **Sakha** (Yakut) shamans' knowledge of the whereabouts of **reindeer**, and **Inuit** shamans' mediation with animals who may have been offended and refuse to give themselves to hunters. This shamanic role is generally overlooked, misunderstood, or taken to be merely symbolic or "spiritual," by many commentators, especially **neo-shamans**.

RHYTHM. Shamans in many cultures make use of rhythmic **music**, songs, **chants**, dances, and movements. Instruments as varied as **drums**, rattles, and bells are used. Claims are sometimes made that shamans always use a constant rhythm in **healing** and in inducing **trances** to facilitate **journeying**. However, not only are different rhythms claimed to be what **Mongolian** or **Saami** or **Native American** or other shamans use (3–4 or 4–7 beats per second are popular among the claimants, especially **Cyberian** and **neo-shamans**), it is not even the case that shamans always use their instruments to make a constant rhythm, pulse, or beat. Drums are often used to make noise without any discernible rhythm. While noise and rhythm may have testable effects on people, not only do these vary considerably but they are also valued differently from culture to culture. **Gilbert Rouget**'s study *Music and Trance* (1985) demonstrates that any effects of music, and especially of rhythm, operate only in the context of other influences acting on those who enter trance or **ecstasy** (between which he distinguishes). Other **ethnomusicologists** agree with this conclusion, if not with everything Rouget proposes.

RIPINSKY-NAXON, MICHAEL. Scholar whose interest in shamanism concerns the use of psychoactives, the **origins of religion**, and the nature of religious experience. In line with established developments in the study of religion that have broadened analysis into indigenous practices without the restrictions of theology and biases of monotheisms, Ripinsky-Naxon agrees that shamanism can suitably be approached as a religion. He argues, though, contra **Mircea Eliade**, that rather than being a relatively recent, degenerate development, **entheogens** are crucial to understanding shamanism (while this might be so in some instances, given that entheogen use in shamanism is restricted to certain areas, particularly **Central America** and **South America**, Ripinsky-Naxon overstates his case). This is in order to establish what he calls the "shamanic metaphor" and its origins, along with the "religious impulse," in an "*ur*-religion"—that is, shamanism. In his volume *The Nature of Shamanism: Substance and Function of a Religious Metaphor* (1993), he suggests, "With the help of trance inducing psychoactive alkaloids, the different magico-religious credos strove to forge a key capable of unlocking the doors to the cosmic arcane." This somewhat jargonistic argument harks back to the outmoded research of **Gordon Wasson** on magic **mushrooms** as the origin of religion and revives the idea that shamanism can be seen as the earliest religion and indeed the origin of religion (arguably, such a metanarrative neglects the diversity of shamanisms and tells us more about the modern Western researcher's predilections than about shamans themselves).

Addressing **neo-shamanisms**, or "**New Age** pop-shamanism" as he puts it, Ripinsky-Naxon agrees with other scholars that simply learning the techniques employed by a shaman does not make one a shaman. He adds that without established shamanisms in the modern West, neo-shamans tend to show "a tremendous lack of awareness, insight and sensitivity into the true shamanic experience." In many instances, he is correct, although other scholars have also presented detailed ethnographic information on neo-shamans such as **Runic John** and **Gordon "the Toad" MacLellan**, whose roles as "shamans" are honorific rather than self-proclaimed, sensitive to other indigenes, and integrated into social relations.

RITUALS. A central function of many shamans is to conduct or preside over rituals. While much attention has been devoted to rituals in which shamans alone **perform**—for example, as **healers** and **journeyers** to **other worlds**—they also play significant roles in community ceremonies and rites of passage in many cultures. Shamans may even be defined as the repositories of the knowledge of the conduct of ceremonies. Such knowledge is likely to be learned from other shamans and from **initiatory** otherworld or **other-than-human persons**.

ROAD MAN. *See* NATIVE AMERICAN CHURCH.

ROCK ART. Paintings (also known as pictographs) and engravings (also known as petroglyphs) on rock surfaces in caves or rock shelters and on boulders and exposed rock in the open landscape. The current "shamanistic interpretation" of some rock **art** traditions was pioneered by scholars in **southern Africa**, principally **David Lewis-Williams** and **Thomas Dowson**, who proposed a link between Southern African rock art accounts of shamanistic practices in ethnographic records of the **San** (Bushmen). There is widespread agreement that this is the most reliable interpretation of much of this art to date.

Lewis-Williams and Dowson went on to draw attention to the similarities between southern African rock art and the **cave art** of the **European Paleolithic**, suggesting that a human neurological bridge might explain the presence of certain geometric shapes in both Southern Africa and European Paleolithic rock art traditions. They proposed a **neuropsychological model** for interpreting cave art that has implications for other rock art worldwide. An important component of the model's application involves the identification of **entoptic phenomena**—complex and diverse geometric images derived from the human central nervous system during some **altered states of consciousness**—in the art. A number of authors subsequently applied the model, and the presence of entoptics in particular, to other rock art traditions, from **North America** and **Aboriginal Australia** to **Siberia**, **Central Asia**, and **Northern Europe**.

A vociferous debate ensued between so-called shamaniacs and shamanaphobes over the reliability of the approach, with a particular focus on the veracity of identifying entoptics. Certainly, a single approach to all rock art as shamanistic, and one which overemphasizes the entoptic component at the expense of other integral parts of the neuropsychological model, is problematic. But where ethnographic data is available, for example, in parts of Southern Africa and the United States, it is widely accepted that the origins of specific rock art traditions are in altered states of consciousness and associated shamanistic practices. In circumstances where there are no ethnographic records, some researchers argue that the neuropsychological model is applicable to determine whether the rock art images originate in altered consciousness, and studies indicate the British cup-and-ring art, for example, is not so derived, while the megalithic art of the passage tomb traditions in the British Isles may be. *See also* CALIFORNIAN ROCK ART; SIBERIAN AND CENTRAL ASIAN ROCK ART.

ROUGET, GILBERT. Ethnomusicologist of the Musée de l'Homme, Paris. Rouget is best known for his book *Music and Trance* (1985), in which he argues for a distinction between **trance** and **ecstasy**. *Trance* is said to involve and be induced by movement, noise, company, crises, sensory overstimulation, and amnesia and to lack hallucinations. *Ecstasy*, on the other hand, is said to be induced by stillness, silence, solitude, lack of crises, sensory **deprivation**, recollection, and hallucinations. Much of Rouget's data relate to fieldwork in **Africa** and may be culturally specific. Alternatively, his use of *ecstasy* may be different from that of **Mircea Eliade**, especially in relation to **Siberian** shamans. Rouget's *trance* may be closer to other scholars' *mysticism*. In some cases, Rouget's terms may apply to phases of shamanic **performance** and thus clarify stages of a shaman's work. Similarly, Rouget's argument that "**possession** trance seems to require, everywhere and at all times, a form of **music** belonging to the most everyday and popular system" may be true in African possession cults but is inapplicable in, for example, **Korea**, where shamanic music is distinct from everyday music, and in **Amazonia**, where shamans **chant** in languages unknown to those who have not been **initiated**. However, his argument that music, especially **rhythm** alone, is insufficient to induce trance or **altered states of consciousness**, and that it does not do so automatically, has been widely accepted among ethnomusicologists in contrast to some **neo-shamans** and **techno-shamans**. Rouget argues that trances and altered states are induced only in those who have made a decision to enter them—and even then a variety of other factors is required both to induce a trance and to make the practitioner's actions meaningful to others. Among the most important of these factors, as Roy Willis (1999) shows, especially in relation to the Ngulu **spirit** cult of Zambia, is the "quality of relations between the individuals making up the trancing group."

RUDGELEY, RICHARD. Independent British scholar of archaeology, anthropology, and religious studies. Rudgeley's volume *The Alchemy of Culture: Intoxicants in Society* (1993) revived interest in **entheogen** use through time, and more recently he has written books on prehistory, the Norse, **Celts**, and **Pagans**.

RUNIC JOHN. A British **Heathen neo-shamanic** practitioner and the author of *The Book of* ***Seidr****: The Native English and Northern European Shamanic Tradition* (2004) whose shamanic work with runes earned him this nickname. Ethnographic records of John's shamanic practices, including **journeying** to the nine **other worlds** of the Ygdrasill world tree and **healing** work at alternative festivals are presented in **Robert Wallis**'s book *Shamans/Neo-Shamans* (2003). Wallis argues that unlike those neo-shamans who decontextualize and psychologize indigenous practices and focus on **individual** empowerment, Runic John's work is more readily comparable with traditional shamanisms, as it is embedded in a specific tradition and involves direct encounters with **spirits** John perceives as "real" rather than aspects of self, as well as the healing of those clients who request his services.

– S –

SAAMI (SÁMI). Also known as Lapps. Indigenous to northern Finland, Norway, Sweden, and northwestern Russia, the Saami's primary traditional mode of subsistence is **reindeer** herding. Their traditional shamanism is sometimes said to have been crushed by **Christian** missionaries (especially the dominant Lutherans) and by royal power (on the grounds that they may have led **political** and cultural opposition). Certainly, however, Saami culture, including shamanism, has enjoyed a resurgence in recent decades.

Traditional Saami shamanism shares elements with circumpolar and Finno-Ugric shamanism, with usually (in the recorded literature) male shamans maintaining harmony in human and nonhuman relations through **journey**s to the **other world**, assisted by a female accomplice. Traditional roles for the *noaydde* (also *noaide*) include **healing** by removing **spirit** intrusions, protecting the reindeer, acting as a psychopomp, engaging in **combat** in **animal** form (such as the bear, a mythical **ancestor** shaman conferring strength) with rival shamans for control of the weather and fertility of the crops, and seeking knowledge. Songs or **chants** (now often accompanied on hand **drums**), *joiks*, derived from shamanic invocations (sung by the shaman's assistant) to and **mediations** with those **other-than-human persons** who control the **predators** of reindeer remain popular. The shaman's drum (known as a "troll-drum") is highly decorated with an elaborate map of the spirit world and is used in **divination** wherein the beater causes lots to move around the surface of the drum. The antiquity of Saami shamanism may stretch back to prehistory, as evinced by **rock art** in the region that depicts shamanistic themes reminiscent of the decoration on shamans' drums (as argued by Knut

Helskog). There appears to have been significant contact with non-Saami peoples of the North since at least Medieval times, including the Vikings, with whom elements of shamanic practice were shared (as recently argued by **Jenny Blain**, **Thomas DuBois**, and **Neil Price**)—including perhaps ***seidr***, although it is unclear to what extent Viking seidr derives from Saami shamanic practices.

SABINA, MARIA (1888–1985). Mazatec Indian *curandera* who was "discovered" in the 1950s by the ethnomycologist **Gordon Wasson**. Wasson held Sabina's *veledas* (**healing** ceremonies involving the ingestion of **psilocybin mushrooms**) to be the archetypical residue of a prehistoric mushroom cult that marked the **origin of religion**, having spread across the globe from Europe via cultural diffusion and evolved into the "high" religions. Sabina's veledas, held in the basement of her home, involved the blessing of pairs of mushrooms in copal incense and the reciting of prayers to **Christian** saints. Those gathered to embark on the healing process consumed the mushrooms in darkness with Sabina, who sang improvised monotonous **chants** accompanied by shouts and claps (recorded by Wasson and released by Smithsonian Folkways). While Sabina stressed the valuable aid of the mushrooms in inducing **purificatory purgation**, Wasson assumed this was an embarrassing side effect preceding the **visions** that he considered the key to shamanism. Wasson's publications in the late 1950s celebrated Mexican mushroom-inspired shamanism and, in poor ethnographic practice, named his informant and her location; flocks of hippies and other psychedelic seekers were soon streaming into Mexico seeking the mushrooms and Sabina, with disastrous consequences for the local community. With the fame promulgated by Wasson, Sabina remains a major figure in studies on Mexican shamanism, despite the unreliability of Wasson's ethnography (focused as he was on fitting Mazatec shamanism into his erroneous concept of a mushroom cult) and the vagaries of Wasson's translation from Mazatec into Spanish and thence into Italian.

SACRED HOOP. *See* MEDICINE WHEEL.

***SACRED HOOP*. Neo-shamanic** journal based in Great Britain and established in 1993 by Nick and Jan Wood, offering "a network magazine for the shamanic community" as well as articles on shamanism,

Native American spirituality, and other material and also operating as a forum for debate on these and related issues. The title of the magazine references the **Native American medicine wheel**.

SACRED SITES. Marking out particular places—from a small cave containing **rock art** to an entire landscape—as being special in some way is a consistent aspect of shamanisms. Small-scale sites such as watering holes, rivers, waterfalls, individual trees, and hills may be identified as places of metaphysical or **otherworldly** potency, the location of important **spirits**, or the site of a major spiritual event. These sacred sites may not be substantially different, to the Western eye, from any other natural location; in some cases, a small shrine may mark out such a place as significant or a building or monument may clearly demark its importance. Most obviously, **Aboriginal Australian** narratives of creation processes ("the **Dreaming**") refer to the making of the landscape by the formative acts of creative beings **ancestral** to all life, and every feature of the landscape is related to traditional knowledge and practices.

Such understandings of sacred landscapes persist in other indigenous traditions. **Paul Devereux** has argued that "ley lines" in Great Britain and elsewhere in the world are not lines of energy or the spiritual "arteries of the Earth" but are instead the routes by which shamans undertake out-of-body **journeys**. Fellow earth mysteries scholar **Alby Stone** has countered some of Devereux's claims, but the hypothesis holds sway among researchers of ley lines. Devereux's Dragon Project of the 1970s scientifically investigated a number of anomalous phenomena at sacred sites, and the recent Dreaming Project, involving a collaboration between Devereux and **Stanley Krippner**, has analyzed people's **dreams** at sacred sites. Michael Dames, discussing the megalithic landscape of Avebury in southern England, has emphasized the sacredness of specific places as marked out in the burial mounds, stone circles, and other monuments constructed in prehistory.

Contemporary **Pagans** and **neo-shamans** have drawn on this and other discourse, such as punk musician Julian Cope's "New Antiquarian" approach, for their own engagements with sacred sites, including the megalithic complexes of Avebury and Stonehenge. The current Sacred Sites, Contested Rights/Rites Project, codirected by **Jenny Blain** and **Robert Wallis**, has been theorizing the meaning of the "sacred" site and examining Pagan engagements with these places in Great Britain. In the United States, "vortex sites" and other places of power, such as Sedona in Arizona, the **Medicine Wheel** in Wyoming, and ancient Pueblo remains in Chaco Canyon in New Mexico, have become pilgrimage sites for **New Agers** (see work by Adrian Ivakhiv and Wallis). A recent scholarly survey of research on sacred sites (mainly in Britain), *Sacred Places: Prehistory and Popular Imagination* (2005), was written by Bob Trubshaw.

SACRED TRUST, THE. "A United Kingdom–based educational organization concerned with the teaching of practical shamanism for modern **women** and men," founded and directed by **Simon Buxton** and headquartered in Penzance in Cornwall. The Sacred Trust began offering workshops and resources (primarily books, **drums**, sage, and so on) in the 1990s and has become the most prominent organization for **neo-shamans** in Great Britain. Buxton is the British faculty for the United States–based **Foundation for Shamanic Studies**, and he offers a program including **core shamanism** workshops. Buxton's practice of "bee shamanism" is outlined in his book *The Shamanic Way of the Bee*, in which he claims to have undergone a 13-year apprenticeship with a "European Bee Master" in the shamanic bee tradition. Buxton teaches a workshop entitled "The Serpent Flight of the Honey Bee: Shamanic **Sexuality** and Sexual Energy" through the auspices of the Sacred Trust. The historical authenticity of this bee shamanism tradition, as with many neo-shamanic practices, cannot be verified, but it marks another example of the vibrant inventiveness of neo-shamanists in the early 21st century.

SAGA OF ERIK THE RED. *See* SEIDR.

SAKHA. *Sakha* may refer to peoples known as the Sakha (formerly Yakut) living in the Sakha region (Yakutia) in northeast **Siberia**; the Sakha language, which belongs to the Turkic family of languages; or the Sakha Republic, the largest independent republic of the Russian Federation, home to more than 80 ethnicities, including such tribes as the hunting, fishing, and herding Sakha, Chukchi, **Evenk** (Tungus), and Tatar, of which some 40 percent of the population is Sakha. Extensive fieldwork in the region began in the mid-19th century, documenting shamanism among the Chukchi, Evenk, and the Sakha, with important reports of Sakha shamanic **performances** involving dialogue between shaman and **spirits** by Ivan Khudiakov. There is much local variation, but consistently, Sakha shamans inherit their vocation from **ancestors** who **elect** shamans, and these shamans undergo an **initiation** involving **illness** and "death." Initiated shamans inhabit a three-**tiered cosmos** in which they travel in **altered states of consciousness** in order to negotiate with **other-than-human helpers** in the **upper world** and **underworld** for the benefit of their communities. The Sakha (and comparably the **Buryat**) distinguish between "**black shamans**" and "**white shamans**," although **Caroline Humphrey** has drawn attention to the problematics of these terms. More recently, **Piers Vitebsky** has discussed the relationship between shamanism and **environmentalism** among the Sakha and the transformation of this relationship in the "global village." Despite widespread persecution under Soviet state atheism, shamanism is today undergoing a reconstitution and revival in the region, with the Sakha Republic seizing on shaman genealogies and other elements of traditional shamanism as part of its emergent nationalism. *See also* CENTRAL ASIAN AND SIBERIAN ROCK ART; SIBERIA, NORTHERN AND EASTERN.

SALADIN D'ANGLURE, BERNARD (1936–). French-born professor of anthropology at the Université Laval in Canada. Since 1956, Saladin d'Anglure has been particularly interested in the traditional and contemporary lives of the peoples of the **Arctic** of **North America**. A fluent speaker of Inuktitut (the language of the **Inuit**), he pioneered dialogical methods in the 1970s, involving Inuit in his research and handing them the data gathered among them (e.g., land use maps, genealogies). Saladin d'Anglure founded Études Inuit and has organized significant international conferences concerned with Arctic issues. In an article entitled "Rethinking Inuit Shamanism through the Concept of 'Third **Gender**'" (1990), he presents a "three-dimensional holistic model" that demonstrates the integration of "kinship, social organization, economics and technology, mythology and worldview, the system of dictates/prohibitions, and **rituals** and shamanism." Shamans are able to **mediate** between other persons (humans or **other-than-human persons**) because they are, in one way or another, "in between" people. While much of Inuit culture is divided in a binary manner (men and **women** have distinct roles, winter tools and summer tools are distinct, and sea and land mammals are distinguished), and while these distinctions are maintained by **taboos**, it is only the **mediating** role provided in a ternary model that makes sense of the culture's dynamics.

SAMUEL, GEOFFREY. Australian professor of **Tibetan** religions, now at Cardiff University in Wales. In addition to important ethnographic discussion of Tibetan shamanism and Tantric **Buddhism**, Samuel has also proposed a "multimodal framework" for approaching and theorizing about indigenous and other knowledges and practices. Rather than seeing rational thought as being opposed to symbolic thought, Samuel proposes that people (as totalities rather than conflicting minds and bodies) live within frameworks that are multiply and variously interconnected and multicentered, like a plant's underground rhizome. Only theoretical approaches that attend to the currents and vortices that swirl around us, move us, and shape us have any hope of leading to a full and rich understanding of particular cultures and societies, worldviews, and lifeways.

SAN. Also known as Bushmen (both terms are problematic). The San are the descendents of the original indigenous inhabitants of **Southern Africa**. Currently, San communities are focused in the Kalahari Desert, but there are people of San origin across the south of **Africa**. The San originally lived as **hunter-gatherers** in a relatively egalitarian society, but this way of life has adapted in regions where Bantu farming predominates, and they have been consistently persecuted, from the European colonizers who perceived the San as childlike if not actually **animals** to the present-day forcible relocation of San communities to make way for transnational diamond mining.

San religion is associated with shamanism primarily due to the nature of the **trance** or **healing** dance that is central to San community life, takes place on a regular, sometimes nightly, basis, and may last for many hours. Members of the community gather around a fire, with mainly **women** seated as they sing and clap out a monotonous **rhythm**. The dancers may be men or women (although they are mainly men) who shuffle and dance in a wider circle around the fire in the desert sand. The effect of the rhythmic singing and clapping, and the dancing which induces **hyperventilation**, contextualized by cultural expectation and interpretation, is to induce a trance or **altered**

state of consciousness. San healers describe how a supernatural potency termed *n|om* boils painfully at the base of the spine and shoots up to the head, resulting in *!kia*, a trance state. In *!kia*, healers collapse to the ground apparently unconscious, while others rally around to rub the limbs of the shaman and thereby rouse him. While "unconscious," shamans **transform** into and communicate with animal **helpers** such as the giraffe and eland, may experience out-of-body travel in the form of birds, control game animals and the rain, or **combat** rival shamans. Jan Platvoet (2001) discusses shamans' responsibility for "chasing off" God and the **ancestors** who made the world a difficult place, that is, one that contains **illnesses** that require the difficult work of healing. San shamans in *!kia* sweat profusely and may experience nasal hemorrhaging due to the intensity of the experience, and these two substances are used in healing.

The exquisite **rock art** produced by the ancestors of today's San depicts various aspects of their shamanic **cosmology** and **performance**, such as **entoptics** and elands. **Thomas Dowson** also discusses the depiction of the shamans' ability to bring rain, which is an important and valued part of San relations with surrounding Bantu pastoralists and agriculturalists.

SAN PEDRO. A cactus (*Trichocereus pachanoi*) indigenous to the northern Andes in **South America**, valued by indigenous **doctors**, *curanderos*, for inducing **vomiting** and **visions**. It is a common source of mescaline, which may account for its long popularity with "hallucinogen **tourists**" from **North America**.

SANTA CLAUS. Also known as Father Christmas, St. Nicholas, or Saint Nick. A popular myth asserts that Santa Claus was originally a shaman among **reindeer** herders and ate fly agaric **mushrooms** (red-and-white spotted fungi that are somewhat hallucinogenic after careful treatment) to enable him to **journey**. **Andy Letcher** has traced the recent origins of this story and demonstrated that it arose no later than the screening of *Miracle on 34th Street* (1947) in which Santa Claus wore the red and white colors of the Coca-Cola brand rather than those of the mushroom.

SANTERÍA. A ceremonial and **trance** or **possession** complex that evolved from the interaction of **African**- and European-derived religious traditions in Cuba. It is sometimes called Lucumí after one of the names applied to African slaves largely but not entirely of Yoruba origin. Since spreading to **North America** with Cuban exiles after the revolution in 1959, Santería has become popular more widely. Its main ceremonies express devotion to deities, the *Orichas*, also known as *Santos*. This blending of Yoruba and popular Spanish terminology reflects the pervasive linking of elements drawn from many originally discrete ethnic and religious backgrounds. Traditionally, ceremonies are open only to appropriately **initiated** persons, and a hierarchical series of initiations permits increasing access to rites that engage with more members of the divine pantheon. **Priestly** leaders not only make offerings but also practice **divination** for clients, seeking knowledge to solve problems and **heal illnesses**. *See also* CARIBBEAN.

SANTO DAIME. A movement that began in Brazil and spread in various organizations to many other countries during the 1990s. Creatively fusing indigenous **Amazonian**, **African** (especially **Umbanda**), **Christian**, Spiritism (especially **Kardecism**), and other inspirations, it makes use of the **vision**- and **vomit**-inducing **help** of **ayahuasca** and similar plants (understood to be shamanic **other-than-human persons** themselves) to **combat** such **illnesses** as alcoholism, cancer, and hepatitis. Like **William Burroughs**, *Daimistas* (practitioners) also value the help of ayahuasca in combating drug addictions and mental disturbances.

SAR. A "**possession** cult" discussed by **Ioan Lewis** that particularly attracts **women** in East **Africa**, giving them a religious role unavailable in locally dominant forms of **Islam**.

SCANDINAVIAN CENTER FOR SHAMANIC STUDIES. Neo-shamanic organization founded in 1986 by **Jonathan Horwitz**. With **Annette Høst**, Horwitz teaches **core shamanism** and other neo-shamanic practices, including ***seidr***.

SCHAEFER, STACY B. Cultural anthropologist specializing in **Mesoamerica**, focusing on **Huichol** (*Wixáritari*) shamanism, **art**, and weaving (and the interface of these). Schaefer's doctoral research examined backstrap loom weaving and the role of **women** in Huichol culture, for which she undertook a five-year apprenticeship to become a master weaver. As well as studying Huichol dyes and dying, she is building an archive of Huichol designs, many of which are derived from the shamanistic **trances** induced by the *mara'akate*'s ingestion of **peyote**. Schaefer's volume exploring these issues is entitled *To Think with a Good Heart: Wixarika Women, Weavers, and Shamans* (2002), and she is also coeditor with **Peter Furst** of *People of the Peyote: Huichol Indian History, Religion and Survival* (1996). Schaefer is director of the Museum of Anthropology and assistant professor of anthropology at California State University, Chico.

SCHIZOPHRENIA. *See* MENTAL HEALTH.

SCHULTES, RICHARD EVANS (1915–2001). The founder of ethnobotany as a scientific discipline. Much of Schultes's work was devoted to the discovery of the active ingredients in plants used by shamans. He was initially interested in **Amazonia** as part of a quest for sources of rubber plants independent of the Southeast Asian (and at that point in World War II, Japanese-occupied) industry. However, his work before and after that frequently engaged with ethnobotany, especially the cultural uses of plants and substances that aided **healing**. Although many have focused on his work about substances that inspire **visions** or **altered states of consciousness**, Schultes's contribution to medical pharmacology is perhaps more significant both for understanding indigenous **doctoring** and for modern health care. His research about **Mazatec** use of **mushrooms**, for example, has resulted in the development of a heart drug. In addition to his own publications, two of his students have written books about or inspired by Schultes: Wade Davis's *One River* (1996) and Mark Plotkin's *Tales of a Shaman's Apprentice* (1994).

SECRECY. Initiation as a shaman often entails the learning of knowledge, practices, and skills that are unknown to other people and are not meant to be revealed to anyone but another shaman. Some of these "secrets" are in fact known to everyone; for instance, the fact that a mask that is experienced and treated as a powerful **other-than-human person** is carried or worn in **rituals** by a known relative may be common knowledge but is treated as less significant than the presence and **performance** of that visiting person. **Paul**

Johnson calls this "secretism," the privileging of the idea of secrets and their known possession by particular, honored individuals or groups; he traces its importance in **possession** traditions in the **Caribbean** in particular. In many places, shamans may be feared because they might know secrets that might endanger uninitiated people or be used to threaten others with **illness**. This is one of the reasons for the suspicion that shamans might be **sorcerers**. Shamans' abilities to find hidden knowledge may be drawn upon when people suspect someone in their community or a neighboring group is causing illness or bad luck. Less threateningly, shamans may tell clients or **patients** things, or give them tasks to perform, that must remain secret in order to be efficacious. Similarly, secrets may be held in common between shamans and their **otherworld helpers**, especially those with whom they form **sexual** and/or marital relationships. Revelation of such secrets may lead to the withdrawal of a shaman's helper and, thus, efficiency.

SECUNDA, BRANT. Founder of the **Dance of the Deer Center for Shamanic Studies** and apprentice to the **Huichol** shaman Don José Matsuwa. Secunda promotes Huichol shamanism in seminars, **vision quests**, and pilgrimages worldwide, with all profits allegedly going to the Huichol themselves. However, scholars including Jay Fikes have drawn attention to the negative impact of this spiritual **tourism**, including the disruption of Huichol communities by **New Age** consumers and the misrepresentation of Huichol "shamanism" (its character dependent on the ethnographer at issue) such as Secunda's inappropriate use of the term *vision quest*.

SEDNA. Inuit otherworld, underwater Mistress of Animals. Part of the job of Inuit shamans, *angakkut* (*See ANGAKKOQ*), is to **mediate** between their communities and Sedna, especially to deal with breaches of **taboos** that have caused Sedna to withhold sea **animals** from **hunters**. Although Sedna is now a well-known name (popularized beyond the **Arctic** by ethnographer **Franz Boas**), other names or titles are also used, and these strongly suggest that "Sedna" is not a proper name but an oblique reference to an **other-than-human person** who can be dangerous to name or encounter. She is also named *Takannaaluk arnaaluk*, "the terrible woman down there," and *Sanna* or *Kanna*, "the one down there." *See also* MASTER OR MISTRESS OF ANIMALS.

SEIDR. An Old Norse term (also spelled *seid* or *sejd*) in the Icelandic myths and sagas conventionally translated as "**sorcery**," "**witchcraft**," or "magic," but more recently interpreted less pejoratively by scholars and **neo-shamans** (e.g., **Jenny Blain**, **Thomas DuBois**, **Annette Høst**, **Diana Paxson**, **Neil Price**, **Robert Wallis**) as a shamanistic practice. In ancient **Heathenry**, the workers of seidr were known variously as *völva* (wand- or staff-bearer), *spakona/spamadr* (seeress/seer), or *seidkona/seidmadr* ("worker of seidr," that is, a seer or shaman). Examples of seidr practitioners are found in the sagas of Kormak, Erik the Red, Vatansdaela, Grettis, Volsunga, Eyrbyggja, Gull-Thoris, Viga-Glum, Heidarviga, and Harald, among others. Snorri Sturluson (1179–1241) records that **Odin** "ruled and practiced the art which is the most powerful of all and is called *seidr*" (Ynglinga saga 7), but we also know that Odin learned this "**women**'s magic" from **Freyja**, for which he is accused of being *ergi* (unmanly).

The most detailed description of a seidr séance is in the 13th-century Saga of Erik the Red, according to which a seeress performed a séance for a **Greenlandic** community suffering a famine during the 10th century. Many features of the tale may be interpreted shamanistically. The völva eats a strange porridge before the **ritual** containing the hearts of various creatures. She wears obscure items, perhaps associated with her **other-than-human** or **spirit helpers**: a black lambskin hood lined with cat fur, cat-skin gloves, and a pouch at her waist probably containing shamanic power objects. She holds a long staff—topped with a brass knob, studded with stones—which may symbolize the world tree Yggdrasill itself. And, she sits on a ritual "high seat" with a cushion of hen feathers beneath her. The verses that enable the spirits to be present are then sung or chanted by the young woman Gudrid, and in communication with that realm, the völva prophesies a better future and answers questions posed to her by each member of the community.

The increasingly popular practice of "oracular seidr" among contemporary Heathens is based primarily around the description in the Saga of Erik the Red, but practices vary. The seidr developed by Paxson's Hrafnar group in California is based around this saga, with a **journey** to the realm of the dead, Hel, as a contemporary innovation based on ancient sources. **Runic John** in England and **Jan Fries** in Germany regard *seidr* as a loose term for shamanistic practice. Blain in Great Britain, on the other hand, has taken Hrafnar-style oracular seidr in an **animistic** direction. In Scandinavia, Høst began learning seidr with the group Yggdrasil, but has taken this in her own direction with an emphasis on the use of *galdr* (magical songs), the staff (which gives the seeress her name, *völva*), and journey to the **other world** of spirits.

SENSORY DEPRIVATION AND STIMULATION. *See* DEPRIVATION AND OVERSTIMULATION.

SEVEN ARROWS. Chief of the Little People (a group of **other-than-human persons** who live inside mountains). Seven Arrows acted as the "**medicine father**" who **elected**, **initiated**, and aided several generations of **Crow** and Shoshone **Native Americans**, including **John Truhujo**, **Thomas Yellowtail**, and **John Pretty on Top**. He is also credited as preserving the Shoshone-Crow Sun Dance during the period when its **performance** was banned (c. 1875–1941) among Native American nations, and then reintroducing it via Truhujo and his successors. It was also his instruction that led to the removal of self-piercing from the Sun Dance in its revived form among the Crow and Shoshone. Yellowtail's biography (as told to and written by Michael Oren) includes an account of Truhujo's **visionary journey** into the **other world**, here located within the mountain, and his adoption and education by Seven Arrows. It also contains a note that Seven Arrows directed Yellowtail's choice of a successor. Yellowtail says of Seven Arrows and his people, "They represent, and pass on, the power of God, the Maker of All Things, and this is something we should not say more about."

SEVERI, BRUNO (1946–). Vice president and scientific coordinator of the Centro Studi Parapsicologici (Center for Parapsychological Studies) of Bologna, Italy, and member of the Faculty of Medicine at the University of Bologna. In addition to research interests in the relationship between **parapsychology** and quantum mechanics, Severi is interested in shamanic and **altered states of consciousness**.

SEVERI, CARLO. Director of research at the Centre National de la Recherche Scientifique (CNRS) social anthropology workshop in Paris. Severi has studied **Native American** shamanistic traditions and dressing rites in **Oceania**. The subtitle of one of his publications serves as an umbrella unifying the diversity of his interests: "A Cognitive Approach to Cultural Complexity." He is particularly interested in the transmission of cultural and ritual knowledge and has done research among the Kuna in Panama and then more widely. He discusses various ways in which shamanic indigenous traditions have engaged with **Christianity**, sometimes opposing Christian proselytism but sometimes adopting Christianity's rhetorics and/or **rituals** to enhance and preserve indigenous knowledge and practices. Severi contests the notion that these are "syncretistic" or inauthentic movements and presents evidence that contributes to understanding the **political** roles played by shamans, especially when confronted by colonialism. In the same article, he argues that however important indigenous terms translated by "**soul**" might be, they are almost always fluid and open to a wide semantic range and diverse uses. They may not be precise scientific terms but they permit a range of communication about important topics not only to do with **healing** but also with being a respectful and mature person.

SEXUALITY. Despite significant interest in the **gender** of shamans, the importance of sexuality in shamanic being and **performance** is commonly overlooked or diminished. In those cultures where shamanic **initiation** and roles involve marital relationships with **otherworld** persons or **spirits**, sexuality is often explicitly involved. References to the gendered nature of a shaman's **drum** and stick are not always only poetic metaphors, especially since they might be (animate) **other-than-human persons** in their own right, and, in ceremonies, engage sexually. In her discussion of shamanizing among the **Siberian Evenk** and **Buryat** peoples, **Roberte Hamayon** argues not only that shamanic séances are "sexual encounters," but also that sexuality between shamans and their otherworld partners is more important than the **journeying** that has gained more attention in both scholarly and **neo-shamanic** contexts. **Nurit Bird-David**'s demonstration that hunting among the **Native American** Cree and among Siberian peoples is frequently spoken of sexually (including "courtship, seduction/abduction, consummation and procreation/reproduction") is especially significant in the light of **Carlos Fausto**'s insistence that shamans and hunters are inseparably linked in **Amazonian** cultures. Thus, the blatant sexuality of many shamanic performances is neither "mere entertainment" (although it does frequently entertain the community) nor marginal to the main purposes or activities of shamans. **Ioan Lewis** concludes an important discussion of "shamans and sex" by saying:

> the shaman [in Siberia and elsewhere] is literally empowered by his marriage to a female **nature** spirit and his erotic, shamanic ecstasy dramatizes this relationship. In **women**'s **possession** cults elsewhere . . . devotees are regularly considered to be "brides" of the spirit—with whom, in their turn, they make love.

An example from **Malaysia** in which a woman claimed to have had a child by her spirit husband demonstrates that such relationships might not be positively valued: the woman was fined by an **Islamic** court for committing adultery. A complete contrast is offered by the initiation accounts of Haitians, who are expected to marry their possessing spirits.

SHALLCRASS, PHILIP "GREYWOLF." British **Druid** and former joint-chief of the British Druid Order. Shallcrass is discussed by **Robert Wallis** as a **neo-shaman** engaging with ancient historic and archaeological sources, which may hint at ancient British shamanisms, in order to reconstruct and inspire contemporary shamanic Druidry. Shallcrass describes how wolf **spirit helpers** and other **other-than-human persons** guide his practice, but while he has worked with **Native Americans**, he was prompted by them to explore the shamanic heritage of Great Britain. The descriptions of **Awenyddion** by Gerald of Wales mark one example of an ancient practice which Shallcrass argues may be shamanic and may, like ***seidr*** for **Heathens**, be reconstructed for contemporary practitioners.

SHAM. Neo-shamanism is often alleged to be a false shamanism, a pretense or self-delusion based on the wish by colonialists to acquire the metaphorical gold of indigenous spirituality. Early travelers and anthropologists were equally persuaded that **Siberian** shamans, **Native American medicine people**, and similar people elsewhere were tricking their communities into believing they had exceptional powers. Allegations that such people were "merely jugglers, sleight-of-hand **tricksters** and ventriloquists" miss the point that indigenous communities, too, were perfectly able to identify these kinds of tricks. In **Gerald Vizenor**'s rendition of 19th-century **Ojibwe** accounts (*Summer in the Spring*), the term *tchissakiwinini* is glossed as "jugglers" and "masters of ventriloquism." The narrator, however, says that "at a given signal all would join in" a **chant**, and a powerful **other-than-human person** "had arrived and was ready to listen to and answer any inquiries they had to make." Similar descriptions of deliberate and open shamming are common elsewhere and can be interpreted as a blend of communal entertainment, preparation, and focusing. Like masks and **costumes**, shamming also served to help the community pay less attention to the presence of the shaman and more to the activities of shamanizing. Unfortunately, much of the shamming of shamanism appears to have been abandoned (shammed, perhaps) under the influence of modernist colonization. However, the mockery of shamans in Soviet pedagogical satires, and the pseudo-shamanic rituals-as-theater in the cultural revitalization movements in post-Soviet republics, can be perceived as genuine moments of shamanic performance that restore the traditional sham to shamanizing.

SHAMANIC CIRCLES. A nonprofit **neo-shamanic** organization initially founded by a group in the United States to support and foster community, with council members worldwide "as far apart as Japan, Ireland and Israel." Its website (http://shamaniccircles.org) hosts the journal *Spirit Talk: A Core Shamanic Newsletter*, provides a list of **drumming** circles worldwide, and organizes community gatherings and workshops.

SHAMANIC STATE OF CONSCIOUSNESS. Michael Harner's preferred term for the **altered state of consciousness** induced by shamans, to distinguish shamanic activity (control over the experience, **journeying** to nonordinary reality, engaging with **animal helpers**) from other altered states such as those induced by drugs, in **mediums**, and through **spirit possession** that, for Harner, lack control and remove important safety barriers. The concept derives in part from **Sergei Shirokogoroff**'s assertion that the shaman is a "**master of spirits**" and hence is in control of the experience. For the teachers of **core shamanism**, the experience can thus be presented as safe for beginners and readily distinguishable from illegal and dangerous drug use. The term is peculiar to core shamanism, since studies on altered consciousness indicate that such states are fluid so that it is difficult to pin down precise shamanic, mediumistic, possession, and other states. Furthermore, the shaman's vocation may be dangerous rather than safe (especially in **Amazonia**, where **sorcery** and **dark shamanism** are prevalent) and shamans may indeed "lose control," become possessed, or go mad. Also, these putative states of consciousness are culturally determined **performative** actions that require cultural knowledge to be effective, recognizable, and meaningful.

SHAMANISTIC APPROACH (TO ROCK ART). *See* DOWSON, THOMAS; ROCK ART; SOUTHERN AFRICA.

SHAMAN'S DRUM. A "journal of experiential shamanism" published by the Cross-Cultural Shamanism Network, a not-for-profit educational organization. The magazine seeks to encourage the study of shamanism from a practical perspective, offering ethnographic papers on contemporary shamanic and **neo-shamanic** practice and experiential anthropology, as well as a forum for debate on the interface between **indigenous** and Western cultures and related issues. Interpretation is predominantly in the vein of transpersonal psychology, insider anthropology, and **entheogenic** performance, and it tends to take a generalist approach to shamanism as "truly a universal human phenomenon, or complex of phenomena, that ultimately transcends culture or tradition"—suggesting that an **Eliadean** and/or **Harnerist** discourse influences the magazine.

SHAMEN, THE. British psychedelic-influenced electronic music group popular with dance/rave culture in Great Britain during the early to mid-1990s. The album *Boss Drum* released in 1992 featured a spoken-word collaboration with **Terence McKenna** entitled "Re:Evolution." The controversial hit "Ebenezer Goode" had clear drug references, particularly to the drug MDMA or ecstasy in the lyric derived from the title "E's Are Good" ("E" referring to ecstasy).

SHAME-ON. A term of ridicule used to refer to **neo-shamans**, especially by **Native Americans** opposed to the movement.

SHANON, BENNY (1948–). Professor of psychology at the Hebrew University of Jerusalem, specializing in the study of human consciousness, cognitive processes, and the philosophy of psychology. Shanon's particular interests in the phenomenology of consciousness have led him to research the **Amazonian** psychoactive brew **ayahuasca** and the special **altered state of consciousness** it induces. His writing carefully documents and reflects on his own experiences and those of many other people following the ingestion of ayahuasca. The main aim of his research is a systematic charting of the phenomenology of the ayahuasca experience to characterize it from a cognitive psychological perspective. Philosophical ramifications are discussed as well. Shanon does not espouse common accounts of the effects of ayahuasca in terms of paranormal abilities and instead characterizes these effects as manifestations of unusual enhancement of cognitive functioning, creativity, and intuition. Empirically, his investigation highlights the significant interpersonal commonalities exhibited by the contents and themes of ayahuasca **visions**, as well as the ideations associated with them.

SHAPE-SHIFTING. While the ability to change shape or take on the appearance of an **animal**, plant, or other being seems to many Westerners to be one of the most outlandish claims made by or on behalf of shamans, it may seem entirely ordinary in other cultures. Indeed, Western discourses that interpret shape-shifting as "a change of appearance" may be entirely misunderstanding a point that is basic in some **animist** cultures. In traditional **Ojibwe** understandings, for example, **transformation** and malleability are definitive of personhood: to be a person (human or **other-than-human**) is to be able to transform oneself. While shamans may learn to change into bears (as in the **Midewiwin**), the ability to transform is available to all persons willing to learn and utilize the power offered by significant other-than-human persons.

More radically, as **Eduardo Viveiros de Castro** demonstrates, it is a fundamental premise of **Amazonian** knowledge that all living persons are cultural and look, to themselves and to shamans, the same as humans look to themselves (and to other-than-human shamans). The shapes perceived by members of another species are deceptive and mask the real personhood (and even humanness) of all beings. The remarkable power that Amazonian shamans seek, then, is not shape-shifting so much as **perspective**-shifting. Seeing as, for instance, a **jaguar** sees enables a shaman to do what shamans need to do. That they may also "be jaguars" or other **predators** is a significant part both of the **ambiguity** of shamans and of the fear that shamans may be **sorcerers**. The prevalence of shape-shifting in many cultures' mythologies has been taken to be a possible indicator of shamanism.

SHARON, DOUGLAS. Following Sharon's now-classic anthropological study *Wizard of the Four Winds* (1978), which brought the Peruvian shaman **Eduardo Calderon** to public attention, Calderon was commercialized by **neo-shaman** and psychologist **Alberto Villoldo** who conducts spiritual **tours** for neo-shamans to meet and practice with the shaman. Donald Joralemon, who has since collaborated with Sharon, considers how Calderon's involvement with neo-shamans brings his reliability as an "authentic" ethnographic informant into question, perhaps even jeopardizing the credibility of Sharon's research. Equally alarming for Joralemon is how Calderon responds to the neo-shamans' requirements by substantially altering his "traditional" practice for them. Calderon thus becomes both a shaman, practicing local Peruvian **healing**, and a neo-shaman, blending **New Age** terminology with local beliefs. At the same time, Joralemon is impressed with the way Calderon shifts between local Peruvian and neo-shamanic modes of understanding **illness** and the supernatural. Adapting to new social and cultural circumstances is indeed what Calderon and countless other shamans have been doing with their "traditions" for generations, and in Peru, where shamans are increasingly urbanized and must engage with **Christianity**, cultural facets blend and new forms of **helper-spirits** include Christian saints.

SHINTO. Japanese religion with a complex history of engagement with **Buddhism**, folk practice, and imperial and international **politics**. Irit Averbuch identifies as shamanic a dance, accompanied by **drums**, cymbals, flutes, and songs, that induces a **trance** and invites *kami*, powerful **other-than-human persons** (perhaps "mysteries"), to **possess** the increasingly frenzied dancer. Stuart Picken suggests that such *Kagura*, ceremonial dances, might be best understood as *chinkon*, ceremonial pacifications of vengeful **spirits**. He also provides two other aspects of Shinto practices that might be considered shamanic: *miko*, entranced female **mediums** through whom kami elect to speak, and *shugenja*, ascetic **purification** in *Shugendo*. Picken also notes that there is speculation that the first empresses were shamans.

SHIROKOGOROFF, SERGEI MIKHAILOVICH (1887–1939). Russian ethnographer whose expertise in psychiatry and extensive field observations of the **Evenk** (Tungus) in the 1930s, including performing the role of shaman's assistant on a number of occasions, led him to challenge the view that shamans were neurotics. He preferred to focus on the **ecstatic** experiences of shamans and their abilities as **masters of spirits** to control as allies the **other-than-human persons** they encountered. In his classic work *Psychomental Complex of the Tungus* (1935), Shirokogoroff discusses the Evenk tribes from whom the term *shaman* derives, and it is from this more focused starting point that such scholars as **Mircea Eliade** picked up, generalized, and popularized the term.

SHUAR. Indigenous people of Ecuadorian **Amazonia**, also known as Jivaro. **Michael Harner** began his anthropological fieldwork among the Shuar in 1956 but focused on their shamanism only after taking **ayahuasca** (***yagé***) with the Peruvian **Conibo** in 1961. Considerable interest has been shown in Shuar uses of ayahuasca, almost to the exclusion of any other issue. Philippe Descola's *Spears of Twilight* (1998) provides a rich account of their shamanic knowledge and practice, along with a discussion of many other elements of their society and culture. He demonstrates that their **cosmology** does not impose absolute coherence on the world but entails **ambiguity** and paradox within which shamans are necessary.

SHULGIN, ALEXANDER (SASHA) (1925–). Pharmacologist and chemist known for his work on **entheogens** and especially as a pioneer of psychedelic research, including the synthesis of new hallucinogenic chemicals. At the University of San Francisco, Shulgin completed postdoctoral work in psychiatry and pharmacology, during which time he experimented with **mescaline**. Shulgin went on to work as research director at BioRad Laboratories as well as a senior research chemist at Dow Chemical Company. He pioneered work on MDMA (ecstasy), and his partner Ann Shulgin used MDMA in psychedelic therapy. In his long and successful career, Shulgin has synthesized and self-tested hundreds of entheogenic chemicals, and his results are published in four books, the most famous of which are *PiHKAL* (1991) and *TiHKAL* (1997), both cowritten with Ann Shulgin. He has also contributed to discourse on the term *entheogen* in the volume *Entheogens and the Future of Religion* (1997) and works as a scientific consultant for such clients as the National Institute on Drug Abuse, the Drug Enforcement Administration, and the National Aeronautics and Space Administration (NASA).

SIBERIA, NORTHERN AND EASTERN. Siberia (a vast landmass stretching from the **Arctic** Ocean in the north to the borders of **Mongolia** and **China** in the south, and eastwards to the Pacific Ocean) is the so-called **locus classicus** of shamanism. The term *shaman* itself derives from the **Evenk** (Tungus) language, carried by explorers in the 18th century to become the German *schamanen* and thence into English. Some of these early accounts characterized shamans through the lens of **Christianity**, such as Nicolas Witsen's well-known illustration (from his *Noord en Oost Tartarye*, 1705) of an Evenk shaman, labeled "Priest of the Devil," with an antler headdress and banging a drum. However, as **Ronald Hutton** points out, the clawed feet of this "priest of the devil" indicate that he is also a demon.

Extensive fieldwork in the region began in the mid-19th century, documenting shamanism across the region, from the Chukchi and Koryak in the north, to the Evenk in the east and the **Sakha** (Yakut) who dwell in the interior of Siberia, one of the coldest places on earth. At the beginning of the 20th century, Waldemar Bogoras published extensively on the Chukchi and Koryak and made detailed accounts of **gender transformations** among Chukchi female and male shamans. **Maria Czaplicka,** who had written several primer books on the diverse peoples of Siberia and **Central Asia**, was one of the first scholars to call shamans "hysterical," which in effect added to the already prevalent criticism of them as being merely charlatans. **Sergei Shirokogoroff** positively characterized shamans as religious specialists who learned to **master spirits**, although it might be more accurate to consider the relationship between shamans and **helpers** (such as **reindeer** among the Chukchi) as reciprocal to varying degrees.

During the Stalinist period of the 1930s, the dissemination of Siberian ethnography became restricted, and Soviet research into shamanism fell into social evolutionary frameworks of Soviet Marxism. The Marxist model characterized shamanism as a condition arising from the inequality of production and the establishment of private property. The Communist Party sent out its own ethnographers who sought out shamans, documented them, and informed on them to be punished. Siberian shamans were banned, imprisoned, or killed under Soviet rule and even today, in post-Soviet times, there are still regions where people will not talk about shamanic knowledge for fear of persecution. Recent scholarship has reclaimed much lost ground, however.

Ioan Lewis points to the consistent occurrence of **possession** in "classic" shamanic **initiatory** and biographical accounts from Siberia. **Marjorie Balzer** and **Bernard Saladin d'Anglure** have both agreed that Siberian shamans are often a **third gender** that **mediates** between human and **other-than-human persons**. Saladin d'Anglure also uses the term *election* to refer to the choosing of their own gender among some Siberian and Arctic peoples. **Roberte Hamayon** goes further, in her discussion of the Evenk and **Buryat**, in arguing that shamanic séances are themselves "**sexual** encounters" and that the "marriage" between shamans and their helpers is more important than the **ecstasy**, mastery of spirits, or **journeying** emphasized by other scholars. The Buryat and Sakha, on the other hand, distinguish between "**black shamans**," who enter **trances** and descend into the **underworld**, and "**white shamans**," who do not enter trances, are more like **priests**, and communicate with the **upper world** (note that there is not a good–bad distinction here). In her work on Siberian shamans, **Caroline Humphrey** assesses the complex **political** relationship between shamans and chiefs and in so doing repositions the shaman as a social being rather than a religious specialist separate from daily life. In parts of post-Soviet Siberia, shamanism is undergoing a reconstitution and revival, with the Sakha in particular seizing this process as part of their emergent nationalism. *See also* SIBERIA, SOUTHERN; SIBERIA, WESTERN.

SIBERIA, SOUTHERN. The **Altai** (Gorno-Altai) in the southwest, **Tuva** in the southeast, and Khakassia to the north are southern Siberian regions consisting of vast steppes and mountains. Altaian peoples are nomadic pastoralists of mixed Turkic-**Mongolian** descent. The Khakass are Turkish-speaking nomadic pastoralists, some of them related to the Kyrgyz who moved to Kyrgyzstan in **Central Asia**. The territories of the Khakass and Altaian peoples were annexed by Russia in the 18th century. Tuvans, to the north of Mongolia, are pastoralists of mixed Turkic-Mongolian descent, and **Chinese** control of Tuva was passed to Russia at the outset of the 20th century. With the advent of Communism, shamanic traditions, like all religions, faced purges, and shamans suffered greatly everywhere across the Soviet Union. Altaic shamanism is famous from the 19th-century accounts of such authors as Wilhelm Radloff and Uno Harva, who describe shamans in **costume** going on voyages to **other worlds**. During the Soviet era, Russian scholars continued to disseminate information, though officially shamanism was considered a dead and archaic practice of a bygone primitive age: for example, L. Potapov extensively published on Altaic shamanism, while Sevyan Vainshtein did the same for Tuvan shamanism.

Shamans today, as well as traditional forms of **music**, are undergoing a major resurgence in Khakassia and Tuva, with shamans practicing openly and **neo-shamanisms** emerging as people draw on the past and renegotiate the role of shamans in society. In the Altai, there is a shamanic revival but there is also a significant revival of Altaic culture and spirituality within the indigenous religious movement called Ak Jang, the "White Faith." *See also* SIBERIA, NORTHERN AND EASTERN; SIBERIA, WESTERN.

SIBERIA, WESTERN. The territory that lies to the east of the Ural Mountains is a vast lowland covered in taiga forest which extends toward the **Arctic** Ocean in the north and, to the east, to the network of rivers in the basin of the Ob, the largest Siberian river. The Khanty (Ostyaks) and Mansi (Voguls) are known as Ob-Ugrian speakers living east of the Urals, and these peoples spread to the great Ob River and its tributaries. Culturally the Khanty and Mansi are closely related, and their languages, together with Hungarian, comprise the Ugrian group of Finno-Ugrian languages, so studies of their shamanism tend to emphasize links to the Suomi (Finns), **Saami** (Lapps), and Hungarian Magyars. To the north of the Khanty and Mansi are the Nenet (Samoyeds) who are a Samoyed-speaking people. All these Western Siberians are hunters and fishers. By the 18th century much of the territory was seized by the encroaching Russians, who sought to control the natural resources of the region beyond the Urals.

The Khanty and Mansi were converted to Orthodox **Christianity**, but much of their indigenous beliefs endured. Two important 19th- and early 20th-century ethnographies about the Ob-Ugrians and Samoyeds were amassed by Alexander Castrén and K. Karjalainen. Khanty, Mansi, and Samoyed shamans wore special hoodlike hats, and they utilized **drums**. Shamanic séances were conducted to recover information from the **spirits** or for **soul retrieval**. Indigenous religious practices, according to **Marjorie Balzer**, involved each **clan** maintaining **sacred sites** in groves within which effigies of **ancestors** and spirits, as well as those of shamans, were placed. Castrén also noted that Khanty shamans spoke to wooden effigies during shamanic ceremonies. Early ethnographers reported that only a shaman was allowed to conduct sacrifices; however, Kustaa Karjalainen demonstrated that this was not always the case. The most famous rite among the Ob-Ugrian peoples was the **bear ceremony**, which has been documented by many investigators and comprises a number of **rituals** involving the sacrifice of a bear that conclude with festivities involving dancing, singing, and satirical dramatic **performances**. More recently, Balzer addressed the significance of **gender** and bear ceremonialism among the Ob-Ugrian peoples. Karjalainen points out that the bear was also an important spirit called upon by Mansi shamans. However, the Ob-Ugrian shamans, and by extension the Finno-Ugrians, are most noted for their ingestion of *Amanita muscaria* or fly agaric **mushrooms**. This practice continues today, as Khanty shamans have been recorded to take *Amanita*, beat their drum, and wait for the **spirit** of the mushroom, *pong*, to arrive. *Pong* acts as the intermediary between the spirits and shaman, transmitting questions and returning answers. *See also* SIBERIA, NORTHERN AND EASTERN; SIBERIA, SOUTHERN.

SIBERIAN AND CENTRAL ASIAN ROCK ART. Within the vast geographical area of **Siberia** and **Central Asia**, among the mountains, hills, and river valleys, there are numerous **rock art** sites. Images argued to be of shamanistic origin and meaning have been engraved and painted onto exposed rock as well as graves. Such images have been used time and again by scholars to illustrate books and articles discussing the prehistory of shamanism in the region—and implicitly to lend visual authenticity to these arguments.

One prominent image consistently referred to is the rock painting of a figure with a **drum** from Sinsk, along the Middle Lena River in the Republic of **Sakha** (Yakutia). This painting was originally documented by Anatoly Okladnikov and V. D. Zaporozhskaya, and their published drawing is used in subsequent books on shamanism, including **Piers Vitebsky**'s *The Shaman* (1995). Another important site dating to the early second millennium BCE (Early Bronze Age) is in the village of Karakol in the **Altai**: archaeological excavations revealed paintings on the stone slabs of graves, consisting of human figures with feathered headdresses and elaborate **costumes**, some with clawlike hands and feet, perhaps referencing shamanic **transformation** and/or costume.

At the Bronze Age engraving site of Mugur-Sargol in **Tuva**, there is a large, complex scene consisting of masklike heads with horns in the upper part of the panel, and human figures and animals below. Ekaterina and Marianna Devlet argue that this panel represents a shamanistic **upper world** dividing the world of **spirits** and **ancestors** from the terrestrial world of humanity. At the site of Tamgaly in Kazakhstan, there is a large mural of six anthropomorphic figures, dating to the later Bronze Age, around 1300 BCE; though traditionally labeled "solar-gods" because of the lines and halos radiating from their enlarged heads, these features are more strongly suggestive of an origin in shamanistic **altered states of consciousness**. Figures with heads radiating lines are found at other sites in Kazakhstan, as well as in Kyrgyzstan and East Turkestan (Xinjiang province, **China**). The antlered deer imagery of the Early Nomadic period in Central Asia, Southern Siberia, and **Mongolia** (800–200 BCE), though often interpreted as "**hunting magic**" or warrior **clan totems** (ethnic markers) or even forms of the "universal goddess," has more recently and coherently been interpreted as shamanistic in origin by Kenneth Lymer, who argues that a number of key scenes from Kazakhstan contain shamanistic elements. Shamanic rock art images have also been produced in recent history; in particular in the Altai region, where there are numerous engravings of humans with distinctive Altaic shamanic drums dating from the 19th century CE. *See also* ART AND ARTIFACTS.

SIIKALA, ANNA-LEENA (1943–). Finnish scholar of the Finnish language and of Eurasian shamanism, especially in Finland, **Siberia**, **Central Asia**, and the **Arctic**. Among her most significant publications is a volume produced with Hungarian scholar **Mihály Hoppál** in which both authors republish their earlier writings concerned with a wide range of issues to do with shamanism. Siikala not only discusses particular ethnographic cases but also considers shamanic songs and **artwork**. In *Suomalainen shamanismi* (1992), Siikala discussed the shaman's **combat** against threats to the village community and its individual members by incantation, magic, and folk **medicine**.

SILVA, RAMÓN MEDINA (193?–1971). Huichol (*Wixáritari*) shaman (*mara'akame*) and **artist** whose narrative yarn paintings depicting **peyote visions** were made famous by anthropologist **Peter Furst**. Furst collaborated with **Barbara Myerhoff**, and both anthropologists worked closely with Silva in their ethnographies of Huichol shamanism. **Carlos Castaneda**'s fictional ethnography of **Don Juan** borrows from Myerhoff's research: the "waterfall jumping" of Don Juan's fellow **sorcerer** Don Genaro replicates Myerhoff's experience of watching Silva perform this feat.

SILVERMAN, JULIAN. *See* MENTAL HEALTH.

SOMÉ, MALIDOMA (1956–). West **African diviner** and "**medicine man**" from Burkina Faso, now living in the United States, whose biographical and how-to books seek to encourage the growth of "**elders** of the new post-modern tribal order" and were initially most influential in the men's movement and among **neo-shamans**. His work with his wife Sobonfu attracted the interest of **women**. Somé is also interested in reestablishing the importance of **ritual** in Western culture. Somé's relationship with the **New Age** (which underpins much neo-shamanism) is complicated by his view that it can be shallow, naive, and overly optimistic. He argues that multicultural gatherings are more important venues for learning precisely because they require recognition of difference and difficulties, especially of the reality of colonial violence.

SORA. An indigenous people of the jungle of Orissa, **India**. **Piers Vitebsky**'s fieldwork-based book, *Dialogues with the Dead* (1993), concerns the **mediatory** role of Sora shamans between the living and their deceased relatives and **ancestors**. He discusses the **gendered** distinction between "great" shamans, mostly **women** and responsible for conducting funerals, and "lesser" shamans, mostly men and responsible for **divination** and **healing**. Funerals and other **rituals** are occasions on which shamans "impersonate ancestors in pantomime" and enter **trances** to allow the dead to speak through them to resolve family and communal issues and tensions. As the dead can also cause **illness**, divination indicates which "dead person is attacking a **patient**," so they can be "fended off with a sacrificial offering" as part of the cure. **Initiation** is the result of the choice by an **elder** shaman of a successor to whom she will pass her powers, but it also requires training, intimate (marital) relationship with **otherworld** persons (especially powerful high-caste **Hindu** spirits such as deceased kings and warriors who have dominated the Sora), and the support of (living human) **helpers**. Among these helpers are other ritualists, who may be called *kuran* just like Sora shamans. Vitebsky also notes, "Christian Soras say that Jesus is more powerful than the **spirits** of their shamans, but that they still believe in the old spirits as these have their own names and all names refer to something."

SORCERY. A term used to refer to the harmful (**combat** or assault) activities associated with some shamans, especially when turned against their own kin or community. While it can be used to distinguish "our shamans" from "enemy sorcerers," the idea of sorcery can also point to the **ambiguity** of shamans in many cultures—people who might be able to either **heal** or cause **illness**. Such allegations and fears are commonplace (e.g., in the **Caribbean** traditions of **Vodou** and **Obeah**), but academics have only recently devoted sustained attention to these issues (most interestingly in relation to **Amazonian "dark shamans"**). Sorcery may even be institutionalized; for example, Johannes Wilbert concludes that the Warao of northeastern Venezuela "separate young shamanic healers from old shamanic sorcerers," noting that these groups formed and performed complementary functions in the confrontation with enemy groups and with the diseases and disruptions of colonialism. For the Warao, both their shamans and sorcerers were good, as opposed to the bad shamans and sorcerers of enemy groups.

SOUL. Many cultures posit the existence of various parts that make up a person (human or **other-than-human**). In addition to possessing arms and noses, or branches and trunks, or fins and gills, as the case may be, particular kinds of person may also possess a soul, or possibly more than one soul. Some writers translate indigenous terms as either *soul(s)* or *spirit(s)*. In some cultures these terms can be equivalent to *psyche*, *consciousness*, or *will*, but they may instead refer to some more mystical aspect that is thought to survive death. The precise location of a soul in relation to other, especially physical, parts of a person varies in different cultural understandings. Since souls are often considered to be detachable aspects of a person, they may be the part that "**journeys**" to **other worlds** to seek knowledge, power, or **help**, or they may be lost. Shamans may **perform** "**soul projection**" to **combat** enemies or to cause **illness** if they are at the **sorcerer** end of the shamanic continuum. When people infringe cultural **taboos**, the resulting "**soul loss**" often requires "**soul retrieval**."

SOUL FLIGHT. *See* JOURNEYING.

SOUL LOSS. Among people who understand that human and **other-than-human persons** may have one or more **souls**, there is a common understanding that all or part of a soul may become detached from the person. **Illnesses** or bad luck may be thought to be caused by damage to a person's soul, perhaps as a result of a breach of a **taboo** or a soul's abduction by **predatory spirits**. In such cases, shamans may be employed for their skill as adepts at **soul projection** (or **journeying**) and thereby capable of **soul retrieval**.

SOUL PROJECTION. Ioan Lewis formulated this term, equivalent to "**journeying**," to describe an aspect of the work of shamans in **combating possession** by powerful **other-than-human persons** or **spirits**.

SOUL RETRIEVAL. In a number of shamanic traditions, **illness** is understood to have supernatural causes, including **soul loss**, the stealing of a **soul** by **spirits**. It is the task of the shaman to undertake the dangerous **journey** to the **other world** (also called "**soul projection**" by **Ioan Lewis**) to retrieve the lost soul, usually with the assistance of spirit **helpers**. The task is usually understood as an arduous and dangerous one, in which the soul of the shaman is also at peril. The shaman persuades, cajoles, forces, or seduces the spirit(s) into returning the soul, which the shaman then recovers—or the shaman's soul itself may be captured, then requiring further soul retrieval work on the part of another shaman, if available. Ideally, with the soul returned to the **patient**, a process of **healing** is initiated.

Soul retrieval has gained currency in **neo-shamanisms**, especially in **core shamanism** and the work of **Sandra Ingerman**, who explains soul retrieval as a process of "mending the fragmented self," wherein various traumas experienced in life, such as sex abuse, can be healed by undertaking the retrieval of that part of the soul lost due to the harrowing event. The process appears, at least rhetorically, to have something in common with psychotherapy, and indeed many core shamanism–trained psychotherapists use it. **Therapists** and neo-shamans have been charged with decontextualizing indigenous concepts of soul loss that involve malevolent spirits and a perilous journey into the spirit world for the shaman, replacing this with a more positive and essentially psychological discourse. Not all core shamanic soul retrieval can be read in this way, and indeed other neo-shamans, particularly those involved in reconstructionist **Paganisms**, take an approach to soul loss that has more in common with indigenous shamanisms. **Chas Clifton** offers an insightful and amusing take on all this in his article "Training Your Soul Retriever." *See also* HEATHENRY; MACLELLAN, GORDON ("THE TOAD"); MATTHEWS, JOHN AND CAITLIN; SEIDR.

SOUTH AMERICA. Many of the most significant developments in the study of shamanism in recent decades have come from those interested in **Amazonia**. Similarly, the influence of South American shamanism on **neo-shamanism** and **Cyberian** shamanism is considerable. While much of the popular interest has been in the use of hallucinogenic, psychotropic, or **vision**-inducing plants, the more fundamental role played by **tobacco** has not received sufficient attention. It is notable, for example, that among the **Araweté**, a non-shaman is called a "noneater of tobacco."

Shamanism in South America is divided, broadly speaking, between Amazonian practices and those of the Andes. Juan Ossio usefully details the major differences. In the Andes, shamans are **healers** hired by clients, and they largely attempt to purify and "raise" (*levantar*) their **patients** by means of instruments displayed on a table. These include elements drawn from indigenous cultures and others associated with **Christianity**, and they are set out in an organizational pattern that replicates the "recurrent Andean representation of order, in which complementary opposites are mediated by a unifying principle." **Trance** is used to identify and expel "evil forces," to aid "**journeying**" toward sources of power, and to facilitate communication with the tabled objects. In Amazonia, by contrast, shamans enforce law and order, especially by **combating sorcery** or **witchcraft** and other assaults on or within communities. Amazonian shamans heal using tobacco and "**sucking** cures." In both areas, shamans may be aided by powerful plants, particularly **ayahuasca** in Amazonia and **San Pedro** in the northern Andes, but further south in the Andes hallucinogens are replaced by coca.

Ossio also notes that these **performative** and ideological differences arise from the nature of their broader cultures. The highly differentiated societies of the northern coast of Peru, with economies and modes of subsistence that generate trade surpluses, have developed hierarchical and bureaucratic **political** systems. "Social control was, and continues to be, a basic responsibility of the state more than that of **ritual** specialists." Amazonian societies are "politically stateless and less differentiated" and "depend basically on shamanism to keep social control." In both areas, shamans are present not only in small villages but also in the cities. This illustrates the ability of shamanism to evolve in relation to broader cultural, political, economic, and epidemiological contexts. For example, **Neil Whitehead** argues that "**dark shamanism**" or **kanaimà** is "an authentic and legitimate form of cultural expression and is mimetically linked to the violence of economic and **political** 'development.'" It is also entangled with experiences of waves of disease that have resulted from European colonization. Shamanic vitality may also be illustrated by the inclusion of outboard motors among the **other-than-human persons** or powers with whom **animist** shamans may now engage. Further, it is significant that shamanic knowledge and practices have influenced the evolution of local forms of Christianity in South America, including the development of groups that use ayahuasca and similar plants sacramentally.

SOUTH AND EAST ASIA. Piers Vitebsky illustrates the wide variety of practices that might be called "shamanism" in this religiously, geographically, ethnically, and **politically** diverse region. He notes that in **Nepal** the term *shamans* can be used to label "people who make **soul journeys** similar to those found in **Siberia** and **Mongolia**, whereas in **Korea** it is used for female **mediums** who control their **trances** but do not make soul journeys." However, even in Nepal there is a distinction between Himalayan peoples, among whom shamans "journey," and the more **Hindu** population of the southern plains, among whom **possessed ecstatics** do not "journey." Vitebsky contributes to discussions of the political relationships of shamans by noting the interaction of **Tibetan Buddhism** and "the shamanistic religion . . . called ***Bon-po***." He also contrasts the historical evidence of shamanic influence among **Chinese** emperors with the marginal and **ambiguous** position of contemporary shamans in Korea (simultaneously alluding to **gender** distinctions). Vitebsky's own fieldwork-based book, *Dialogues with the Dead* (1993), concerns the role of shamans among the **Sora** of Eastern **India**, whose most significant role is as **mediators** between the living and their deceased relatives and **ancestors**. Other shamanic complexes in the region include those among the **Hmong** of Laos; the Mru of Vietnam; the **Chewong**, Batek, and Temiar of **Malaysia**; the Iban of Brunei; the **Wana** and **Dayak** of **Indonesia**; and Taiwanese groups.

SOUTHERN AFRICA. Application of the term *shaman* in this vast region of **Africa** (ranging from desert and semiarid areas to rain forest and temperate zones and comprising the countries of Angola, Zimbabwe, Botswana, Zambia, Malawi, Mozambique, South Africa, and Namibia) is controversial since purist scholars restrict shamanism to the **locus classicus** of **Siberia** and the **Arctic**. Nonetheless, **Ioan Lewis** has convincingly argued that shamanisms exist in Southern Africa and points to examples where **possession** states are integral to practice for some shamans. The most obvious candidate for shamanistic practice in Southern Africa today is found among the **San** (Bushmen) of the Kalahari Desert (of Botswana and Namibia), namely, their **healing** and **trance** dances. Similarly, the exquisite **rock art** produced by their **ancestors** has generated much of the debate about the possible shamanistic interpretation of **rock art**. This art also draws attention to the intercultural relationship between the San and surrounding Bantu peoples, for example, depicting shamans' abilities to bring rain to these pastoralists and agriculturalists, and thus illustrates another dimension of the **political** nature of shamanism. South African **healing** and anti-**witchcraft** movements (e.g., Sangoma) have also been considered shamanic. The Zulu writer **Credo Mutwa** has had considerable influence on **neo-shamans** internationally.

SPACE ALIENS. Parallels are sometimes found between narratives of shamanic **initiation** and those of **alien abduction**. UFOs may also be found in the colorful, **ayahuasca**-inspired **visionary art** of ex-*vegetalista* **Pablo Amaringo**. **Credo Mutwa** has claimed that the Zulu and other **African** peoples and traditions derive from contact with space aliens.

SPARE, AUSTIN OSMAN (1887–1956). Artist and occultist who was born and lived in London. His automatic drawing, esoteric system of "atavistic resurgence," and other **trance**-derived techniques such as the "death posture" have been likened to shamanistic practices. Spare was the youngest exhibitor ever at the Royal Academy in 1904 (with a bookplate drawn at the age of 14), won a scholarship to the Royal College of Art (among other awards), was hailed as an artistic genius by John Singer Sargent and Augustus John, and was an official war artist from 1914 to 1918. As a prolific draftsman throughout his life, he published much of his work in a series of volumes, including *Earth Inferno* (1905), *A Book of Satyrs* (1907), *The Book of Pleasure* (1909–13), and *The Focus of Life* (1921), as well as in the journals *Form* and *The Golden Hind* of which Spare was coeditor. Many of these publications detailed Spare's occult philosophy, and although he was associated for a brief time with fellow occultist **Aleister Crowley** and his Argentum Astrum (Order of the Silver Star), Spare developed his own idiosyncratic system of atavistic resurgence, which incorporated **sexual** excitation and orgasm combined with "will" and "image" in a technique of **ecstasy**. **Spirit** familiars were encountered, and automatic drawings of them made, and the **Native American** spirit "Black Eagle" was a major source of Spare's ecstatic inspiration. Spare's automatic work preceded that of the surrealists by some years, and he developed an artistic technique he termed "siderealism," wherein portraits especially became strangely distorted from naturalistic representation, as if being viewed through an **otherworldly** lens.

Spare claimed that much of his occultism derived from a relationship with the enigmatic "**witch**" Mrs. Patterson. After a period of obscurity and poverty in the 1920s, Spare returned to some prominence with his **visionary** pastel drawings of the 1950s during a wider revival of interest in the occult, around the time Spare became acquainted with the magicians Kenneth and Steffi Grant, who have done much to promote Spare's work since his death. There have been several important posthumous works, including the "Book of Ugly

Ecstasy" (1989), which evince the **altered-state-of-consciousness** derivation of Spare's dark, grotesque imagery. **Chaos Magickians** and other occultists in the 1980s and 1990s associated aspects of Spare's occult practices—particularly his techniques of automatic drawing and sigil magic, the "death posture," and "free belief"—with an acultural "shamanism."

SPIRIT PATHS. *See* DEVEREUX, PAUL; SACRED SITES; STONE, ALBY.

SPIRIT WORLD. *See* OTHER WORLDS; SPIRITS.

SPIRITS. A term that commonly appears in ethnographic and religious discourse but remains of uncertain and/or misleading reference. Not only does it translate a wide range of terms for entirely different and distinct types of **other-than-human persons**, but it also clearly privileges the metaphysical, nonempirical, or "spiritual" nature of significant beings. While particular shamans *may* refer to invisible, nonphysical, **otherworld** beings in ways that encourage translators to use words like "spirit" or "**soul**," in many cases this is not their intention. More often, words rendered as "bear spirit" or "tree spirit" might be better expressed simply as "bear" or "tree" or by collocations such as "bear person" or "tree person." In either case, the point is that it is the particular, physical bear or tree who is addressed, asked for **help**, or offered a gift. Just as it is not usual to speak in similar circumstances of "human spirits," it is often unhelpful to mask the personhood of a being by imputing the existence of spirits where the concept is unwarranted. When shamans do speak of beings that are invisible under normal circumstances, they usually claim the ability to see them. **Napoléon Chagnon**, for instance, writes in considerable detail of the size, beauty, preferences, habits, characters, hungers, and other far-from-nonempirical traits of the *hekura* invited to dwell within **Yanomamo** shamans.

An understanding of the **animism** of shamanic cultures and practitioners along the lines proposed by **Irving Hallowell**, **Nurit Bird-David**, and **David Abram** promises to enrich the understanding of shamanism by making terms like *spirit* redundant in many contexts. Conversely, neurophysiology, psychobiology, and other forms of psychology may ask interesting questions about brain states, chemistries, capabilities, and behaviors, but they focus attention on one aspect of shamanic **performance** and knowledge.

SPIRITUAL BAPTISTS. A movement that originated in Saint Vincent in the **Caribbean** but is now also growing in the United States, especially among Vincentian immigrants. Blending elements of **African** indigenous religions with revivalist Protestant **Christianity**, it has been identified as a **possession** cult, but may more properly be characterized as centered on **purification** and the enabling of alterations of **perspective** or the ability to "see" properly.

STOLLER, PAUL. Anthropologist best known for his studies of the Hauka movements among the Songhay in Niger, West **Africa**. He not only describes shamanic **healing** and **possession** phenomena but also discusses the **political** ramifications of these movements in their confrontation with colonialism. Like **Edith Turner**, he is also significant for his experiential engagement and practice.

STONE, ALBY. In response to **Paul Devereux**'s reinterpretation of "ley lines" as the **spirit** tracks used by shamans on out-of-body **journeys**, Stone wrote *Straight Track, Crooked Road: Leys, Spirit Paths and Shamanism* (1998), offering an alternative, though not mutually exclusive, argument. Stone cites numerous sources that indicate that the path of shamanic extracorporeal travel is as likely, if not more likely, to be crooked as it is straight, and so he does not refute Devereux's claim but does contribute positively to the argument—and Devereux has since responded with more nuanced discussions of shamanic spirit paths. Stone has also written the highly accessible volume *Explore Shamanism* (2003), and while he critically discusses a number of issues and debates—including what a shaman is, **gender** and **sex**, and the shamanistic interpretation of **rock art**—Stone mainly deals with shamanism among Uralic- and **Altaic**-speaking peoples of **Central Asia** and **Siberia** (with a brief excursion into **Northern Europe**); that is, he tends to prefer what might be perceived as the "safe" territory of the **locus classicus**. Stone's dismissal of the role of shamanism in the production and consumption of rock art, focusing as it does on the argument of **David Lewis-Williams**, neglects recent developments in the shamanistic approach offered by **Thomas Dowson** and others—and recent engagements of these scholars with **animism** indicate that the interpretation is gaining renewed analytical strength. Stone goes on to engage with practices at the interface of indigenous and **neo-shamanisms**, problematizing the authenticity of neo-shamans vis-à-vis his understanding of shamans in Central Asia and Siberia.

STORM, HYEMEYOHSTS (WOLF). A significant influence in the **Deer Tribe**, among the first to teach non-**Native American** people about **Medicine Wheel** teachings, and explicitly cited among those targeted by the **Lakota** Declaration of War and by the **American Indian Movement**'s opposition to the activities of "**plastic medicine people**." Storm's response labels its authors "religious hate mongers," encourages a vision of cooperation and harmony, and proposes that all spiritual traditions are systems that promote personal growth. His book *Seven Arrows* (1972) remains popular among **neo-shamans** attracted to "**Native American spirituality**." Responses to it from Native Americans point out that what they object to is not Storm's encouragement of cooperation but his invention of practices that they do not recognize as ever having been traditional.

STUTLEY, MARGARET. In her short volume on shamanism, Stutley states that shamanism is "one of the world's most ancient, notorious and frequently misrepresented spiritual traditions," but *Shamanism: An Introduction* (2003) is problematic in not offering convincing corrections to this imbalance. Instead, the book reifies the modernist principle of identifying similarities across space and time as an "ur-shaman-ism." Claiming that "recent research indicates that shamanism represents the earliest religious experiences of mankind and therefore is important for the understanding of all human culture" (4), Stutley neglects the diversity of shamanisms, not to mention human cultures more generally, in favor of a metanarrative that locates "shamanism" as the single primordial, primitive religion and the **origin of religion**. In the vein of **Mircea Eliade**, this approach tells us very little about shamans in their specific community contexts or about the complexity of engagements between shamans and their communities. Furthermore, there is no discussion of postcolonial shamanism or the dynamic, if controversial, interface between indigenous shamans and **neo-shamans**. Rather than informing us about shamans past and present, this approach epitomizes the positioning of shamanism as "one of the phenomena against which modern western civilization has defined itself" (Hutton 2001, viii).

SUCKING. A common method of **healing illnesses** employed by shamans while **performing** their duties as **doctors**. It is commonly understood that illness results from the **intrusion** of projectiles shot or forced into **patient**'s bodies by **witches**, **sorcerers**, or other **predators** such as animal shamans, **other-than-human persons**, and other aggressors. Healing shamans may first **purify** the patient—for example, in **Amazonia**, they may blow **tobacco** smoke over them—and then suck (with or without the aid of tubes) to remove pathogenic objects, such as **darts**, or "**spirits**" (illnesses understood as other-than-human persons). Sucking has also become part of the repertoire of **neo-shamans**.

SUN BEAR. Among the most well-known **Native American medicine people** who have been willing, indeed eager, to teach non-Native people about their practices and worldview. In response to his condemnation (by the **American Indian Movement**, among others) as inauthentic, especially on the grounds of his charging clients to participate in **sweat lodges** and other ceremonies, Sun Bear argued vociferously that cooperation, sharing, and global harmony were more important than what he saw as parochialism and meanness. His Bear Tribe Medicine Society continues, as does the **Deer Tribe**, in the founding of which he had some influence. Both are largely run by and attractive to non-Native people interested in **neo-shamanism** of a clearly **New Age** kind.

SWEAT LODGES. Many **Native American** nations make use of a **ritual** complex in which people enter a heated confined space in order to seek **purification**. The ceremony itself involves communication with powerful **other-than-human persons** or **helpers**, most centrally the heated rocks onto which water is sprinkled to produce steam. In fact, many Native Americans identify the ritual structures not as "sweat lodges" but as "stone people lodges," clearly aligning themselves with an **animist cosmology**. The combination of sensory **deprivation and overstimulation** (i.e., the darkness and heat) may induce a light **trance**, but the key here is the practice of **altered styles of communication**, or "prayer." Further ceremonies normally follow from the purification achieved in "the sweat," such as **vision quests**. In **New Age** and **neo-shamanic** contexts, sweat lodges may also be considered **initiatory** but more often enable self-knowledge than communication with other-than-humans. While many Native Americans welcome non-Natives into their lodges, they generally see neo-shamanic sweat lodges as an offensive appropriation by "**wannabe Indians**" facilitated by exploitative "**plastic medicine people**."

– T –

TABOO (TABU; TAPU). All cultures distinguish between appropriate and inappropriate behaviors. Rules govern the ways in which people should or should not engage with others and with places, times, objects, and ideas. The word *taboo* derives from **Polynesian** languages and refers to prohibitions that may be either temporary or permanent. Shamans in many cultures, for example, among the **Inuit** of the **Arctic**, are deemed necessary to **mediate** between humans and powerful **other-than-human persons** who have been offended by breaches of taboo (whether deliberate or inadvertent).

TANTRA. *See* BUDDHISM; SAMUEL, GEOFFREY; TIBET.

TART, CHARLES T. (1937–). Professor and core faculty member of the Institute of Transpersonal Psychology, Palo Alto, California. Tart is internationally known for his psychological work on the nature of consciousness—particularly **altered states of consciousness**—especially the volume *Altered States of Consciousness* (1969), as well as his research in scientific **parapsychology**. He is one of the founders of the field of transpersonal psychology, and his book *Transpersonal Psychologies* (1975) was instrumental in integrating the field into modern psychology. With his interests in the interface between scientific and spiritual communities, Tart edits the online journal *TASTE*, "dedicated to exploring the transcendent experiences of scientists."

TAUSSIG, MICHAEL. Professor of anthropology at Columbia University. Taussig's book *Shamanism, Colonialism, and the Wild Man: A Study of Terror and Healing* (1987) provides the foremost consideration of the work of **Amazonian** shamans confronted by and confronting the devastation of colonialism. It not only discusses **healing**, **performance**, and **sorcery** but also considers shamans' **political** and cultural leadership (even when they may be marginal, **ambiguous**, and even feared members of their communities). Taussig also documents the widespread suspicion that European colonialism itself is a form of sorcery or "*magia*" that shamans, some using **ayahuasca** (***yagé***), can attempt to **combat**. Similar accusations against those who succeed or become rich are significant aspects of **witchcraft** discourse not only in Amazonia but also in **Africa** and elsewhere. All of this contributes to an understanding of the resilience of indigenous cultures, especially as they incorporate elements of originally discrete cultural practices and knowledge. Taussig's work is an important challenge to romantic views of shamans as heroic and exceptional characters. His earthy, bawdy, and matter-of-fact confrontation with the devastating facts of colonial life roots his books in a more gritty reality, albeit sometimes in a **trickster**-like manner.

TECHNO-SHAMANS. The rise of "acid-house" rave parties, "techno" electronic music with repetitive and monotonous beats, and the use of the drug ecstasy (MDMA) in the late 1980s and early 1990s have given rise to the term *techno-shamans*, referring to participants in "dance culture" who use the drug and/or the aural driving of the **rhythmic** music to enter **altered states of consciousness**. MDMA stimulates heightened sensory perception, excitement, and endurance, allowing "ravers" to dance for prolonged periods. The internet had an increasingly prominent role, as ravers used this medium for dialogue, to establish virtual communities beyond the rave, and to disseminate information about dance venues. A government crackdown on rave culture and other alternative movements in Great Britain, with the Criminal Justice Act (1988) in particular, took pure (as opposed to club) "rave" underground; yet it has also had a major influence on popular music of the 1990s and to the present. *See also* CYBERIA; PSYCHONAUTS.

TEDLOCK, BARBARA AND DENNIS. Barbara Tedlock is professor of anthropology at the State University of New York (SUNY), Buffalo, a researcher among Guatemalan Maya, and the author of articles and books about shamans, especially **women** shamans. Dennis

Tedlock is professor of English and anthropology at SUNY Buffalo and a linguist, poet, and translator of Mayan literature (the *Popol Vuh* [1996] and *Rabinal Achi* [2003]). The Tedlocks have both trained and been initiated by Mayan shamans and written reflexively about that process and its implications.

THERAPY. If therapy is understood broadly as equivalent to **healing**, the term is certainly applicable to much of what shamans do. This is illustrated in the common preference for terms related to ***doctors*** and ***medicine*** in indigenous references to shamans and their work. However, *therapy* often suggests a more psychological approach to the **mental health** of an individual's mind or psyche. In this sense, the term is most applicable to **neo-shamanic** practices that privilege individual interiority, especially under the influence of **Carl Jung** and his heirs. A good example of this is Sylvia Perera's representation of the *Descent to the Goddess* (*see DESCENT OF INANNA*) as a shamanic **initiation** narrative that may then provide a model for those seeking self-knowledge and personal growth. Visualization and self-reflection play the role of **underworld journeying** in the service of **individuation**.

THERIOMORPHISM. In **animist** contexts in which the ability to **transform** is understood to be a defining characteristic of persons, or specifically of powerful persons, the ability of some humans to transform themselves into animal forms or to imagine themselves as **animals** (so as to understand and anticipate their actions and intentions) may be important both to shamans and to **hunters**. Brian Morris (2000) discusses this as an aspect of human–animal relationships in Malawi in **Southern Africa**. **David Lewis-Williams** and **Thomas Dowson** discuss the interpretation of **rock art** depictions of some therianthropes, part-human and part-animal beings, as shamanic. *See also* SHAPE-SHIFTING.

THIRD GENDER. Marie Czaplicka, **Marjorie Balzer**, and **Bernard Saladin d'Anglure** demonstrate the importance of broadening the notion of **gender** to include not only male and female but also various mediating positions and roles. Czaplicka, for example, notes that shamans are a "third class," separate from males and females. This separation enables shamans to **mediate** because they are already, by nature or **initiation**, "in-between" persons. This use of the term *third* *gender* to refer to shamans as a gender separate from male and female overlaps its use as a reference to homosexuality as a third gender. The marriage of some shamans to **otherworld** partners sometimes leads to their practice of **transvestitism**, but can also result in homosexual marriages in the "ordinary world." Whether this is acceptable within the wider culture or a specific aspect of the strangeness of shamans varies from culture to culture, and perhaps from village to village.

THORN APPLE. *See* DATURA.

TIBET. Himalayan country with a long historical influence in the region, especially stretching northward into **Buryatia** and **Mongolia** and south into **Nepal** and **India**. **Buddhist** authorities, lamas, sometimes acted against shamans but at other times creatively blended elements of earlier Buddhist and shamanic traditions into distinctive new forms. Buddhism and **Bön-po** are sometimes considered to be distinct religions, but a more useful understanding is that Bön-po is one of the local, shamanic forms Buddhism takes in Tibet and its diaspora. Buddhism's best-known ecstatic form, Tantra, is sometimes considered to be a form of shamanism. **Geoffrey Samuel**'s discussions of Tibetan religion are important not only for descriptions but also for their elucidation of appropriate academic approaches to these and other religious complexes.

TIERED COSMOS. Among some, but far from all, societies that employ shamans, the **cosmos** is understood to be layered, often in three levels: an **upper world**, middle world, and **underworld**. Ordinary humans live entirely in the middle world, unless their **souls** are taken by **otherworld** persons or **spirits**. Shamans work in all three worlds, **mediating** between their communities and **other-than-human persons** of many kinds, including **animals**. **Neo-shamans** often conceive of these other worlds as inner (psychological) and **imaginal** realms requiring **Jungian**-style **therapeutic** and **individuated** interpretations.

TOBACCO. Indigenous to the Americas, tobacco is a sacred and powerful plant in many indigenous cultures. Its intoxicating effects were well known and rarely used for recreational purposes. In some cultures, it was never smoked or ingested in sufficient quantities to cause intoxication or addiction, but was utilized as a means of making smoke that was understood to carry invocations and prayers to respected or powerful **other-than-human persons**. Many **North American** indigenous ceremonies and events are initiated by the communal smoking of a tobacco pipe. These **animist** actions are the broad context or milieu of more specifically shamanic **performances** and understandings.

However, many **Amazonian** shamans make extreme use of tobacco's intoxicating powers. **Carlos Fausto** notes that tobacco consumption is "the hallmark of shamanic activity" in Amazonia and that it is used more widely and more commonly than any other psychoactive plants or derivatives. While contrasting Amazonian and Andean shamanism in **South America**, Juan Ossio notes that inhalation of sufficient quantities of tobacco to induce the **vomiting** of copious phlegm for **healing** purposes, alongside **sucking** as a curative practice, is commonplace in the Amazonia lowlands but not in the Andes. Similarly, **Eduardo Viveiros de Castro**'s observation that, among the Amazonian **Araweté**, "the usual way of saying that someone is not a shaman is *petĩ ã-ĩ*, a 'noneater of tobacco'" demonstrates the centrality of intoxication among shamans. In nighttime communal rituals, men are served large cigars by their wives or female friends and smoke ("eat") tobacco until they become "translucent enough to experience shamanic visions." New **initiates** smoke almost until they faint, but the tobacco that "slays" them in this way is also a means of reviving those who have fainted and, perhaps, lost their **souls**. The smell of tobacco and the unpleasant odor given off by the bodies of shamans made dangerously ill by overconsumption of tobacco and, via smoke, nicotine may mask the stench of **blood** and thus disguise the malevolent activities of "**dark shamans**."

TOTEMISM. Often confused with the exceptionally close or "spiritual" relationship of a shaman with a particular **animal** or plant, *totem* derives from an Algonquian term for "**clan**." Many indigenous cultures understand that clans are not merely kinship groups larger than families, but groups of persons related across species boundaries. That is, a clan includes both human and **other-than-human persons** and may be known by the priority it gives to a particular type of such person, for example, the "bear clan." Totemism expresses the understanding that all beings share responsibility for the well-being of every person who lives in an area. It is a particular form of sociality emerging from a broader **animism**. This provides the larger context in which shamans form intimate relationships with other-than-humans within and beyond their clans; those relationships are better indicated by terms like ***power animal*** or ***helper** plant*. The use of totems among **neo-shamans** in this more **individualized** sense derives from anthropological debates that found the notion of interspecies clans difficult and conceived of totemism as a peculiar way of *thinking* about animals, humans, and the **cosmos**. Both forms of totemism indicate something about the "true self" of the individual as construed by animist and modernist cultures.

TOURISM. Shamanic **performances** and shamanic use of **vision**-inducing plant derivatives have attracted both scholars and enthusiasts seeking **initiation**, education, and entertainment. While shamanism tourism and hallucinogen tourism have seriously disrupted indigenous cultures, communities, and environments, some critics have exaggerated the distinction between shamanic work and entertainment. **Humor**, carnivalesque drama, and the telling of **trickster** tales are common elements of shamans' roles. Shamans' traditional clients and neighbors frequently evidence entirely **pragmatic** and even skeptical approaches to shamanic claims and indicate that good performance can be a sign of an adept shaman. Similarly, while some indigenous shamans work only for their **clan**, village, or kin group, others serve any clients willing to pay. Since scholars have struggled to understand indigenous knowledge and have sometimes imported modernist preconceptions into their interpretations, it is not surprising that hallucinogen tourists and others have misunderstood the **purity** aspects of **purgative** (**vomit**-inducing) plant **helpers**. Similarly, many **neo-shamanic** tourists have clearly interpreted their experiences among indigenous shamans in, for example, **South America** or **Nepal**, entirely in line with Western modernist ideas about **therapeutic** and **Jungian**-style psychology. Shamanic- and **entheogen**-related tourism have been promoted by **Brant Secunda**, **Alberto Villoldo**, and many leading neo-shamans, while being strongly criticized by **Marlene Dobkin de Rios** and Jay Fikes. *See also* AYAHUASCA; HUICHOL; MAZATEC; PSILOCYBIN; SABINA, MARIA; WASSON, GORDON.

TOWNSEND, JOAN. Professor emeritus in anthropology at the University of Manitoba, Canada. Broadly concurring with **Michael Harner**'s definition of **core shamanism** as the essential character of indigenous shamanisms, Townsend's analysis of "modern shamanic spirituality" draws distinctions between "traditional" shamanism, core shamanism, and **neo-shamanism**. She accurately notes the emphasis on **individual** empowerment in neo-shamanisms, in contrast to traditional shamanisms. Core shamanism is singled out for special treatment, but it must also be seen as a Western construct: while it is possible to strip away the differences that constitute "shamanisms" across cultures, it is improbable that the core shamanism that remains is anything but a neo-shamanism made accessible (safe, acultural, apolitical) to a Western audience. It is cultural difference and diversity which makes shamans, in all their nuances, "shamans."

TRANCE. Shamans are sometimes distinguished from other religious or cultural leaders by their ability to deliberately enter **altered states of consciousness**. A trance may be considered a dissociative state of mind in which actors become unaware of their ordinary or physical surroundings. It has been assessed in completely contradictory ways: as either the equivalent or the opposite of **possession**. However, the work of **Ioan Lewis** and **Caroline Humphrey**, among others, demonstrates that both are **performed** behaviors and that the **individual**'s inner "state of mind" is hardly an issue for shamans, their clients, or communities. Both trance and possession, if they can be distinguished, are culturally recognizable patterns of behavior that demonstrate the presence and activity of **otherworld** beings, **spirits**, or other powerful **other-than-human persons**. That is, while many Western observers are interested in "trance" as a state of mind, what is significant to shamans and their (**animist**) communities is the active engagement or relationship between the shamans and their **helpers** and enemies. Since "entranced" shamans are supposed to be fully in control of their **journeying** in places and ways inaccessible to onlookers, and of their actions for others, to speak of "dissociation" is to miss what shamans consider most significant: their powerful association with helpers and clients. Trance is also important in a host of religious communities that are not normally considered shamanic except by those who equate shamanism with trance (and thus overgeneralize both terms).

TRANSFORMATION. Many shamans are purported to be able to transform themselves, either at will or with the aid of **otherworld** and **other-than-human persons**, or **spirits**, into forms other than their own. They may do so in order to **journey**. In **Amazonia** and in many other indigenous and especially **animist** societies, all powerful persons are able to appear in different material forms, so that shamans are required to alter **perspective**, to see as others see, in order to know the true nature of an approaching **animal**, human, or spirit. **Theriomorphism**, shamanic transformation into certain animal forms, such as bears, is significant, especially where **bear ceremonialism** is important. *See also* SHAPE-SHIFTING.

TRANSVESTITISM. Shamans in many cultures **perform** alternative **gender** and other cultural, societal, and kinship roles different from those locally deemed "normal." Some male shamans adopt the **costume** of **women**, while some female shamans adopt that of men. They may do so to indicate their difference from the rest of the community or to show that they have formed an intimate, even sexual and/or marital, relationship with an **otherworld**, **other-than-human**, or **spirit** person of the same gender. Transvestitism may be temporary, a part of specific performances, or permanent, a sign of a distinctive everyday identity.

TRICKSTERS. The **animist** worldviews or **cosmologies** within which shamans are required **ritualists**, **mediators**, **healers**, or **combatants** usually posit co-creation by a wide community of persons. At least some of these are "tricksters." Generally, tricksters are **other-than-human persons** who create or transform the world as a result of strange and even antisocial behavior. In stories and ceremonies they are usually gluttonous, lascivious, greedy, deceptive, destructive, and foolish. Tricksters are creative or transformative either to achieve self-serving ends or simply by accident. Nonetheless, the results of their actions benefit others, especially humans.

Trickster tales and rituals may be playfully celebratory even as they warn against unacceptable and transgressive behavior. It is not that tricksters are "evil," but more that they are ambiguous, although Coyote (an almost ubiquitous trickster in **North America**) is heavily involved in the **witchcraft** traditions of some areas. Part of the **ambiguity** and marginality of shamans lies in their close kinship with tricksters. This is played out in their **performance** of **gender** and results in their ability to mediate, but it is also demonstrated in the common suspicion that shamans may also be **sorcerers** or witches. They may cure, but they can also inflict **illness**. They can warn against enemy **cannibalism**, but they may also aid bloodthirsty deities.

For all the amusement that is gained from trickster tales, they should not be mistaken for "just-so" stories told purely for entertainment. The Navajo storyteller Yellowman told Barre Toelken that although his stories of the trickster Ma'i contained **humorous** episodes and were told in amusing ways, they were not funny but vitally important for educating children in appropriate behavior and for "making everything possible." Similarly, Ellen Basso links **Amazonian** Kalapalo understandings of tricksters with the pervasive "**perspectivism**" that requires shamans to be able to see as others see. The confusion of trickster tales with funny stories may also result from the inclusion of "fools" in collections such as *American Indian Trickster Tales* (coedited by **Richard Erdoes** and Alfonso Ortiz in 1998). The short-story collections of **Gerald Vizenor** not only retell and embellish traditional **Ojibwe** trickster tales but also make them powerfully relevant to contemporary urban, mixed-blood, and marginal contexts and communities; indeed, he makes full use of the transgressive and metaphorical power of tricksters as he demolishes stereotypes and liberates his stories and readers to reimagine and reform the world. James Welch's *Fools Crow* (1986) offers further examples of shamanic-trickster engagements.

TRUHUJO, JOHN (c. 1883–1985). Shoshone (**Native American**) **medicine man** and Sun Dance chief who was **elected** and aided by **Seven Arrows** (chief of the Little People, a group of **other-than-human persons** who live inside mountains) and initiated **Thomas Yellowtail** (of the **Crow**) to reintroduce the Sun Dance to his people. His biography is a significant part of Fred Vogt's account of *The Shoshoni-Crow Sun Dance* (1984). In Yellowtail's biography (as told to Michael Oren), Truhujo is called Trehero, and there is some debate about his birthdate.

TUKANO. Shamans, or *payé*, among the Tukano of Colombia use **tobacco** and **ayahuasca** in order to engage with such **other-than-human persons** as the powerful **jaguar**. Key research among the payé was conducted by Colombian anthropologist **Gerardo Reichel-Dolmatoff**, who wrote the classic *The Shaman and the Jaguar* (1975) in which he summarized that the

> principal spheres of a *payé* are the curing of disease, the obtaining of game **animals** and fish from their supernatural **masters**, the presiding over **rituals** in the individual life cycle, and defensive or aggressive action against personal enemies. In all these aspects the role of the *payé* is essentially that of a **mediator** and moderator between superterrestrial forces and society, and between the need for survival of the individual and the forces bent on his destruction—sickness, hunger and the ill will of others.

Reichel-Dolmatoff's work on **entoptic phenomena** in the geometric art of the Tukano was also influential on the shamanistic approach to **rock art**.

TURNER, EDITH. University of Virginia symbolic anthropologist who has written extensively about indigenous **healing** practices in **Africa** and the **Arctic**. Turner's reflections on her participation in healing work among the Ndembu of Zambia and the Inupiat of Alaska have been important contributions to new experiential approaches to ethnography and knowledge. She demonstrates the value of an understanding of indigenous knowledge of taking the existence and activities of **spirits** seriously.

TUVA. Tuva lies north of **Mongolia**, east of **Central Asia**, and south of Southern **Siberia**, and the Tuvans are pastoralists of mixed Turkic-Mongolian descent with genealogical ties going back to Chinggis (Genghis) Khan. The area was under the control during the 17th century of Oriot (Western Mongol) Khans, who became **Buddhist** and established Lamaist monasteries, and local shamanism faced opposition from the new religious order, as it did in Mongolia and **Buryatia**. With the defeat of the Oriots, the area passed into **Chinese** control and was then annexed by the Russians at the beginning of the 20th century. During the Communist era, shamanic traditions were persecuted across the Soviet Union, including in Tuva. Despite restrictions on scholarship on shamans, however, Soviet scholar Sevyan Vainshtein published extensively on Tuvan shamanism. More recently, the Tuvinian historian Nikolai Abaev has argued that religion in Tuva is not shamanism in the "strict sense of the term," since their **cosmology** includes an idea of "god" (*burhan*) and not just **spirits**.

Benedikte Kristensen (as also discussed by **Caroline Humphrey** and **Piers Vitebsky**) agrees that "shamanism" gives a misleading impression of a single unified system and of the shaman as a "singular **ritual** practitioner," while Tuvinian traditions termed "shamanism" are consistently flexible and fluid and include several religious specialists in addition to shamans. Kristensen retains the term *shamanism* because the Duha Tuvinians use a similar concept—*böögiin sjasjin*, meaning "shamanic religion or faith." But, Tuvinians sometimes made a distinction between böögiin sjasjin as "faith in shamans" and as other engagements with spirits, and some Tuvinians informed Kristensen that they did not believe in "shamanism" because they did not trust shamans today and there were no powerful (*xuchtei*) shamans left—although this did not alter their belief in spirits. Drawing on Humphrey, Kristensen uses *shamanism* to mean "the entire conglomeration of ideas about beings in the world which includes the shaman" and not in the Duha Tuvinians' strict understanding of the term ("faith in living shamans").

Since the collapse of the Soviet Union, Tuva, among other now-independent nations of Central Asia, has revived traditions that Communism sought to eradicate. **Mongush Kenin-Lopsan** has played a key role in this revival. Shamanism has reemerged with new vigor as part of a Tuvan nationalist agenda: lending an atmosphere of authenticity, shamans in the city hold clinics that operate much like a Western physician's surgery, with a shamanic consultation requiring the shaman to wear a white coat and the **patient** to have a general medical exam before the **healing** séance. This change in tradition might indicate why some Tuvinians do "not trust shamans today." While aspects of Tuvan shamanism derive from traditional practices (e.g., **drumming**, **chanting**, engaging with spirits), Western **core shamanic** elements have been adopted to fill in where traditions have been lost, and the U.S.-based **Foundation for Shamanic Studies** has been offering its services in the area. This situation raises issues of neocolonialism, on the one hand, and processes of creative fusion, on the other.

– U –

UMBANDA. Religious movement originating in Brazil in the early 20th century creatively bringing together themes from **Christianity**, **African** (especially Angolan and Yoruba-derived), and indigenous **Amazonian** religions along with **Kardecist** Spiritism. **Other-than-human persons** of various geographical and cultural origins are honored in particular "houses" by **initiated** "fathers" or "mothers," in **rituals** that may involve **possession** and **divination** as well as **healing**.

UNDERWORLDS. Among the **other worlds** of many shamanic **cosmologies**, the existence of realms under the earth are significant. Shamanic **initiations** and **journeys** may entail a visit to these places. **Piers Vitebsky** writes about the frequent and calm **ritual** descents of **Sora** shamans into the underworld to converse with **ancestors**. To do so, shamans prepare themselves by ceremonial means and then enter a **trance** and become monkeys climbing down a huge tree. Since the Sora underworld is the home of the dead, the shaman must be careful not to become trapped or obligated to remain there, for example, by eating the food of the dead or playing with children there. This not only illustrates the common understanding that underworlds are dangerous places but also reinforces the notion that shamans are distinct from other people in their familiarity with death. **Heathen** shamans also enter the underworld in trance ceremonies or ***seidr***. A common initial experience of **core shamanism**, as taught by **Michael Harner** and his colleagues, is a descent into the underworld to discover one's **power animal** or **helper**. Light trance is induced by **rhythmic drumming** (sometimes prerecorded) and initiates are guided to **visualize** themselves descending. A similar combination of visualization and guided meditation or self-reflection is utilized in **Jungian therapeutic** contexts. Sylvia Perera, for example, turned the ancient Sumerian poem ***Descent of Inanna*** into a powerful therapeutic tool, emphasizing allegedly shamanic themes.

UPPER WORLDS. Among the **other worlds** of many shamanic **cosmologies**, the existence of realms above the earth are significant. Shamanic **initiations** and **journeys** may entail a visit to these places. Among the ascent routes noted by **Piers Vitebsky** are the use of a branch lowered from the sky to aid Khanty shamans, the crossing of a bridge made of smoke by Nenets shamans, and the Chukchi shaman's riding on **reindeer**. He also notes that in addition to being aided by birds or flying **animals** in their ascents, shamans sometimes become their own vehicles for dramatic locomotion. Some even draw on nontraditional vehicles such as airplanes and trains to aid their journeys. **Mircea Eliade**'s construction of shamanic cosmology privileges the upper world and ascent journeys to the extent that he twists an **Aboriginal Australian "Dreaming"** narrative and denigrates **underworld** and this-worldly journeys as "degenerate."

– V –

VEGETALISTAS. Shamans of the upper **Amazon** who are inspired and **helped** by **ayahuasca** and chakruna, plants that are considered to be shamanic persons in their own right (*see* ANIMISM). Although the colorful and dramatic art that has become famous in recent decades draws attention to the visionary results of shamanic ingestion of these plants, they are also significant as enablers of communication between shamans and significant **other-than-human persons**. The paintings of **Pablo Amaringo**, for example, are often more famous than his assertion that ayahuasca enables him to hear Amazonian trees weeping as they are cut down.

VILLOLDO, ALBERTO. Psychologist who pioneered **neo-shamanic tourism** in the Peruvian **Amazon**. *See also* SHARON, DOUGLAS.

VISION. Shamans are often required to be visionaries, sometimes aided by powerful **otherworld** or **other-than-human persons** or by plants such as **ayahuasca**. The ability to alter **perspective** is a vital skill for many **Amazonian** shamans, as discussed by **Eduardo Viveiros de Castro**. A note of caution should be attached to all claims that shamans make use of substances that induce visions and **altered states of consciousness**, especially when these are labeled "hallucination" by Western observers. Indigenous understandings may not overly privilege vision over other senses and may seek the aid of plants not simply to alter consciousness but to aid communication with others in the wider-than-human **cosmos**.

VISION QUESTS. For many **Native Americans**, traditional **initiation rituals**, especially those celebrated at puberty, are marked by a **vision** quest, in which a person goes to a remote and possibly sacred place and seeks to encounter a powerful **other-than-human helper**. This may be an animal or a **spirit** being and may be seen after prolonged sensory **deprivation**, for example, fasting and continuous wakefulness. **Neo-shamans** often demonstrate their **New Age** credentials by presenting vision quests as opportunities for self-discovery, seeking the "**soul**" or true inner self, rather than **altered styles of communication** in an **animist** world. Neo-shamans such as **Sun Bear** have been strongly criticized (and labeled "**plastic medicine men**") by the **American Indian Movement**, among others, for charging clients to participate in vision quests and related, **purificatory sweat lodges**.

VISIONARY PLANTS. *See* ENTHEOGENS.

VISUALIZATION. The use of intense visual concentration in order to focus on a guided meditation through an imaginative narrative is popular among many **New Agers**, **Pagans**, and **neo-shamans**. The experient is usually encouraged to sit comfortably or lie down, with eyes closed, in a safe space and to focus on a particular scenario, perhaps walking down a path into the woods where they encounter **otherworldly** beings who offer advice and instruction. The imagination is understood by these practitioners to be a powerful tool for self-help, improvement, and **therapy** and has much in common with the **imaginal** realm of neo-**Jungian** psychologists and psychotherapists. Visualization might also be used to approach **soul retrieval**, as it is taught by the **Foundation for Shamanic Studies**, pioneered by **Sandra Ingerman** in particular, for "**healing** the fragmented self"—seeking out and healing the traumatic experiences of one's past (understood as the lost parts of one's **soul**) in order to become a healthy, whole person. Shamanic **journeying**, as taught by **core shamanists**, might also be read as a form of visualization, since the practice has more in common with guided meditation than exuberant indigenous shamanic **rituals**. By contrast, core shamanists often argue that since the visualization is free-form rather than stipulated step by step, journeying is shamanism, not guided meditation. While the power of the imagination (in producing healing, otherworldly experiences, **art**, and so on) must be acknowledged, the more introductory forms of core shamanism, soul retrieval, Pagan ritual, and New Age–style guided meditation are markedly different from the intense **ecstatic** rituals of indigenous shamans and contemporary Pagans drawing on such sources, as seen in the work of **Gordon "the Toad" MacLellan**, for instance. *See also* VISION.

VITEBSKY, PIERS. Anthropologist and head of social sciences at the Scott Polar Research Institute, University of Cambridge, Great Britain. Vitebsky has written a detailed ethnography of the **Sora** of India and conducted research in **Siberia** (the recent *The Reindeer People* [2005]) and Sri Lanka and has also written one of the most useful single-volume introductions to the practices and contexts of shamans. In *The Shaman* (1995), he introduces a wide range of cultures and debates, along with invaluable photographic and textual material. Additionally, in a 1995 article on the **Sakha** (Yakut) discussing the relationship between shamanism and **environmentalism**, he sets out four "key characteristics which it is reasonable to see as distinctively shamanic" and elaborates on shamanism's "local, holistic, eristic and dissident" features. This setting out of key characteristics and use of "the shaman" in the singular might initially be read as a monolithic understanding of "shamanism," yet his insistence on the diversity of shamanic phenomena and their engagement with varied social and **political** contexts is important, especially in contrast with the tendency of scholars such as **Mircea Eliade** and **neo-shamanic** practitioners to construct universal and "spiritual" definitions. Vitebsky eloquently writes, "Shamanism is a chameleon-like phenomenon, reappearing across diverse regional traditions, in varied historical and political settings, and co-existing, sometimes uneasily, with major world religions."

VIVEIROS DE CASTRO, EDUARDO. Brazilian anthropologist at the Museu Nacional of Rio de Janeiro, Brazil, and director of the Núcleo de Transformações Indígenas research group. Viveiros de Castro has held important posts in Cambridge, England, and Paris and has written extensively about **Amazonian** indigenous peoples, especially the **Araweté**. His publications include *From the Enemy's Point of View: Humanity and Divinity in an Amazonian Society* (1992) and "Cosmological Deixis and Amerindian Perspectivism" (1998). Viveiros de Castro's discussion on **perspectivism** is among the most important recent writings on shamanism and has also influenced cultural critics and theorists such as Bruno Latour.

VIZENOR, GERALD (1934–). Enrolled member of the Minnesota Chippewa Tribe, White Earth Reservation, a prolific poet and author of academic and imaginative works, and professor of ethnic studies at the University of California, Berkeley. Vizenor's writing is multifaceted and complex, but often turns on the relationship of presence and absence in conversations, myths, films, writing, and politicking and other discourses and contexts. His work is full of neologisms that provocatively challenge dominant preconceptions; for example, the term *postindians* rejects the identification of Native people, especially urban "mixed bloods," with the "Indians" invented (not "discovered") by Columbus and his followers. This is significant to the roles played by shamans in Vizenor's works. In *Earthdivers* (1981), drawing on traditional knowledge and practices, especially **Ojibwe** ceremonial complexes like the **Midewiwin**, and narratives like those of the **trickster** Nanabozo or Nanabush, he writes:

> Some shaman sprites and tricksters are spiritual **healers**, with warm hands and small **medicine bundles** loaded with secret remedies, and some shaman spirits are clowns who can tell and reveal the opposites of the world in sacred reversals, natural tilts in double **visions**, interior glories. The shaman clowns and tricksters are transformed in familiar places and spaces from common grammars, the past and the present are shapes of **animals** and birds.

However, as in the short stories of Sherman Alexie, these "familiar places and spaces" are not those of traditional or reservation villages but urban environments. In following Jacques Lacan's liberation of "signifiers" from too close an identification with "the signified," Vizenor's trickster-shamans are "comic holotropes." Although they may possess a "thick memory" of tribal and continental history, they reject the posture of homogeneity and spirituality and insist on trickster revelations of the presence of varying, complex, and real-life Native people. Characters such as "Captain Shammer" (a name resonant of accusations that shamans "**sham**" and that **neo-shamans** are pseudo-shamans at best) satirize contemporary academic postures, while "Bagese" brings **bear ceremonialism** into impoverished urban places.

VODOU. Also Vodu, Vodun, Vudu, and similar. Various related forms of **animist ancestor** veneration and **possession** cult that originated in West and Central **Africa** and evolved by integrating elements derived from **Christianity** in the **Caribbean** and its diaspora during and after the slavery era.

VOMITING. Shamans in many cultures seek the aid of powerful plants (sometimes understood to be **other-than-human persons** and even shamans in their own right). While many of these plants are labeled by Westerners (whether academics or enthusiasts) as hallucinogenic, psychotropic, **entheogenic**, or **vision** inspiring, it is as **purgatives**—vomit inducers—that they are valued by many indigenous shamans. **Gordon Wasson** and others interested in **Central American mushrooms** were apologetic and embarrassed about having to vomit under the influence of mushrooms, but the *curandera* (**doctor**), **Maria Sabina**, was insistent that vomiting is not only part of the **healing** process but in fact *the* most important **help** offered by the mushrooms. She said, "If the **patient** fails to vomit, I have to vomit for them." As **Andy Letcher** demonstrates in relation to **psilocybin**, the positive value now attached by Westerners to the visions resulting from ingestion of such plants is of recent origin. Previously both the nausea and the "hallucinations" (false dreams) were considered signs of poisoning. With the global spread of movements like the **ayahuasca**-centered **Santo Daime** and increasing knowledge of the **peyote**-centered **Native American Church**, perhaps purgative **purification** will be revalued, too. Until then, vomiting should be added to **Carlos Fausto**'s list of signs that distinguish indigenous shamanisms from **neo-shamanism**.

– W –

WALLIS, ROBERT J. (1972–). Associate professor of visual culture at Richmond University in London, where he coordinates the master's program in **art** history, and associate lecturer in the humanities with the Open University. Wallis has published extensively on shamanistic art, including critical discussions of the shamanistic approach to **rock art**. He argues that, while critics have accurately bemoaned the monolithic application of "shamanism" to various rock art traditions, the origin of some rock art imagery in **altered states of consciousness** is widely accepted among rock art researchers, with the shamanistic approach proposed by **Thomas Dowson** embracing the diversity of shamans and offering more nuanced and sophisticated interpretations than such previous explanations as "**hunting magic**" and "art for art's sake." Having held a research fellowship in archaeology and coordinated the master's in the archaeology and anthropology of rock art at the University of Southampton, Wallis also specializes in the representation of the past in the present, particularly among **neo-shamans** and contemporary **Pagans**, and he has published widely on neo-shamanic engagements with archaeology and indigenous communities. Wallis suggests that neo-shamans have been dismissed too easily by scholars as fringe and inauthentic, pointing to Western practitioners whose worldviews compare favorably with indigenous shamans, and he argues that we should take neo-shamanic engagements with anthropology and archaeology seriously.

Building on this research, Wallis is currently codirecting the Sacred Sites, Contested Rites/Rights: Contemporary Pagan Engagements with the Past project with **Jenny Blain**, a collaboration of archaeology and anthropology. Wallis and Blain theorize about what a **sacred site** is, examine the emergence of sacred sites in heritage management discourse, and point to the variety of alternative perspectives on the past with which archaeologists, heritage managers, and other professionals must now constructively engage, foregrounding the issue of **animism** and living landscapes as emerging worldviews among neo-shamans and other "**new-indigenes**." Wallis and Blain have also collaborated on research discussing neo-shamans and **gender**, and the **performance** of neo-shamanic ritual. In his current work, Wallis is critically examining the discourse on shamans and image making, ranging from prehistoric **cave art** to contemporary art.

WALSH, ROGER N. Professor of psychiatry and behavior at the University of California at Irvine, whose research interests in transpersonal psychology involve the psychology of religion, Asian religion, and shamanism. In his volume *The Spirit of Shamanism* (1990), Walsh examines the role of **healing** in shamanism, arguing that some shamanic practices foreshadow contemporary medical and psychological techniques. This research is in the vein of other psychological approaches to shamanism as a **therapeutic** technique valid for modern Westerners. Historically, this trend of psychologizing shamanism influenced the development of **Michael Harner**'s **core shamanism**. *See also* ACHTERBERG, JEANNE; EXTRA PAY; GOODMAN, FELICITAS; GROF, STANISLAV; INGERMAN, SANDRA; KRIPPNER, STANLEY; NEUROTHEOLOGY; PETERS, LARRY G.; TART, CHARLES T.

WANA. Native to the interior region of eastern Central Sulawesi in **Indonesia**, the Wana have *tau kawalia* "people **spirits**" who **mediate** between the worlds of human and **other-than-human persons**, and the *mabolong* or "**drumming** ceremony" is especially popular. In her ethnography on the Wana, **Jane Atkinson** focuses on the effectiveness of shamanic **ritual** and **performance**, and the dynamic between shaman, **patient**, and audience/community, critically engaging with symbolic, **therapeutic**, and performance-based anthropological readings.

WANNABE INDIANS. Although this term derives from **Native Americans** (see principally Green 1988) who have criticized non-Native writers for marketing their work as if it were actually by a Native author—"simulations of tribal identities in the literature of dominance," as **Gerald Vizenor** has put it—the "wannabe" label is sometimes applied to all **neo-shamans**, **New Agers**, **Pagans**, and others who can be seen by Native Americans as appropriating their spiritual traditions. Such well-known neo-shamanic writers as **Carlos Castaneda**, **Lynn Andrews**, and **Sun Bear** have been singled out for specific criticism as "wannabe Indians" by the **American Indian Movement**.

WARFARE. While many commentators recognize that shamans may protect their communities by gaining advance knowledge of attack by enemies or **predators**, **Carlos Fausto** argues that "there is an intrinsic link between warfare and shamanism." Among many **Amazonian** peoples, shamans are those who can gain the **perspective** of dangerous "others." In a thoroughly animate world, shamans "are capable of interacting [with nonhuman entities] verbally and establishing relationships of adoption or alliance, which permit them to act upon the world in order to cure, to fertilize, and to kill." Such alterations of perspective are, like warfare and hunting, aggressive acts that turn enemies into "pets" or "prey," that is, beings that can be used to sustain shamans and their kin and allies. As warriors engage with human enemies and gain power (which may be understood both socially and mystically) from such relationships, shamans engage principally with **other-than-human** enemies (e.g., **animal** or "**spirit**" persons).

WASSON, R. GORDON (1898–1996). American banker and amateur mycologist whose study of "ethnomycology" with his wife Valentina began on a delayed honeymoon in the Catskill Mountains of New York. The Wassons became convinced that the human religious impulse began with a Paleolithic magic **mushroom** cult that spread globally via cultural diffusion and evolved into "higher religions," and that fossil residues of this cult endured in folk traditions around the world. They found a wealth of sources for the use of fly agaric, **psilocybin**, and other hallucinogenic mushrooms across cultures and used the terms *mycophobic* (mushroom-hating) and *mycophilic* (mushroom-loving) to delineate positive and negative attitudes. From 1953, Wasson made 10 trips into the **Mazatec** hinterlands of Mexico, where he found and engaged in indigenous mushroom **rituals**. His greatest discovery was the "shaman" (*curandera*) **Maria Sabina**, who, like other Mazatec *curanderos*, held *veledas* (**healing** ceremonies) using psilocybin mushrooms.

Wasson's "Seeking the Magic Mushroom," his 1957 article in *Life*, along with *Mushrooms, Russia and History* (published in a very limited deluxe edition), were influential on the psychedelic counterculture, and visitors seeking Sabina and magic mushrooms streamed into Mexico in the early 1960s, with disastrous consequences for the local inhabitants of Huautlaand. This applied to Sabina in particular, whose community-oriented, **Christian** Catholic-inspired mushroom ceremonies were disrupted by self-interested, convention-flouting hippies seeking psychedelic "trips."

The results of Wasson's investigations in the Middle and Far East after retirement were published in 1969 as *Soma: The Divine Mushroom of Immortality*, in which the "soma: of the *Rig Veda* was (erroneously) identified as fly agaric. Wasson collaborated on the volumes *The Road to Eleusis: Unveiling the Secret of the Mysteries* (1978) and *Persephone's Quest:* ***Entheogens*** *and the* ***Origins of Religion*** (1986), which reified the mushroom cult thesis that remained popular outside of academia. The approaches of cultural diffusion and evolution and the Frazerian comparative method were all outmoded at the time Wasson was writing, and the metanarrative of a worldwide mushroom cult cannot be sustained. Indeed, **Andy Letcher** demonstrates that Wasson not only overemphasized the importance of fly agaric use but also tailored evidence to fit his theory. Nonetheless, Wasson was awarded an honorary research fellowship at Harvard Botanical Museum, as well as the Addison Emery Verrill Medal for Distinction in the Field of Natural History in 1983. Wasson and colleagues also contributed the term *entheogen* (literally, "to inspire god within") to replace the pejorative terms *hallucinogenic* or *psychedelic*, *psychoactive*, or *drug*. Wasson's greatest contribution, according to Letcher, was not the misplaced notion of the origins of religion in a prehistoric mushroom cult, but the inauguration of a modern mushroom cult in the 20th century.

WAYAPÍ. An **Amazonian** indigenous people. **Alan Campbell**'s ethnography is particularly interested in the Wayapí's use of the term *payé*, which, though roughly cognate with ***piya*** (a term for shamans elsewhere in the region), acts as a verb or adjective rather than a noun. That is, there are no "shamans" among the Wayapí, but anyone can access, utilize, and be affected by powers that can be called "shamanistic." Similarly, any person (human or **other-than-human** in this **animist** community) can be "very shamanistic" or only "slightly shamanistic."

WHITE SHAMANS. The **Buryat** and Yakut peoples of **Mongolia** and **Siberia** distinguish between two types of shaman: **black shamans** and white shamans. Although the distinction is never entirely systematic or absolute, white shamans do not enter **trances** but seek benefits from **upper-world** beings for their communities and **animals**. **Piers Vitebsky** notes that they may be called "**priests**" in other places. **Caroline Humphrey** (informed by **Urgunge Onon** and citing **Galina Galdanova**) notes that white shamans are comparable to the **ritualists**, *bagchi*, of the Daur Mongols in distinction from their shamans, *yadgan*, except that Daur bagchi are not shamans whereas white shamans are. A variety of distinctions in the **performance**, **costume**, and social roles of the two groups is also evident. *Black* and *white* are not equivalent to "good" and "bad," unlike the **Amazonian** distinction between curing shamans and **dark shamans**.

WHITEHEAD, NEIL. Professor of anthropology at the University of Wisconsin, Madison. His research and publications are mostly concerned with **Amazonian** peoples and the influence of Amerindian cultures on academic and Western thought and culture. His book *Dark Shamans* (2002), discussing "**dark shamanism**," especially **Kanaimà**, and books he has coedited with colleagues about **witchcraft** and **sorcery** contribute significantly to the growing interest in the more **ambiguous** roles played by shamans both in practice and in imagination or fear. He also contributes to discussions of the **political** positioning and relationships of shamans, especially in relation to the devastation of genocidal colonialism.

WHITESHAMANISM. A term like ***plastic medicine men*** that alleges that some or all **neo-shamans** are frauds. In articles called "The Great Pretenders: Further Reflections on Whiteshamanism" and "Just What's All This Fuss about Whiteshamanism Anyway?" Wendy Rose carefully explains the problematic dynamics of the continuing colonization of indigenous peoples and their practices by a globalized culture founded on a notion that knowledge is universal property. In asking for respectful interactions between indigenous people and those who wish to learn about or from them, she proffers a useful parallel. She might be happy to write imaginatively about the Roman Catholic Mass, but she would not pretend to be a **priest** or attempt to persuade others that she can facilitate their experience of the transubstantiation of the Host. Equally, she demonstrates that indigenous cultures have protocols, boundaries, rules, expectations, and requirements that cannot be set aside, especially in favor of those who demonstrably ignore existing indigenous ceremonial leaders and writers who usually offer more complex introductions to the kinds of events and experiences desired by "**wannabe Indians**."

WICCA. A form of **Paganism**, also known as **witchcraft** but distinct from the practice of malevolent magic or **sorcery**. Following its creation as a popularized blend of esotericism with **ecstatic** practices, a number of Pagan witches have increased the shamanic content of their tradition. Victor Anderson was influential on a number of American traditions of witchcraft (especially "the Feri Faith" or "Faerie Tradition," but also the development of Huna as a **neo-shamanic** form of **Hawaiian** shamanism). In Great Britain, **Gordon MacLel-**

lan is one of several Wiccans who blend shamanism with **environmental** education and activism.

WILBY, EMMA. Much of the data on early medieval **witches** is unreliable, extracted under conditions of torture and permeated by witch-hunt propaganda discourse—originating not with witches but with "learned" or "elite" medieval theologians. In this light, the suggestion by Montague Summers (1880–1948) that Medieval sources on witches are accurate factual accounts must be viewed as eccentric, and **Margaret Murray**'s thesis that these sources reveal an "old religion" of fertility worship which endured for thousands of years has been deconstructed by scholars such as **Ronald Hutton**. Nonetheless, Wilby, following in the vein of **Carlo Ginzburg**, argues in *Cunning Folk and Familiar Spirits* (2005) that the consistency of encounter narratives between witches, or "**cunning folk**," and their **spirit** familiars or devils in these early Medieval sources indicates that this feature must be considered seriously as evidence for actual belief and practice. Wilby's revisiting of the sources is detailed and meticulous, although she gives the misleading impression that the disparate sources across Great Britain and through two centuries are coherent and related. Wilby concludes that a veneer—albeit an all-pervading, official one—of **Christianity** overlay enduring traditions of pre-Christian shamanic practice among the populace of Great Britain and that "coherent and vigorous 'shamanistic **visionary** traditions' existed in many parts" of the country. While her approach to shamanism perhaps overemphasizes visionary experience and the induction of **altered states of consciousness**, there is compelling discussion of the overlap between what shamans and witches do in their engagements with communities of human and **other-than-human persons**. The replacing of the "fertility cult" hypothesis with "shamanistic visionary traditions," however, may be too much of an interpretative leap for some scholars of witchcraft and of shamanism.

WINKELMAN, MICHAEL. Professor in anthropology at Arizona State University, former president of the Society for the Anthropology of Consciousness, and founder of the Anthropology of Religion Section of the American Anthropological Association. Winkelman's research focuses on shamans and medical anthropology, with particular emphasis on **neurotheology**—the idea that the impulse behind shamanism and other religions originates in **brain chemistry**. Having demonstrated consistencies in shamanism and other **healing** practices across cultures (*Shamans, **Priests** and **Witches***, 1992), Winkelman has explained (in *Shamanism: The Neural Ecology of Consciousness and Healing*, 2000) such similarities in terms of a biological imperative: since all humans are capable of altering consciousness and such **altered states of consciousness** are derived from the human central nervous system, so shamanism specifically is "humanity's original healing practice." As such, he sees **neo-shamanisms** as indicative of the persistent significance and **pragmatism** of altered consciousness in the psychobiology of healing, with particular value currently in substance abuse rehabilitation. Winkelman's approach aligns with the shamanistic approach in **rock art** studies, which deploys **neuropsychological** data in order to analyze some rock art imagery as originating in altered consciousness. For postmodernist researchers, the danger with a psychobiological approach is of biological reductionism and the reification of metanarrative (e.g., shamanism as the **origin of religion**), but proponents of the shamanistic approach to rock art in particular tend to embed the broader psychobiological research in specific community contexts in order to embrace cultural diversity.

WIRIKÙTA. *See* HUICHOL.

WITCHCRAFT. Shamans in many cultures are expected to **combat** users of malevolent magic, witches, or **sorcerers**—or they may be suspected of being witches or sorcerers themselves. **Obeah**, for example, is commonly portrayed as the practice of witchcraft, but its practitioners consider it equivalent to other shamanic **trance** and **ritual** complexes utilized for **healing** and other socially valued actions. Among the **Amazonian** Parakanã, discussed by **Carlos Fausto**, no one admits to being a shaman but only to being a **dreamer**, because although only the former can heal people from the intrusion of *karowara*, "**spirits**," even to admit to having seen *karowara* is to admit the possibility of being a witch. **Ioan Lewis** argues that, as "**possession** is the means by which the underdog bids for attention," so "witchcraft accusations provide the countervailing strategy by which such demands are kept within bounds." In addition to providing another illustration of the **political** roles of shamans, this also unveils the essential **ambiguity** of notions of shamanic power and sources of power, especially among socially marginal individuals and groups. If marginal people can access power to heal the victims of unwanted possession, what power will they wield when they voluntarily become possessed and actively control or **master the spirits**? The **otherworld** persons involved here are themselves ambiguous, **tricksters** at best, and "they can scarcely be expected to have shed completely their capacity to harm." Lewis concludes that one who "can cast out malign spirits is *ipso facto* a witch," and shamans cannot be entirely distinguished from such sinister and dangerous beings. By rejecting this possibility and allying itself with only positive values and actions, **neo-shamanism** undercuts its claims to access similar sources of power and its assertion of sharing a similar **cosmology**. These uses of the "witch" and "witchcraft" should be distinguished from **Pagan** witchcraft or **Wicca**.

WIXÁRITARI/WIXÁRIKA. *See* HUICHOL.

WOMEN. In some cultures, only men can serve as shamans, while in others, shamanism is almost entirely women's business, and in still others, the role is open to anyone **elected** by **otherworld** persons or **spirits**. Similarly, women or men or both can be the main clients of shamans in particular cultures. Often the status of shamans and shamanism is higher when it is a largely male preserve.

It is important to note that many cultures see **gender** quite differently from what seems normal in the West, sometimes recognizing more than two genders, sometimes classing shamans in a **third gender** of their own, and sometimes distinguishing animate and inanimate genders rather than **sexual** genders. That all these possibilities have **cosmological** implications is clearly argued in the work of **Bernard Saladin d'Anglure**, especially in relation to the **Inuit**. The study of women's shamanic roles, authority, **performance**, and participation has been a particular focus of study by scholars such as **Jeanne Achterberg**, **Jenny Blain**, **Laurel Kendall**, **Ioan Lewis**, **Barbara Myerhoff**, **Stacey Schaefer**, Susan Sered, **Barbara Tedlock**, and **Piers Vitebsky**. *See also* BORI; HUICHOL; KOREA; NAYAKA; SAN; SAR; SEIDR; SORA; ZAR.

WOUNDED HEALER. Many recorded examples of shamanic **initiation** involve a debilitating or life-threatening **illness**, recovery from which is facilitated only by the assistance of **spirits** who instruct the novice that in return for this **healing** s/he must become a shaman. The consistency of this initiatory illness and subsequent healing has led to the application of the term *wounded healer* as a characteristic feature of shamanisms. Nonetheless, such a general term and monolithic approach should be treated with caution since the diversity of indigenous realities resists simplistic classification. The German **performance** artist and "shaman" **Joseph Beuys**'s urge to "show your wound" is reminiscent of the shaman as a wounded healer.

– Y –

YAGÉ. Common **Amazonian** name for the *Banisteriopsis* vine, also known in Quechua as **ayahuasca**.

YAKUT. *See* SAKHA; SIBERIA, NORTHERN AND EASTERN; SIBERIAN AND CENTRAL ASIAN ROCK ART.

YANOMAMO. An **Amazonian** people whose traditional homeland spans the border of Venezuela and Brazil and who remained so remote that **Napoléon Chagnon** could claim that in 1990–91 he spent time in "villages that had never before been visited by outsiders." Partly influenced by Chagnon's writings, and partly due to media and **Christian** missionary presentations, the Yanomamo have been portrayed as an intensely violent society. More recent research challenges this perception.

Among the Yanomamo, the role of shaman carries significant status and is sought by more than a few men of each village. A major part of the shaman hopeful's training involves extreme fasting and instruction by older men in what Chagnon calls the "attributes, habits, songs, mysteries and fancies of the *hekura* **spirits**." These **other-than-human persons** are diminutive and "somewhat coy and fickle," for example, disliking it if their **elected** trainee shamans have **sex**. Hekura have to be attracted and tempted to take up residence in the inner geography (including mountains, streams, and forests) within the shaman. Once a trainee has successfully persuaded the hekura to move in, via the chest, and gains **mastery** over his indwelling **helpers**, he too is called *hekura*. **Illnesses** can be caused or cured by hekura (either the shamans or the spirits they control), sometimes by taking hallucinogens. Reliance on the consumption of **ebene** snuff seems to decrease with experience, but shamanic **performance** always requires self-decoration to attract hekura helpers. As with other hallucinogens, ebene causes **vomiting** and the discharge of copious quantities of nasal mucus, "laden with green powder." This is often described as an unpleasant distraction by ethnographers who are more interested in **visionary** effects than in messy embodiment. Indigenous interpretations rarely divide these results in such a prissy manner.

As elsewhere in Amazonia, Chagnon notes that Yanomamo shamans "cure the sick with magic, **sucking**, singing [cosmological creative **chant** epics involving hekura and "marvelous and fabulous events"], or massaging; diagnose illness and prescribe a magical remedy; and generally intercede [**mediate**] between humans and spirits in the context of health versus sickness." Shamans may also be suspect, at least, of sending "malevolent *hekura*" to cause illness or death. As elsewhere, shamans and hekura are essential **ambiguous**, but they are typically honored "at home."

YAQUI. Calling themselves Yoeme ("people"), the more widely known term *Yaqui* derives from "Hiakim," the Yaqui term for their land, encompassing the southern coastal Mexican region of Sonora and part of southern Arizona. Forming a remote northern outpost of prehistoric **Mesoamerica**, the Yaqui's ancestors remained independent of the Toltec and Aztec empires and fought successfully against the Spanish conquistadors until **Christian** conversion conducted by Jesuits, when they settled in the eight towns of Pótam, Vícam, Tórim, Bácum, Cóorit, Huirivis, Belem, and Rahum. **Carlos Castaneda**'s "informant" **Don Juan** was described by him as a Yaqui **sorcerer**, but there is little correspondence between Castaneda's **entheogenic** and **New Age** shamanism pitched at a Euro-American psychedelic audience, and the Yaqui religion, a creative fusion of Catholicism and indigenous practices. A more useful insight into Yaqui religion can be gained from Larry Evers and Felipe Molina's *Yaqui Deer Songs* (1987).

YELLOWTAIL, THOMAS (1903–1993). Medicine man (*akbaalia*) and Sun Dance chief of the Absaroke (**Crow**). He succeeded the

Shoshone medicine man and Sun Dance chief **John Truhujo** (Trehero) and was himself succeeded by **John Pretty on Top** in 1985. In 1972 Yellowtail adopted Michael Fitzgerald and told him everything he needed to know in order to write the biography *Yellowtail* (1991). This details the process by which Yellowtail and the other medicine men were **initiated** and employed. He also contributed four stories to Rodney Frey's *Stories That Make the World* (1995). Yellowtail "**doctored**" as well as worked as a **ritual** leader, but he notes that not all "medicine people" are **healers**. He not only conducted Sun Dances but also presided over the opening of **medicine bundles**. Although Yellowtail presented the "**peyote** way" or **Native American Church** as incompatible with the Sun Dance religion, on the basis of a **visionary** test by the "**medicine father**," **Seven Arrows**, he was a member of a Baptist **Christian** church. Both positions are rooted in an understanding of what "roads" will enable people to travel furthest and of what rites fit with the cultural needs of Plains people: peyote's attachment to Mexico and the Southwest of the United States made it, in his opinion, less adaptable than the less spatially located Baptist tradition.

YOPO. Amazonian snuff prepared from the seeds or nuts of a tree (*Anadenanthera peregrine*) mixed with ash. Its cultural usage is similar to that of **ebene** and **ayahuasca**.

– Z –

ZAR. Discussed by **Ioan Lewis** as a "**possession** cult" that particularly attracts **women** in East **Africa**, giving them a religious role unavailable in locally dominant forms of **Islam** and **Christianity**.

Bibliography

As the scope of the dictionary entries and extent of this bibliography make clear, there is a huge range of literature on shamans, from introductory works, general discussions on such topics as definition, and culture-specific ethnographic works on shamans and their communities across all continents, to "how-to" neo-shaman manuals and psychological analyses. This bibliography is divided into sections loosely based around the geographical regions engaged within the dictionary itself, as well as a number of key themes, but as a matter of course these sections should not be seen as definitive. A "global" approach might risk homogenizing shamans in the specified regions, especially when considering that shamanisms in Africa or Siberia, among other areas, are so vast and so diverse. Nonetheless, while any breakdown of a bibliography into sections risks such metanarrative, a regional approach, at the very least, evinces some of the variety of shamanisms and represents the way in which shamans have been identified in many cultures across the globe.

In addition to these regional sections, the sections on introductory works and general discussions offer examples of some accessible and sometimes classic works on shamans to readers unfamiliar with the topic. While it would be unwieldy to break the bibliography down further into all the themes mentioned in the dictionary entries, there are sections on the key themes of performance, gender, altered consciousness, rock art, neo-shamans, and animism, all of which are, arguably, at the cutting edge of current research. It is important to note not only that shamanism is a construct applied globally but also that the process of globalization has itself had a significant impact on shamanism, no less given the interest of neo-shamans in indigenous and prehistoric cultures, and the accessibility afforded to these and other researchers by the internet as well as shamanism tourism. Inevitably, then, some works are duplicated in more than one section in order, for instance, to connect them with both a theme and a region. The remainder of this introduction to the bibliography briefly orients readers on its structure, pointing to important authors, their works, and key themes and offering critical analysis of the literature where relevant.

INTRODUCTORY WORKS AND GENERAL DISCUSSIONS

A section each on introductory works and more general discussion provides readers unfamiliar with shamanism with an entry point as well as an overall insight into research into the topic. Introductory works tend to be of two types: volumes written by scholars with material aimed at the general reader, and books by neo-shamanic practitioners offering general information alongside instructions for contemporary practice. With such a diversity of shamanistic practices worldwide, those in the former category often risk stripping away what makes each shaman in context so different from another, in order to present a singular "shamanism." For example, although Mircea Eliade's major volume *Shamanism* (1964 [1951]) describes a huge variety of shamanic practices, in the end it tells us more about Eliade's preoccupation with shamanism as an archaic religion originating in the locus classicus of Central Asia and Siberia than it does about shamans themselves. Other authors have tended to reify Eliade's singular, monolithic, and archaic "shamanism" (e.g., Lommel 1967, Harner 1990 [1980]), despite numerous revisions of this problematic approach.

Other recent overviews of shamanism often take one particular approach to shamans—usually the shaman as a healer (e.g., Halifax 1982, Villoldo and Krippner 1986, Krippner and Welch 1992, McClennon 1997) or a master of altered states of consciousness (e.g., Walsh 1990)—once again overgeneralizing what shamanism is. These books serve an important purpose in representing the variety of interpretations scholars bring to the subject, but they should not be seen as stand-alone authoritative or definitive works. Other books, specifically written as introductions to the subject, must be approached with greater caution. Margaret Stutley's *Shamanism: An Introduction* (2003), for instance, despite its recent publication, neglects recent theorizing of the subject and generalizes what shamanism is, in the end reifying Eliade's metanarrative of shamanism as an "ur-religion." Of course, it is difficult to avoid generalizing when attempting to introduce a subject as diverse as shamanism, but other introductions go some way to achieving this, such as Piers Vitebsky's *The Shaman* (1995). Other volumes, rather than attempting to introduce shamanism in its entirety, choose, perhaps more appropriately, to offer a reader on the subject, such as Graham Harvey's *Shamanism: A Reader* (2003).

Just as caution is required when approaching any volume that claims to represent an introduction to shamanism, such critical engagement is in order with regard to introductory manuals written by contemporary Western practitioners, or "neo-shamans." The classic work in this area, perhaps the neo-shamanic equivalent of Eliade, is Michael Harner's manual *The Way of the Shaman* (1990 [1980]). However, Harner's "core shamanism" should not be seen as a value-free, objective concept, but rather as a construct that draws on Eliade's understanding that the shamanic "journey" to other worlds is a definitive feature of shamanism. In addition, core shamanism strips away cultural nuance to provide a technique Westerners can more readily consume. Yet journeying is not universal to all shamans, and cultural specificity is crucial to understanding what shamans do and why they do it. One exceptional neo-shamanic work, Gordon MacLellan's *Shamanism* (1999), does not claim to represent shamanism in its entirety but focuses on other important components of shamanism, especially the role of shamans in their communities as people who negotiate harmonious relations between human people and other-than-human people. Since books like MacLellan's blur the boundary between what might otherwise be too easily dichotomized as "shamans" and "neo-shamans," they are included alongside other introductions and general works as well as in the section listing neo-shamanic works and studies on neo-shamans.

The vast majority of literature on shamans consists of culture-specific ethnographies of shamans, from shorter articles to extensive volumes, with some in multiple volumes and perhaps covering the lifetime of a particular ethnographer who worked with one shamanistic community. Rather than offer a section of ethnographic works, readers will find ethnographies on shamans scattered throughout the regional and thematic sections, as well as the section on general discussions. A short word here on especially significant volumes of an ethnographic nature, then, is in order, especially since these works cover at least 300 years of discourse on shamans so that, interestingly and importantly, a book always speaks of the era in which it was written.

Sergei Shirokogoroff's classic *Psychomental Complex of the Tungus* (1935), for example, stands out for revising the notion that shamans are psychotic, preferring instead to see shamans as accomplished masters of the spirits and/or the altered conscious states with which they engage. But at the same time as attempting to more positively represent these shamans, it might be argued that Shirokogoroff also stereotyped them in another way, distancing practices involving possession states in which shamans lose control (i.e., "possession") or mediate spirits (i.e., "mediumship"). Regarding the latter, Vitebsky's ethnography of the Sora attends to people he defines as shamans who do indeed mediate spirits of the dead. Vitebsky has also, more recently, written an extensive and accessible ethnography on the northeast Siberian Eveny, *The Reindeer People: Living with Animals and Spirits in Siberia* (2005), paying special attention to shamanism since the Russian Revolution. Addressing this theme, along with Siberian shamanism in Western discourse, is Ronald Hutton's volume *Shamans: Siberian Spirituality and the Western Imagination* (2001), a theme taken up earlier by Gloria Flaherty in her important work *Shamanism and the Eighteenth Century* (1992). While neither of these two books is an ethnographic work as such, they are crucial reading (in English) for understanding Siberian shamanism and its reception and subsequent influence in the West.

Caroline Humphrey's work with Urgunge Onon, *Shamans and Elders* (1996), also stands out—not only for being a collaborative work with an indigenous practitioner but also for repositioning the shaman (in Mongolia) as a social player rather than focusing on altered consciousness or shamans as religious specialists separate from daily life. In a similar vein, Michael Taussig's volume *Shamanism, Colonialism, and the Wild Man: A Study in Terror and Healing* (1987) also situates shamans in the Colombian Putomayo in the social arena as active agents negotiating the colonial encounter. Taussig also addresses the tension inherent in, and unstructured nature of, shamanic performance, wherein the outcome may be unpredictable, thereby disrupting perceived notions of shamanism as universally benevolent and successful, and shamans themselves as consistently "in control."

Finally in this section, considering the prevalence of Western interests in indigenous shamans, especially direct encounters between shamans and neo-shamans—both at the positive, creative interface and in neocolonial situations—it is important for scholars to analyze these contemporary expressions. Only rarely is this the case in traditional ethnographies, where what is perceived to be the "authentic" indigenous tradition is accentuated over what is new and allegedly inauthentic and intrusive. But it is worth noting that there have been a few ethnographic comments on neo-shamans, including Merete Demant Jakobsen's (1999) contrasting of practices among the Greenlandic *angakkoq* and core shamanists. Jenny Blain's *Nine Worlds of Seid-Magic* (2002) provides a detailed theorization of contemporary Heathen reconstructions of *seidr* vis-à-vis ancient North European shamanism, a topic also taken up by Galina Lindquist (1997) with reference to urban Sweden and by Robert Wallis in *Shamans/Neo-Shamans* (2003). Wallis examines seidr alongside "Celtic shamanism" (past and present) and neo-shamanic appropriations of Native American spirituality. Along with a variety of papers commenting on the indigenous/neo-shamanic interface (e.g., Clifton 1989, Joralemon 1990, Rose 1992, Geertz 1993, Smith 1994, Johnson 1995, Hoppál 1996, Harvey 1998, Wallis 2000, Townsend 2005), this work indicates that in the "global village" it is imperative to critically theorize the permeability of boundaries between what might once have been rigidly and misleadingly defined as either "indigenous" (authentic/valid) or "new" (inauthentic/invalid).

As the ethnographic works mentioned above attest, the complexities of shamanism worldwide have been a rich source for anthropological and archaeological theorizing. The remaining sections introduce this work.

PERFORMANCE

Shamans are performers in that they may conduct or lead public and dramatic events, ceremonies, or rituals. A number of scholars have studied shamanic practices, and rituals in particular, as a form of performance (e.g., Balzer 1995,

Csordas 1996, Bogoras 1972 [1958], Laderman 1991, Lindquist 1997, Schieffelin 1996, 1998), with the positive assertion that shamans and their communities (of human and other-than-human people) are active agents in the success of the rite. There is a risk that such analyses focus on the externally observed acts of rituals at the expense of internal understandings or knowledge, psychological processes, or the "reality" of encountering spirits. Early travelers and ethnographers often focused on shamans' tricks such as ventriloquism and juggling and concluded that everything shamans did must therefore be a sham. Neo-shamanic author Jonathan Horwitz (1995) has criticized the recent redefinition of shamans as performers as dismissive of the efficacy of shamanic experience, with the logical comparison of shamanic séances with role-play or the acting out of a play on a stage. While shamans do often deploy acting abilities and trickery in their work, though not necessarily in order to deceive clients or audiences, Blain and Wallis (drawing on Csordas 1996 and Schieffelin 1996, 1998) have recently argued (2006a) that the recognition of shamanic ritual as the "active accomplishment of meaning" embraces the creative, agentic nature of performance and the power of practice of all performers involved—including "spirits."

GENDER

Just as gender issues have been at the forefront of anthropological and related research in the humanities and social sciences in recent decades, so shamanism studies have also benefited from the theoretical positioning offered by feminism, gender studies, and queer theory. The issue is far more complex than identifying a preponderance of male shamans in one community (e.g., Siberia) and women shamans in another (e.g., Korea), with gender indicative of status, authority, and ability. Nor is the issue a simple matter of identifying homosexual activity or cross-dressing among shamans. Early literature on shamans, sex, and gender assumed that instances of cross-dressing were indicative of transvestitism, homosexuality, or bisexuality. Such colonial narratives, in line with other Western stereotypes, misleadingly equated the representation of gender as being synonymous with sexual preference. More nuanced analysis has approached shamans traversing both male and female genders or adopting third, fourth, or even multiple genders. Maria Czaplicka (1914) and Marjorie Balzer (1996b) have written about the way in which many Siberian shamans embody a "third class" or gender that may mediate between other persons. Further, Bernard Saladin d'Anglure (1990) notes that a binary model (opposing male and female genders) is insufficient for engaging sensitively with multiple genders among shamans: his "ternary" model offers a more fluid or dynamic perception of gender.

Such comments have challenged the Western binary "male or female" requirement, in which sex and gender are usually synonymous and heterosexuality is presumed to be normative. Far from being universal, these categories are disrupted by shamans who may embody a third or other multiple gender—without reference to sexuality. Other shamans contravene Western dichotomies further, by engaging in heterosexual family life in the "real" world while simultaneously being "married" to a helper of the same sex in the "spirit" world, or vice versa. While the addition of the suffix *-ka* to represent women shamans as *shamanka* serves principally to reify normative Western dichotomies of gender among some neo-shamans (e.g., Matthews 1995), indigenous discourses often offer creative and empowering precedents for other practitioners. For instance, both gay and heterosexual seidr practitioners in Heathenry engage with the concept of *ergi* from ancient sources in order to understand and negotiate their identities in the present (e.g., Blain and Wallis 2000).

ALTERED CONSCIOUSNESS

Ascribing *trance*, *altered states of consciousness*, and related terms to shamanic practices has become de rigueur to the point that these terms are almost synonymous with shamans in some of the literature. Harner's (1990 [1980]) idea of a "shamanic state of consciousness" marks a good example, not only making altered states inseparable from shamanism but also privileging an alleged shamanic state from others—indeed, harking back to Shirokogoroff's (1935) view that shamans are able to control their spirits and altered states of consciousness while other engagements with spirits (i.e., possession and mediumship) do not. The vast literature on shamans and related practices from which this bibliography selects indicates that such an emphasis on one specific altered state of consciousness is too restrictive.

Returning to Vitebsky's (1993) ethnography on the Sora who mediate spirits, or attending to the possession practices in Vodou, a more nuanced term might be *altered consciousness* (see Blain and Wallis 2006a). Moreover, while to Western eyes altered consciousness appears to be in play during many shamanic practices, it must be remembered that such terminology is specific to the compartmentalizing attitude of the West: many shamans themselves will not use this nomenclature, preferring instead to speak of other worlds, spirits, and other-than-human persons who enable them to negotiate harmony in their everyday community setting. It is important to be sensitive to shamans' own understandings since the overuse of such terms as *altered states of consciousness* risks a psychologizing process, as some scholars focus on the neuropsychology—even neurotheology—at the expense of what it is that shamans do in their communities (e.g., Winkelman 2000). Roberte Hamayon (e.g., 1993,

1996, 1998), in notable contrast, argues that, in Siberia, the "marriage" between shamans and their helpers is more significant in understanding what these shamans do than the "ecstasy," "mastery of spirits," or "journeying" emphasized by other scholars.

ROCK ART

The association between rock art and shamanism is enduring, with the "sorcerer" in the cave of Les Trois Freres in the Dordogne, France, often being cited as a Paleolithic shaman. Such an association is exaggerated by the perception that shamanism is humanity's oldest religion (e.g., Riches 1994, Ripinsky-Naxon 1993, McClennon 1997) and that cave art marks the origin of art (e.g., Lommel 1967). This, alongside recent theorizing of a shamanistic interpretation of rock art in an extensive body of literature, indicates that a separate section of the bibliography on rock art is pertinent.

As the dictionary entry suggests, it is important to consider that the recent shamanistic interpretation of rock art has prompted much debate, with the emotive terms *shamaniac* and *shamanophobe* being exchanged between scholars. After David Lewis-Williams and Thomas Dowson (1988) made the initial suggestion of a neuropsychological model for interpreting Southern African rock art and Upper Paleolithic cave art, many rock art scholars applied the model to other traditions across the globe (e.g., Sales 1992, Whitley 1992, Dronfield 1996, Bradley 1997, Patterson 1998). Overall, this risked the shamanistic interpretation becoming a metanarrative, as various commentators argued (e.g., Bahn 1998, Solomon 2000). In response, Lewis-Williams and Dowson and other scholars (e.g., Wallis 2002) have refined the shamanistic approach with a sensitive understanding of shamanism as diverse and culturally nuanced. The latest development involves the sophisticated deployment of animism by Dowson, offering a broader frame within which to interpret shamans and rock art in community contexts.

NEO-SHAMANS

Scholars are often quick to make a distinction between what is indigenous or prehistoric and what is an appropriation of these traditions by Westerners—that is, "neo-shamanism." In instances where there is cultural theft, such a distinction is apt (e.g., Geertz 1993, Hobson 1978, Johnson 1995, Kehoe 1990, Wallis 2003). For example, some neo-shamans, New Agers, Pagans, and others (e.g., Storm 1972, Hungry Wolf 1973) have ignored Native American objections and protests (e.g., Green 1988, Rose 1992, Smith 1994). However, while there are differences between some neo-shamanisms and some indigenous shamanisms, as well as differences between particular indigenous shamanisms, it is misleading to exaggerate these differences into some supposedly definitive statement—especially one embroiled in notions of authenticity. In offering a section of the bibliography on neo-shamans, the intention is not to distance contemporary Western practices from other shamanisms or to indicate that indigenous shamanisms are pristine and authentic, uninfluenced by the West, including by neo-shamans. Rather, this section offers readers examples of literature on neo-shamans by scholars, and key works by neo-shamans on shamanism, in an effort to represent the diversity of neo-shamanisms and the interface between neo-shamanisms, indigenous shamanisms, and prehistoric shamanisms.

ANIMISM

If studies on shamans always tend to reflect current discourses in academe, then at the time of writing, one of the most significant developments has been the theorization of "animism" and its contribution to our understanding of shamans. In the 19th century, Edward Tylor defined *animism* (what would now be termed "old animism") as "the belief in spirits." He presented this as the essence of religion and alleged that "primitive" people made a mistake in believing in "spirits." The concept has been revisited by Nurit Bird-David (e.g., 1993, 1999), Eduardo Viveiros de Castro (e.g., 1992, 1998, 1999), Signe Howell (e.g., 1984, 1989), Graham Harvey (2005), and others who offer a "new animism": animism as a relational ontology, the recognition that the world is full of persons, only some of whom are human. Shamans act as mediators in order to broker harmonious relations between human and other-than-human people. Harvey (2005) has argued that animism makes shamans both possible and necessary because their roles are about dealing with the problems of living in a relational world. Carlos Fausto (e.g., 2004), furthermore, points to the darker side of animism in the Amazon: in a living world where warfare and hunting are preferred means of affirming one's agency and intentionality, rather than being used or preyed upon by other persons, shamans interact relationally with powerful other-than-human persons, especially jaguars—resulting in "a predatory animism."

Just as neo-shamans have engaged with scholarship on shamans with regard to gender, postcolonial critiques, and performance, so new animism has become a resource for identity formation, and Blain and Wallis have termed Pagan practitioners engaging with "living landscapes" as "new/indigenes" (2002, 2006b). New animism offers a critically engaged methodology for examining indigenous realities and moves analysis beyond the rather paradigm-restrictive "shamanistic communities," which assumes that the worldview of the community at issue is "shamanistic" and that shamans are the most important persons in such communities. In contrast, animism situates shamans (and all human people) within a wider network or web of relationships with other-than-human people, which are dynamic, relational, and creatively agentic.

INTRODUCTORY WORKS

Eliade, Mircea. 1964 [1951]. *Shamanism: Archaic Techniques of Ecstasy*. New York: Pantheon.

Flaherty, Gloria. 1992. *Shamanism and the Eighteenth Century*. Princeton, N.J.: Princeton University Press.

Halifax, Joan. 1979. *Shamanic Voices: A Survey of Visionary Narratives*. London: Arkana.

———. 1982. *Shaman: The Wounded Healer*. London: Thames and Hudson.

Harvey, Graham, ed. 2000. *Indigenous Religions: A Companion*. London: Cassell.

———, ed. 2002. *Readings in Indigenous Religions*. London: Continuum.

———, ed. 2003. *Shamanism: A Reader*. London: Routledge.

———. 2005. *Animism: Respecting the Living World*. London: Hurst; New York: Columbia University Press; Adelaide: Wakefield Press.

Hoppál, Mihály, ed. 1984. *Shamanism in Eurasia*. Göttingen: Edition Herodot.

Hutton, Ronald. 1993. *The Shamans of Siberia*. Glastonbury, Somerset: Isle of Avalon Press.

———. 2002. *Shamans: Siberian Spirituality and the Western Imagination.* London: Hambledon.

Lewis, Ioan M. 1989. *Ecstatic Religion: A Study of Shamanism and Spirit Possession*. 2nd ed. London: Routledge.

MacLellan, Gordon. 1999. *Shamanism*. London: Piatkus.

Price, Neil S., ed. 2001. *The Archaeology of Shamanism*. London: Routledge.

Ripinsky-Naxon, Michael. 1993. *The Nature of Shamanism: Substance and Function of a Religious Metaphor*. Albany: State University of New York Press.

Stutley, Margaret. 2003. S*hamanism: An Introduction*. London: Routledge.

Thomas, Nicholas, and Caroline Humphrey, eds. 1994. *Shamanism, History, and the State*. Ann Arbor: University of Michigan Press.

Vitebsky, Piers. 1995. *The Shaman*. London: Macmillan.

Wallis, Robert J. 2003. *Shamans/Neo-Shamans: Ecstasy, Alternative Archaeology and Contemporary Pagans*. London: Routledge.

Walsh, Roger N. 1990. *The Spirit of Shamanism*. Los Angeles: Jeremy Tarcher.

GENERAL DISCUSSIONS

Abram, David. 1997. *Spell of the Sensuous*. New York: Vintage Books.

Achterberg, Jeanne. 1985. *Imagery in Healing: Shamanism and Modern Medicine*. Boston: Shambhala.

——. 1991. *Woman As Healer*. Boston: Shambhala.

Adamec, Ludwig W. 2001. *Historical Dictionary of Islam*. Lanham, Md.: Scarecrow Press.

Allegro, John. 1970. *The Sacred Mushroom and the Cross*. Garden City, N.Y.: Doubleday.

Atkinson, Jane M. 1992. "Shamanisms Today." *Annual Review of Anthropology* 21:307–30.

Bailey, Michael. 2003. *Historical Dictionary of Witchcraft*. Lanham, Md.: Scarecrow Press.

Blain, Jenny, and Robert J. Wallis. 2006a. "Ritual Reflections, Practitioner Meanings: Disputing the Terminology of Neo-Shamanic 'Performance.'" *Journal of Ritual Studies* 20 (1): 21–36.

Boas, Franz. 1955. *Primitive Art*. New York: Dover.

Bourguignon, Erika. 1976. *Possession*. San Francisco: Chandler and Sharp.

Boyer, L. B. 1969. "Shamans: To Set the Record Straight." *American Anthropologist* 71:307–9.

Brown, Michael F. 1988. "Shamanism and Its Discontents." *Medical Anthropology Quarterly* 2 (2): 102–20.

——. 1989. "Dark Side of the Shaman." *Natural History* (November): 8–10.

Butt, A., S. Wavell, and N. Epton. 1966. *Trances*. London: Allen & Unwin.

Calestro, Kenneth. 1972. "Psychotherapy, Faith Healing, and Suggestion." *International Journal of Psychiatry* 10 (2): 83–113.

Campbell, Joseph. 1949. *The Hero with a Thousand Faces.* Princeton, N.J.: Princeton University Press.

——. 1959. *The Masks of God: Primitive Mythology.* New York: Viking Press.

Carrasco, David, and J. M. Swanberg, eds. 1985. *Waiting for the Dawn: Mircea Eliade in Perspective*. Boulder, Colo.: Westview Press.

Csordas, Thomas J. 1996. "Imaginal Performance and Memory in Ritual Healing," in Carol Laderman and Marina Roseman, eds., *The Performance of Healing*, 91–114. London: Routledge.

Deleuze, Gilles, and Félix Guttari. 1972. *A Thousand Plateaus: Capitalism and Schizophrenia*. Minneapolis: University of Minnesota Press.

Devereux, George. 1956. "Normal and Abnormal: The Key Problem of Psychiatric Anthropology," in J. B. Casagrande and T. Gladwin, eds., *Some Uses of Anthropology: Theoretical and Applied*, 22–48. Washington, D.C.: Anthropological Society of Washington.

——. 1961. "Shamans as Neurotics." *American Anthropologist* 63 (5): 1088–90.

Devereux, Paul. 1992. *Shamanism and the Mystery Lines: Ley Lines, Spirit Paths, Shape-Shifting and Out-of-Body-Travel*. London: Quantum.

——. 1997. *The Long Trip: A Prehistory of Psychedelia*. New York: Arkana.

——. 2001. "Did Ancient Shamanism Leave a Monumental Record on the Land as Well as in Rock Art?" in Robert J. Wallis and Kenneth Lymer, eds. *A Permeability of Boundaries? New Approaches to the Archaeology of Art, Religion and Folklore*, BAR International Series 936, 1–7. Oxford: British Archaeological Reports.

Diderot, Denis, et al. 2001 [1765]. "Shamans Are Imposters Who Claim They Consult the Devil—And Who Are Sometimes Close to the Mark," in Jeremy Narby and Francis Huxley, eds., *Shamans through Time: 500 Years on the Path to Knowledge*, 32–35. London: Thames & Hudson.

Downton, J. V. 1989. "Individuation and Shamanism." *Journal of Analytic Psychology* 34:73–88.

Eliade, Mircea. 1961. "Recent Works on Shamanism." *History of Religions* 1 (1): 152–86.

——. 1964 [1951]. *Shamanism: Archaic Techniques of Ecstasy*. New York: Pantheon.

Flaherty, Gloria. 1988. "The Performing Artist as the Shaman of Higher Civilisation." *Modern Language* 103 (3): 519–39.

——. 1989. "Goethe and Shamanism." *Modern Language* 104 (3): 580–96.

——. 1992. *Shamanism and the Eighteenth Century*. Princeton, N.J.: Princeton University Press.

Forte, Robert, ed. 1997. *Entheogens and the Future of Religion*. San Francisco: Council on Spiritual Practices.

Francfort, Henri-Paul, and Roberte N. Hamayon, eds. 2001. *The Concept of Shamanism: Uses and Abuses*. Budapest: Akadémiai Kiadó.

Frazer, James. 1890. *The Golden Bough*. London: Macmillan.

——. 1975. *Hallucinogens and Culture*. Novato, Calif.: Chandler and Sharp.

——. 1978. "The Art of 'Being Huichol,'" in K. Berrin, ed., *Art of the Huichol Indians*, 18–34. San Francisco: Fine Arts Museum of San Francisco.

——. 2003. *Visions of a Huichol Shaman*. Philadelphia: University of Pennsylvania.

Furst, Peter T., ed. 1972. *Flesh of the Gods: The Ritual Use of Hallucinogens*. London: Allen & Unwin.

Gilberg, R. 1984. "How to Recognise a Shaman among Other Ritual Specialists?" in Mihály Hoppál, ed., *Shamanism in Eurasia*, 21–27. Göttingen: Edition Herodot.

Gmelin, Johann G. 2001 [1751]. "Shamans Deserve Perpetual Labor for Their Hocus-Pocus," in Jeremy Narby and Francis Huxley, eds., *Shamans through*

Time: 500 Years on the Path to Knowledge, 27–28. London: Thames & Hudson.

Groesbeck, C. Jess. 1989. "C. G. Jung and the Shaman's Vision." *Journal of Analytical Psychology* 34 (3): 255–75.

Grof, Stanislav. 1975. *Realms of the Human Unconscious: Observations from LSD Research*. London: Souvenir Press.

——. 1980. *LSD Psychotherapy*. Pomona, Calif.: Hunter House.

——. 1998. *The Cosmic Game*. Albany: State University of New York Press.

——. 2000. *Psychology of the Future*. Albany: State University of New York Press.

Guenther, Mathias G. 1999. "From Totemism to Shamanism: Hunter-Gatherer Contributions to World Mythology and Spirituality," in Richard B. Lee and Richard Daly, eds., *The Cambridge Encyclopedia of Hunters and Gatherers*, 426–33. Cambridge: Cambridge University Press.

Halifax, Joan. 1979. *Shamanic Voices: A Survey of Visionary Narratives*. London: Arkana.

——. 1982. *Shaman: The Wounded Healer*. London: Thames & Hudson.

Handelman, Donald. 1968. "Shamanizing on an Empty Stomach." *American Anthropologist* 70:353–56.

Harner, Michael, ed. 1973. *Hallucinogens and Shamanism*. Oxford: Oxford University Press.

Harvey, Graham, ed. 2000. *Indigenous Religions: A Companion*. London: Cassell.

——, ed. 2002. *Readings in Indigenous Religions*. London: Continuum.

——, ed. 2003. *Shamanism: A Reader*. London: Routledge.

——. 2005. *Animism: Respecting the Living World*. London: Hurst; New York: Columbia University Press; Adelaide: Wakefield Press.

Harvey, Graham, and Karen Ralls, eds. 2001. *Indigenous Religious Musics*. Aldershot, England: Ashgate.

Hayden, Brian. 2003. *Shamans, Sorcerers and Saints: A Prehistory of Religion*. Washington, D.C.: Smithsonian Books.

Heinze, Ruth-Inge, ed. 1991. *Shamans of the 20th Century*. New York: Irvington.

Herle, Anita. 1993. "Views: Shaman Insights." *Museums Journal* (December): 24.

Holm, Nils G., ed. 1980. *Religious Ecstasy*. Stockholm: Almqvist & Wiksell.

——, ed. 2000. *Ethnography Is a Heavy Rite: Studies of Comparative Religion in Honor of Juha Pentikäinen*. Turku, Finland: Åbo Akademi.

Hoppál, Mihály, ed. 1984. *Shamanism in Eurasia*. Göttingen: Edition Herodot.

Hoppál, Mihály, and Keith Howard, eds. 1993. *Shamans and Cultures*. Budapest: Akadémiai Kiadó.

Hoppál, Mihály, and Otto von Sadovszky, eds. 1989. *Shamanism: Past and Present*. Budapest: Hungarian Academy of Sciences.

Houston, Jean. 1987. "Foreword: The Mind and Soul of the Shaman," in Shirley Nicholson, ed., *Shamanism: An Expanded View of Reality*, vii–xiii. Wheaton, Ill.: Quest Books.

Hultkrantz, Åke. 1973. "A Definition of Shamanism." *Temenos* 9:25–37.

——. 1998a. "The Meaning of Ecstasy in Shamanism," in Helmut Wautischer, ed., *Tribal Epistemologies: Essays in the Philosophy of Anthropology*, 163–73. Aldershot, England: Ashgate.

——. 1998b. "On the History of Research in Shamanism," in Juha Pentikäinen, T. Jaatinen, I. Lehtinen, and M.-R. Saloniemi, eds., *Shamans*, 51–70. Tampere Museums Publications 45. Tampere, Finland: Tampere Museums.

——. 1998c. "Rejoinder," in Helmut Wautischer, ed., *Tribal Epistemologies: Essays in the Philosophy of Anthropology*, 188–90. Aldershot, England: Ashgate.

Hutton, Ronald. 2001. *Shamans: Siberian Spirituality and the Western Imagination.* London: Hambledon.

Huxley, Aldous. 1932a. *The Art of Seeing*. New York: Harper.

——. 1932b. *Brave New World*. London: Chatto & Windus.

——. 1946. *The Perennial Philosophy*. New York: Harper.

——. 1952. *The Devils of Loudon*. London: Chatto & Windus.

——. 1954. *The Doors of Perception*. New York: Harper.

——. 1956. *Heaven and Hell*. London: Chatto & Windus.

——. 1962. *Island*. London: Chatto & Windus.

Insoll, Timothy. 2001. *Archaeology and World Religion*. London: Routledge.

Jakobsen, Merete Demant. 1999. *Shamanism: Traditional and Contemporary Approaches to the Mastery of Spirits and Healing*. Oxford: Berghahn Books.

Jensen, Alan F. 1996. "Possible Criteriological Categories Used in the Judgement of the Authenticity of Shamanism," in D. G. Bromley and Lewis F. Carter, eds., *Religion and the Social Order: The Issue of Authenticity in the Study of Religions*, 191–206. Official Publication of the Association for the Sociology of Religion, vol. 6. Greenwich, Conn: JAI Press.

Jeter, Kris. 1990. "The Shaman: The Gay and Lesbian Ancestor of Humankind." *Marriage and Family Review* 14 (2–3): 317–34.

Jilek, W. G. 1971. "From Crazy Witch Doctor to Auxiliary Psychotherapist: The Changing Image of the Medicine Man." *Psychiatric Clinician* 4:200–220.

Kalweit, Holger. 1988. *Dreamtime and Inner Space: The World of the Shaman.* Boston: Shambhala.

——. 2000. *Shamans, Healers and Medicine Men.* Boston: Shambhala.

Kapferer, Bruce. 1995. "From the Edge of Death: Sorcery and the Motion of Consciousness," in Anthony P. Cohen and Nigel Rapport, eds., *Questions of Consciousness*, 134–52. London: Routledge.

——. 1997. *The Feast of the Sorcerer: Practices of Consciousness and Power.* Chicago: University of Chicago Press.

Kehoe, Alice B. 2000. *Shamans and Religion: An Anthropological Exploration in Critical Thinking*. Prospect Heights, Ill.: Waveland Press.

Kiev, Ari. 1964. *Magic, Faith, and Healing*. New York: Free Press.

Krippner, Stanley, and Alberto Villoldo. 1977. *The Realms of Healing.* Berkeley, Calif.: Celestial Arts.

Krippner, Stanley, and Patrick Welch. 1992. *Spiritual Dimensions of Healing: From Tribal Shamanism to Contemporary Health Care*. New York: Irvington.

Kroeber, Alfred L. 1940. "Psychotic Factors in Shamanism." *Character and Personality* 8:204–15.

La Barre, Weston. 1972. "Hallucinogens and the Shamanic Origins of Religion," in Peter T. Furst, ed., *Flesh of the Gods: The Ritual Use of Hallucinogens*, 261–78. New York: Praeger.

Latour, Bruno. 2004. *Politics of Nature*. Cambridge, Mass.: Harvard University Press.

Laufer, Berthold. 1917. "Origin of the Word Shaman." *American Anthropologist* 19:361–71.

Letcher, Andy. 2006. *Shroom: A Cultural History of the Magic Mushroom*. London: Faber & Faber.

Levy, Mark. 1993. *Technicians of Ecstasy: Shamanism and the Modern Artist*. Norfolk, Conn.: Bramble Books.

Lewin, Louis. 1924. *Phantastica: Die Betäubende und Erregenden Genussmittel.* Berlin: Georg Stilke.

——. 1931. *Phantastica: Narcotic and Stimulating Drugs, Their Use and Abuse.* New York: Dutton and Co.

Lewis, Ioan M. 1984. "What Is a Shaman?" in Mihály Hoppál, ed., *Shamanism in Eurasia*, 3–12. Göttingen: Edition Herodot.

——. 1986. *Religion in Context: Cults and Charisma*. Cambridge: Cambridge University Press.

——. 1989. *Ecstatic Religion: A Study of Shamanism and Spirit Possession*. 2nd ed. London: Routledge.

——. 1991 [1988]. "Shamanism," in Stewart Sutherland, Leslie Houlden, and Peter Clarke, eds., *The World's Religions: The Study of Religion, Traditional and New Religion*, 67–77. London: Routledge.

——. 1999a. *Arguments with Ethnography*. London: Athlone.

——. 1999b. "Shamans and Sex: A Comparative Perspective," in Ioan M. Lewis, *Arguments with Ethnography*, 106–14. London: Athlone.

——. 2003. "Trance, Possession, Shamanism and Sex." *Anthropology of Consciousness* 14 (1): 20–39.

Lommel, Andreas. 1967. *Shamanism: The Beginnings of Art*. New York: McGraw-Hill.

MacLellan, Gordon. 1999. *Shamanism*. London: Piatkus.

McClennon, James. 1997. "Shamanic Healing, Human Evolution, and the Origin of Religion." *Journal for the Scientific Study of Religion* 36 (3): 345–54.

——. 2001. *Wondrous Healing: Shamanism, Human Evolution and the Origin of Religion*. DeKalb: Northern Illinois University Press.

Métraux, Alfred. 1949. "Religion and Shamanism," in Julian H. Steward, ed., *Handbook of South American Indians*, 5:559–99. Washington, D.C.: GPO.

——. 1957. "Dramatic Elements in Ritual Possession." *Diogenes* 11:18–36.

Mitrani, Phillipe. 1992. "A Critical Overview of the Psychiatric Approaches to Shamanism." *Diogenes* 158:145–64.

Morris, Romma H. 1995. "Woman as Shaman: Reclaiming the Power to Heal." *Women's Studies* 24:573–84.

Morrison, Jim. 1971. *The Lords and the New Creatures.* New York: Simon and Schuster.

——. 1995. *An American Prayer.* Los Angeles: Western Lithographers.

Neu, Jerome. 1975. "Levi-Strauss on Shamanism." *Man* 10 (1): 285–92.

Noel, Daniel C. 1990. *Paths to the Power of Myth: Joseph Campbell and the Study of Religion.* New York: Crossroad.

——. 1997. *The Soul of Shamanism: Western Fantasies, Imaginal Realities*. New York: Continuum.

Nolan, E. P. 1985. "The Forbidden Forest: Eliade as Artist and Shaman," in David Carrasco and Jane M. Swanberg, eds., *Waiting for the Dawn: Mircea Eliade in Perspective*, 108–22. Boulder, Colo.: Westview Press.

Noll, Richard. 1983. "Shamanism and Schizophrenia: A State-Specific Approach to the 'Schizophrenia Metaphor' of Shamanic States." *American Ethnologist* 10:443–59.

——. 1985. "Mental Imagery Cultivation as a Cultural Phenomenon: The Role of Visions in Shamanism." *Current Anthropology* 26:443–61.

——. 1989. "What Has Really Been Learned about Shamanism?" *Journal of Psychoactive Drugs* 21 (1): 47–50.

Osterreich, T. K. 1966. *Possession: Demoniacal and Other*. Secaucus, N.J.: Citadel Press.

Pas, Julian F. 1998. *Historical Dictionary of Taoism*. Lanham, Md.: Scarecrow Press.

Perkinson, James W. 2005. *Shamanism, Racism and Hip Hop Culture.* New York: Palgrave Macmillan.

Peters, Larry G., and Douglass Price-Williams. 1980. "Towards an Experiential Analysis of Shamanism." *American Anthropologist* 9:21–46.

Petrovich, Awakum. 2001 [1672]. "The Shaman: 'A Villain of a Magician Who Calls Demons,'" in Jeremy Narby and Francis Huxley, eds., *Shamans through Time: 500 Years on the Path to Knowledge*, 18–20. London: Thames & Hudson.

Pilch, John J. 2005. "Holy Men and Their Sky Journeys: A Cross-Cultural Model." *Biblical Theology Bulletin* 5:106–11.

Porterfield, Amanda. 1987. "Shamanism: A Psychosocial Definition." *Journal of the American Academy of Religion* 55 (4): 721–39.

Prebish, Charles S. 1993. *Historical Dictionary of Buddhism*. Lanham, Md.: Scarecrow Press.

Price, Neil S. 2001a. "An Archaeology of Altered States: Shamanism and Material Culture Studies," in Neil Price, ed. *The Archaeology of Shamanism*, 3–16. London: Routledge.

——, ed. 2001b. *The Archaeology of Shamanism*. London: Routledge.

Prince, Raymond, ed. 1968. *Trance and Possession States*. Montreal: R. M. Bucke Memorial Society.

——. 1982a. "Introduction to Shamans and Endorphins." *Ethos* 10 (4): 299–302.

——. 1982b. "Shamans and Endorphins: Hypothesis for a Synthesis." *Ethos* 10 (4): 409–23.

Reinhard, Johan. 1976. "Shamanism and Spirit Possession: The Definition Problem," in John T. Hitchcock and Rex L. Jones, eds., *Spirit Possession in the Nepal Himalayas*, 12–20. Warminster, England: Aris & Phillips.

Riches, David. 1994. "Shamanism: The Key to Religion." *Man* 29:381–405.

Ripinsky-Naxon, Michael. 1989. "Hallucinogens, Shamanism, and the Cultural Process: Symbolic Archeology and Dialectics." *Anthropos* 84:219–24.

——. 1993. *The Nature of Shamanism: Substance and Function of a Religious Metaphor*. Albany: State University of New York Press.

Roney-Dougal, Serena. N.d. "Walking between the Worlds: Links between Psi, Psychedelics, Shamanism and Psychosis—An Overview of the Literature." www.psi-researchcentre.co.uk/article_1.html.

Rouget, Gilbert. 1985. *Music and Trance*. Chicago: University of Chicago Press.

Rudgeley, Richard. 1993. *The Alchemy of Culture: Intoxicants in Society*. London: British Museum Press.

Rushkoff, Douglas. 1994. *Cyberia: Life in the Trenches of Hyperspace*. San Francisco: HarperCollins.

Samuel, Geoffrey. 1990. *Mind, Body and Culture: Anthropology and the Biological Interface*. Cambridge: Cambridge University Press.

Sarris, Greg. 1993. *Keeping Slug Woman Alive*. Berkeley: University of California Press.

——. 1994a. *Grand Avenue*. New York: Penguin.

——. 1994b. *Mabel McKay: Weaving the Dream*. Berkeley: University of California Press.

Schieffelin, Edward. 1996. "On Failure in Performance: Throwing the Medium out of the Séance," in Carol Laderman and Marina Roseman, eds., *The Performance of Healing*, 59–90. London: Routledge.

——. 1998. "Problematising Performance," in Felicia Hughes-Freeland, ed., *Ritual, Performance, Media*, 194–207. London: Routledge.

Senn, Harry A. 1989. "Jungian Shamanism." *Journal of Psychoactive Drugs* 21 (1): 113–21.

Sered, Susan S. 1992. *Women as Ritual Experts: The Religious Lives of Elderly Jewish Women in Jerusalem*. Oxford: Oxford University Press.

Severi, Bruno. 1994. "Parapsychological Publications in Non-Parapsychology Journals." *European Journal of Parapsychology* 10:104–29.

Shapiro, Warren. 1998. "Ideology, 'History of Religions' and Hunter-Gatherer Studies." *Journal of the Royal Anthropological Institute* 4 (3): 489–510.

Sherratt, Andrew. 1995a. "Alcohol and Its Alternatives: Symbol and Substance in Pre-Industrial Cultures," in Paul E. Lovejoy, Jordan Goodman, and Andrew Sherratt, eds., *Consuming Habits: Drugs in History and Anthropology*, 11–46. London: Routledge.

——. 1995b. "Introduction: Peculiar Substances," in Paul E. Lovejoy, Jordan Goodman, and Andrew Sherratt, eds., *Consuming Habits: Drugs in History and Anthropology*, 1–10. London: Routledge.

Shulgin, Alexander, and Ann Shulgin. 1991. *PiHKAL (Phenethylamines I Have Known and Loved): A Chemical Love Story.* Berkeley, Calif.: Transform Press.

——. 1997. *TiKHAL (Tryptamines I Have Known and Loved): The Continuation.* Berkeley, Calif.: Transform Press.

Siegel, Ronald K. 1977. "Hallucinations." *Scientific American* 237:132–40.

Siikala, Anna-Leena, and Mihály Hoppál. 1998. *Studies on Shamanism.* Helsinki: Finnish Anthropological Society; Budapest: Akadémiai Kiadó.

Silverman, Julian. 1967. "Shamans and Acute Schizophrenia." *American Anthropologist* 69:21–31.

Smith, Jonathan Z. 1987. *To Take Place: Toward a Theory of Ritual*. Chicago: University of Chicago Press.

Smith, Linda T. 1999. *Decolonizing Methodologies: Research and Indigenous Peoples*. London: Zed Books; Dunedin, New Zealand: University of Otago Press.

Stoller, Paul. 1997. *Sensuous Scholarship*. Philadelphia: University of Pennsylvania Press.

Stone, Alby. 2003. *Explore Shamanism.* Loughborough, United Kingdom: Explore Books.

Stutley, Margaret. 2003. *Shamanism: An Introduction*. London: Routledge.

Tart, Charles T. 1969. *Altered States of Consciousness*. New York: E. P. Dutton.

——. 1975. *Transpersonal Psychologies*. London: Routledge & Kegan Paul.

Tedlock, Barbara. 2005. *The Woman in the Shaman's Body*. New York: Bantam.

Tepperman, Lorne, and Jenny Blain. 2005. *Think Twice: Sociology Looks at Current Social Issues.* Englewood Cliffs, N.J.: Prentice Hall.

Thomas, Nicholas, and Caroline Humphrey, eds. 1994. *Shamanism, History, and the State*. Ann Arbor: University of Michigan Press.

Tucker, Michael. 1992. *Dreaming with Open Eyes: The Shamanic Spirit in Contemporary Art and Culture*. London: HarperCollins.

Turner, Edith. 1992. "The Reality of Spirits." *ReVision* 15 (1): 28–32. Reprinted in Graham Harvey, ed., *Shamanism: A Reader* (London: Routledge, 2003), 145–52.

——. 1993. "The Reality of Spirits: A Tabooed or Permitted Field of Study?" *Anthropology of Consciousness* 3 (1): 9–13.

Villoldo, Alberto, and Stanley Krippner. 1986. *Healing States: A Journey into the World of Spiritual Healing and Shamanism*. New York: Simon & Schuster.

Vitebsky, Piers. 1995. *The Shaman*. London: Macmillan.

——. 2000. "Shamanism," in Graham Harvey, ed., *Indigenous Religions: A Companion*, 55–67. London: Cassell.

Voigt, V. 1984. "Shaman—Person or Word?" in Mihály Hoppál, ed., *Shamanism in Eurasia*, 13–20. Göttingen: Edition Herodot.

Wallis, Robert J. 2003. *Shamans/Neo-Shamans: Ecstasy, Alternative Archaeology and Contemporary Pagans*. London: Routledge.

——. 2004. "Shamanism and Art," in Mariko N. Walter and Eva N. Fridman, eds., *Shamanism: An Encyclopedia of World Beliefs, Practices, and Culture*, 1:21–28. Santa Barbara, Calif.: ABC-CLIO.

Walsh, Roger N. 1989. "What Is a Shaman? Definition, Origin and Distribution." *Journal of Transpersonal Psychology* 21 (1): 1–11.

——. 1990. *The Spirit of Shamanism*. Los Angeles: Jeremy Tarcher.

Wasson, R. Gordon. 1969. *Soma: The Divine Mushroom of Immortality*. New York: Harcourt, Brace and World.

——. 1978. *The Road to Eleusis: Unveiling the Secret of the Mysteries*. New York: Harcourt, Brace and Jovanovich.

——. 1986. *Persephone's Quest: Entheogens and the Origins of Religion*. New Haven, Conn.: Yale University Press.

Winkelman, Michael. 1986. "Trance States: A Theoretical Model and Cross-Cultural Analysis." *Ethos* 14:174–203.

——. 1989. "A Cross-Cultural Study of Shamanistic Healers." *Journal of Psychoactive Drugs* 21 (1): 17–24.

——. 1992. *Shamans, Priests and Witches: A Cross-Cultural Study of Magico-Religious Practitioners*. Tempe: Arizona State University Press.

——. 1999. "Altered States of Consciousness and Religious Behavior," in Stephen D. Glazier, ed., *Anthropology of Religion: A Handbook*, 393–428. Westport, Conn.: Praeger.

——. 2000. *Shamanism: The Neural Ecology of Consciousness and Healing*. Westport, Conn.: Bergin & Garvey.

Winkler, Gershom. 2003. *Magic of the Ordinary: Recovering the Shamanic in Judaism*. Berkeley, Calif.: North Atlantic Books.

Wright, Peggy A. 1989. "The Nature of the Shamanic State of Consciousness: A Review." *Journal of Psychoactive Drugs* 21 (1): 25–33.

Young, David E., and Jean-Guy Goulet, eds. 1994. *Being Changed by Cross-Cultural Encounters: The Anthropology of Extraordinary Experience*. Peterborough, Ont.: Broadview Press.

Zelenin, D. 1937. "Zur Frage der Entwicklungeschichte der primitiven Religionen." *Ethnos* 2 (3): 74–91.

REGIONS

Africa

Clune, Francis J. 1973. "A Comment on Voodoo Deaths." *American Anthropologist* 75 (1): 32.

Crapanzano, Vincent. 1980. *Tuhami: Portrait of a Moroccan*. Chicago: University of Chicago Press.

Deren, Maya. 1975. *The Voodoo Gods*. St. Albans, England: Paladin.

Dowson, Thomas A. 1989. "Dots and Dashes: Cracking the Entoptic Code in Bushman Rock Art." *South African Archaeological Society Goodwin Series* 6:84–94.

——. 1994a. "Hunter-Gatherers, Traders, and Slaves: The 'Mfecane' Impact on Bushmen, Their Ritual and Art," in Carolyn Hamilton, ed., *The Mfecane Aftermath: Reconstructive Debates in South Africa's History*, 51–70. Johannesburg: Witwatersrand University Press; Pietermaritzberg: Natal University Press.

——. 1994b. "Reading Art, Writing History: Rock Art and Social Change in Southern Africa." *World Archaeology* 25 (3): 332–45.

——. 1998a. "Like People in Prehistory." *World Archaeology* 29 (3): 333–43.

Dowson, Thomas, and J. David Lewis-Williams, eds. 1994. *Contested Images: Diversity in Southern African Rock Art Research*. Johannesburg: Witwatersrand University Press.

Emboden, William. 1978. "The Sacred Narcotic Lily of the Nile: *Nymphaea caerulea*." *Economic Botany* 32:395–407.

——. 1989. "The Sacred Journey in Dynastic Egypt: Shamanistic Trance in the Context of the Narcotic Water Lily and the Mandrake." *Journal of Psychoactive Drugs* 21:61–75.

Evans-Pritchard, Edward E. 1937. *Witchcraft, Oracles and Magic among the Azande*. Oxford: Oxford University Press.

Fatunmbi, A. Falokun. 1991. *Ìwa-pèlé: Ifá Quest; The Search for the Source of Santería and Lucumí*. New York: Original.

Hall, James. 1994. *Sangoma: My Odyssey into the Spirit World of Africa*. New York: Tarcher/Putnam.

Katz, Richard. 1973. "Education for Transcendence: Lessons from the Kung Zhu/Twasi." *Journal of Transpersonal Psychology* 2:136–55.

——. 1982. *Boiling Energy: Community Healing among the Kalahari !Kung*. Cambridge, Mass.: Harvard University Press.

Katz, Richard, Megan Biesele, and Verna St. Denis. 1997. *Healing Makes Our Hearts Happy: Spirituality and Cultural Transformation among the Kalahari Ju|'hoansi*. Rochester, Vt.: Inner Traditions International.

Lachman, Sheldon J. 1983. "A Psychophysiological Interpretation of Voodoo Illness and Voodoo Death." *Omega* 13 (4): 345–59.

Lewis, Ioan M. 1989. "South of North: Shamanism in Africa." *Paideuma* 35:181–88.

Lewis-Williams, J. David. 1975. "The Drakensberg Rock Paintings as an Expression of Religious Thought," in E. Anati, ed., *Les réligions de la préhistoire*, 413–26. Capo di Ponte, Brescia, Italy: Centro Camuno di Studi Preistorici.

——. 1981. *Believing and Seeing: Symbolic Meanings in Southern San Rock Paintings*. London: Academic Press.

——. 1992. "Ethnographic Evidence Relating to 'Trance' and 'Shamans' among Northern and Southern Bushmen." *South African Archaeological Bulletin* 47:56–60.

——. 1998. "Quanto? The Issue of 'Many Meanings' in Southern African San Rock Art Research." *South African Archaeological Bulletin* 53:86–97.

Lewis-Williams, J. David, and Thomas A. Dowson. 1999 [1989]. *Images of Power: Understanding Bushman Rock Art*. Johannesburg: Southern Book Publishers.

Morris, Brian. 2000. *Animals and Ancestors: An Ethnography*. Oxford: Berg.

Mutwa, Credo. 1996. *Songs of the Stars: The Lore of a Zulu Shaman*. New York: Station Hill Press.

——. 2003. *Zulu Shaman: Dreams, Prophecies, and Mysteries (Song of the Stars)*. Rochester, Vt.: Destiny Books.

Nadel, S. F. 1965 [1958]. "A Study of Shamanism in the Nuba Hills," in William A. Lessa and Evon Z. Vogt, eds., *Reader in Comparative Religion*, 464–79. New York: Harper & Row.

Platvoet, Jan G. 1999. "At War with God: Ju/'hoan Curing Dances." *Journal of Religion in Africa* 29 (1): 2–61.

——. 2001. "Chasing Off God: Spirit Possession in a Sharing Society," in Karen Ralls and Graham Harvey, eds., *Indigenous Religious Musics*, 123–35. Aldershot, England: Ashgate.

Solomon, Anne. 2000. "On Different Approaches to San Rock Art." *South African Archaeological Bulletin* 55:77–78.

Somé, Malidoma P. 1997. *Ritual: Power, Healing and Community: The African Teachings of the Dagara*. London: Penguin Arkana.

——. 1998. *The Healing Wisdom of Africa*. New York: Penguin.

Stoller, Paul. 1989. *Fusion of the Worlds: An Ethnography of Possession among the Songhay of Niger*. Chicago: University of Chicago Press.

——. 1995. *Embodying Colonial Memories: Spirit Possession, Power and the Hauka in West Africa*. London: Routledge.

Stoller, Paul, and Cheryl Olkes. 1987. *In Sorcery's Shadow*. Chicago: University of Chicago Press.

Turner, Edith. 1994. "A Visible Spirit Form in Zambia," in David E. Young and Jean-Guy Goulet, eds., *Being Changed by Cross-Cultural Encounters: The Anthropology of Extraordinary Experience*, 71–95. Peterborough, Ont.: Broadview Press. Reprinted in Graham Harvey, ed., *Readings in Indigenous Religions* (London: Continuum, 2002), 149–73.

Turner, Victor. 1968. *The Drums of Affliction*. Oxford, England: Clarendon.

Willis, Roy. 1999. *Some Spirits Heal, Others Only Dance: A Journey into Human Selfhood in an African Village*. Oxford: Berg.

Young, A. 1975. "Why Amhara Get Kureyna: Sickness and Possession in an Ethiopian Zar Cult." *American Ethnologist* 2:567–84.

The Americas: North, Central, and South America

Anderson, Edward. 1996. *Peyote: The Divine Cactus*. Tucson: University of Arizona Press.

Bahr, Donald, Juan Gregorio, David Lopez, and Albert Alvarez. 1974. *Piman Shamanism and Staying Sickness*. Tucson: University of Arizona Press.

Banfield, Annika, ed. 2005. *They Call Us "Indians."* Stockholm: The World in Our Hands.

Basso, Ellen. 1987. *In Favor of Deceit: A Study of Tricksters in an Amazonian Society*. Tucson: University of Arizona Press.

Black Elk, Wallace H., and William S. Lyon. 1990. *Black Elk: The Sacred Ways of a Lakota.* New York: Harper & Row.

Brown, Joseph Epes. 1971. *The Sacred Pipe*. Baltimore: Penguin.

Brown, Michael T. 1986. *Tsewa's Gift: Magic and Meaning in an Amazonian Society.* Washington, D.C.: Smithsonian Institution Press.

——. 2003. *Who Owns Native Culture?* Cambridge, Mass.: Harvard University Press.

Burroughs, William S., and Allen Ginsberg. 1963. *The Yage Letters*. San Francisco: City Lights Books.

Campbell, Alan T. 1995. *Gettting to Know Waiwai.* London: Routledge.

Carrasco, David. 2002. "Aztec Religion: Sacred Cities, Sacred Actions," in Lawrence E. Sullivan, ed., *Native Religions and Cultures of Central and South America*, 9–32. New York: Continuum.

Castaneda, Carlos. 1968. *The Teachings of Don Juan: A Yaqui Way of Knowledge*. Berkeley: University of California Press.

——. 1971. *A Separate Reality*. London: Bodley Head.

——. 1972. *Journey to Ixtlan: The Lessons of Don Juan*. New York: Simon & Schuster.

——. 1974. *Tales of Power*. New York: Penguin Books.

Castaneda, Margaret R. 1997. *A Magical Journey with Carlos Castaneda*. Victoria, B.C.: Millennia Press.

Castile, George P. 1996. "The Commodification of Indian Identity." *American Anthropologist* 98 (4): 743–49.

Chagnon, Napoléon. 1968. *Yanomamo: The Fierce People*. Austin, Tex.: Holt, Rinehart & Winston.

Churchill, Ward. 1992. *Fantasies of the Master Race*. Monroe, Maine: Common Courage Press.

——. 1994. *Indians Are Us? Culture and Genocide in Native North America.* Monroe, Maine: Common Courage Press.

Clifton, James, ed. 1990. *The Invented Indian: Cultural Fictions and Government Policies*. New Brunswick, N.J.: Transaction.

Clune, Francis J. 1973. "A Comment on Voodoo Deaths." *American Anthropologist* 75 (1): 32.

Coltelli, Laura. 1990. *Winged Words: American Indian Writers Speak*. Lincoln: University of Nebraska Press.

Crocker, John C. 1985. *Vital Souls: Bororo Cosmology, Natural Symbolism, and Shamanism*. Phoenix: University of Arizona Press.

Crow Dog, Leonard, and Richard Erdoes. 1995. *Crow Dog: Four Generations of Sioux Medicine Men*. New York: HarperCollins.

Cushing, Frank H. 1897. "Remarks on Shamanism." *American Philosophical Society Proceedings* 36:183–92.

Davis, Wade. 1996. *One River*. London: Simon & Schuster.

Deloria, Barbara, Kristen Foehner, and Sam Scinta, eds. 1999. *Spirit and Reason: The Vine Deloria, Jr., Reader*. Golden, Colo.: Fulcrum.

Deloria, Philip J. 1998. *Playing Indian*. New Haven, Conn.: Yale University Press.

Deloria, Vine, Jr. 1969. *Custer Died for Your Sins: An Indian Manifesto*. Norman: University of Oklahoma Press.

——. 1973. *God Is Red*. Golden, Colo.: Fulcrum.

——, ed. 1984. *A Sender of Words: Essays in Memory of John G. Neihardt*. Salt Lake City: Howe Brothers.

——. 1997. "Anthros, Indians and Planetary Reality," in Thomas Biolsi and Larry J. Zimmerman, eds., *Indians and Anthropologists: Vine Deloria Jr. and the Critique of Anthropology*, 209–21. Tucson: University of Arizona Press.

——. 1998. "Comfortable Fictions and the Struggle for Turf: An Essay Review of *The Invented Indian: Cultural Fictions and Government Policies*," in Devon A. Mihesuah, ed., *Natives and Academics: Researching and Writing about American Indians*, 65–83. Lincoln: University of Nebraska Press.

——. 1999. *For This Land*. New York: Routledge.

——. 2000. *Singing for a Spirit: A Portrait of the Dakota Sioux*. Santa Fe, N.M.: Clear Light.

Deloria, Vine, Jr., and Clifford Lytle. 1983. *American Indians, American Justice*. Austin: University of Texas Press.

DeMallie, Raymond. 1984. *The Sixth Grandfather: Black Elk's Teachings Given to John G. Neihardt*. Lincoln: University of Nebraska Press.

Deren, Maya. 1975. *The Voodoo Gods*. St. Albans, England: Paladin.

Descola, Philippe. 1998. *Spears of Twilight: Life and Death in the Amazon Jungle*. New York: New Press.

Dobkin de Rios, Marlene. 1972. *Visionary Vine: Hallucinogenic Healing in the Peruvian Amazon*. Prospect Heights, Ill.: Waveland Press.

———. 1974. "The Influence of Psychotropic Flora and Fauna on Mayan Religion." *Current Anthropology* 15:147–64.

———. 1984. *Hallucinogens: Cross-Cultural Perspectives*. Prospect Heights, Ill.: Waveland Press.

———. 1992. *Amazon Healer: The Life and Times of an Urban Shaman*. Prospect Heights, Ill.: Waveland Press.

Douglas, Mary. 1980. "The Authenticity of Castaneda," in Richard de Mille, ed., *The Don Juan Papers: Further Castaneda Controversies*, 25–32. Santa Barbara, Calif.: Ross-Erikson.

Dow, James. 1986. *The Shaman's Touch: Otomí Indian Symbolic Healing*. Salt Lake City: University of Utah Press.

Erdoes, Richard, and Alfonso Ortiz, eds. 1998. *American Indian Trickster Tales*. New York: Viking.

Evers, Larry, and Felipe Molina. 1987. *Yaqui Deer Songs: A Native American Poetry*. Tucson: Sun Tracks and the University of Arizona Press.

Fausto, Carlos. 2004. "A Blend of Blood and Tobacco: Shamans and Jaguars among the Parakanã of Eastern Amazonia," in Neil L. Whitehead and Robin Wright, eds., *In Darkness and Secrecy*, 157–78. Durham, N.C.: Duke University Press.

Felici, Maria L. 2001. "Alcuni caratteri dello sciamanesimo presso gli Indiani del Nord America." *Luce e Ombra*, no. 4.

Fitzgerald, Michael. 1991. *Yellowtail: Crow Medicine Man and Sun Dance Chief*. Norman: University of Oklahoma Press.

Frey, Rodney. 1995. *Stories That Make the World: Oral Literature of the Indian Peoples of the Inland Northwest as Told by Lawrence Aripa, Tom Yellowtail and Other Elders*. Norman: University of Oklahoma Press.

Garza, Mercedes de la. 2002. "Sacred Forces of the Mayan Universe," in Lawrence E. Sullivan, ed., *Native Religions and Religious Cultures of Central and South America*, 93–176. New York: Continuum.

Geertz, Armin W. 1983. "Book of the Hopi: The Hopi's Book?" *Anthropos* 78:547–56.

———. 1987. "Prophets and Fools: The Rhetoric of Hopi Indian Eschatology." *Native American Studies* 1 (1): 33–45.

——. 1994. *The Invention of Prophecy: Continuity and Meaning in Hopi Indian Religion*. Berkeley: University of California Press.

——. 1996. "Contemporary Problems in the Study of Native North American Religions with Specific Reference to the Hopis." *American Indian Quarterly* 20 (3–4): 393–414.

Gibson, Kean. 2001. *Comfa Religion and Creole Language in a Caribbean Community.* Albany, N.Y.: SUNY.

Green, Rayna. 1988. "The Tribe Called Wannabee." *Folklore* 99 (1): 30–55.

Grim, John. 1983. *The Shaman: Patterns of Religious Healing among the Ojibway Indians*. Norman: University of Oklahoma Press.

Hallowell, A. Irving. 1960. "Ojibwa Ontology, Behavior and World View," in Stanley Diamond, ed., *Culture in History*, 19–52. New York: Columbia University Press. Reprinted in Graham Harvey, ed., *Readings in Indigenous Religions* (London: Continuum, 2002), 17–49.

Handelman, Donald. 1967. "The Development of a Washo Shaman." *Ethnology* 6:444–64.

Harner, Michael. 1984 [1972]. *The Jivaro: People of the Sacred Waterfalls*. Berkeley: University of California Press.

Holler, Clyde, ed. 2000. *The Black Elk Reader.* Syracuse, N.Y.: Syracuse University Press.

Hollimon, Sandra E. 2004. "Bear Shamanism and Social Control in Native California Societies." *Society for California Archaeology Newsletter* 38 (3): 26–31.

Hungry Wolf, Adolf. 1973. *The Good Medicine Book*. New York: Warner Paperback Library.

Jocks, Christopher R. 1996. "Spirituality for Sale: Sacred Knowledge in the Consumer Age." *American Indian Quarterly* 20 (3): 415–31.

Johnson, Paul C. 2002. *Secrets, Gossip and Gods: The Transformation of Brazilian Candomblé*. Oxford: Oxford University Press.

Joralemon, Donald. 1984. "The Role of Hallucinogenic Drugs and Sensory Stimuli in Peruvian Ritual Healing." *Culture, Medicine, and Psychiatry* 8:399–430.

Joralemon, Donald, and Douglas Sharon. 1993. *Sorcery and Shamanism: Curanderos and Clients in Northern Peru*. Salt Lake City: University of Utah Press.

Krech, Shepherd. 1999. *The Ecological Indian: Myth and History*. New York: W. W. Norton.

La Barre, Weston. 1962. *They Shall Take Up Serpents: Psychology of the Southern Snake-Handling Cult*. Minneapolis: University of Minnesota Press.

——. 1989 [1938]. *The Peyote Cult*. Norman: University of Oklahoma Press.

Lachman, Sheldon J. 1983. "A Psychophysiological Interpretation of Voodoo Illness and Voodoo Death." *Omega* 13 (4): 345–59.

Lame Deer, John (Fire), and Richard Erdoes. 1972. *Lame Deer: Seeker of Visions.* New York: Simon & Schuster.

Lang, Julian. 1994. *Ararapíkva: Creation Stories of the People*. Berkeley, Calif.: Heyday Books.

Lang, Sabine. 1998. *Men as Women, Women as Men: Changing Gender in Native American Cultures*. Austin: University of Texas Press.

Linderman, Frank B. 1932. *Red Mother*. Reprinted as *Pretty-Shield: Medicine Woman of the Crows* (Lincoln: University of Nebraska Press, 2000).

Locke, Raymond Friday. 1976. *The Book of the Navajo*. Los Angeles: Mankind.

Loeb, E. M. 1924. "The Shaman of Nieu." *American Anthropologist* 26:393–402.

———. 1929. "Shaman and Seer." *American Anthropologist* 31:60–84.

Luna, Luis E. 1986. *Vegetalismo: Shamanism among the Mestizo Population of the Peruvian Amazon*. Stockholm: Almqvist & Wiksell.

Luna, Luis E., and Pablo Amaringo. 1991. *Ayahuasca Visions: The Religious Iconography of a Peruvian Shaman*. Berkeley, Calif.: North Atlantic Books.

Lyon, William S. 1996. *Encyclopedia of Native American Healing*. New York: W. W. Norton.

Matson, Erin R. 1980. "De Mille Does Not Exist," in Richard de Mille, ed., *The Don Juan Papers: Further Castaneda Controversies*, 174–77. Santa Barbara, Calif.: Ross-Erikson.

Métraux, Alfred. 1959. *Voodoo in Haiti*. New York: Schocken.

Metzner, Ralph. 1999. *Ayahuasca: Hallucinogens, Consciousness and the Spirit of Nature*. New York: Thunder's Mouth Press.

———. 2005. *Sacred Mushroom of Visions: Teonanacatl*. El Verano, Calif.: Green Earth Foundation.

Murphy, Jane M. 1964. "Psychotherapeutic Aspects of Shamanism on St. Lawrence Island, Alaska," in Ari Kiev, ed., *Magic, Faith and Healing: Studies in Primitive Psychiatry Today*, 53–83. London: Free Press.

Myerhoff, Barbara. 1974. *Peyote Hunt: The Sacred Journey of the Huichol Indians*. Ithaca, N.Y.: Cornell University Press.

Neihardt, John G., ed. 1961. *Black Elk Speaks: Being the Life Story of a Holy Man of the Oglala Sioux*. Lincoln: University of Nebraska Press.

Noel, Daniel C., ed. 1976. *Seeing Castaneda: Reactions to the "Don Juan" Writings of Carlos Castaneda.* New York: Capricorn Books.

Olden, Sarah E. 1918. *The People of Tipi Sapa (The Dakotas).* Milwaukee, Wis.: Morehouse.

Opler, Morris E. 1936. "Some Points of Comparison and Contrast between the Treatment of Functional Disorders by Apache Shamans and Modern Psychiatric Practice." *American Journal of Psychiatry* 92:1371–87.

———. 1947. "Notes on Chiricahua Apache Culture 1: Supernatural Power and Shaman." *Primitive Man* 20 (1–2): 1–14.

———. 1961. "On Devereux's Discussion of Ute Shamanism." *American Anthropologist* 63:1091–93.

Ossio, Juan M. 2002. "Contemporary Indigenous Life in Peru," in Lawrence E. Sullivan, ed., *Native Religions and Religious Cultures of Central and South America*, 200–20. New York: Continuum.

Patterson, Carol. 1998. "Seeking Power at Willow Creek Cave, Northern California." *Anthropology of Consciousness* 9 (1): 38–49.

Pendleton, Reece. 1995. "A Ghostly Splendor: John G. Neihardt's Spiritual Preparation for Entry into Black Elk's World." *American Indian Culture and Research Journal* 19 (4): 213–29.

Perkinson, James W. 2005. *Shamanism, Racism and Hip Hop Culture.* New York: Palgrave Macmillan.

Press, Irwin. 1971. "The Urban Curandero." *American Anthropologist* 73:741–56.

Reichel-Dolmatoff, Gerardo. 1972. "The Cultural Context of an Aboriginal Hallucinogen: *Banisteriopsis Caapi*," in Peter T. Furst, ed., *Flesh of the Gods: The Ritual Use of Hallucinogens*, 83–113. New York: Praeger.

———. 1974. *Amazonian Cosmos: The Sexual and Religious Symbolism of the Tukano Indians*. Chicago: University of Chicago Press.

———. 1975. *The Shaman and the Jaguar: A Study of Narcotic Drugs among the Indians of Colombia*. Philadelphia: Temple University Press.

———. 1978. "Drug-Induced Optical Sensations and Their Relationship to Applied Art among Some Colombian Indians," in Michael Greenhalgh and Vincent Megaw, eds. *Art in Society: Studies in Style, Culture and Aesthetics*, 289–304. London: Duckworth.

———. 1987. *Shamanism and Art of the Eastern Tukanoan Indians, Colombian Northwest Amazon*. Iconography of Religions vol. 9, no. 1. Leiden, Netherlands: Brill.

———. 1996. *The Forest Within: The World-view of the Tukano Amazonian Indians*. Totnes, Devon, England: Themis Books.

———. 1997. *Rainforest Shamans: Essays on the Tukano Indians of the Northwest Amazon*. Totnes, Devon, England: Themis Books.

Reuben, Paul P. 2003. "Early Twentieth Century—Black Elk." Chap. 7 of *PAL: Perspectives in American Literature—A Research and Reference Guide*, www.csustan.edu/english/reuben/pal/chap7/blackelk.html.

Roscoe, Will. 1996. "How to Become a Berdache: Toward a Unified Analysis of Gender Diversity," in Gilbert Herdt, ed., *Third Sex Third Gender: Beyond Sexual Dimorphism in Culture and History*, 329–71. New York: Zone Books.

———. *Changing Ones: Third and Fourth Genders in North America*. London: Macmillan, 1998.

Saler, Benson. 1979 [1967]. "Nagual, Witch, and Sorcerer in a Qhiché Village," in John Middleton, ed., *Magic, Witchcraft and Curing*, 69–100. Austin: University of Texas Press.

Schaefer, Stacy B. 2002. *To Think with a Good Heart: Wixarika Women, Weavers, and Shamans*. Salt Lake City: University of Utah Press.

Schaefer, Stacy B., and Peter T. Furst. 1996. *People of the Peyote: Huichol Indian History, Religion and Survival.* Albuquerque: University of New Mexico Press.

Schultes, Richard Evans, and Robert F. Raffauf. 1992. *Vine of the Soul: Medicine Men, Their Plants and Rituals in the Colombian Amazonia*. Santa Fe, N.M.: Synergetic.

Schweder, Richard. 1972. "Aspects of Cognition in Zinacanteco Shamans: Experimental Results," in William A. Lessa and Evon Z. Vogt, eds., *Reader in Comparative Religion: An Anthropological Approach*, 407–12. New York: Harper & Row.

——. 1993. "Talking about Souls: On the Pragmatic Construction of Meaning in Kuna Chants," in Pascal Boyer, ed., *Cognitive Aspects of Religious Symbolism*, 165–81. Cambridge: Cambridge University Press.

——. 1996. "Ayahuasca: La medicina dell'anima; Viaggio ed esperienze tra gli sciamani Shipibo-Conibo del Perù [Ayahuasca: The drug of the soul; Journey and experiences among the Shipibo-Conibo shamans of Peru]." *Quaderni di Parapsicologia* 27 (1): 15–27.

——. 2002a. *The Antipodes of the Mind: Charting the Phenomenology of the Ayahuasca Experience*. Oxford: Oxford University Press.

——. 2002b. "Memory, Reflexivity and Belief." *Social Anthropology* 10 (1): 23–40.

Shanon, Benny. 1993. *The Representational and the Presentational: An Essay on Cognition and the Study of Mind.* London: Harvester-Wheatsheaf.

Sharon, Douglas. 1972. "The San Pedro Cactus in Peruvian Folk Healing," in Peter T. Furst, ed., *Flesh of the Gods: The Ritual Use of Hallucinogens*, 114–35. New York: Praeger.

——. 1978. *Wizard of the Four Winds: A Shaman's Story.* New York: Free Press.

Simard, Jean-Jacques. 1990. "White Ghosts, Red Shadows: The Reduction of North American Natives," in James Clifton, ed., *The Invented Indian: Cultural Fictions and Government Policies*, 333–70. New Brunswick, N.J.: Transaction.

Smith, Andy. 1994. "For All Those Who Were Indian in a Former Life," in Carol J. Adams, ed., *Ecofeminism and the Sacred*, 168–71. New York: Continuum.

Snell, Alma. 2000. *Grandmother's Grandchild: My Crow Indian Life.* Lincoln: University of Nebraska Press.

Spicer, Edward. 1969. "Review of C. Castaneda 1968. *The Teachings of Don Juan: A Yaqui Way of Knowledge*. Berkeley and Los Angeles: University of California Press." *American Anthropologist* 71 (2): 320–22.

Stoll, David. 1987. "Smoky Trails: On Taussig's 'Shamanism, Colonialism and the Wild Man.'" *Anthropology Today* 3 (6): 9–10.

Sullivan, Lawrence E., ed. 2002. *Native Religions and Religious Cultures of Central and South America*. New York: Continuum.

Taussig, Michael. 1987. *Shamanism, Colonialism, and the Wild Man: A Study in Terror and Healing*. Chicago: University of Chicago Press.

Tedlock, Dennis. 1996. *Popol Vuh: The Mayan Book of the Dawn of Life*. New York: Simon & Schuster.

———. 2003. *Rabinal Achi: A Mayan Drama of War and Sacrifice*. Oxford: Oxford University Press.

Toelken, Barre. 1976. "The 'Pretty Languages' of Yellowman: Genre, Mode, and Texture in Navaho Coyote Narratives," in Dan Ben-Amos, ed., *Folklore Genres*, 145–70. Austin: University of Texas Press.

Villoldo, Alberto, and Erik Jendresen. 1990. *The Four Winds: A Shaman's Journey into the Amazon*. New York: Harper & Row.

Viveiros de Castro, Eduardo. 1992. *From the Enemy's Point of View: Humanity and Divinity in an Amazonian Society*. Chicago: University of Chicago Press.

———. 1998. "Cosmological Deixis and Amerindian Perspectivism." *Journal of the Royal Anthropological Institute* 4:469–88.

Vizenor, Gerald. 1981. *Earthdivers: Tribal Narratives on Mixed Descent*. Minneapolis: University of Minnesota Press.

———. 1990. *Bearheart: The Heirship Chronicles*. Minneapolis: University of Minnesota Press.

———. 1993. *Summer in the Spring: Anishinaabe Lyric Poems and Stories*. New ed. Norman: University of Oklahoma Press.

———. 1994. *Manifest Manners: Postindian Warriors of Survivance*. Hanover, N.H.: University Press of New England.

Vogt, Fred. 1984. *The Shoshoni-Crow Sun Dance*. Norman: University of Oklahoma Press.

Welch, James. 1986. *Fools Crow*. New York: Viking Penguin.

Werlang, Guilherme. 2000. "Emerging Amazonian Peoples: Myth-Chants," in Karen Ralls and Graham Harvey, eds., *Indigenous Religious Musics*, 167–82. Aldershot, England: Ashgate.

Whitehead, Harriet. 1993. "The Bow and the Burden Strap: A New Look at Institutionalized Homosexuality in Native North America," in Henry Abelove, Michele A. Barde, and David M. Halperin, eds., *The Lesbian and Gay Studies Reader*, 498–527. London: Routledge.

Whitehead, Neil L. 2002. *Dark Shamans: Kanaimà and the Politics of Violent Death*. Durham, N.C.: Duke University Press.

Whitley, David S. 1992. "Shamanism and Rock Art in Far Western North America." *Cambridge Archaeological Journal* 2:89–113.

———. 2000. *The Art of the Shaman: Rock Art of California*. Salt Lake City: University of Utah Press.

Wilbert, Johannes. 1972. "Tobacco and Shamanistic Ecstasy among the Waro Indians of Venezuela," in Peter T. Furst, ed., *Flesh of the Gods: The Ritual Role of Hallucinogens*, 55–83. New York: Praeger.

——. 2004. "The Order of Dark Shamans among the Warao," in Neil L. Whitehead and Robin Wright, eds., *In Darkness and Secrecy*, 21–50. Durham, N.C.: Duke University Press.

Wilcox, Joan P. 1999. *Keepers of the Ancient Knowledge: The Mystical World of the Q'ero Indians of Peru*. Shaftesbury, England: Element.

Wilk, S. 1980. "Don Juan on Balance," in Richard de Mille, ed., *The Don Juan Papers: Further Castaneda Controversies*, 154–57. Santa Barbara, Calif.: Ross-Erikson.

Arctic, Central Asia, and Siberia

Anisimov, A. F. 1963. "The Shaman's Tent of the Evenks and the Origin of the Shamanistic Rite," in M. Henry, ed., *Siberian Shamanism*, 84–123. Toronto: Toronto University Press.

Anokhin, A. V. 1924. *Materialy po shamanstvu u Altaitsev* [Materials on shamanism of the Altaians]. Leningrad: n.p.

Balikci, Asen. 1963. "Shamanistic Behavior among the Netsilik Eskimos." *Southwestern Journal of Anthropology* 16:380–96.

Balzer, Marjorie M., ed. 1990. *Shamanism: Soviet Studies of Traditional Religion in Siberia and Central Asia.* Armonk, N.Y.: M. E. Sharpe.

——. 1993. "Two Urban Shamans: Unmasking Leadership in Fin-de-Soviet Siberia," in George E. Marcus, ed., *Perilous States: Conversations on Culture, Politics, and Nation*, 131–64. Chicago: University of Chicago Press.

——. 1995. "The Poetry of Shamanism," in Tae-Gon Kim and Mihály Hoppál, eds., *Shamanism in Performing Arts*, 171–87. Budapest: Akadémiai Kiadó. Reprinted in Graham Harvey, ed., *Shamanism: A Reader* (London: Routledge, 2003), 307–23.

——, ed. 1996a. *Shamanic Worlds: Ritual and Lore of Siberia and Central Asia*. Armonk, N.Y.: North Castle Books.

——. 1996b. "Sacred Genders in Siberia: Shamans, Bear Festivals and Androgyny," in Sabrina P. Ramet, ed., *Reversals and Gender Cultures*, 164–82. London: Routledge. Reprinted in Graham Harvey, ed., *Shamanism: A Reader* (London: Routledge, 2003), 242–61.

——. 1999. "Shamans in All Guises: Exploring Cultural Repression and Resilience in Siberia." *Curare* 22 (2): 129–34.

——. 2001. "Healing Failed Faith? Contemporary Siberian Shamanism." *Anthropology and Humanism* 26 (2): 134–49.

——. 2002. "Shamans across Space, Time and Language Barriers." *Shaman* 10 (1–2): 7–20.

——, ed. 2006. *Religion and Politics in the Russian Federation*. Armonk, N.Y.: M. E. Sharpe.

Banzarov, Dorji. 1981–1982. "The Black Faith or Shamanism among the Mongols (1846)." English translation. *Journal of the Anglo-Mongolian Society* 7:3–91.

Basilov, Vladimir N. 1976. "Shamanism in Central Asia," in A. Bharati, ed., *The Realm of the Extra-Human: Agents and Audiences*, 149–57. The Hague: Mouton.

——. 1978. "Vestiges of Transvetism in Central-Asian Shamanism," in Vilmos Diószegi and Mihály Hoppál, eds., *Shamanism in Siberia*, 281–90. Budapest: Akadémiai Kiadó.

——. 1984. *Izbranniki Dukhov*. Moscow: Politizdat.

——. 1992. *Shamanism of the Peoples of Central Asia and Kazakhstan* (in Russian). Moscow: Nauka.

——. 2001. "Chosen by the Spirits," in Marjorie M. Balzer, ed., *Shamanic Worlds: Rituals and Lore of Siberia and Central Asia*, 3–49. Armonk, N.Y.: North Castle Books.

Boas, Franz. 1904. "The Eskimo of Baffin Island and Hudson Bay." *Bulletin of the American Museum of Natural History* 15 (1): 1–370.

——. 1907. "Second Report on the Eskimo of Baffin Island and Hudson Bay." *Bulletin of the American Museum of Natural History* 15 (2): 371–570.

——. 1964 [1888]. *The Central Eskimo*. Lincoln: University of Nebraska Press.

Bogoras, Waldemar. 1909. *The Chukchee*. Memoirs of the American Museum of Natural History, vol. 11. New York: American Museum of Natural History.

——. 1972 [1958]. "Shamanic Performance in the Inner Room," in William A. Lessa and Evon Z. Vogt, eds., *Reader in Comparative Religion*, 382–87. New York: Harper & Row.

Brown, D. N.d. "Traditional Healing Returns to Tuva," *Washington Post*. Available at www.fotuva.org/misc/shamanism/clinic.html.

Castagné, Jean. 1930. "Magie et exorcisme chez les Kazak-Kirghizes et autres peuples turcs orientaux." *Revue des études Islamiques*, 53–151.

Chadwick, Nora K. 1936a. "Shamanism among the Tatars of Central Asia." *Journal of the Royal Anthropological Institute of Great Britain and Ireland* 66:75–112.

——. 1936b. "The Spiritual Ideas and Experiences of the Tatars of Central Asia." *Journal of the Royal Anthropological Institute of Great Britain and Ireland* 66:291–329.

Czaplicka, Maria A. 1914. *Aboriginal Siberia: A Study in Social Anthropology*. Oxford, England: Clarendon.

Devlet, Ekaterina. 2001. "Rock Art and the Material Culture of Siberian and Central Asian Shamanism," in Neil Price, ed., *The Archaeology of Shamanism*, 43–55. London: Routledge.

Diószegi, Vilmos. 1963. "Ethnogenic Aspects of Darkhat Shamanism." *Acta Orientalia Hungarica* 16:55–81.

——, ed. 1968. *Popular Beliefs and Folklore Tradition in Siberia*. Uralic and Altaic Series, vol. 57. Bloomington: Indiana University Press.

Diószegi, Vilmos, and Mihály Hoppál, ed. 1996. *Shamanism in Siberia*. Budapest: Akadémiai Kiadó.

Dugarov, D. S. 1991. *Istoricheskie korni belogo shamanstva* [The historical roots of whiteshamanism]. Moscow: Nauka.

Fridman, Eva J. N. 1999. "Buryat Shamanism: Home and Hearth—a Territorialism of the Spirit." *Anthropology of Consciousness* 10 (4): 45–56.

Galdanova, Galina R. 1987. *Dolamaiskiye verovaniya Buryat*. Novosibirsk: Nauka.

Hamayon, Roberte N. 1993. "Are 'Trance,' 'Ecstasy' and Similar Concepts Appropriate in the Study of Shamanism?" *Shaman* 1 (2): 3–25.

——. 1994. "The Eternal Return of the Everybody-for-Himself Shaman: A Fable." *Diogenes* 166 (4) 2/2: 99–109.

——. 1996. "Shamanism in Siberia: From Partnership in Supernature to Counter-power in Society," in Nicholas Thomas and Caroline Humphrey, eds., *Shamanism, History, and the State*, 76–89. Ann Arbor: University of Michigan Press.

——. 1998. "'Ecstasy' or the West-Dreamt Siberian Shaman," in Helmut Wautischer, ed., *Tribal Epistemologies: Essays in the Philosophy of Anthropology*, 175–87. Aldershot, England: Ashgate.

——. 2003. "Game and Games, Fortune and Dualism in Siberian Shamanism," in Graham Harvey, ed., *Shamanism: A Reader*, 63–68. London: Routledge.

Harva, Uno. 1938. *Die Religiösen vorstellungen der Altaischen völker*. Helsinki: Suomalainen Tiedeakatemia.

Haslund-Christensen, Henning. 1971 [1943]. *The Music of the Mongols*. New York: Da Capo Press.

——. 2001. *Mongolian Adventure: 1920s Danger and Escape among the Mounted Nomads of Central Asia*. Milton Keynes, England: Lightning Source.

Heissig, Walther. 1953. "A Mongolian Source to the Lamaist Suppression of Shamanism in the 17th Century." *Anthropos* 48:1–29, 493–536.

——. 1998. *The Religions of the Mongols*. London: Routledge & Kegan Paul, 1980.

Hoppál, Mihály, ed. 1998. *Shamanism: Selected Writings of Vilmos Diószegi*. Budapest: Akadémiai Kiadó.

Hoppál, Mihály, and Juha Pentikäinen, eds. 1992. *Northern Religions and Shamanism*. Budapest: Akadémiai Kiadó.

Hultkrantz, Åke. 1978. "Ethnological and Phenomenological Aspects of Shamanism," in Vilmos Diószegi and Mihály Hoppál, eds., *Shamanism in Siberia*, 27–58. Budapest: Akadémiai Kiadó.

Humphrey, Caroline. 1974. "Some Ritual Techniques in the Bull-Cult of the Buriat-Mongols." *Proceedings of the Royal Anthropological Institute for 1973*, 15–28.

——. 1994. "Shamanic Practices and the State in Northern Asia: Views from the Centre and Periphery," in Nicholas Thomas and Caroline Humphrey, eds., *Shamanism, History, and the State*, 191–228. Ann Arbor: University of Michigan Press.

——. 1999. "Shamans in the City." *Anthropology Today* 15 (3): 3–10.

Humphrey, Caroline, with Urgunge Onon. 1996. *Shamans and Elders: Experience, Knowledge, and Power among the Daur Mongols*. Oxford: Oxford University Press.

Hutton, Ronald. 1993. *The Shamans of Siberia*. Glastonbury, England: Isle of Avalon Press.

——. 2002. *Shamans: Siberian Spirituality and the Western Imagination.* London: Hambledon.

Jakobsen, Merete Demant. 1999. *Shamanism: Traditional and Contemporary Approaches to the Mastery of Spirits and Healing*. Oxford: Berghahn Books.

Jordan, Peter. 2001. "The Materiality of Shamanism as a 'World-view': Praxis, Artifacts and Landscape," in Neil Price, ed., *The Archaeology of Shamanism*, 87–104. London: Routledge.

Khangalov, M. 1959. *Sobraniye Sochinenii, v 3–kh tomakh* [Collected works in 3 volumes]. Ulan-Ude, Buryat Republic: Buryatskoye Knizhnoye Izdatel'stvo.

Khazanov, Anatoly M. 1996. "Nationalism and Neoshamanism in Yakutia," in Kathryn Lyon, Laada Bilaniuk, and Ben Fitzhugh, eds., *Post-Soviet Eurasia: Anthropological Perspectives on a World in Transition*, 77–86. Michigan Discussions in Anthropology, vol. 12. Ann Arbor: Department of Anthropology, University of Michigan.

Krader, Lawrence. 1956. "A Nativistic Movement in Western Siberia." *American Anthropologist* 58:282–92.

——. 1978. "Shamanism: Theory and History in Buryat Society," in Vilmos Diószegi and Mihály Hoppál, eds., *Shamanism in Siberia*, 181–236. Budapest: Akadémiai Kiadó.

Kristensen, Benedikte M. 2004. *The Living Landscape of Knowledge: An Analysis of Shamanism among the Duha Tuvinians of Northern Mongolia*. www.anthrobase.com/Txt/K/Kristensen_B_02.htm.

Lymer, Kenneth. 2002. "The Deer Petroglyphs of Arpauzen, South Kazakhstan," in Andrej Rozwadowski and Maria M. Kośko, eds., *Spirits and Stones: Shamanism and Rock Art in Central Asia and Siberia*, 80–95. Poznań, Poland: Instytut Wschodni.

Michael, Henry. 1963. *Studies in Siberian Shamanism*. Toronto: Toronto University Press.

Mikhalilov, Taras M. 1980. *Iz istorii buryatskogo shamanizma* [From the history of Buryat shamanism]. Novosibirsk: Izdatel'stvo "Nauka," Sibirskoe Otdelenie.

Okladnikov, A. P., and V. D. Zaporozhskaya. 1972. *Petroglify Srendei Leny* [Petroglyphs of the Middle Lena]. Leningrad: Nauka.

Oosten, Jarich. 1989. "Theoretical Problems in the Study of Inuit Shamanism," in Mihály Hoppál and Otto von Sadovszky, eds., *Shamanism Past and Present (Part 2)*, 331–41. Budapest, Hungary: Ethnographic Institute, Hungarian Academy of Sciences; Fullerton, Calif.: International Society for Trans-Oceanic Research.

Pentikäinen, Juha. 1998. *Shamanism and Culture*. Helsinki: Etnika.

Pentikäinen, Juha, with Hanna Saressalo and Chuner M. Taksami, eds. 2001. *Shamanhood: Symbolism and Epic*. Budapest: Akadémiai Kiadó.

Poncelet, C., and N. Poncelet. 1994. "Expedition to Buryatia." *Shamanism* 7 (1): 21.

Rasmussen, Knud. 1929. *Intellectual Culture of the Inglulik Eskimos: Report of the Fifth Thule Expedition, 1921–1924*. Vol. 7. Copenhagen: Gyldendalske Boghandel, Nordisk Forlag.

——. 1930. *Observations on the Intellectual Culture of the Caribou Eskimos: Inglulik and Caribous Eskimo Texts. Report of the Fifth Thule Expedition, 1921–1924*. Vol. 7 (2–3). Copenhagen: Gyldendalske Boghandel, Nordisk Forlag.

——. 1931. *The Netsilik Eskimos: Social Life and Spiritual Culture. Report of the Fifth Thule Expedition, 1921–1924*. Vol. 7 (1–2). Copenhagen: Gyldendalske Boghandel, Nordisk Forlag.

Rozwadowski, Andrej. 2001. "Sun Gods or Shamans? Interpreting the 'Solar-Headed' Petroglyphs of Central Asia," in Neil Price, ed., *The Archaeology of Shamanism*, 65–86. London: Routledge.

Rozwadowski, Andrej, and Maria M. Kośko, eds. 2002. *Spirits and Stones: Shamanism and Rock Art in Central Asia and Siberia*. Poznań, Poland: Instytut Wschodni.

Saladin d'Anglure, Bernard. 1990. "Rethinking Inuit Shamanism through the Concept of 'Third Gender,'" in Mihály Hoppál and Juha Pentikäinen, eds., *Northern Religions and Shamanism*, 146–50. Budapest: Akadémai Kiadó. Reprinted in Graham Harvey, ed., *Shamanism: A Reader* (London: Routledge, 2003), 235–41.

Shirokogoroff, Sergei. M. 1923. "General Theory of Shamanism among the Tungus." *Journal of the Royal Asiatic Society of Great Britain and Ireland, North China Branch (Shanghai)*, 54:246–49.

——. 1924. "What Is Shamanism?" *China Journal of Sciences and Arts* 2 (3–4): 275–79, 328–71.

——. 1935. *Psychomental Complex of the Tungus*. London: Kegan Paul.

Siikala, Anna-Leena. 1978. *The Rite Technique of the Siberian Shaman*. Helsinki: FF Communications 220.

——. 1992. *Suomalainen shamanismi*. Helsinki: Suomalaisen Kirjallisuuden Seura.

Stern, Pamela. 2004. *Historical Dictionary of the Inuit*. Lanham, Md.: Scarecrow Press.

Sutherland, Patricia. 2001. "Shamanism and the Iconography of Palaeo-Eskimo Art," in Neil Price, ed., *The Archaeology of Shamanism*, 135–45. London: Routledge.

Taylor, J. G. 1989. "Shamanic Sex Roles in Traditional Labrador Inuit Society," in Mihály Hoppál and Otto von Sadovsky, eds., *Shamanism Past and Present (Part 2)*, 297–306. Budapest, Hungary: Ethnographic Institute, Hungarian Academy of Sciences; Fullerton, Calif.: International Society for Trans-Oceanic Research.

Turner, Edith. 1989. "From Shamans to Healers: The Survival of an Inupiaq Eskimo Skill." *Anthropologica* 31:3–24.

——. 1996. *The Hands Feel It: Healing and Spirit Presence among a Northern Alaskan People*. DeKalb: Northern Illinois University Press.

Uccusic, P. 1996. "Second Foundation Expedition to Tuva: July 1994." *Shamanism* 8 (1): 4–9.

Van Deusen, Kira. 1997a. "Buryat Shamans and Their Stories." *Shamanism* 10 (1): 7–11.

——. 1997b. "Shamanism in Khakassia Today." *Shamanism* 10 (1): 11–16.

Vinogradov, Andrei. 1999. "After the Past, before the Present: New Shamanism in Gorny Altai." *Anthropology of Consciousness* 10 (4): 36–45.

——. 2003. "Ak Jang in the Context of Altai Religious Tradition." Master's thesis, University of Saskatchewan. Available at library.usask.ca/theses/available/etd-01192005-154827/unrestricted/tezispdf.pdf.

Vitebsky, Piers. 1995. "From Cosmology to Environmentalism: Shamanism as Local Knowledge in a Global Setting," in Richard Fardon, ed., *Counterworks: Managing the Diversity of Knowledge*, 182–203. London: Routledge. Reprinted in Graham Harvey, ed., *Shamanism: A Reader* (London: Routledge, 2003), 276–98.

——. 2005. *The Reindeer People: Living with Animals and Spirits in Siberia*. London: Houghton Mifflin.

Whaley, Arthur. 1955. *The Nine Songs: A Study of Shamanism in Ancient China*. London: Allen & Unwin.

Europe

Aswynn, Freyja. 1994. *Leaves of Yggdrasil*. Saint Paul, Minn.: Llewellyn.

Backman, L. 1987. "The Noaidie: The Sami Shaman," in M. M. J. Fernandez-Vest, ed., *Kalevala et traditions orales du monde*, 53–59. Paris: Colloques Internationaux du CRNS.

Bates, Brian. 1983. *The Way of Wyrd*. London: Arrow.

——. 1996. *The Wisdom of the Wyrd: Teachings for Today from Our Ancient Past*. London: Rider.

———. 1996–1997. "Wyrd: Life Force of the Cosmos." *Sacred Hoop* 15 (Winter): 8–13.

———. 2002. *The Real Middle Earth.* London: Sidgwick & Jackson.

Blain, Jenny. 1998. "Presenting Constructions of Identity and Divinity: Ásatrú and Oracular Seidhr," in S. Grills, ed., *Fieldwork Methods: Accomplishing Ethnographic Research*, 203–27. Thousand Oaks, Calif.: Sage.

———. 1999a. "The Nine Worlds and the Tree: Seiðr as Shamanistic Practice in Heathen Spirituality." *Spirit Talk* 9 (Early Summer): 14–19.

———. 1999b. "Seidr as Shamanistic Practice: Reconstituting a Tradition of Ambiguity." *Shaman* 7 (2): 99–121.

———. 2001. "Shamans, Stones, Authenticity and Appropriation: Contestations of Invention and Meaning," in Robert J. Wallis and Kenneth Lymer, eds., *A Permeability of Boundaries: New Approaches to the Archaeology of Art, Religion and Folklore*, 47–55. BAR International Series 936. Oxford: British Archaeological Reports.

———. 2002. *Nine Worlds of Seid-Magic: Ecstasy and Neo-shamanism in North European Paganism*. London: Routledge.

Blain, Jenny, and Robert J. Wallis. 2000. "The 'Ergi' Seidman: Contestations of Gender, Shamanism and Sexuality in Northern Religion Past and Present." *Journal of Contemporary Religion* 15 (3): 395–411.

———. 2002. "A Living Landscape? Pagans and Archaeological Discourse." *3rd Stone* 43 (Summer): 20–27.

———. 2004a. "Sacred Sites, Contested Rites/Rights: Contemporary Pagan Engagements with the Past." *Journal of Material Culture* 9 (3): 237–61.

———. 2004b. "Sites, Texts, Contexts and Inscriptions of Meaning: Investigating Pagan 'Authenticities' in a Text-Based Society." *Pomegranate* 6 (2): 231–52.

———. 2006b. "Re-Presenting Spirit: Heathenry, New-Indigenes, and the Imaged Past," in Ian A. Russel, ed., *Image, Simulation and Meaning in Archaeology: On Archaeology and the Industrialisation and Marketing of Heritage and Tourism*, 89–118. London: Springer.

Bradley, Richard. 1997. *Signing the Land: Rock Art and the Prehistory of Atlantic Europe*. London: Routledge.

Buxton, Simon. 2004. *The Shamanic Way of the Bee.* Rochester, Vt.: Inner Traditions.

Chadwick, Nora K. 1934. "Imbas Forosnai." *Scottish Gaelic Studies* 4:98–135.

———. 1942. *Poetry and Prophecy*. Cambridge: Cambridge University Press.

———. 1966. *The Druids*. Cardiff: University of Wales Press.

Clifton, Chas S., and Graham Harvey, eds. 2004. *The Paganism Reader*. London: Routledge.

Clottes, Jean, and J. David Lewis-Williams. 1998. *The Shamans of Prehistory: Trance and Magic in the Painted Caves*. New York: Harry N. Abrams.

Cowan, Tom. 1993. *Fire in the Head: Shamanism and the Celtic Spirit*. San Francisco: HarperCollins.

Creighton, John. 1995. "Visions of Power: Imagery and Symbols in Late Iron Age Britain." *Britannia* 26:285–301.

———. 2000. *Coins and Power in Late Iron Age Britain*. Cambridge: Cambridge University Press.

Davenport, Demorest, and Michael A. Jochim. 1988. "The Scene in the Shaft at Lascaux." *Antiquity* 62:559–62.

Devereux, Paul. 1992. *Shamanism and the Mystery Lines: Ley Lines, Spirit Paths, Shape-Shifting and Out-of-Body-Travel*. London: Quantum.

———. 1997. *The Long Trip: A Prehistory of Psychedelia*. New York: Arkana.

Dickinson, Tania M. 1993. "An Anglo-Saxon 'Cunning Woman' from Bidford-on-Avon," in Martin Carver, ed., *In Search of Cult: Archaeological Investigations in Honour of Philip Ratz*, 45–54. Woodbridge, Suffolk, England: Boydell Press.

Dowson, Thomas A., and Martin Porr. 2001. "Special Objects—Special Creatures: Shamanistic Imagery and the Aurignacian Art of South-west Germany," in Neil Price, ed., *The Archaeology of Shamanism*, 165–77. London: Routledge.

Dronfield, Jeremy. 1996. "Entering Alternative Realities: Cognition, Art and Architecture in Irish Passage Tombs." *Cambridge Archaeological Journal* 6 (1): 37–72.

Dubois, Thomas A. 1999. *Nordic Religions in the Viking Age*. Philadelphia: University of Pennsylvania Press.

Favret-Saada, Jeanne. 1980. *Deadly Words: Witchcraft in the Bocage*. Cambridge: Cambridge University Press.

Fries, Jan. 1993. *Helrunar: A Manual of Rune Magic*. Oxford: Mandrake Press.

———. 1996. *Seidways: Shaking, Swaying and Serpent Mysteries*. Oxford: Mandrake.

———. 2001. *Cauldron of the Gods: Manual of Celtic Magick*. Oxford: Mandrake.

Ginzburg, Carlo. 1983. *The Night Battles: Witchcraft and Agrarian Cults in the Sixteenth and Seventeenth Centuries*. Baltimore: Johns Hopkins University Press.

———. 1991. *Ecstasies: Deciphering the Witches' Sabbath*. London: Hutchinson.

Glosecki, Stephen O. 1986. "Wolf Dancers and Whispering Beasts: Shamanic Motifs from Sutton Hoo?" *Mankind Quarterly* 26:305–19.

———. 1988. "Wolf of the Bees: Germanic Shamanism and the Bear Hero." *Journal of Ritual Studies* 2 (1): 31–53.

———. 1989. *Shamanism and Old English Poetry*. New York: Garland.

Grambo, R. 1989. "Unmanliness and Seiðr: Problems Concerning the Change of Sex," in Mihály Hoppál and Otto von Sadovszky, eds., *Shamanism: Past and Present (Part 1)*, 103–13. Budapest: Ethnographic Institute, Hungarian Academy of Sciences; Fullerton, Calif.: International Society for Trans-Oceanic Research.

Green, Miranda. 1997. *Exploring the World of the Druids*. London: Thames & Hudson.

Gundarsson, Kveldulf. 2001. "Spae-Craft, Seiðr, and Shamanism." www.thetroth.org/resources/kveldulf/spaecraft.html.

Gyrus Orbitalis. 2000. "On Prehistoric Rock Art and Psychedelic Experiences." dreamflesh.com/essays/rockpsych.

Hoppál, Mihály, and Juha Pentikäinen, eds. 1992. *Northern Religions and Shamanism*. Budapest: Akadémiai Kiadó.

Howard, Michael. 1985. *The Wisdom of the Runes*. London: Rider.

Hübener, Gustav. 1935. "Beowulf and Germanic Exorcism." *Review of English Studies* 11:163–81.

Hutton, Ronald. 1991. *The Pagan Religions of the Ancient British Isles: Their Nature and Legacy*. Oxford, England: Blackwell.

Johnson, Nathan J., and Robert J. Wallis. 2005. *Galdrbok: Practical Heathen Runecraft, Shamanism and Magic*. London: Wykeham Press.

Jones, Leslie Ellen. 1998. *Druid, Shaman, Priest: Metaphors of Celtic Paganism*. Enfield Lock, England: Hisarlik Press.

Karjala, M. Y. 1992. "Aspects of the Other World in Irish Folk Tradition," in Mihály Hoppál and Juha Pentikäinen, eds., *Northern Religions and Shamanism*, 176–80. Budapest: Akadémiai Kiadó.

Knüsel, Christopher, and Kathryn Ripley. 2000. "The *Berdache* or Man-woman in Anglo-Saxon England and Early Medieval Europe," in William O. Frazer and Andrew Tyrell, eds., *Social Identity in Early Medieval Britain*, 157–91. Leicester, England: Leicester University Press.

Larrington, Carolyne, trans. 1996. *The Poetic Edda*. Oxford: Oxford University Press.

Laurie, Erynn R., and Timothy White. 1997. "Speckled Snake, Brother of Birch: Amanita Muscaria Motifs in Celtic Literature." *Shaman's Drum* 44:52–65.

Leto, Stephen. 2000. "Magical Potions: Entheogenic Themes in Scandinavian Mythology." *Shaman's Drum* 54:55–65.

Lonigan, Paul. 1985. "Shamanism in the Old Irish Tradition." *Eire-Ireland* 20 (3): 109–29.

MacEowen, Frank H. 1998. "Rekindling the Gaelic Hearthways of Oran Mor." *Shaman's Drum* 49 (Summer): 32–39.

———. 2004. *The Spiral of Memory and Belonging: A Celtic Path of Soul and Kinship*. Novato, Calif.: New World Library.

Mack, J. 1992. "Shetland Finn-Men: Interpretations of Shamanism?" in Mihály Hoppál and Juha Pentikäinen, eds., *Northern Religions and Shamanism*, 181–87. Budapest: Akadémiai Kiadó.

MacLellan, Gordon. 1995. "Dancing on the Edge: Shamanism in Modern Britain," in Graham Harvey and Charlotte Hardman, eds., *Paganism Today: Wiccans, Druids, the Goddess and Ancient Earth Traditions for the Twenty-First Century*, 138–48. London: Thorsons.

Matthews, Caitlin. 1996. "Following the Awen-Celtic Shamanism and the Druid Path in the Modern World," in Philip Carr-Gomm, ed., *The Druid Renaissance*, 223–36. London: Thorsons.

Matthews, John. 1991a. *The Celtic Shaman: A Handbook*. Shaftesbury, England: Element Books.

———. 1991b. *The Song of Taliesin: Stories and Poems from the Books of Broceliande*. London: Aquarian.

———. 1991c. *Taliesin: Shamanism and the Bardic Mysteries in Britain and Ireland*. London: Aquarian.

Mattingly, Harold, trans. 1948. *Tacitus on Britain and Germany*. London: Penguin.

Meadows, Kenneth. 1996. *Rune Power*. Shaftesbury, England: Element Books.

Meaney, Audrey L. 1981. *Anglo-Saxon Amulets and Curing Stones*. BAR British Series 96. Oxford: British Archaeological Reports.

———. 1989. "Women, Witchcraft and Magic in Anglo-Saxon England," in D. G. Scragg, ed., *Superstition and Popular Medicine in Anglo-Saxon England*, 9–40. Manchester, England: Manchester Centre for Anglo-Saxon Studies.

Melia, Daniel F. 1983. "The Irish Saint as Shaman." *Pacific Coast Theology* 18:37–42.

Metzner, Ralph. 1994. *The Well of Remembrance: Rediscovering the Earth Wisdom Myths of Northern Europe*. Boston: Shambhala.

Morris, Katherine. 1991. *Sorceress or Witch? The Image of Gender in Medieval Iceland and Northern Europe*. New York: University of America Press.

Murray, Margaret. 1921. *The Witch-Cult in Western Europe*. London: Oxford University Press.

———. 1931. *The God of the Witches*. London: Sampson Low, Marston.

Naddair, Kaledon. 1990. "Pictish and Keltic Shamanism," in Prudence Jones and Caitlin Matthews, eds., *Voices from the Circle: The Heritage of Western Paganism*, 93–108. Wellingborough, England: Aquarian Press.

Nagy, Joseph F. 1981. "Shamanic Aspects of the *Bruidhean* Tale." *History of Religions* 20:302–22.

Paxson, Diana L. 1993. "Heide: Witch-Goddess of the North," *Sagewoman*, Fall 1993. Available at www.hrafnar.org/goddesses/heide.html.

———. 1998. "'This Thou Dost Know . . .': Oracles in the Northern Tradition." *Idunna: A Journal of Northern Tradition*, n.p.

Pennick, Nigel. 1989. *Practical Magic in the Northern Tradition*. Wellingborough, England: Aquarian.

———. 1992. *Rune Magic: The History and Practice of Ancient Runic Traditions*. London: Thorsons.

Piggott, Stuart. 1962. "From Salisbury Plain to South Siberia." *Wiltshire Magazine* 58:93–97.

———. 1968. *The Druids*. London: Pelican.

Pollington, Stephen. 2000. *Leechcraft: Early English Charms, Plantlore and Healing*. Hockwold-cum-Wilton, England: Anglo-Saxon Books.

Price, Neil S. 2000. "Shamanism and the Vikings?" in William W. Fitzhugh and Elisabeth I. Ward, eds., *Vikings: The North Atlantic Saga*, 70–71. Washington, D.C.: Smithsonian Institution.

———. 2002. *The Viking Way: Religion and War in Late Iron Age Scandinavia*. Department of Archaeology and Ancient History, University of Uppsala, Sweden.

Ross, Anne. 1967. *Pagan Celtic Britain*. London: Constable.

Shell, Colin A. 2000. "Metalworker or Shaman: Early Bronze Age Upton Lovell G2a Burial." *Antiquity* 74:271–72.

Shepherd, Colin. 1998. *A Study of the Relationship between Style I Art and Socio-Political Change in Early Medieval Europe*. BAR International Series 745. Oxford: British Archaeological Reports.

Sherratt, Andrew. 1991. "Sacred and Profane Substances: The Ritual Use of Narcotics in Later Neolithic Europe," in Paul Garwood, David Jennings, Robin Skeates, and Judith Toms, eds., *Sacred and Profane: Conference Proceedings*, 50–64. Oxford University Monograph 32. Oxford: Oxford University Press.

Shetelig, Haakon, and Hjalmur Falk. 1937. *Scandinavian Archaeology*. Oxford, England: Clarendon.

Simek, Rudolf. 1993. *A Dictionary of Northern Mythology*. Bury St. Edmunds, England: St. Edmundsbury Press.

Solli, Brit. 1999. "Odin the *Queer*? On *Ergi* and Shamanism in Norse Mythology," in Andy Gustafsson and Hàkan Karlsson, eds., *Glyfer och arkeologiska rum—en vänbok till Jarl Nordbladh*, Gotarc Series A, 3:341–49. Göteborg, Sweden: University of Göteborg.

Stoodley, Nick. 1999. *The Spindle and the Spear: A Critical Enquiry into the Construction and Meaning of Gender in the Early Anglo-Saxon Burial Rite*. BAR British Series 288. Oxford: British Archaeological Reports.

Strömbäck, Dag. 1935. *Sejd: Textstudier i nordisk religionshistoria*. Nordiska texter och undersökningar 5. Stockholm: Hugo Gebers Förlag.

Wallis, Robert J. 2000. "Queer Shamans: Autoarchaeology and Neo-shamanism." *World Archaeology* 32 (2): 251–61.

———. 2001. "Waking the Ancestors: Neo-shamanism and Archaeology," in Neil Price, ed., *The Archaeology of Shamanism*, 213–30. London: Routledge. Reprinted in Graham Harvey, ed., *Shamanism: A Reader* (London: Routledge, 2003), 402–23.

———. 2003. *Shamans/Neo-Shamans: Ecstasy, Alternative Archaeology and Contemporary Pagans*. London: Routledge.

Wallis, Robert J., and Jenny Blain. 2003. "Sites, Sacredness, and Stories: Interactions of Archaeology and Contemporary Paganism." *Folklore* 114 (3): 307–21.

Wilby, Emma. 2005. *Cunning Folk and Familiar Spirits: Shamanistic Visionary Traditions in Early Modern British Witchcraft and Magic*. Brighton, England: Sussex Academic Press.

Indian Subcontinent, Nepal, and Tibet

Hardman, Charlotte. 2000. *Other Worlds: Notions of Self and Emotion among the Lohorung Rai*. Oxford, England: Berg.

——. 2002. "Beer, Trees, Pigs and Chickens: Medical Tools of the Lohorung Shaman and Priest," in P. A. Baker and G. Carr, eds., *Practitioners, Practices and Patients: New Approaches to Medical Archaeology and Anthropology*, 81–108. Oxford, England: Oxbow.

Harper, Edward. 1957. "Shamanism in South India." *Southwestern Journal of Anthropology* 13:267–87.

Holmberg, David H. 1989. *Order in Paradox: Myth, Ritual, and Exchange among Nepal's Tamang*. Ithaca, N.Y.: Cornell University Press.

Mumford, Stan R. 1989. *Himalayan Dialogue: Tibetan Lamas and Gurung Shamans in Nepal*. Madison: University of Wisconsin Press.

Opler, Morris E. 1958. "Spirit Possession in a Rural Area of Northern India," in William A. Lessa and Evon Z. Vogt, eds., *Reader in Comparative Religion*, 553–66. New York: Harper & Row.

Peters, Larry G. 1981. *Ecstasy and Healing in Nepal: An Ethnopsychiatric Study of Tamang Shamanism*. Malibu, Calif.: Undena.

——. 1982. "Trance, Initiation, and Psychotherapy in Tamang Shamanism." *American Ethnologist* 9 (1): 21–46.

——. 1997. "The Tibetan Healing Rituals of Dorje Yüdronma: Fierce Manifestation of Feminine Cosmic Force." *Shaman's Drum* 45:36–47.

Samuel, Geoffrey. 2004. *Tantric Revisionings: New Understandings of Tibetan Buddhism and Indian Religion*. Aldershot, England: Ashgate.

Spilman, S. 1999. "Lhamo Dolkar: A Tibetan Exorcist in Nepal." *Shaman's Drum* 51:51–57.

Sullivan, Bruce M. 1997. *Historical Dictionary of Hinduism*. Lanham, Md.: Scarecrow Press.

Vitebsky, Piers. 1993. *Dialogues with the Dead: The Discussion of Mortality among the Sora of Eastern India*. Cambridge: Cambridge University Press.

Walter, Damien. 2001. "The Medium of the Message: Shamanism as Localized Practice in the Nepal Himalayas," in Neil Price, ed., *The Archaeology of Shamanism*, 105–19. London: Routledge.

Pacific and Southeast Asia

Atkinson, Jane M. 1989. *The Art and Politics of Wana Shamanship*. Berkeley: University of California Press.

Averbuch, Irit. 1998. "Shamanic Dance in Japan: The Choreography of Possession in Kagura." *Asia Folklore Studies* 57 (2): 293–329.

Berndt, Roland M., and Catherine H. Berndt. 1993. *A World That Was: The Yaraldi of the Murray River and the Lakes, South Australia*. Carlton, Australia: Melbourne University Press.

Blacker, Carmen. 1999. *The Catalpa Bow: A Study of Shamanistic Practices in Japan*. 3rd ed. London: Japan Library.

Chippindale, Christopher, Benjamin Smith, and Paul S. C. Taçon. 2000. "Visions of Dynamic Power: Archaic Rock-Paintings, Altered States of Consciousness and 'Clever Men' in Western Arnhem Land (NT), Australia." *Cambridge Archaeological Journal* 10 (1): 63–101.

Elkin, Adolphus P. 1977. *Aboriginal Men of High Degree: Initiation and Sorcery in the World's Oldest Tradition*. 2nd ed. St. Lucia, Australia: University of Queensland Press.

Flood, Bo. 2001. *Marianas Island Legends: Myth and Magic*. Honolulu: Bess Press.

Heinze, Ruth-Inge. 1997. *Trance and Healing in Southeast Asia Today*. Bangkok: White Lotus.

Herdt, Gilbert. 1977. "The Shamans 'Calling' among the Sambia of New Guinea." *Journal de la Société des Océanistes* 33:153–67.

Howell, Signe. 1984. *Society and Cosmos: Chewong of Peninsular Malaysia*. Oxford: Oxford University Press.

——. 1989. "'To Be Angry Is Not to Be Human, But to Be Fearful Is': Chewong Concepts of Human Nature," in Signe Howell and Roy Willis, eds., *Societies at Peace: Anthropological Perspectives*, 45–59. London: Routledge.

Jullerat, Bernard. 1979. *Spirit Possession: Shamans and Trance in New Guinea*. Paris: Société de Oceane.

Katz, Richard. 1999. *The Straight Path of the Spirit: Ancestral Wisdom and Healing Traditions in Fiji*. Rochester, Vt.: Park Street Press.

Kendall, Laurel. 1981. "Supernatural Traffic: East Asian Shamanism." *Culture Medicine and Psychiatry* 5:171–91.

——. 1985. *Shamans, Housewives, and Other Restless Spirits: Women in Korean Ritual Life*. Honolulu: University of Hawaii Press.

——. 1988. *The Life and Hard Times of a Korean Shaman*. Honolulu: University of Hawaii Press.

——. 1996. "Korean Shamanism and the Spirits of Capitalism." *American Anthropologist* 98 (3): 512–27.

Laderman, Carol. 1991. *Taming the Wind of Desire: Psychology, Medicine, and Aesthetics in Malay Shamanistic Performance*. Berkeley: University of California Press.

Lattas, Andrew. 1993. "Sorcery and Colonialism: Illness, Dreams and Death as Political Languages in West New Britain." *Man* 28 (1): 51–77.

Layard, John W. 1930a. "Malakula: Flying Tricksters, Ghosts, Gods and Epileptics." *Journal of the Royal Anthropological Institute* 60:501–24.

———. 1930b. "Shamanism: An Analysis Based on Comparison with the Flying Tricksters of Malakula." *Journal of the Royal Anthropological Institute* 60:525–50.

Lewis, Ioan M. 1993. "Malay Bomohs and Shamans." *Man* 28: 361.

Naoko, Takiguchi. 1984. *Miyako Shamanism: Shamans, Clients, and Their Interactions*. Los Angeles: Department of Anthropology, University of California.

Ohnuki-Tierney, Emiko. 1980. "Shamans and Imu: Among Two Ainu Groups." *Ethos* 8 (3): 204–28.

Picken, Stuart B. 2002. *Historical Dictionary of Shinto*. Lanham, Md.: Scarecrow Press.

Sales, Kim. 1992. "Ascent to the Sky: A Shamanic Initiatory Engraving from the Burrup Peninsula, Northwest Western Australia." *Archaeology Oceania* 27:22–35.

Spiro, Melford E. 1952. "Ghosts, Ifaluk, and Teleological Functionalism." *American Anthropologist* 54 (4): 497–503.

Stephen, Michelle. 1979. "Dreams of Change: The Innovative Role of Altered States of Consciousness in Traditional Melanesian Religion." *Oceania* 50 (1): 3–22.

———, ed. 1987. *Sorcerer and Witch in Melanesia*. New Brunswick, N.J.: Rutgers University Press.

Strathern, Andrew. 1994. "Between Body and Mind: Shamans and Politics among the Anga, Baktaman and Gebusi in Papua New Guinea." *Oceania* 64 (4): 288–301.

Tanaka, Sakurako (Sherry). 2000. *The Ainu of Tsugaru: The Indigenous History and Shamanism of Northern Japan*. Vancouver: University of British Columbia.

———. 2003. "Ainu Shamanism: A Forbidden Path to Universal Knowledge." *Cultural Survival Quarterly*, Issue 27 (2) (June 15) www.cs.org/publications/csq/csq-article.cfm?id=1667.

Thomas, Nicholas. 1989. "Marginal Powers: Shamanism and the Disintegration of Hierarchy." *Critique of Anthropology* 8 (3): 53–74.

———. 1994. "Marginal Powers: Shamanism and Hierarchy in Eastern Oceania," in Nicholas Thomas and Caroline Humphrey, eds., *Shamanism, History, and the State*, 15–31. Ann Arbor: University of Michigan Press.

Tonkinson, Robert. 1981. "Sorcery and Social Change in Southeast Ambrym, Vanuatu." *Social Analysis* 8:77–88.

Trompf, Gary. 1991. *Melanesian Religion*. Cambridge: Cambridge University Press.

Wallis, Robert J. 2002. "The *Bwili* or 'Flying Tricksters' of Malakula: A Critical Discussion of Recent Debates on Rock Art, Ethnography and Shamanisms." *Journal of the Royal Anthropological Institute* 8 (4): 735–60.

Zelenietz, Marty, and Shirley Lindenbaum, eds. 1981. *Sorcery and Social Change in Melanesia*, Special Issue of *Social Analysis* 8.

THEMES

Altered Consciousness

Blain, Jenny. 2002. *Nine Worlds of Seid-Magic: Ecstasy and Neo-shamanism in North European Paganism*. London: Routledge.

Blain, Jenny, and Robert J. Wallis. 2006a. "Ritual Reflections, Practitioner Meanings: Disputing the Terminology of Neo-shamanic 'Performance.'" *Journal of Ritual Studies* 20 (1): 21–36.

Boddy, J. 1994. "Spirit Possession Revisited: Beyond Instrumentality." *Annual Review of Anthropology* 23:407–34.

Bourguignon, Erika. 1967. "World Distribution and Pattern of Possession States," in Raymond Prince, ed., *Trance and Possession States*, 3–34. Montreal: R. M. Bucke Memorial Society.

———. 1974. "Cross-Cultural Perspectives on the Religious Use of Altered States of Consciousness," in Irving I. Zaretsky and Mark P. Leone, eds., *Religious Movements in Contemporary America*, 228–43. Princeton, N.J.: Princeton University Press.

———. 1976. *Possession*. San Francisco: Chandler & Sharp.

Butt, A., S. Wavell, and N. Epton. 1966. *Trances*. London: Allen & Unwin.

Clottes, Jean, and J. David Lewis-Williams. 1998. *The Shamans of Prehistory: Trance and Magic in the Painted Caves*. New York: Harry N. Abrams.

Dowson, Thomas A. 1998b. "Rock Art: Handmaiden to Studies of Cognitive Evolution," in Colin Renfrew and Chris Scarre, eds., *Cognition and Material Culture: The Archaeology of Symbolic Storage*, 67–76. Cambridge, England: McDonald Institute Monographs.

———. 1999b. "Rock Art and Shamanism: A Methodological Impasse," in Andrej Rozwadowski, Maria M. Kośko, and Thomas A. Dowson, eds., *Rock Art, Shamanism and Central Asia: Discussions of Relations* (in Polish), 39–56. Warsaw: Wydawnictwo Academickie.

Goodman, Felicitas D. 1986. "Body Posture and the Religious Altered State of Consciousness: An Experimental Investigation." *Journal of Humanistic Psychology* 26 (3): 81–118.

——. 1988. "Shamanic Trance Postures," in Gary Doore, ed., *Shaman's Path: Healing, Personal Growth, and Empowerment*, 53–61. Boston: Shambhala.

Gyrus Orbitalis. 2000. "On Prehistoric Rock Art and Psychedelic Experiences." dreamflesh.com/essays/rockpsych.

Hamayon, Roberte N. 1993. "Are 'Trance,' 'Ecstasy' and Similar Concepts Appropriate in the Study of Shamanism?" *Shaman* 1 (2): 3–25.

——. 1996. "Shamanism in Siberia: From Partnership in Supernature to Counter-power in Society," in Nicholas Thomas and Caroline Humphrey, eds., *Shamanism, History, and the State*, 76–89. Ann Arbor: University of Michigan Press.

——. 1998. "'Ecstasy' or the West-Dreamt Siberian Shaman," in Helmut Wautischer, ed., *Tribal Epistemologies: Essays in the Philosophy of Anthropology*, 175–87. Aldershot, England: Ashgate.

Harner, Michael. 1988. "What Is a Shaman?" in Gary Doore, ed., *Shaman's Path: Healing, Personal Growth, and Empowerment*, 7–15. Boston: Shambhala.

——. 1990 [1980]. *The Way of the Shaman*. London: HarperCollins.

Heusch, Luc de. 1982. "Possession and Shamanism," in Luc de Heusch, *Why Marry Her? Society and Symbolic Structures*, 151–64. Cambridge: Cambridge University Press.

Holm, Nils G., ed. 1980. *Religious Ecstasy*. Stockholm: Almqvist & Wiksell.

Hultkrantz, Åke. 1998. "The Meaning of Ecstasy in Shamanism," in Helmut Wautischer, ed., *Tribal Epistemologies: Essays in the Philosophy of Anthropology*, 163–73. Aldershot, England: Ashgate.

Jakobsen, Merete Demant. 1999. *Shamanism: Traditional and Contemporary Approaches to the Mastery of Spirits and Healing*. Oxford, England: Berghahn Books.

Johnson, Nathan J., and Robert J. Wallis. 2005. *Galdrbok: Practical Heathen Runecraft, Shamanism and Magic*. London: Wykeham Press.

Kehoe, Alice B. 1981. "Women's Preponderance in Possession Cults: The Calcium Deficiency Hypothesis Extended." *American Anthropologist* 83:549–61.

——. 2000. *Shamans and Religion: An Anthropological Exploration in Critical Thinking*. Prospect Heights, Ill.: Waveland Press.

Lewis, I. M. 2003. "Trance, Possession, Shamanism and Sex." *Anthropology of Consciousness* 14 (1): 20–39.

Lewis-Williams, J. David. 1992. "Ethnographic Evidence Relating to 'Trance' and 'Shamans' among Northern and Southern Bushmen." *South African Archaeological Bulletin* 47:56–60.

Lewis-Williams, J. David, and Thomas A. Dowson. 1988. "The Signs of All Times: Entoptic Phenomena in Upper Paleolithic Art." *Current Anthropology* 29 (2): 201–45.

Lex, Barbara. 1984. "Recent Contributions to the Study of Ritual Trance." *Reviews in Anthropology* 11:44–51.

Métraux, Alfred. 1957. "Dramatic Elements in Ritual Possession." *Diogenes* 11:18–36.

Noll, Richard. 1983. "Shamanism and Schizophrenia: A State-Specific Approach to the 'Schizophrenia Metaphor' of Shamanic States." *American Ethnologist* 10:443–59.

———. 1985. "Mental Imagery Cultivation as a Cultural Phenomenon: The Role of Visions in Shamanism." *Current Anthropology* 26:443–61.

———. 1989. "What Has Really Been Learned about Shamanism?" *Journal of Psychoactive Drugs* 21 (1): 47–50.

Osterreich, T. K. 1966. *Possession: Demoniacal and Other*. Secaucus, N.J.: Citadel Press.

Price, Neil S. 2001a. "An Archaeology of Altered States: Shamanism and Material Culture Studies," in Neil Price, ed., *The Archaeology of Shamanism*, 3–16. London: Routledge.

———, ed. 2001b. *The Archaeology of Shamanism*. London: Routledge.

Prince, Raymond, ed. 1968. *Trance and Possession States*. Montreal: R. M. Bucke Memorial Society.

Reinhard, Johan. 1976. "Shamanism and Spirit Possession: The Definition Problem," in John T. Hitchcock and Rex L. Jones, eds., *Spirit Possession in the Nepal Himalayas*, 12–20. Warminster, England: Aris & Phillips.

Rouget, Gilbert. 1985. *Music and Trance*. Chicago: University of Chicago Press.

Tart, Charles T. 1969. *Altered States of Consciousness*. New York: E. P. Dutton.

Wallis, Robert J. 1999. "Altered States, Conflicting Cultures: Shamans, Neoshamans and Academics." *Anthropology of Consciousness* 10 (2–3): 41–49.

———. 2002. "The *Bwili* or 'Flying Tricksters' of Malakula: A Critical Discussion of Recent Debates on Rock Art, Ethnography and Shamanisms." *Journal of the Royal Anthropological Institute* 8 (4): 735–60.

———. 2003. *Shamans/Neo-Shamans: Ecstasy, Alternative Archaeology and Contemporary Pagans*. London: Routledge.

———. 2004. "Shamanism and Art," in Mariko N. Walter and Eva N. Fridman, eds., *Shamanism: An Encyclopedia of World Beliefs, Practices, and Culture*, 1:21–28. Santa Barbara, Calif.: ABC-CLIO.

Winkelman, Michael. 1986. "Trance States: A Theoretical Model and Cross-Cultural Analysis." *Ethos* 14:174–203.

———. 1999. "Altered States of Consciousness and Religious Behavior," in Stephen D. Glazier, ed., *Anthropology of Religion: A Handbook*, 393–428. Westport, Conn.: Praeger.

——. 2000. *Shamanism: The Neural Ecology of Consciousness and Healing*. Westport, Conn.: Bergin & Garvey.

Wright, Peggy A. 1989. "The Nature of the Shamanic State of Consciousness: A Review." *Journal of Psychoactive Drugs* 21 (1): 25–33.

Animism

Bird-David, Nurit. 1993. "Tribal Metaphorization of Human–Nature Relatedness: A Comparative Analysis," in Kay Milton, ed., *Environmentalism: The View from Anthropology*, 112–25. London: Routledge.

——. 1999. "'Animism Revisited': Personhood, Environment, and Relational Epistemology," *Current Anthropology* 40:67–91. Reprinted in Graham Harvey, ed., *Readings in Indigenous Religions* (New York: Continuum, 2002), 72–105.

Blain, Jenny, and Robert J. Wallis. 2002. "A Living Landscape? Pagans and Archaeological Discourse." *3rd Stone* 43 (Summer): 20–27.

——. 2006b. "Re-Presenting Spirit: Heathenry, New-Indigenes, and the Imaged Past," in Ian A. Russel, ed., *Image, Simulation and Meaning in Archaeology: On Archaeology and the Industrialisation and Marketing of Heritage and Tourism*, 89–118. London: Springer.

Fausto, Carlos. 2004. "A Blend of Blood and Tobacco: Shamans and Jaguars among the Parakanã of Eastern Amazonia," in Neil L. Whitehead and Robin Wright, eds., *In Darkness and Secrecy*, 157–78. Durham, N.C.: Duke University Press.

Hallowell, A. Irving. 1960. "Ojibwa Ontology, Behavior and World View," in Stanley Diamond, ed., *Culture in History*, 19–52. New York: Columbia University Press. Reprinted in Graham Harvey, ed., *Readings in Indigenous Religions* (London: Continuum, 2002), 17–49.

Harvey, Graham. 2005. *Animism: Respecting the Living World*. London: Hurst; New York: Columbia University Press; Adelaide: Wakefield Press.

Howell, Signe. 1984. *Society and Cosmos: Chewong of Peninsular Malaysia*. Oxford: Oxford University Press.

——. 1989. "'To Be Angry Is Not to Be Human, But to Be Fearful Is': Chewong Concepts of Human Nature," in Signe Howell and Roy Willis, eds., *Societies at Peace: Anthropological Perspectives*, 45–59. London: Routledge.

Johnson, Nathan J., and Robert J. Wallis. 2005. *Galdrbok: Practical Heathen Runecraft, Shamanism and Magic*. London: Wykeham Press.

Viveiros de Castro, Eduardo. 1992. *From the Enemy's Point of View: Humanity and Divinity in an Amazonian Society*. Chicago: University of Chicago Press.

——. 1998. "Cosmological Deixis and Amerindian Perspectivism." *Journal of the Royal Anthropological Institute* 4:469–88.

——. 1999. "Comment on Nurit Bird-David's "Animism Revisited.'" *Current Anthropology* 40:S79–80.

Gender

Balzer, Marjorie M. 1996b. "Sacred Genders in Siberia: Shamans, Bear Festivals and Androgyny," in Sabrina P. Ramet, ed., *Reversals and Gender Cultures*, 164–82. London: Routledge. Reprinted in Graham Harvey, ed., *Shamanism: A Reader* (London: Routledge, 2003), 242–61.

Basilov, Vladimir. 1978. "Vestiges of Transvestism in Central-Asian Shamanism," in Vilmos Diószegi and Mihály Hoppál, eds., *Shamanism in Siberia*, 281–90. Budapest: Akadémiai Kiadó.

Blain, Jenny, and Robert J. Wallis. 2000. "The 'Ergi' Seidman: Contestations of Gender, Shamanism and Sexuality in Northern Religion Past and Present." *Journal of Contemporary Religion* 15 (3): 395–411.

Cruden, Loren. 1995. *Coyote's Council Fire: Contemporary Shamans on Race, Gender, and Community*. Rochester, Vt.: Destiny Books.

Czaplicka, Maria A. 1914. *Aboriginal Siberia: A Study in Social Anthropology*. Oxford, England: Clarendon.

Grambo, R. 1989. "Unmanliness and Seiðr: Problems Concerning the Change of Sex," in Mihály Hoppál and Otto von Sadovszky, eds., *Shamanism: Past and Present (Part 1)*, 103–13. Budapest: Ethnographic Institute, Hungarian Academy of Sciences; Fullerton, Calif.: International Society for Trans-Oceanic Research.

Hamayon, Roberte N. 1993. "Are 'Trance,' 'Ecstasy' and Similar Concepts Appropriate in the Study of Shamanism?" *Shaman* 1 (2): 3–25.

——. 1996. "Shamanism in Siberia: From Partnership in Supernature to Counter-power in Society," in Nicholas Thomas and Caroline Humphrey, eds., *Shamanism, History and the State*, 76–89. Ann Arbor: University of Michigan Press.

Lang, Sabine. 1998. *Men as Women, Women as Men: Changing Gender in Native American Cultures*. Austin: University of Texas Press.

Lewis, Ioan M. 1999. "Shamans and Sex: A Comparative Perspective," in *Arguments with Ethnography*, 106–14. London: Athlone.

——. 2003. "Trance, Possession, Shamanism and Sex." *Anthropology of Consciousness* 14 (1): 20–39.

Morris, Katherine. 1991. *Sorceress or Witch? The Image of Gender in Medieval Iceland and Northern Europe*. New York: University of America Press.

Reichel-Dolmatoff, Gerardo. 1974. *Amazonian Cosmos: The Sexual and Religious Symbolism of the Tukano Indians*. Chicago: University of Chicago Press.

Roscoe, Will. 1996. "How to Become a Berdache: Toward a Unified Analysis of Gender Diversity," in Gilbert Herdt, ed., *Third Sex Third Gender: Beyond Sexual Dimorphism in Culture and History*, 329–71. New York: Zone Books.

———. 1998. *Changing Ones: Third and Fourth Genders in North America*. London: Macmillan.

Saladin d'Anglure, Bernard. 1990. "Rethinking Inuit Shamanism through the Concept of 'Third Gender,'" in Mihály Hoppál and Juha Pentikäinen, eds., *Northern Religions and Shamanism*, 146–50. Budapest: Akadémai Kiadó. Reprinted in Graham Harvey, ed., *Shamanism: A Reader* (London: Routledge, 2003), 235–41.

Stoodley, Nick. 1999. *The Spindle and the Spear: A Critical Enquiry into the Construction and Meaning of Gender in the Early Anglo-Saxon Burial Rite*. BAR British Series 288. Oxford: British Archaeological Reports.

Taylor, J. G. 1989. "Shamanic Sex Roles in Traditional Labrador Inuit Society," in Mihály Hoppál and Otto von Sadovsky, eds., *Shamanism Past and Present (Part 2)*, 297–306. Budapest: Ethnographic Institute, Hungarian Academy of Sciences; Fullerton, Calif.: International Society for Trans-Oceanic Research.

Whitehead, Harriet. 1993. "The Bow and the Burden Strap: A New Look at Institutionalized Homosexuality in Native North America," in Henry Abelove, Michele A. Barde, and David M. Halperin, eds., *The Lesbian and Gay Studies Reader*, 498–527. London: Routledge.

Neo-Shamanisms

Allegro, John M. 1970. *The Sacred Mushroom and the Cross*. London: Hodder & Stoughton.

Andrews, Lynn. 1982. *Medicine Woman.* San Francisco: Harper & Row.

Aswynn, Freyja. 1994. *Leaves of Yggdrasil*. Saint Paul, Minn.: Llewellyn.

Bates, Brian. 1983. *The Way of Wyrd*. London: Arrow.

———. 1996. *The Wisdom of the Wyrd: Teachings for Today from Our Ancient Past.* London: Rider.

———. 1996–1997. "Wyrd: Life Force of the Cosmos." *Sacred Hoop* 15 (Winter): 8–13.

Beals, R. L. 1978. "Sonoran Fantasy or Coming of Age?" *American Anthropologist* 80:355–62.

Beaumont, R., and O. Kharitidi. 1997. "The Secrets of Siberian Shamanism." *Kindred Spirit Quarterly* 38:47–50.

Bend, C., and Tanya Wiger. 1987. *Birth of a Modern Shaman*. Saint Paul, Minn.: Llewellyn.

Blain, Jenny. 1998. "Presenting Constructions of Identity and Divinity: Ásatrú and Oracular Seidhr," in S. Grills, ed., *Fieldwork Methods: Accomplishing Ethnographic Research*, 203–27. Thousand Oaks, Calif.: Sage.

———. 1999a. "The Nine Worlds and the Tree: Seiðr as Shamanistic Practice in Heathen Spirituality." *Spirit Talk* 9 (Early Summer): 14–19.

———. 1999b. "Seidr as Shamanistic Practice: Reconstituting a Tradition of Ambiguity." *Shaman* 7 (2): 99–121.

———. 2001. "Shamans, Stones, Authenticity and Appropriation: Contestations of Invention and Meaning," in Robert J. Wallis and Kenneth Lymer, eds., *A Permeability of Boundaries: New Approaches to the Archaeology of Art, Religion and Folklore*, 47–55. BAR International Series 936. Oxford: British Archaeological Reports.

———. 2002. *Nine Worlds of Seid-Magic: Ecstasy and Neo-shamanism in North European Paganism*. London: Routledge.

Blain, Jenny, and Robert J. Wallis. 2000. "The 'Ergi' Seidman: Contestations of Gender, Shamanism and Sexuality in Northern Religion Past and Present." *Journal of Contemporary Religion* 15 (3): 395–411.

———. 2004a. "Sacred Sites, Contested Rites/Rights: Contemporary Pagan Engagements with the Past." *Journal of Material Culture* 9 (3): 237–61.

———. 2004b. "Sites, Texts, Contexts and Inscriptions of Meaning: Investigating Pagan 'Authenticities' in a Text-Based Society." *Pomegranate* 6 (2): 231–52.

———. 2006a. "Ritual Reflections, Practitioner Meanings: Disputing the Terminology of Neo-Shamanic 'Performance.'" *Journal of Ritual Studies* 20 (1): 21–36.

———. 2006b. "Re-Presenting Spirit: Heathenry, New-Indigenes, and the Imaged Past," in Ian A. Russel, ed., *Image, Simulation and Meaning in Archaeology: On Archaeology and the Industrialisation and Marketing of Heritage and Tourism*, 89–118. London: Springer.

Brown, Michael F. 1997. *The Channeling Zone: American Spirituality in an Anxious Age*. Cambridge, Mass: Harvard University Press.

———. 2003. *Who Owns Native Culture?* Cambridge, Mass.: Harvard University Press.

Brown, Mick. 1998. "In February of This Year I Received a Curious and Completely Unexpected Invitation . . . Would I Like to Interview Carlos Castaneda?" *Daily Telegraph Saturday Magazine* (1 August): 38–42.

Butler, Beverley. 1996. "The Tree, the Tower and the Shaman: The Material Culture of Resistance of the No M11 Link Roads Protest of Wanstead and Leytonstone, London." *Journal of Material Culture* 1 (3): 337–63.

Buxton, Simon. 2004. *The Shamanic Way of the Bee*. Rochester, Vt.: Inner Traditions.

Carroll, Phil J. 1987. *Liber Null and Psychonaut: An Introduction to Chaos Magic*. 2 vols. York Beach, Maine: Samuel Weiser.

Castaneda, Carlos. 1968. *The Teachings of Don Juan: A Yaqui Way of Knowledge*. Berkeley: University of California Press.

———. 1971. *A Separate Reality*. London: Bodley Head.

———. 1972. *Journey to Ixtlan: The Lessons of Don Juan*. New York: Simon & Schuster.

———. 1974. *Tales of Power*. New York: Penguin Books.

Castaneda, Margaret R. 1997. *A Magical Journey with Carlos Castaneda*. Victoria, B.C.: Millennia Press.

Chryssides, George D. 2001. *Historical Dictionary of New Religious Movements*. Lanham, Md.: Scarecrow Press.

Clifton, Chas S. 1989. "Armchair Shamanism: A Yankee Way of Knowledge," in T. Schultz, ed., *The Fringes of Reason: A Whole Earth Catalogue*, 43–49. New York: Harmony Books.

———, ed. 1994. *Witchcraft and Shamanism: Witchcraft Today, Book Three*. Saint Paul, Minn.: Llewellyn.

———. 1995. "Training Your Soul Retriever." www.chasclifton.com/columns/column13.html.

Clifton, Chas S., and Graham Harvey, eds. 2004. *The Paganism Reader*. London: Routledge.

Cowan, Tom. 1993. *Fire in the Head: Shamanism and the Celtic Spirit*. San Francisco: HarperCollins.

Cox, James L. 2003. "Contemporary Shamanism in Global Contexts: 'Religious' Appeals to an Archaic Tradition?" *Studies in World Christianity* 9 (1): 69–87.

Crowley, Aleister. 1906. *The Book of the Law*. Reprinted in Chas S. Clifton and Graham Harvey, eds., *The Paganism Reader* (London: Routledge, 2004), 67–79.

———. 1929. *Moonchild*. London: Mandrake Press.

———. 1973. *Magick*. London: Routledge and Kegan Paul.

Cruden, Loren. 1995. *Coyote's Council Fire: Contemporary Shamans on Race, Gender, and Community*. Rochester, Vt.: Destiny Books.

de Mille, Richard. 1976. *Castaneda's Journey: The Power and the Allegory*. Santa Barbara, Calif.: Capra Press.

———, ed. 1980. *The Don Juan Papers: Further Castaneda Controversies*. Santa Barbara, Calif.: Ross-Erikson.

Deloria, Philip J. 1998. *Playing Indian*. New Haven, Conn.: Yale University Press.

Douglas, Mary. 1980. "The Authenticity of Castaneda," in Richard de Mille, ed., *The Don Juan Papers: Further Castaneda Controversies*, 25–32. Santa Barbara, Calif.: Ross-Erikson.

Drury, Nevill. 1982. *The Shaman and the Magician: Journeys between the Worlds*. London: Routledge.

———. 1989. *The Elements of Shamanism*. Shaftesbury, England: Element Books.

———. 1993. *Pan's Daughter: The Magical World of Rosaleen Norton*. Oxford, England: Mandrake.

———. 2003. *Magic and Witchcraft: From Shamanism to the Technopagans*. London: Thames & Hudson.

Fikes, Jay C. 1993. *Carlos Castaneda, Academic Opportunism and the Psychedelic Sixties*. Victoria, B.C.: Millennia Press.

Fries, Jan. 1992. *Visual Magick: A Manual of Freestyle Shamanism*. Oxford, England: Mandrake.

———. 1993. *Helrunar: A Manual of Rune Magic*. Oxford, England: Mandrake.

———. 1996. *Seidways: Shaking, Swaying and Serpent Mysteries*. Oxford, England: Mandrake.

———. 2001. *Cauldron of the Gods: Manual of Celtic Magick*. Oxford, England: Mandrake.

Geertz, Armin W. 1983. "Book of the Hopi: The Hopi's Book?" *Anthropos* 78:547–56.

———. 1993. "Archaic Ontology and White Shamanism." *Religion* 23:369–72.

———. 1994. *The Invention of Prophecy: Continuity and Meaning in Hopi Indian Religion*. Berkeley: University of California Press.

Gibson, William. 1984. *Neuromancer*. London: Victor Gollancz.

Glass-Coffin, B. 1994. "Viewpoint: Anthropology, Shamanism, and the 'New Age.'" *Chronicle of Higher Education* (June 15): A48.

Goodman, Felicitas D. 1986. "Body Posture and the Religious Altered State of Consciousness: An Experimental Investigation." *Journal of Humanistic Psychology* 26 (3): 81–118.

———. 1988. "Shamanic Trance Postures," in Gary Doore, ed., *Shaman's Path: Healing, Personal Growth, and Empowerment*, 53–61. Boston: Shambhala.

———. 1989. "The Neurophysiology of Shamanic Ecstasy," in Mihály Hoppál and Otto von Sadovszky, eds., *Shamanism Past and Present (Part 2)*, 377–79. Budapest: Ethnographic Institute, Hungarian Academy of Sciences; Fullerton, Calif.: International Society for Trans-Oceanic Research.

———. 1990. *Where the Spirits Ride the Wind: Trance Journeys and Other Ecstatic Experiences*. Bloomington: Indiana University Press.

Grant, Kenneth. 1973. *Aleister Crowley and the Hidden God*. London: Frederick Muller.

———. 1975. *Cults of the Shadow*. London: Frederick Muller.

———. 1980. *Outside the Circles of Time*. London: Frederick Muller.

———. 1991 [1972]. *The Magical Revival*. London: Skoob Books.

Grant, Kenneth, and Steffi Grant. 1998. *Zos Speaks: Encounters with Austin Osman Spare*. London: Fulgur.

Green, Rayna. 1988. "The Tribe Called Wannabee." *Folklore* 99 (1): 30–55.

Greenwood, Susan. 2000. *Magic, Witchcraft and the Otherworld*. Oxford: Berg.

———. 2005. *The Nature of Magic: An Anthropology of Consciousness*. Oxford: Berg.

Grimaldi, Susan. 1996. "Learning from a Master: An Ulchi Shaman Teaches in America." *Shamanism* 9 (2): 7–11.

———. 1997. "Open Dialogue: Observations on Daniel Noel's *The Soul of Shamanism*—A Defense of Contemporary Shamanism and Michael Harner." *Shaman's Drum* 46:4–9.

Gyrus Orbitalis. 2000. "On Prehistoric Rock Art and Psychedelic Experiences." dreamflesh.com/essays/rockpsych.

Harner, Michael. 1988a. "Shamanic Counseling," in Gary Doore, ed., *Shaman's Path: Healing, Personal Growth, and Empowerment*, 179–87. Boston: Shambhala.

———. 1988b. "What Is a Shaman?" in Gary Doore, ed., *Shaman's Path: Healing, Personal Growth, and Empowerment*, 7–15. Boston: Shambhala.

———. 1990 [1980]. *The Way of the Shaman*. London: HarperCollins.

———. 1994. "The Foundation's Expedition to Tuva." *Shamanism* 7 (1): 1–2.

Harvey, Graham. 1995. "Heathenism: A North European Pagan Tradition," in Graham Harvey and Charlotte Hardman, eds., *Paganism Today: Wiccans, Druids, the Goddess and Ancient Earth Traditions for the Twenty-First Century*, 49–64. London: Thorsons.

———. 1997. *Listening People, Speaking Earth: Contemporary Paganism*. London: Hurst; Adelaide: Wakefield; New York: New York University Press (under the title *Contemporary Paganism: Listening People, Speaking Earth*).

———. 1998. "Shamanism in Britain Today." *Performance Research 'On Ritual'* 3 (3): 16–24.

Hobson, Geary. 1978. "The Rise of the White Shaman as a New Version of Cultural Imperialism," in Geary Hobson, *The Remembered Earth*, 100–108. Albuquerque, N.M.: Red Earth Press.

Hoppál, Mihály. 1996. "Shamanism in a Postmodern Age." *Folklore*, haldjas.folklore.ee/folklore/vol2/hoppla.htm.

Horwitz, Jonathan. 1989. "On Experiential Shamanic Journeying," in Mihály Hoppál and Otto von Sadovszky, eds., *Shamanism Past and Present (Part 2)*, 373–76. Budapest: Ethnographic Institute, Hungarian Academy of Sciences; Fullerton, Calif.: International Society for Trans-Oceanic Research.

———. 1995. "The Absence of 'Performance' in the Shamanic Rite: Shamanic Rites Seen from a Shamanic Perspective II," in Tae-Gon Kim and Mihály Hoppál, eds., *Shamanism in Performing Arts*, 231–42. Budapest: Akadémiai Kiadó.

Høst, Annette. 1999. *Exploring Seidhr: A Practical Study of the Seidhr Ritual*. Paper presented at "Religious Practices and Beliefs in the North Atlantic Area" seminar, Århus University.

———. 2001. "What's in a Name? Neo Shamanism, Core Shamanism, Urban Shamanism, Modern Shamanism, or What?" *Spirit Talk* 14:1–4.

Howard, Michael. 1985. *The Wisdom of the Runes*. London: Rider.

Hungry Wolf, Adolf. 1973. *The Good Medicine Book*. New York: Warner Paperback Library.

Hunt, Dave, and T. A. McMahon. 1988. *America, the Sorcerer's New Apprentice: The Rise of New Age Shamanism*. Eugene, Ore.: Harvest House.

Hutton, Ronald. 1991. *The Pagan Religions of the Ancient British Isles: Their Nature and Legacy*. Oxford, England: Blackwell.

———. 1996. "Introduction: Who Possesses the Past?" in Philip Carr-Gomm, ed., *The Druid Renaissance*, 17–34. London: Thorsons.

———. 1999. *The Triumph of the Moon: A History of Modern Pagan Witchcraft*. Oxford: Oxford University Press.

———. 2002. *Shamans: Siberian Spirituality and the Western Imagination.* London: Hambledon.

Ingerman, Sandra. 1991. *Soul Retrieval: Mending the Fragmented Self.* San Franciso: HarperCollins.

Jakobsen, Merete Demant. 1999. *Shamanism: Traditional and Contemporary Approaches to the Mastery of Spirits and Healing*. Oxford, England: Berghahn Books.

Jocks, Christopher R. 1996. "Spirituality for Sale: Sacred Knowledge in the Consumer Age." *American Indian Quarterly* 20 (3): 415–31.

Johnson, Nathan J., and Robert J. Wallis. 2005. *Galdrbok: Practical Heathen Runecraft, Shamanism and Magic*. London: Wykeham Press.

Johnson, Paul C. 1995. "Shamanism from Ecuador to Chicago: A Case Study in Ritual Appropriation." *Religion* 25:163–78.

Jones, Leslie Ellen. 1994. "The Emergence of the Druid as Celtic Shaman." *Folklore in Use* 2:131–42.

———. 1998. *Druid, Shaman, Priest: Metaphors of Celtic Paganism*. Enfield Lock, England: Hisarlik Press.

Joralemon, Donald. 1990. "The Selling of the Shaman and the Problem of Informant Legitimacy." *Journal of Anthropological Research* 46 (2): 105–18.

Kehoe, Alice B. 1990. "Primal Gaia: Primitivists and Plastic Medicine Men," in James Clifton, ed., *The Invented Indian: Cultural Fictions and Government Policies*, 193–209. New Brunswick, N.J.: Transaction.

———. 2000. *Shamans and Religion: An Anthropological Exploration in Critical Thinking*. Prospect Heights, Ill.: Waveland Press.

Kelly, Karen. 1997. "Blessing of the Reindeer Camps." *Sacred Hoop* 18:24–25.

———. 1999. "Close to Nature: An Interview with Annette Høst." *Spirit Talk* 9 (Early Summer): 5–9.

Kharitidi, Olga. 1997. *Entering the Circle: Ancient Secrets of Siberian Shamanism Discovered by a Russian Psychiatrist*. London: Thorsons.

King, Serge Kahili. 1990. *Urban Shaman: A Handbook for Personal and Planetary Transformation Based on the Hawaiian Way of the Adventurer*. New York: Simon & Schuster.

———. 2003. *Kahuna Healing*. Stuttgart: Lüchow Verlag.

Leary, Timothy. 1970. *The Politics of Ecstasy*. St. Albans, England: Paladin.

Leary, Timothy, Ralph Metzner, and Richard Alpert. 1964. *The Psychedelic Experience: A Manual Based on the Tibetan Book of the Dead*. New Hyde Park, N.Y.: University Books.

Lee, Matt. 2003. "Memories of a Sorcerer: Notes on Gilles Deleuze-Felix Guattari, Austin Osman Spare and Anomalous Sorceries." *Journal for the Academic Study of Magic* 1:102–30.

Letcher, Andy. 2001. "The Scouring of the Shire: Fairies, Trolls and Pixies in Eco-Protest Culture." *Folklore* 112:147–61.

Lindquist, Galina. 1997. *Shamanic Performance on the Urban Scene: Neo-Shamanism in Contemporary Sweden*. Stockholm Studies in Social Anthropology 39. Stockholm: University of Stockholm.

Linzie, Bil. 1999. "Seething: Where Does a Seiðrman Go?" *Spirit Talk* 9 (Early Summer): 27–29.

MacEowen, Frank H. 1998. "Rekindling the Gaelic Hearthways of Oran Mor." *Shaman's Drum* 49 (Summer): 32–39.

———. 2004. *The Spiral of Memory and Belonging: A Celtic Path of Soul and Kinship*. Novato, Calif.: New World Library.

MacLellan, Gordon. 1994. *Small Acts of Magic*. Manchester, England: Creeping Toad.

———. 1995. "Dancing on the Edge: Shamanism in Modern Britain," in Graham Harvey and Charlotte Hardman, eds., *Paganism Today: Wiccans, Druids, the Goddess and Ancient Earth Traditions for the Twenty-First Century*, 138–48. London: Thorsons.

———. 1996. *Talking to the Earth*. Chieveley, England: Capall Bann.

———. 1997. *Sacred Animals*. Chieveley, England: Capall Bann.

———. 1998. "A Sense of Wonder." *Performance Research 'On Ritual'* 3 (3): 60–63.

———. 1999. *Shamanism*. London: Piatkus.

Matson, Erin R. 1980. "De Mille Does Not Exist," in Richard de Mille, ed., *The Don Juan Papers: Further Castaneda Controversies*, 174–77. Santa Barbara, Calif.: Ross-Erikson.

Matthews, Caitlin. 1995. *Singing the Soul Back Home: Shamanism in Daily Life*. Shaftesbury, England: Element Books.

———. 1996. "Following the Awen—Celtic Shamanism and the Druid Path in the Modern World," in Philip Carr-Gomm, ed., *The Druid Renaissance*, 223–36. London: Thorsons.

———. 1997. "Midwifing the Soul." *Sacred Hoop* 19:14–17.

Matthews, John. 1991a. *The Celtic Shaman: A Handbook*. Shaftesbury, England: Element Books.

———. 1991b. *The Song of Taliesin: Stories and Poems from the Books of Broceliande*. London: Aquarian.

———. 1991c. *Taliesin: Shamanism and the Bardic Mysteries in Britain and Ireland*. London: Aquarian.

McKenna, Terence. 1992. *Food of the Gods: The Search for the Original Tree of Knowledge: A Radical History of Plants, Drugs, and Human Evolution.* New York: Bantam.

Meadows, Kenneth. 1989. *Earth Medicine: A Shamanic Way to Self-Discovery*. Shaftesbury, England: Element Books.

———. 1991. *Shamanic Experience: A Practical Guide to Contemporary Shamanism.* London: Element Books.

———. 1996. *Rune Power*. Shaftesbury, England: Element Books.

Metzner, Ralph. 1994. *The Well of Remembrance: Rediscovering the Earth Wisdom Myths of Northern Europe*. Boston: Shambhala.

Moore, J. H. 1973. "Book Review: S. Hyemeyohsts *Seven Arrows*." *American Anthropologist* 75:1040–42.

Murphy, R. 1981. "Book Review: M. Harner *The Way of the Shaman*." *American Anthropologist* 83:714–17.

Naddair, Kaledon. 1990. "Pictish and Keltic Shamanism," in Prudence Jones and Caitlin Matthews, eds., *Voices from the Circle: The Heritage of Western Paganism*, 93–108. Wellingborough, England: Aquarian Press.

Noel, Daniel C., ed. 1976. *Seeing Castaneda: Reactions to the "Don Juan" Writings of Carlos Castaneda.* New York: Capricorn Books.

———. 1990. *Paths to the Power of Myth: Joseph Campbell and the Study of Religion.* New York: Crossroad.

———. 1997. *The Soul of Shamanism: Western Fantasies, Imaginal Realities*. New York: Continuum.

———. 1998. "Open Dialogue: A Response to Susan Grimaldi's critique of *The Soul of Shamanism*." *Shaman's Drum* 48:4–8.

Olson, Alan M. 1978. "From Shaman to Mystic: An Interpretation of the Castaneda Quartet." *Soundings* 1:47–66.

Paxson, Diana L. 1992. *The Seid Project: A Report on Experiences and Findings*. Hrafnar Monograph #1 (unpublished).

———. 1993. "Heide: Witch-Goddess of the North," *Sagewoman*, Fall 1993. Available at www.hrafnar.org/goddesses/heide.html.

———. 1997. "The Return of the Volva: Recovering the Practice of Seidh." Available at www.seidh.org/articles/seidh.html.

———. 1998. "'This Thou Dost Know . . .': Oracles in the Northern Tradition." *Idunna: A Journal of Northern Tradition*, n.p.

———. 1999. "Seeing for the People: Working Oracular Seiðr in the Pagan Community." *Spirit Talk* 9 (Early Summer): 10–13.

Pearce, Joseph C. 1976. "Don Juan and Jesus," in Daniel C. Noel, ed., *Seeing Castaneda: Reactions to the "Don Juan" Writings of Carlos Castaneda*, 191–219. New York: Capricorn Books.

Pedersen, M. 1999. "The Return of the Seiðr: Experiences of Seiðr in Modern Denmark." *Spirit Talk* 9 (Early Summer): 25–27.

Pennick, Nigel. 1989. *Practical Magic in the Northern Tradition*. Wellingborough, England: Aquarian.

———. 1992. *Rune Magic: The History and Practice of Ancient Runic Traditions*. London: Thorsons.

———. 1999. *The Complete Illustrated Guide to Runes*. Shaftesbury, England: Element Books.

Pennick, Nigel, and Nigel Jackson. 1992. *The Celtic Oracle: A Complete Guide to Using the Cards*. London: Aquarian.

Perera, Sylvia B. 1981. *Descent to the Goddess: A Way of Initiation for Women*. Toronto: Inner City Books.

Pilch, John J. 2002. "Altered States of Consciousness in the Synoptics," in Wolfgang Stegemann, Bruce J. Malina, and Gerd Theissen, eds., *The Social Setting of Jesus and the Gospels*, 103–16. Minneapolis, Minn.: Fortress.

Pinchbeck, Daniel. 2002. *Breaking Open the Head: A Visionary Journey from Cynicism to Shamanism*. London: Flamingo.

Pitts, Mike. 1996. "The Vicar's Dewpond, the National Trust and the Rise of Paganism," in David Morgan, Peter Salway, and David Thackray, eds., *The Remains of Distant Times: Archaeology and the National Trust*, 116–31. Woodbridge, Suffolk, England: Boydell Press for the Society of Antiquaries of London and the National Trust.

Plotkin, Bill. 2003. *Soulcraft: Crossing into the Mysteries of Nature and Psyche*. Novato, Calif.: New World Library.

Plotkin, Mark J. 1994. *Tales of a Shaman's Apprentice*. New York: Penguin.

Reid-Wolfe, Adrian. 1997. "Teach an Alais." *Sacred Hoop* 18:28–29.

Rose, Wendy. 1978. "An Old-Time Indian Attack Conducted in Two Parts: Part One: Imitation 'Indian' Poems; Part Two: Gary Snyder's Turtle Island," in Geary Hobson, ed., *Remembered Earth: An Anthology of Contemporary Native American Literature*, 211–16. Albuquerque, N.M.: Red Earth Press.

———. 1984. "Just What's All This Fuss about Whiteshamanism, Anyway?" in Bo Schöler, ed., *Coyote Was Here: Essays on Contemporary Native American Literary and Political Mobilization*, 13–24. Aarhus, Norway: University of Aarhus.

———. 1992. "The Great Pretenders: Further Reflections on Whiteshamanism," in M. Annette Jaimes, ed., *The State of Native America: Genocide, Colonization, and Resistance*, 403–21. Boston: South End.

Roth, Gabriella. 1990. *Maps to Ecstasy: Teachings of an Urban Shaman*. Wellingborough, England: Crucible.

——. 1997. *Sweat Your Prayers: Movement as a Spiritual Practice*. New York: Tarcher/Putnam.

Rothenberg, Jerome, ed. 1985. *Technicians of the Sacred: A Range of Poetry from Africa, America, Asia, Europe, and Oceania*. Berkeley: University of California Press.

Runic John. 2004. *The Book of Seidr: The Native English and Northern European Shamanic Tradition*. Chieveley, England: Capall Bann.

Rutherford, Leo. 1993. "To All Races and Colours: About the Release of the Ancient Teachings." *Sacred Hoop* 1:8–9.

——. 1996. *Principles of Shamanism*. London: Thorsons.

Santana, Carlos. 2002. *Shaman*. Arista CD. B00006L8G8.

Shallcrass, Philip. 1998. "A Priest of the Goddess," in Joanne Pearson, Richard H. Roberts, and Geoffrey Samuel, eds., *Nature Religion Today: Paganism in the Modern World*, 157–69. Edinburgh: Edinburgh University Press.

——. 2000. *Druidry*. London: Piaktis.

Smith, Andy. 1994. "For All Those Who Were Indian in a Former Life," in Carol J. Adams, ed., *Ecofeminism and the Sacred*, 168–71. New York: Continuum.

Spare, Austin O. 1905. *Earth Inferno*. Privately published.

——. 1907. *A Book of Satyrs*. London: Co-operative Printings Society.

——. 1909–13. *The Book of Pleasure*. London: Co-operative Printing Society.

——. 1921. *The Focus of Life: The Mutterings of AOS*. London: Morland Press.

——. 1993. *From the Inferno to Zos: The Writings and Images of Austin Osman Spare*. Vol. 1. Seattle: First Impressions.

Spicer, Edward. 1969. "Review of C. Castaneda 1968. *The Teachings of Don Juan: A Yaqui Way of Knowledge*. Berkeley and Los Angeles: University of California Press." *American Anthropologist* 71 (2): 320–22.

Stafford, Greg. 1990. "The Medicine Circle of Turtle Island," in Prudence Jones and Caitlin Matthews, eds., *Voices from the Circle: The Heritage of Western Paganism*, 83–92. Wellingborough, England: Aquarian.

Stone, Alby. 1998. *Straight Track, Crooked Road: Leys, Spirit Paths and Shamanism*. Loughborough, United Kingdom: Heart of Albion Press.

Storm, Hyemeyohsts. 1972. *Seven Arrows*. New York: Ballantine.

Stuckrad, Kocku von. 2002. "Reenchanting Nature: Modern Western Shamanism and Nineteenth-Century Thought." *Journal of the American Academy of Religion* 70 (4): 771–99.

Tisdall, Caroline. 1976. *Joseph Beuys—Coyote*. Munich: Schirmer Mosel.

——. 1979. *Joseph Beuys*. New York: Solomon R. Guggenheim Museum; London: Thames & Hudson.

——. 1998. *Joseph Beuys—We Go This Way*. London: Violette Editions.

Torrey, E. Fuller. 1974. "Spiritualists and Shamans as Psychotherapists: An Account of Original Anthropological Sin," in Irving I. Zaretsky and Mark P. Leone, eds., *Religious Movements in Contemporary America*, 330–37. Princeton, N.J.: Princeton University Press.

Townsend, Joan. 1988. "Neo-shamanism and the Modern Mystical Movement," in Gary Doore, ed., *Shaman's Path: Healing, Personal Growth and Empowerment*, 73–83. Boston: Shambhala.

———. 1997. "Core Shaman and Neopagan Leaders of the Mystical Movement in Contemporary Society." *Dialogue and Alliance* 13 (1): 100–22.

———. 1999. "Western Contemporary Core and Neo-shamanism and the Interpenetration with Indigenous Societies." *Proceedings of the International Congress "Shamanism and Other Indigenous Spiritual Beliefs and Practices"* 5 (2): 223–31.

———. 2005. "Individualist Religious Movements: Core and Neo-shamanism." *Anthropology of Consciousness* 15 (1): 1–9.

Trubshaw, Bob. 2005. *Sacred Places: Prehistory and Popular Imagination.* Loughborough, United Kingdom: Heart of Albion Press.

Vitebsky, Piers. 1995a. "From Cosmology to Environmentalism: Shamanism as Local Knowledge in a Global Setting," in Richard Fardon, ed., *Counterworks: Managing the Diversity of Knowledge*, 182–203. London: Routledge. Reprinted in Graham Harvey, ed., *Shamanism: A Reader* (London: Routledge, 2003), 276–98.

———. 1995b. *The Shaman*. London: Macmillan.

Wallis, Robert J. 1999. "Altered States, Conflicting Cultures: Shamans, Neo-shamans and Academics." *Anthropology of Consciousness* 10 (2–3): 41–49.

———. 2000. "Queer Shamans: Autoarchaeology and Neo-shamanism." *World Archaeology* 32 (2): 251–61.

———. 2001. "Waking the Ancestors: Neo-shamanism and Archaeology," in Neil Price, ed., *The Archaeology of Shamanism*, 213–30. London: Routledge. Reprinted in Graham Harvey, ed., *Shamanism: A Reader* (London: Routledge, 2003), 402–23.

———. 2003. *Shamans/Neo-Shamans: Ecstasy, Alternative Archaeology and Contemporary Pagans*. London: Routledge.

———. 2004. "Between the Worlds: Autoarchaeology and neo-Shamans," in Jenny Blain, Douglas Ezzy, and Graham Harvey, eds., *Researching Paganisms: Religious Experiences and Academic Methodologies*, 191–215. Walnut Creek, Calif.: AltaMira.

Wallis, Robert J., and Jenny Blain. 2003. "Sites, Sacredness, and Stories: Interactions of Archaeology and Contemporary Paganism." *Folklore* 114 (3): 307–21.

Wilk, S. 1980. "Don Juan on Balance," in Richard de Mille, ed., *The Don Juan Papers: Further Castaneda Controversies*, 154–57. Santa Barbara, Calif.: Ross-Erikson.

Willis, Roy. 1994. "Narrative: New Shamanism." *Anthropology Today* 10 (6): 16–18.

Wood, Nicholas. 1998. "News from the Hoop: Carlos Castaneda—1925–1998." *Sacred Hoop* 22:8.

Woodman, Justin. 1998. "Conference Review of Shamanism in Contemporary Society, Department of Religious Studies, University of Newcastle upon Tyne, 23–26 June 1998." *Anthropology Today* 14 (6): 23–24.

York, Michael. 2003. *Historical Dictionary of New Age Movements*. Lanham, Md.: Scarecrow Press.

Zinser, Hartmut. 1987. "'Schamanismus im New Age': Zur Wiederkehr Schamanistischer Praktiken und Seancen in Europa." *Zeitschrift fur Religions und Geistes-Geschichte* 39 (1): 319–27.

Performance

Balzer, Marjorie M. 1995. "The Poetry of Shamanism," in Tae-Gon Kim and Mihály Hoppál, eds., *Shamanism in Performing Arts*, 171–87. Budapest: Akadémiai Kiadó. Reprinted in Graham Harvey, ed., *Shamanism: A Reader* (London: Routledge, 2003), 307–23.

Blain, Jenny, and Robert J. Wallis. 2006a. "Ritual Reflections, Practitioner Meanings: Disputing the Terminology of Neo-Shamanic 'Performance.'" *Journal of Ritual Studies* 20 (1): 21–36.

Bogoras, Waldemar. 1972 [1958]. "Shamanic Performance in the Inner Room," in William A. Lessa and Evon Z. Vogt, eds., *Reader in Comparative Religion*, 382–87. New York: Harper & Row.

Coates, Marcus. 2005. *Journey to the Lower World.* Edited by Alec Finlay. Newcastle upon Tyne, United Kingdom: Morning Star Platform Projects.

Csordas, Thomas J. 1996. "Imaginal Performance and Memory in Ritual Healing," in Carol Laderman and Marina Roseman, eds., *The Performance of Healing*, 91–114. London: Routledge.

Flaherty, Gloria. 1988. "The Performing Artist as the Shaman of Higher Civilisation." *Modern Language* 103 (3): 519–39.

Harvey, Graham. 1998. "Shamanism in Britain Today." *Performance Research 'On Ritual'* 3 (3): 16–24.

Horwitz, Jonathan. 1995. "The Absence of 'Performance' in the Shamanic Rite: Shamanic Rites Seen from a Shamanic Perspective II," in Mihály Hoppál and Tae-Gon Kim, eds., *Shamanism in Performing Arts*, 231–42. Budapest: Akadémiai Kiadó.

Kim, Tae-Gon, and Mihály Hoppál, eds. 1995. *Shamanism in Performing Arts*. Budapest: Akadémiai Kiadó.

Laderman, Carol. 1991. *Taming the Wind of Desire: Psychology, Medicine, and Aesthetics in Malay Shamanistic Performance*. Berkeley: University of California Press.

Lindquist, Galina. 1997. *Shamanic Performance on the Urban Scene: Neo-Shamanism in Contemporary Sweden*. Stockholm Studies in Social Anthropology 39. Stockholm: University of Stockholm.

MacLellan, Gordon. 1998. "A Sense of Wonder." *Performance Research 'On Ritual'* 3 (3): 60–63.

Schieffelin, Edward. 1996. "On Failure in Performance: Throwing the Medium out of the Séance," in Carol Laderman and Marina Roseman, eds., *The Performance of Healing*, 59–90. London: Routledge.

——. 1998. "Problematising Performance," in Felicia Hughes-Freeland, ed., *Ritual, Performance, Media*, 194–207. London: Routledge.

Rock Art

Bahn, Paul G. 1997. "Membrane and Numb Brain: A Close Look at a Recent Claim for Shamanism in Palaeolithic Art." *Rock Art Research* 14 (1): 62–68.

——. 1998. "Stumbling in the Footsteps of St Thomas." *British Archaeology* (February): 18.

Bradley, Richard. 1997. *Signing the Land: Rock Art and the Prehistory of Atlantic Europe*. London: Routledge.

Chippindale, Christopher, Benjamin Smith, and Paul S. C. Taçon. 2000. "Visions of Dynamic Power: Archaic Rock-Paintings, Altered States of Consciousness and 'Clever Men' in Western Arnhem Land (NT), Australia." *Cambridge Archaeological Journal* 10 (1): 63–101.

Chippindale, Christopher, and Paul S. C. Taçon, eds. 1998. *The Archaeology of Rock-Art*. Cambridge: Cambridge University Press.

Clottes, Jean, and J. David Lewis-Williams. 1998. *The Shamans of Prehistory: Trance and Magic in the Painted Caves*. New York: Harry N. Abrams.

Davenport, Demorest, and Michael A. Jochim. 1988. "The Scene in the Shaft at Lascaux." *Antiquity* 62:559–62.

Devereux, Paul. 1992. *Shamanism and the Mystery Lines: Ley Lines, Spirit Paths, Shape-Shifting and Out-of-Body-Travel*. London: Quantum.

——. 1997. *The Long Trip: A Prehistory of Psychedelia*. New York: Arkana.

——. 2001. "Did Ancient Shamanism Leave a Monumental Record on the Land as Well as in Rock Art?" in Robert J. Wallis and Kenneth Lymer, eds., *A Permeability of Boundaries? New Approaches to the Archaeology of Art, Religion and Folklore*, BAR International Series 936, 1–7. Oxford: British Archaeological Reports.

Devlet, Ekaterina. 2001. "Rock Art and the Material Culture of Siberian and Central Asian Shamanism," in Neil Price, ed., *The Archaeology of Shamanism*, 43–55. London: Routledge.

Dowson, Thomas A. 1989. "Dots and Dashes: Cracking the Entoptic Code in Bushman Rock Art." *South African Archaeological Society Goodwin Series* 6:84–94.

——. 1994a. "Hunter-Gatherers, Traders, and Slaves: The 'Mfecane' Impact on Bushmen, Their Ritual and Art," in Carolyn Hamilton, ed., *The Mfecane Aftermath: Reconstructive Debates in South Africa's History*, 51–70. Johannesburg: Witwatersrand University Press; Pietermaritzberg: Natal University Press.

——. 1994b. "Reading Art, Writing History: Rock Art and Social Change in Southern Africa." *World Archaeology* 25 (3): 332–45.

——. 1998a. "Like People in Prehistory." *World Archaeology* 29 (3): 333–43.

——. 1998b. "Rock Art: Handmaiden to Studies of Cognitive Evolution," in Colin Renfrew and Chris Scarre, eds., *Cognition and Material Culture: The Archaeology of Symbolic Storage*, 67–76. Cambridge, England: McDonald Institute Monographs.

——. 1999a. "Interpretation in Rock Art Research: A Crisis in Confidence." *Ley Hunter* 133:21–23.

——. 1999b. "Rock Art and Shamanism: A Methodological Impasse," in Andrej Rozwadowski, Maria M. Kośko, and Thomas A. Dowson, eds., *Rock Art, Shamanism and Central Asia: Discussions of Relations* (in Polish), 39–56. Warsaw: Wydawnictwo Academickie.

Dowson, Thomas, and J. David Lewis-Williams, eds. 1994. *Contested Images: Diversity in Southern African Rock Art Research*. Johannesburg: Witwatersrand University Press.

Dowson, Thomas A., and Martin Porr. 2001. "Special Objects—Special Creatures: Shamanistic Imagery and the Aurignacian Art of South-west Germany," in Neil Price, ed., *The Archaeology of Shamanism*, 165–77. London: Routledge.

Dronfield, Jeremy. 1996. "Entering Alternative Realities: Cognition, Art and Architecture in Irish Passage Tombs." *Cambridge Archaeological Journal* 6 (1): 37–72.

Francfort, Henri-Paul, and Roberte N. Hamayon, eds. 2001. *The Concept of Shamanism: Uses and Abuses*. Budapest: Akadémiai Kiadó.

Gyrus Orbitalis. 2000. "On Prehistoric Rock Art and Psychedelic Experiences." dreamflesh.com/essays/rockpsych.

Lewis-Williams, David. 2002. *The Mind in the Cave: Consciousness and the Origins of Art.* London: Thames and Hudson.

Lewis-Williams, J. David. 1975. "The Drakensberg Rock Paintings as an Expression of Religious Thought," in E. Anati, ed., *Les réligions de la préhistoire*, 413–26. Capo di Ponte, Brescia, Italy: Centro Camuno di Studi Preistorici.

——. 1981. *Believing and Seeing: Symbolic Meanings in Southern San Rock Paintings*. London: Academic Press.

——. 1991. "Wrestling with Analogy: A Problem in Upper Palaeolithic Art Research." *Proceedings of the Prehistoric Society* 57 (1): 149–62.

——. 1992. "Ethnographic Evidence Relating to 'Trance' and 'Shamans' among Northern and Southern Bushmen." *South African Archaeological Bulletin* 47:56–60.

——. 1998. "Quanto? The Issue of 'Many Meanings' in Southern African San Rock Art Research." *South African Archaeological Bulletin* 53:86–97.

Lewis-Williams, J. David, and Thomas A. Dowson. 1988. "The Signs of All Times: Entoptic Phenomena in Upper Paleolithic Art." *Current Anthropology* 29 (2): 201–45.

——. 1993. "On Vision and Power in the Neolithic: Evidence from the Decorated Monuments." *Current Anthropology* 34:55–65.

——. 1999 [1989]. *Images of Power: Understanding Bushman Rock Art*. Johannesburg: Southern Book Publishers.

Lymer, Kenneth. 2002. "The Deer Petroglyphs of Arpauzen, South Kazakhstan," in Andrej Rozwadowski and Maria M. Kośko, eds., *Spirits and Stones: Shamanism and Rock Art in Central Asia and Siberia*, 80–95. Poznań, Poland: Instytut Wschodni.

Okladnikov, A. P., and V. D. Zaporozhskaya. 1972. *Petroglify Srendei Leny* [Petroglyphs of the Middle Lena]. Leningrad: Nauka.

Patterson, Carol. 1998. "Seeking Power at Willow Creek Cave, Northern California." *Anthropology of Consciousness* 9 (1): 38–49.

Price, Neil S., ed. 2001. *The Archaeology of Shamanism*. London: Routledge.

Rozwadowski, Andrej. 2001. "Sun Gods or Shamans? Interpreting the 'Solar-Headed' Petroglyphs of Central Asia," in Neil Price, ed., *The Archaeology of Shamanism*, 65–86. London: Routledge.

Rozwadowski, Andrej, and Maria M. Kośko, eds. 2002. *Spirits and Stones: Shamanism and Rock Art in Central Asia and Siberia*. Poznań, Poland: Instytut Wschodni.

Sales, Kim. 1992. "Ascent to the Sky: A Shamanic Initiatory Engraving from the Burrup Peninsula, Northwest Western Australia." *Archaeology Oceania* 27:22–35.

Solomon, Anne. 2000. "On Different Approaches to San Rock Art." *South African Archaeological Bulletin* 55:77–78.

Wallis, Robert J. 2002. "The *Bwili* or 'Flying Tricksters' of Malakula: A Critical Discussion of Recent Debates on Rock Art, Ethnography and Shamanisms." *Journal of the Royal Anthropological Institute* 8 (4): 735–60.

——. 2004. "Shamanism and Art," in Mariko N. Walter and Eva N. Fridman, eds., *Shamanism: An Encyclopedia of World Beliefs, Practices, and Culture*, 1:21–28. Santa Barbara, Calif.: ABC-CLIO.

Whitley, David. S. 1992. "Shamanism and Rock Art in Far Western North America." *Cambridge Archaeological Journal* 2:89–113.

——. 2000. *The Art of the Shaman: Rock Art of California*. Salt Lake City: University of Utah Press.

About the Authors

Graham Harvey is a lecturer in religious studies at the Open University in Great Britain. His research interests include discourses and performances of identity creation and maintenance among Jews, Pagans, and indigenous peoples. Some of his publications also engage with shamanisms of various kinds or discuss the contexts in which shamans are needed, valued, or understandable. These include *Listening People, Speaking Earth: Contemporary Paganism* (1997; 2nd ed., 2006), *Indigenous Religions: A Companion* (2000), *Readings in Indigenous Religions* (2002), *Indigenous Religious Musics* (coedited with Karen Ralls, 2001), *The Paganism Reader* (coedited with Chas S. Clifton, 2004), and *Indigenous Diasporas and Dislocations* (coedited with Charles D. Thompson, 2005). His edited *Ritual and Religious Belief: A Reader* (2005) invites a reconsideration of the importance of ritual in religious and cultural life. Two of his books have an even closer relationship with shamans and their activities and worldviews than these. *Shamanism: A Reader* (2003) brings together significant writings about shamans and the study of shamanism. Most recently, *Animism: Respecting the Living World* (2005) focuses on the cultural context of shamans and argues that animism could make significant contributions to some of the major issues of concern today.

Robert J. Wallis is associate professor of visual culture at Richmond University, London, where he is associate director of the master's program in art history. He is also an associate lecturer in the humanities with the Open University. His research interests include archaeological and anthropological approaches to art, especially prehistoric and indigenous art in (perceived) shamanistic and animistic contexts, as well as the representation of the past in the present, principally with regard to the engagements of contemporary Pagans with the ancient past and archaeological sites. Many of his publications examine shamans and neo-shamans in various ways, from altered consciousness in rock art and the discourse on modern artists as "shamans" to negotiations over various forms of access to Stonehenge and other "sacred sites." His books include *A Permeability of Boundaries: New Approaches to the Archaeology of Art, Religion and Folklore* (2001, coedited with Kenneth Lymer) and *Shamans/Neo-Shamans: Ecstasy, Alternative Archaeologies and Contemporary Pagans* (2003). With Jenny Blain, he codirects the Sacred Sites, Contested Rites/Rights: Contemporary Pagan Engagements with the Past project, and their volume of the same title will be published by Sussex Academic Press in 2007. He is currently working on a book critically examining the discourse on shamans and image making, ranging from prehistoric cave paintings to contemporary art.